SOPHOKLES
The Complete Plays

AIAS

ANTIGONÊ

THE WOMEN OF TRACHIS

OEDIPUS TYRANNOS

ÊLEKTRA

PHILOKTÊTÊS

OEDIPUS AT KOLONOS

Translated by
CARL R. MUELLER and
ANNA KRAJEWSKA-WIECZOREK

with a Preface by Hugh Denard

GREAT TRANSLATIONS SERIES

A Smith and Kraus Book

A Smith and Kraus Book
Published by Smith and Kraus, Inc.
177 Lyme Road, Hanover, NH 03755

Cover and Text Design by Julia Hill Gignoux, Freedom Hill Design
Cover Art: Kore, 510 BC, Acropolis Museum, Athens

First Edition: September 2000
10 9 8 7 6 5 4 3 2

The Library of Congress Cataloging-In-Publication Data
Sophocles.
[Plays. English]
Sophokles : the complete plays / translated by Carl R. Mueller and Anna Krajewska-Wieczorek. —1st ed.
p. cm. — (Great translations series)
Includes bibliographical references.
Contents: Aias — Antigonê — The Women of Trachis — Oedipus tyrannos — Êlektra — Philoktêtês — Oedipus at Kolonos.
ISBN 1-57525-265-1
1. Sophocles—Translations into English. 2. Mythology, Greek—Drama.
I. Mueller, Carl Richard. II. Krajewska-Wieczorek, Anna. III. Title.
PA4414.A1 M84 2000
882'.01—dc21   00-044570

For
JAN KOTT
and
THE EUROPEAN CULTURAL CENTRE OF DELPHI

CONTENTS

PREFACE

Sophoklean Tragedy represents a monumental theatrical and interpretative challenge. It is one of the great and enduring glories of ancient Athenian civilization. By the fifth century B.C.E., that city-state had already invented and consolidated the system of government it called democracy, a system of justice based on trial by jury, and the novel cultural practice that came to be known as theater. It now embarked upon a period of the most extraordinary achievement in virtually every field of human endeavor and, through patronage of the arts, reached unparalleled heights in philosophical inquiry, sculpture, architecture, and poetry. Nowhere are these achievements better represented than in the Tragedies of Sophokles. The sweeping, coruscating poetic expanse of his choral odes; the swift, piercing agonistic exchanges; the sudden moment of reversal or of luminous transcendence; the power and the subtlety of characterization; the unerring mastery of dramatic moment, of ironic aperture; it is our tragedy that only seven of his Tragedies and some fragmentary Satyr plays are all that remain of his life's work.

However, there is a darker side to this civilization. Its "glories" were built with the blood of slaves. Athenian culture glorified aggressive imperialism and relished exploiting and oppressing weaker states in the service of its own economic and strategic advantage. Through its maritime supremacy, this proud mini-nation controlled much of the Greek world, ruthlessly and bloodily crushing would-be secessionist states and hungering for absolute control of the Greek world. Indeed, for the last twenty-five years of Sophokles' life, Athens was continuously at war with other Greek states. Meanwhile, the citizen-class— free, Athenian, adult males—collectively presides over a slave-based economy, institutional xenophobia, and extreme patriarchy. Funded by tributes exacted from subject-states, the great iconic pinnacles of Athenian civilization, such as the Parthenon, and Tragedy itself, are also monuments of oppression. And the urbane, much-loved poet was himself a loyal servant of this barbaric culture. As Public Treasurer between 443 and 442, he presided over the Treasury of tributes levied from the subject-states, and shortly afterwards was elected General responsible for Athenian forces at Samos (indeed, one source attributes this election to the success of the *Antigonê*). Throughout his life he continued to be involved in the affairs of state, serving as Crisis Commissioner in 413 when he was already an old man.

The conjunction of civilized and barbaric extremes that was Athens is reflected in Sophoklean Tragedy. Though set in a mystical past, these Tragedies display preoccupations which unmistakably belong to the fifth century: war, the nature of justice and of power, the glory of Athens, tyranny, the relationship between gods, and mortals. But through theater, the Athenian city-state did not only glorify and celebrate itself; it also questioned itself. Characteristically ironic and elucidating irreconcilable conflicts between equal rights, mapping out stories of grievance, revenge, and redemption, probing the nature of leadership, patriotism, and heroism, often intruding the imagined perspective of the socially marginalized, Sophoklean Tragedy served Athens by subjecting it to an oblique, yet piercing critique.

It is not only Athens, however, that has found the Sophoklean legacy of service. Since antiquity, Sophoklean theater has attracted the attentions of more thinkers and artists, perhaps, than any other playwright except Shakespeare. The *Antigonê* alone is among the most performed, read, adapted, and analyzed of all classical texts, while from Aristotle to Freud and beyond, the *Oedipus Tyrannos* has acquired the status of Ur-text within Western culture and thought. Less potent, though no less provocative, are the Tragedies of *Aias*, *The Women of Trachis*, *Êlektra*, *Philoktêtês*, and the *Oedipus at Kolonos*. Each reading reinvents Sophokles under the pressure of the civilities and barbarisms of its own time.

To read, watch, or perform Sophoklean Tragedy is to enter into a dialogue between past and present, which may be at once fascinating and repellent, inspiring, and troubling.

Hugh Denard
School of Theatre Studies
University of Warwick

SOPHOKLES AND THE ATHENIAN THEATER

By Carl R. Mueller

Sophokles' life spanned the century commonly known as the Golden Age of Athens, the fifth century B.C.E. (Before the Common Era). In the early days of the century, Athens, and Greece in general, was threatened by Persian invasions from the east. The involvement of mainland Greeks in the revolt of Asiatic Greeks against Persion domination precipitated this conflict. Persia already ruled many European Greeks in Thrace and Makedonia, and the most salient reason for its desire to conquer all Greece was the knowledge that there would be no security as long as some Greeks remained independent.

The first major battle between Greeks and Persians occurred in 490 at Marathon, a *deme* or territorial district on the northeast coast of Attika. It was here that 10,000 Greeks and their allies met a Persian force of nearly double that number. The battle, delayed by the Greeks while they waited for the Spartans to arrive, eventually took place without them, most likely because the Greeks learned that the Persians had begun a march on Athens. Having won the battle, the Greeks pursued the remaining Persians to their ships, capturing seven vessels in the process. If reports are correct, the Persians lost 6,400 men, the Greeks a total of 192. Aeschylus (525–456), the first of the great Athenian tragedians, fought in that battle.

The second, and decisive, encounter was fought in 480 at Salamis, an island in the Saronic Gulf off the western coast of Attika. Precisely what happened at this battle is obscure; in any event the Greek fleet, based on the island, thoroughly defeated the Persians, forcing them to withdraw to Asia Minor. It was at the ceremonial celebration of that victory that a gloriously naked sixteen-year-old Sophokles marched, playing the pipes, the chosen representative of the youth of Athens.

With these two astonishing victories, Greece achieved a half-century of comparative peace and unparalleled prosperity during which, especially in Athens, it developed a society and state that has been the wonder of the world ever since. The foundation of a democratic state at Athens had been established in the previous century, a "direct" as opposed to a "representative" or "parliamentary" democracy, a democracy run by the people: the rule (*kratos*) of the people (*demos*). What this meant, and it was a highly cherished right, was that every (male) Athenian citizen was directly involved in the governance of the state.

THEATER BEFORE SOPHOKLES

As far as theater was concerned, around 550 Thespis (if he ever existed) is said to have introduced at Athens the first speaker into the dithyramb chorus. This is also the time of the archaic orchestra in the agora at Athens as well as the establishment of the precinct sacred to Dionysos on the south side of the hill of the Akropolis. In 534 Pisistratos introduced drama into the state festivals of Athens. Then around 500 the site of dramatic performances was moved from the Agora to the precinct of Dionysos, where it remained, and on which site it went through numerous structural transformations.

SOPHOKLES: MAN OF THE THEATER

Sophokles' life was as remarkable in its length (?496–406) as it was in its productivity. His first dramatic competition, in 468, was against Aeschylus; his last was in the City Dionysia in 406. The first was ten years before Aeschylus' death; the last a commemoration of the recent death of Euripides (484–406). His own death followed shortly after.

It is estimated that his dramatic output consisted of more than 120 plays, of which a minimum of twenty won first prize, eighteen of them at the Great or City Dionysia in Athens. But Sophokles was more than merely a playwright. Like every male Athenian citizen, he was vitally involved in the governance of his city-state; in addition to which, in his fifties, he also served as a general with his great friend the Athenian politician Perikles during the revolt of Samos, most likely in 441 to 440. His renown was such that after his death he was rewarded with the honor of a hero cult.

Of his 120 plays only seven have come down to posterity; and of those only two can be positively dated: the *Philoktêtês* in 409, and the *Oedipus at Kolonos* in 406, the latter a posthumous victory produced by his grandson. He had several victories in 447 and 438, as well as with *Antigonê* at an unknown date. The dates for *Aias, Oedipus Tyrannos, Êlektra,* and *The Women of Trachis* are unknown, while the date for *Antigonê* is largely anecdotal.

Earlier in the twentieth century (most likely influenced by the idealizing tendency of nineteenth-century German philologists), Sophokles was considered to be "stable, harmonious, and at ease with experience," as *The Oxford Classical Dictionary* (1996) correctly reports. In reality, however, the plays of Sophokles are rife with examples of violence, discomfort, pain, and mental anguish, all of which are primary aspects of the vital theatricality that earlier times denied him simply by not wanting to recognize them. John Gould speaks of Sophokles as

> . . . the master of the enacted metaphor—metaphors of blindness in the two Oedipus plays and *Antigone*, of bestiality in *Trachiniae*—which is momentarily "realized" in the text as it is performed. The theatricality of such pervasive dramatic metaphors emerges in moments such as the messenger speech of *Oedipus Tyrannus* and the immediately following scene with the entry of the now blinded but "seeing" Oedipus . . .

One wonders at the perception of earlier critics who called Sophokles' dramaturgy "middling," because there are few more powerful, more dramatic and theatrical moments in the history of world theater than those found in his plays.

Cedric Whitman expresses this misreading as well and as eloquently as any.

> After the glibness of the classic assumption, with its easy ethic and its clichés about piety, serenity, and sophrosyne, a return to the mystery of the virile and passionate lines of Sophocles himself is a disquieting and bracing experience. What kind of serene simplicity can embrace the world of Oedipus, or conceive the terrible lines which close the *Trachiniae?* What lessons of prudent restraint can we draw from the fierce and openly justified extremes of Antigone and Electra? Once more, like Mozart, Sophocles veiled his passions in elegance, but they are only the more fearful for being veiled. It is an error to take elegance for meaning, to mistake the artistry for the art and leave the veil drawn. Yet the answer is not to tear the veil and separate the two; elegance is part of meaning, and artistry is necessary to art. If the tragic spirit is to penetrate to the central mysteries of life, it must, in order to remain intelligible, do so within a formal scheme. And the stricter the scheme the better, for thus the mystery grows incandescent by contrast with the innocence of the form.

SOPHOKLEAN THEATRICALITY

Consider, from a theatrical standpoint, the prologue of the *Aias* in which Athêna's voice is heard seemingly from nowhere, while Odysseus looks for traces of Aias' tracks in the sandy soil of the beach outside Aias' hut. Odysseus looks around in the early morning fog to locate the voice, which eventually takes on bodily form out of the mist. Or the "baiting game" that Athêna plays with Odysseus in the same play, leading him by the proverbial nose, condescending in tone and arch in attitude, making the most of his fear of being exposed to the "raving" Aias inside his hut. And when Aias is finally coaxed out of his dwelling by her, she manipulates him like a puppet at the end of her strings. These are moments of brilliant (perhaps even iconoclastic) theatricality. Like any master dramatic creator, Sophokles gives us not the expected but the unexpected possibility.

There are many other purely functional aspects of Sophokles' plays that he transforms into theatrical gold. One of them has to do with the theatrical prop. In *Êlektra* Sophokles plays a wonderfully extended theatrical "game" with what must be considered one of the major props in any of his plays: the funeral urn that ostensibly contains Orêstes' ashes. Once Êlektra is told of her brother Orêstes' death in the Pythian Games at Delphi (a false tale to hide the fact that Orêstes is indeed present), and once she is given the urn, she cannot be parted from it, the last remains of her beloved brother whom she once saved from destruction, and who was to be the avenger of their father Agamemnon's murder. All that she once held dear, her hopes, her love, her expectation, is now in that urn that she grieves and laments over inconsolably. Even when Orêstes tries to reveal himself to his sister and take the urn from her, she refuses to relinquish it. The brilliant use of this central prop resides in the fact that the living Orêstes is present on stage throughout her lamentation. Gould's succinct summation of this coup-de-théâtre is apropos: "The fusing of game-playing, irony, and intensity of tragic emotion is mediated through the simple 'prop.'"

Other major examples of theatrically conceived props in Sophokles are the sword in *Aias,* the gift of his enemy, the Trojan Hektor, with which Aias will kill himself and the magically endowed bow of Heraklês in *Philoktêtês,* without which the Trojan War will not be won by the Greeks.

ENTRANCES AND EXITS

Given the presumed layout of the Greek theater of Sophokles' time, entrances and exits are endowed with particular theatrical power and effectiveness, quite apart from the exact configuration of the theatrical space. The entrance of the blinded Oedipus through the main doors of the palace immediately following one of the greatest messenger speeches in Greek drama is nothing less than shattering in its effect. Its near equal is the final entrance of Kreon in *Antigonê.* Just seconds after the silent exit of his wife Eurydikê who has only just learned of her son Haimon's death, Kreon enters carrying the body of that son. Almost immediately following Kreon's entrance, the Messenger reenters with news of Eurydikê's suicide, followed by the immediate appearance of her dead body pushed out through the central doors on the scenic device known as the *ekkyklêma,* a platform on wheels to "reveal" a sight inside the house. The rapid juxtaposition of these moments of destruction and devastation are the work of a master poet of the theater. If it is Sophokles' intention to repay Kreon for his unbending stubbornness and for causing the deaths of three people closest to him, then he has done it with a sense of brilliant theatricality. These are only a few of many examples, some of the last of which are in *Philoktêtês.* The eponymous hero's initial entrance onto the scene is announced by his groans and laments from far off, striking fear into the hearts of the chorus of sailors, and his exit from Lemnos is equally dramatic: four times attempted and four times aborted, it is realized only at the fifth attempt.

THE ART OF NARRATIVE SPEECHES

Sophokles is also a master of the narrative speech usually, but not always, delivered by a messenger. The description of the death of Iokastê and the blinding of Oedipus has already been mentioned as the most theatrically effective in all of Greek drama. Certainly no less moving, though of a different tone altogether, is the speech describing the death and apotheosis of the aged Oedipus in the sacred grove of the goddesses at Kolonos. In *Êlektra,* the Tutor of Orestês narrates to Êlektra a description of the chariot race at the Pythian Games in Delphi in which Orestês is supposed to have been killed. It is possible to see this speech as not only excessively long but tedious, and adding nothing to the story. What this point of view fails to consider is that it is not the story narrated in the speech that is the main object of the narration, but the effect that it has on the person it most directly concerns, namely Êlektra, whose entire world is annihilated in that speech so that she welcomes death to be one with the brother she loves.

But not only Êlektra is affected; so, too, is the audience. The spectator, after all, not only knows that Orêstes is present to carry out his revenge for his father's murder, he or she also knows that the narration is a sheer fabrication. This creates a grand expectation from the spectator regarding the time when Êlektra will herself learn the truth, the expectation of which is so great that Sophokles is not only inspired to, but does write a scene of such ecstatic dimensions that it can only be rendered in song. With this understanding in place, the false narration of Orêstes' death becomes a central moment in the structure of this play, as well as a major irony. In addition, as will be discussed below, it is possible that the Chorus "acted out" these narrative speeches.

THE IMPORTANCE OF PLACE

One of the principal aspects of playwriting that Sophokles never fails to make use of is that of place. Ideally, the dramatic action of a play should occur in the one place in which it can logically transpire, no other being possible. Each of Sophokles' extant works observes this requirement. But his most organic applications of it are in *Philoktêtês* and *Oedipus at Kolonos*. In *Philoktêtês* the deserted island of Lemnos is at all events the logical location. But master craftsman that he is, Sophokles makes metaphoric connections between the play's eponymous hero and the setting.

In *Oedipus at Kolonos* the presence on stage of the sacred precinct of the goddesses is put to sublime use. That the ancient, blind, and ragged Oedipus enters unknowingly upon this ground is a divinely inspired event, and the mystery of its sanctity is enhanced when Antigonê describes its near-paradisiacal peace and beauty, and when the citizens of Kolonos attempt frantically to remove him from it, unsuccessfully at first, then successfully through persuasion. The very length of this confrontation, all having to do with the place's holiness, is a highly effective example of masterly stagecraft.

RECOGNITION SCENES

Surely the most distinctive aspect of Sophokles' dramaturgy is the idea of recognition (*anagnorisis*), a factor little found in Aeschylus and Euripides, but considered by Aristotle as an essential of tragedy and at the center of Sophokles' view of existence. No extant play of Sophokles is without its central recognition scene, a scene in which "one or more characters is brought to a realization that he or she has misperceived the nature of reality and the realization is almost always associated with pain, suffering, and death," as Gould has pointed out. This misperceived communication is not only between humans, but between humans and the gods, whose oracles and other communications, such as dreams and the readings of signs by prophets, are almost always either false or so clouded in ambiguity that they are an invitation to misunderstanding and a preamble to destruction.

Cedric Whitman calls this syndrome in the Sophoklean scheme of things "late learning." Both Dêianeira and Heraklês in *The Women of Trachis* understand too late the nature and meaning of oracles, learning the truth only after the action is taken and the tragic fall into chaos and death has been set in motion. In *Aias* the proper reading/understanding of Athêna's intention comes too late to prevent the tragic death of Aias. And so, too, in the other five plays of Sophokles. "Learning too late," writes Whitman, "is nothing new in Greek poetry."

THEATER FORM IN SOPHOKLEAN ATHENS

When we think of the structure of the Greek theater in antiquity, the first image that comes to mind is the "traditional" one of a *skênê* or building with from one to three doors in it to serve as a background to the action, and in front of which is a circular acting area made of pounded earth circled in stone and known as the orchestra. But modern scholarship has given cause to question that conventional image. And yet one aspect of the Greek theater is more than fairly certain, that from its inception as a formal entity it has had a very strong visual component.

Antiquity was constantly modifying and rebuilding its theater structures, to the degree that it is virtually impossible to know for certain what the theater space in Athens consisted of in the time of the Classical dramatists of the fifth century. As for the ubiquitous circular orchestra that we tend always to envision, there is no evidence for it prior to about 330 in the great theater at Epidauros, justly famous for its graceful symmetry and aesthetic beauty. As for the Theater of Dionysos in Athens in the fifth century, it is possible to conceive of a much larger and more elaborate version of the tiny provincial deme-theaters at Thorikos and Trachones in Attika. This would mean that in the Theater of Dionysos the audience in the fifth century was seated on wooden benches in a rectilinear arrangement in close proximity to the acting area, which, too, may have been loosely rectilinear, or, even more likely, trapezoidal, with only two sides being parallel.

In any event, it is the orchestra (literally, dancing-place) that is the central focal point at the time of Sophokles, the flat space of pounded earth on which took place the Chorus' song and choreography. Where the action proper of the fifth century Athenian tragic play occurred is not as certain, archeological evidence lacking. Most likely it was at orchestra level, with at most a low wooden platform in front of the *skênê,* and a flight of steps leading into the orchestra. Later in the century a *proskênion* (row of columns) was added to the front of the *skênê.* In any event, the history of the Theater of Dionysos in Athens from its crude beginnings in the latter part of the sixth century is a much debated subject. What cannot be argued, however, is that during the time of the great Classical dramatists it was architecturally still simple and undeveloped.

The stage and stage building (*skênê*) were most likely wooden and rebuilt each year for the occasion. And, as Richard Green points out, vase paintings from the late fifth and early fourth centuries suggest that "the stage [of this period] was about a metre high with a flight of steps in the center communicating with the orchestra." In the *skênê,* which could represent a palace (*Oedipus*

Tyrannos), tent or hut (*Aias*), temple (*Iphigenia in Tauris*), cave (*Philoktêtês*), or the Brazen Threshold of Earth (*Oedipus at Kolonos*), among other sites, were a maximum of three doors, the central one for major entrances and exits, the two flanking ones for less important comings and goings, and yet some (most recently David Wiles) maintain there was only a single door during this period. Behind the central door was housed the *ekkyklêma,* a wheeled platform device measuring about 2.5 by 1.5 meters, which could be rolled out onto the stage to display scenes usually of carnage, such as the body of the murdered Agamemnon, the inside of Aias' hut with scores of slaughtered cattle surrounding him, and the newly dead body of Eurydikê, but also of Oedipus after his self-blinding, lying on the platform. At the right edge of the stage was a crane or machine used to lift gods and heroes onto the stage or fly them off, a device used only once, or perhaps never, by Sophokles. The *logeion* or *skênê* roof was used for the appearance of gods, though as late as mid-fifth century for use by mortals, as, for example, the Watchman in the opening of Aeschylus' *Agamemnon.* To quote Richard Green once more: "The contrast between the hidden interior of the stage building and the daylight outside, between gods on high and the actors on stage, and between these and the chorus, half-way to the audience and virtually within its territory, are all physical facts which the playwrights exploited." It was not until 350–330 that Lycurgos gave Athens the Theater of Dionysos that we generally call to mind before its later Hellenistic remodeling by the Romans in the second centuy. It is a gleaming theater of stone: stone *skênê,* stone *stoa,* and stone auditorium (*theatron*—literally, seeing-place) built into the southern slope of the hill of the Akropolis. Still, this was not the theater of Sophokles' day.

All this said, and supported by scholars, a recent book by David Wiles, *Tragedy in Athens,* gives good reason to suppose from internal evidence in the plays that the wooden *skênê* of Sophokles' time was not raised, but on the same level as the circular orchestra of pounded earth. Furthermore, the *skênê* may either have been immediately behind the orchestra circle, or placed so as to cut off a small part of its upper edge. This is the assumption taken as the model for the present translation, though modern producers, working on a modern stage, will, of course, make their own decisions in this regard.

FIFTH-CENTURY STAGING TRADITION

What tragedy looked like in the age of Sophokles is no easy task to decipher. Though there are many vase paintings almost certainly dealing with stage representations of the myths that served as the basis of the tragedies, these images most likely exceed what might have been seen on stage. What we may be fairly certain of is that costumes were rich, elaborate, and formal, as evidenced by the Pronomos vase from the end of the fifth century. Although it depicts a satyr play, the Pronomos vase also shows costumes that could well have been worn by characters in tragedy of the second half of the fifth century.

MASKS

Most notable in the staging of fifth-century tragedy is the use of the mask. There is ample evidence in Greece of the use of masks in cult ceremonies, everything from the grotesque mask worn in adolescent rites of passage in Sparta, to animal masks in the cult of Dêmêtêr and Dêspoina at Lycosura. Closer to home are the masks frequently worn in the cult of Dionysos, from which the mask in Greek tragedy most likely derives. It is often suggested that the theatrical mask also amplified the voice of the actor to reach, in some theaters, many thousands of spectators. In any case, dramatic masks are frequently depicted from the fifth century onwards. Made generally of linen, the mask covered the entire head and, in fifth-century tragedy, was basically naturalistic and represented types rather than individuals.

TRAGEDY INSIDE AND OUTSIDE ATHENS AND THE FESTIVALS

What we know about the production of tragedy in Greece is almost totally confined to Attika, though other areas were also active producers. In any event, from the close of the sixth century and throughout the fifth century, tragedy was primarily performed as part of the Spring or City Dionysia in Athens, though tragedy was also a part of the Rural Dionysia during the winter months, when access to Athens was inhibited because of weather. But tragedy was not the sole reason for these festivals. They also scheduled processions, sacrifices in the theater, libations, the parade of war orphans, and the performance of dithyramb and comedy. As summary, the final day was devoted to a review of the conduct of the festival and to the awarding of prizes.

Three tragedians competed with three plays each plus a satyr play, all chosen by the *archon,* a state official who also appointed the three *chorêgoi,* who undertook the expense of equipping and training the choruses, the actors and playwrights being paid for by the state. One judge from each of the ten tribes or *demes* of Athens was chosen to determine the winners of the competition, and the winning playwright was crowned with a wreath of ivy in the theater. Till about the middle of the fifth century, the three tragedies of each day's performance comprised a trilogy; eventually each of the three plays had a different subject, and many of Sophokles' plays were written as independent plays.

THE CHORUS IN TRAGEDY

Of all the elements of theatrical practice, the importance of the chorus cannot be overestimated. It was, after all, the chief financial responsibility of the *chorêgoi*. In Athens, especially, there was a long tradition, even before tragedy, of and emphasis on the competition of dithyramb choruses, which consisted of both song and dance. Even in the days of tragedy, there were separate competitions devoted to the dithyramb in which each of the ten *demes* of Athens participated. In Aeschylus' day, the tragic chorus numbered twelve, then Sophokles added three more for a total of fifteen. In his *Tragedy in Athens,* Wiles gives a brilliant and convincing exposition of the degree to which the tragic chorus participated in the event. He posits (with help from other scholars) that not only was the choreographed movement of the chorus not in straight lines or highly formalized, as previously thought, but that it was often particularly active. When, for example, the split chorus in the *Aias* enters through both *eisodoi* searching for Aias, they enter in an agitated and most likely disordered state (choreographed disorder, to be sure). And when the chorus of old men enters for the first time in *Oedipus at Kolonos,* they, too, are highly agitated, as their text clearly indicates, and dart wildly about the orchestra in search of the intruder into the Sacred Grove. Finally, Wiles makes a most insightful deduction when he posits that the subject of each choral ode is acted out by the chorus in choreographed dance. And even more startling, that during long narrative speeches, such as the Messenger's speech describing Oedipus' self-blinding, and Eurydikê's death scene in *Antigonê,* and one might also add the Tutor's narrative of Orêstes' fictitious "death" at Delphi in *Êlektra,* the chorus was actively acting out a choreography that visually complemented the verbal narration. The brilliance of this deduction is staggering in indicating the participation of the chorus in Athenian tragedy: they were seldom inactive, and not only did they wear the persona of their first function as Elders or Trachian Women or women friends of Êlektra, they also represented an abstract or distanced body that acted out the subject of others' narration of which in no event could they have any foreknowledge. It helps one to understand why, when Athenians attended the theater at festival times, they spoke of going to the "choreography" rather than to the play.

THE TRAGIC MASK AND
THE DOUBLING OF ROLES

Considering that tragedy was a masked entertainment, it was only practical to confine the number of speaking parts in any one scene to three actors, the reason most likely being, as Patricia Easterling suggests, to enable the audience to tell "where each voice is coming from," inasmuch as facial movements were obscured by masks. This practical limitation, however, permitted an actor to be double- and perhaps even triple-cast, a practice much used and most often, one must assume, to very good effect. In any case, even though the primary reason for only three actors was very likely a financial consideration, to have a single actor play, for example, the roles of Pentheus as well as his mother Agavê, or Dêianeira and Hêrakles, offers resonances that are far-reaching and highly intriguing. One must also not forget that masks were helpful in disguising the male actor who traditionally assumed female roles, women being excluded from performing. As for the numbers of nonspeaking actors on stage, there was no limit, and exciting stage effects with scores of "extras" would not have been unusual. It was Sophokles, by the way, who introduced the third actor to the theater of his time, thus opening up the possibility of infinitely more flexible scenes than with the previously traditional two.

MUSIC IN TRAGEDY

Of music in Archaic and Classical Greece we know very little. Some music scores survive, but they are largely fragmentary and date from the Hellenistic period or later. Although the Greeks were knowledgeable about a great many musical instruments, especially from their eastern neighbors, they adopted only two main sorts: a stringed instrument (lyre) and a wind instrument or pipe (aulos), not a flute but sounded with a reed (single and double). In tragedy of the fifth century, the double-pipe aulos was the instrument of choice to accompany the musical sections of the dramatic action.

The musical element in the performance of fifth-century tragedy was of primary importance, and its similarity to modern opera is not unnoticed. Every one of the extant tragedies has built into it a number of choral sections (usually five) that cover generally short passages of time and in which the singing and dancing chorus holds the center of attention in the orchestra. In addition, there are sections in which song is exchanged between characters, as well as an alternation between spoken dialogue and recitative or song, the latter often between a character or characters and the chorus. As Easterling rightly points out, these sections exist in the same time frame as the scenes of exclusively spoken dialogue. The rationale behind this practice being "to intensify emotion or to give a scene a ritual dimension, as in a shared lament or song of celebration." Solo singing by individual characters became increasingly more important with the passage of time, and Euripides is famous for his monodies.

TRAGEDY AND THE AUDIENCE

Whatever shape the Greek theater structure may have assumed at any given point in time, two elements were constant: it was an open-air event more or less centered around an open area in which the chorus could dance. Furthermore the performance took place in daylight (and probably not from dawn to dusk as frequently thought). This peculiarity alone endows the performance of the fifth century with a particular reference, namely the audience. The audience was there, the audience could not be hidden in the neutrality of a darkened auditorium, and thus the audience had to be dealt with as modern audiences generally need not be and seldom are.

With this as a given, playwrights went to great lengths never to ignore the spectator, and Sophokles in particular made every effort to create a strong bond between the audience and the chorus that was almost always present on stage. In Sophokles the chorus becomes the audience's onstage extension, or to put it another way, the audience becomes the extension of the chorus in the *theatron*. There is no better way to explain the communal experience elicited by the performance of Greek tragedy in its natural environment.

TRAGIC ACTING STYLE

In a theater structure the size of the one used by Sophokles in fifth-century Athens, the mode of presentation could never have been intimate, even though intimate subjects are dealt with. The size of the seating area and the large number of spectators demanded a style of acting that was unqualifiedly extraverted. Gestures must have been broad and easily read by many thousands of people. Even the masks that covered the entire head of the tragic actor (including a wig) must have been an attempt to communicate with spectators at great distances.

TRAGIC SUBJECT MATTER

As for subject matter, fifth-century tragedy for the most part borrowed from the heroic past, stories found in the Homeric epics and in the tales narrated by rhapsodes from Archaic times. But at no time did this borrowing evidence an antiquarian interest.

Athens being in Attika, it is not to be wondered at that many of the heroes used as the basis for Attic tragedy were figures worshipped in Attic cult, for example—to mention only a few characters from the plays of Sophokles— Thêseus, Heraklês, Oedipus.

TRAGEDY AND POLITICS

Many of the extant plays of fifth-century Athens show signs of learning from or, perhaps better, mirroring the thriving political life of its day. Critics have recently stressed the ideological and didactic content of tragedy, finding vital connections between various aspects of tragic discourse and discourse in the law-making body of the Athenian assembly and the law courts. One need merely glance at Sophokles' *Êlektra,* as only one example among many, to see to what extent the rhetoric and discourse of these bodies may have influenced the first scene in which Êlektra and Klytaimnêstra meet.

THE PLAYS

AIAS

Sophokles' first play, *Aias*, is based on a rich and extensive literary tradition, which includes a great variety of tales and legends concerning its eponymous hero. He figures conspicuously in Homer's *Iliad*, where he is referred to repeatedly as of formidable stature, towering head and shoulders over every other Greek at Troy. He is also spoken of as the greatest of the Greek heroes after Achilleus and is a frequent point of reference in the odes of the fifth-century lyric poet Pindar.

The Aias of legend is a figure very close and dear to the Athenian heart. His ancient kingdom was the island of Salamis situated just off the west coast of Attika, an island that in the sixth century, during the age of Solon and Pisistratos, became an Athenian possession, thanks to the propagandist use of Aias' name. He is proudly referred to by classical Athenians as the "bulwark of Athens." A very late example of his almost sacred connection to that city is the dedication of a Phoenician ship to him at Salamis, a ship from among the spoils of the great victory over the Persians at Salamis in 480. And he was named a patron hero of one of the Athenian tribes in the late sixth century.

Aias is also known as the possessor of an extraordinarily headstrong and self-centered nature. And it is in that guise that we meet him in Sophokles' play. With the death of Achilleus, as legend has it, the armor of that hero, which was made by Hephaistos, the god of fire and metal-working, was to be awarded to the most worthy of the Greek heroes who survived him. Given his reputation as the greatest hero after Achilleus, Aias had good reason to expect it. He was thwarted, however, when the Greek leaders awarded it to Odysseus.

In his rage, Aias determines to take revenge by murdering the generals Agamemnon and Menelaos, as well as his archenemy Odysseus. But Athêna steps in and scrambles Aias' mind, causing him instead, in the dead of night, to descend on the cattle and sheep of the Greek camp at Troy. Those that he doesn't slaughter in the field, he leads back to his tent where he proceeds to torment and slaughter them, thinking they are his intended prey, the generals, Agamemnon and Menelaos, and Odysseus. It is at this point that we enter Sophokles' drama.

This play—most likely the earliest of the seven surviving plays of

Sophokles, but by no means an early work—opens with one of the truly remarkable scenes in extant Greek tragedy. The time is just before dawn. The night is cold and visibility is poor. Odysseus is seen tracing Aias' tracks in the sandy soil of the Trojan seashore outside Aias' tent. Then, at first unseen by him, the voice of Athêna breaks the silence. Odysseus is startled, eventually recognizing the voice of his protector, and there follows a remarkable scene in which a petulant and vindictive Athêna is seen to play condescendingly with Odysseus as if he were a child, taunting him regarding his fear of seeing the "mad" Aias; and cruelly with Aias, still in his delirium, making a fool of him in the midst of his slaughtered "captives."

Emerging from his divinely inspired madness, Aias is shamed by his action and determines that his dignity, his warrior and hero status—his *arete*—can only be restored if he commits suicide and thus escape the opprobrium of his action. His wife Tekmêssa pleads with him to reconsider, as do his sailors from Salamis, but to no avail. At this point one of the two supreme speeches in this play is delivered by Aias: the speech to his very young son on what to expect from the vengeful Greeks and how to live a life of honor. The other speech comes later, at the seashore, just before Aias commits suicide with the sword given him by his most formidable enemy, the Trojan Hektor.

Aias' body is discovered by his wife Tekmêssa and the chorus of sailors, and upon the entrance of Teükros, Aias' brother, they set about to bury his body. They are prevented, however, by Menelaos and later by Agamemnon, who maintain a profound hatred for Aias in general, and in particular for his recent attempt on their lives. His body will not be buried, they insist, but thrown out to be devoured by animals. It is only through the reconciling intervention of Odysseus, no less an enemy of Aias, that the brother generals are mollified only slightly and allow the burial.

It is this final third of the play that has been the victim of severe criticism. Many have said that the two parts of the play, the before and after of Aias' suicide, are a polarity between Aias and Odysseus. But nothing could be further from the truth. Neither of these two parts is an entity unto itself. The subject of both parts is quite simply a single one. John Moore has said, and rightly, that the death of Aias "taken quite simply in itself, completes nothing; the play's action is complete only when the spectator is brought to an altered estimate of the meaning of Ajax's career and destiny." He continues:

> The major dramatic subject, the weight and heft of it, is Ajax. The greatness of his demand upon life is the thing that we must, above all, be made to feel; and Sophocles places this theme before us by the full dramatization

he gives of Ajax's suffering and resolution, of the dismay and pathetic dependence of those around him, and of their desolation when his protection is removed.

Pindar, writing before Sophokles, chose to omit the insane slaughter of the livestock and the shame it brought, allowing Aias' sole motivation for suicide to be the profound humiliation of not being awarded Achilleus' armor—a slight of no minor dimension in the Homeric Age of Heroes. Sophokles, however, being a dramatist, saw far greater theatrical purchase in the more conventional version. Not only is the sight of Aias in his tent, surrounded by the gore of scores of slaughtered beasts and himself befouled with the mess, a powerful image for the spectator, but it sets up an enormously difficult dramaturgical problem for Sophokles, namely to bring us round by the play's end to seeing Aias as the true hero he always was. Concerning that scene of slaughter, says Moore, "it is a fearful and summary image of total degradation not merely of heroic, but of all human, value. The process by which this image is transformed and Ajax's disaster irradiated by his recovery of heroic strength and human relatedness is the true action of the play." By the end of the extended scene in which we first see the slaughter inside the tent, followed by the speech to his small son Eurysakes, Aias has begun to reassert his noble, heroic self. He realizes the depravity of his action and knows that only death can wipe his hero's slate clean. It is a harsh and uncompromising ethic. "[E]ven the address to Eurysakes, one feels, is an uncompromising assertion of the quality of Ajax more than a response to the child."

The second part of the reassertion of Aias' honor comes at the seashore where he sets up the scene for his suicide. The earlier bravado has tempered. He begins, perhaps for the first time, to think of those close to him—his son, his wife, whom he treated so cruelly in the previous scene, and of his mother and father back on Salamis—and how each will take the news of his death. He asks the divine powers for a quiet death, and for his brother Teükros to find his body first so as not to shock others with the sight. All in all, he makes his peace with life and with his death in the world below. What he does not do, of course, as Moore points out, is make his peace with his enemies. Such an act does not exist in Sophokles' scheme of things when one dies and is survived by the same enemies.

There is no question that the squabbles (and that is probably the correct word) between Teükros, Menelaos, and Agamemnon over the burial of Aias' body are couched in a language that is a far cry from that of the first part of the play. Rather than seeing it as an artistic lapse, it is most likely more accurate to assume that Sophokles is merely matching form and content. The speeches are unconscionably long, and the pettiness of the Greek leaders is an embarrassment, and meant to be precisely that. And yet, it is this part of the play that is most likely to have enlisted the rapt attention of the Athenian audience of its time. First of all, the Classical Athenian loved debate and long speeches. Every male Athenian citizen heard thousands, year in, year out, in the Assembly on the Pnyx. Second, the subject is that of burial, a topic that is the central issue in Sophokles' play soon to come, *Antigonê*. It was a topic of vital concern for the Athenian populace, whose attitude toward the right to burial even of one's enemies was deeply held. For the modern audience, however, of equal, if not more interest, is the renewed image of the heroic Aias that emerges slowly, but with great specificity and passion, out of the series of debates.

But what are we to make of the announcement of Athêna, as related by the Greek seer Kalchas, that if Aias is to survive, he must remain in his tent under the watch of his fellows for one whole day, otherwise his time is up? This is a shrewd move on Athêna's part; it testifies to what degree she knows Aias: totally. It is also in keeping with the cruelty she displays toward Aias in the play's prologue. As Cedric Whitman sees it, one day's disgrace for Aias, at home, in his tent, under the watch of his men and Tekmêssa, will mean that he "will have done the sensible thing—reason things out, yield honor lost, and reckon life worth more." But such a decision on Aias' part—such "reasoning"—is an impossibility. If it were possible, he would no longer be Aias, the man of action, the doer. For Athêna to command him to stay in his tent for an entire day is simply to say that Aias "cannot endure one day's disgrace." That is his *arête*, his honor, his greatness. That is why Aias refuses Athena's help in battle to lead him to victory. An insane act of "superhuman pride and self-sufficiency," but self-sufficiency it is, and the hero, like no other mortal, has no choice but to be proud of his self-sufficiency, even if it means that he is headed straight into destruction—and self-destruction in the search for personal glory is at the very core of the Greeks' understanding of the heroic temperament. If that is hubris, then so be it, and hubris must then be a defense of *arête*. The hero is nothing more nor less than the self-made man, and he has only himself to account to.

All of this "excess" was considered "godlike" to Homer. It was the stuff of which Achilleus was made, and the stuff of which Aias, the greatest hero at Troy after Achilleus, was also made. In them and in every true hero there is a *daimon*, an inner spirit or spark that animates him to an act or series of acts or life that is above the ordinary, a force we today might in more pejorative terms call daemonic. To quote Whitman again:

> The heroic assumption means precisely this—the possession of a standard which becomes a kind of fatal necessity that drives toward self-destruction. . . . It seems excessive and culpable only if one's standard is life and common sense; if one's standard is arete, it is an inevitable course. The true Greek hero raises the standard of his own excellence so high that he is no longer appropriate to life.

Which leads to the figure of Odysseus in Sophokles' play, the wily, clever, ever devious, and pragmatic Odysseus. If Aias is the image of the uncompromising Homeric hero of centuries past, then Odysseus in this work is the paradigm of the ethic and temper of the time in which Sophokles created him. He is a hero of compromise, an attribute not uncommon to the mid-fifth century Athenian, and by no means free of sophistry. Athens was beginning the decline that would lead to her ultimate collapse with the conclusion of the Peloponnesian War in 404. If one were to think of a salient reason why Aias and Odysseus should, from a character standpoint, be enemies, the vital ethical question of compromise would serve splendidly. Aias could never have understood Odysseus and what motivates him. And so, we are left at the end of the play with a settlement that is tenuous at best and with, let us say, a vivid, indeed blinding afterimage of a true hero of the past, and the direct image of the new hero in whom there is a mighty falling-off. The play's ending is deeply ironic, as well as deeply felt by its author, and its closing moments lament the passing of greatness.

ANTIGONÊ

If, as it is assumed, *Antigonê* was written roughly past the middle of the fifth century, during Sophokles' own vigorous middle years, it is not surprising to see it as a young man's play. The work fairly bursts with youthful vitality and passion in the characters of Antigonê and her fiancé Haimon—a fact that is apparent no matter when the play is performed.

The central conflict of the work revolves around the question: Who is right among two passionately held principles of Right—Kreon, who puts all of his belief in the integrity of the State or Antigonê, for whom political expediency is secondary, and who sides with compassion and piety to the dead in keeping with what she understands to be the eternal law of Justice? The issue is the burial or nonburial of her brother Polyneikês who invaded Thebes in an attempt to reclaim the throne that was rightly his by agreed-upon arrangement, but denied him by his younger brother Eteoklês. In the night prior to the opening of the dramatic action both brothers kill each other in battle, and Kreon, the new king of Thebes, has issued an edict that assures full rights of military burial to Eteoklês and denies them to the invader Polyneikês. Anyone caught burying the body of Polyneikês is condemned to be stoned to death in the town square. Antigonê refuses obedience to the edict and carries out a ritual burial of her brother's naked corpse left lying on the field of battle. She is caught, defends herself against what she considers Kreon's tyranny, and is walled up in a cavern to die, where she kills herself.

The issue of whose action in this dramatic conflict is correct has been debated down the millennia. Some say Kreon, others Antigonê, and still others that both are equally right and equally wrong, and that the stubbornness of both brings about the devastating tragedies suffered by each in turn: Antigonê dies as does her loyal fiancé Haimon, and Kreon loses his son and his wife in the process and longs for death to take him.

Kreon is shown as one who mouths principles of right government, all the right words—law and order—but then roundly contradicts himself in action. He speaks of the necessity of listening to good advice in the governance of the state, but when it comes time to do precisely that—as in the blazing scene with Haimon—he lashes out against such advice, both from his father-devoted son and from the citizens of Thebes who, Haimon tells him, are afraid of him and who murmur behind his back that what he is doing to Antigonê is reprehensible. Bowra in his *Sophoclean Tragedy* identifies Kreon as the typical tyrant, and Whitman sees him as nothing less, and in very historical terms: "His quickness to wrath, his rejection of criticism, his suspicion of corruption among the people, his resentment of women, and his demand for utter servitude all find their parallels in the familiar habits of the great Greek tyrants."

The *Antigonê* was presented to an Athenian audience in the Theater of Dionysos at the height of the administration of Periklês, the benevolence and brilliance of whose rule is legendary in the history of Classical Athens, and at a time when questions of Justice and Right and Statecraft were fiercely debated. No Athenian of the time could have countenanced a man who, as Whitman writes, "behaved like a tyrant, and talked like an oligarch, however he sometimes prefaced his real sentiments with fine-sounding doctrines about the stability of the state." The government of the military state of Sparta was the contemporary exemplar of such a state, whose stability was based on "repression, control from above, and suspicion," in all of which Kreon is well versed. Again Whitman:

It is therefore clear that Antigone's famous stubbornness, the fault for which she has been so roundly reproved, is really moral fortitude. She does not go "too far." How far should one go in resisting the tyranny of evil? Given real political arete, how much allegiance can one give to an illegal master? It is useless to speak of the defects of Antigone's qualities; there are no defects. Nor need there be any fault whereby her fall is justified. It is as foolish to try to justify it as it would be to try to defend the legal murder of Socrates.

The idea that Kreon shares a tragic fate with Antigonê is to grasp at straws. Indeed he may fall and his world collapse around him, but there is nothing in him that is even remotely tragic. The tragedy belongs to those who are destroyed by his evil stupidity, and especially to Antigonê whose devotion to justice is unshakable. If modern history offers a solitary bravery in face of adversity to match hers, it is that of the student unflinchingly facing down the on-coming tanks in Tiananmen Square on the occasion of another more recent demonstration of brutal tyranny.

Each reader, each critic, each actor and director will continue to make individual decisions on these issues, but one question remains: Is it so impossible that sheer evil and sheer good are capable of a tragic conflict that will send sparks flying in the dark night of a moral dilemma?

THE WOMEN OF TRACHIS

In *The Women of Trachis* Sophokles sets himself much the same structural-dramaturgical problem as he did in his earlier *Aias*. One of his main characters, Dêianeira, makes her final exit to death two-thirds of the way through the play (line 812 in the Greek text, Aias at line 865).

In *Aias* the question is less who is the main character, but in *The Women of Trachis* it is precisely that—Dêianeira or Heraklês? And Sophokles gives us precious little help when it comes to the title, which refers neither to Dêianeira nor to Heraklês, but to one of the least organic choruses in his extant oeuvre, a chorus that contributes virtually nothing to the dramatic action. The title, then, suggests that it is a deliberate evasion of the issue.

Many critics have also questioned whether Sophokles intended that Heraklês, Dêianeira's husband, would, at his death by fire, undergo apotheosis for his sufferings and join the pantheon of Olympian gods. It was a given in Greek mythology, but there is no mention of it in *The Women of Trachis,* nor is there any implication that it is imminent upon the play's conclusion, or even somewhere down the trajectory of time. Does Sophokles expect the mythologically well-versed audience in the Theater of Dionysos to forget what it knows regarding the most famous hero of Greek mythology? If so, why?

Another problem, or surprise (depending on how one sees it), is the use of Heraklês in a tragedy. He appears many times on the Classical Athenian stage, but primarily as a comic figure, even as a buffoon, and not infrequently in an inebriated state. His conventional genre is comedy or the satyr play. In Euripides' *Alkêstis* he appears as a comic figure despite the play's serious nature; but in *The Women of Trachis,* he is seen as a fully serious character in a single mode, as a man in excruciating pain dying because of a fatal but well-intentioned error on the part of his wife.

As for Dêianeira, she is without question one of Sophokles' (and Greek tragedy's) most finely and sensitively etched portraits of woman: kind, gentle, generous, keenly responsive to the feelings of others, and, above all, loving—even of a husband whose treatment of her has been nothing but boorish and insensitive, not alone through his almost constant absence, but as the result of his ubiquitous and flagrant philandering. In this play, he sends his latest concubine on ahead before his arrival for his wife to tend to.

If any leading female character in tragedy has an excuse to extinguish her husband for crudeness and cruelty it is Dêianeira. She is almost as highly motivated toward that end as Klytaimnêstra and more so even than Medea. And that is precisely what mythic tradition made of her prior to Sophokles—a strong, aggressive character in the mold of the two characters mentioned above, a kind of latter-day Amazon, whose name translates as nothing less than "husband killer." Though he kept the name, this is not the character that Sophokles chose to place at the center of *The Women of Trachis.*

From a purely dramaturgical standpoint, Dêianeira is the play's central, pivotal character. It is she who is the play's protagonist, she who is the doer, she who sets the tragedy in motion; without her there is no play as Sophokles wrote it. To be sure, she acts in response to Heraklês' inciting action: his (repeated) absence and his (repeated) provocative spousal behavior; but it is Dêianeira who acts, who observes, contemplates, decides, and, again, acts in front of the spectators in that Theater of Dionysos in Athens.

Had Sophokles wanted, he could very well have omitted the physical appearance of the Heraklês character entirely and reported his fate in one of his famous messenger speeches, and in so doing have avoided the critical problem that has troubled critics and spectators through the millennia. He might also have avoided the Dêianeira character and dwelt entirely on the death of Heraklês. But he did neither. Or was he of two minds regarding who was the central character, as some have asked? Unfortunately, there is no definitive answer to this question and only speculation remains. What, then, may Sophokles have had in mind?

Cedric Whitman has noted that with *The Women of Trachis* there enters into Sophokles' work a "gloomy change . . . an apparently sudden failure of the faith that gives the earlier works their reassuring brightness." And he places *The Women of Trachis* in the same category as the play that will follow it, *Oedipus Tyrannos*, as being "another large step on [investigating] the metaphysics of evil, to which Sophocles devoted his life . . . "

Bitterness and destruction are the hallmarks of the plays of Sophokles' middle period, and they are "poisoned by a kind of universal despair," a despair that arises in the search for truth, for knowledge. Whitman calls them plays of "tragic knowledge," but knowledge that comes too late, as it does in both *The Women of Trachis* and *Oedipus Tyrannos;* knowledge that brings with it not liberation and enlightenment, but the worst kind of loss.

For Sophokles "humanity still wears its jewel of *arête,* but no apotheosis, like that of *Antigonê,* follows." Knowledge always comes, and the characters struggle to see that it comes in time, but it always comes too late. The world to Sophokles in these plays is an irrational place in which his protagonists, Dêianeira and Oedipus, are "examples of high-minded humanity which wills the best and achieves the worst." Both of them suffer through no fault of their own; both are guiltless; and both lose everything: Dêianeira her life, and Oedipus all but his life—but that scrap of life is totally outweighed by his lost reputation, his humiliation, and his abject state, a condition that is infinitely worse than the relative kindness of Dêianeira's death. But some years had passed between those plays, and Sophokles' view of life had changed or, rather, evolved. Antigonê's death is likened by Sophokles to that of a goddess; for Dêianeira there is no such comforting comparison, not even in her own mind.

The long scene of Heraklês' death agony that ends *The Women of Trachis* is a cruel and brilliant move on the part of Sophokles to allow Dêianeira no restitution. The vulgar and egocentric Heraklês cares nothing about her motivations and refuses to listen to his son Hyllos' attempt to explain them. It takes no stretch of understanding to see that Dêianeira is everywhere present in the last third of the play. If her corpse had been dumped onstage, she could not be more present. What we see is the result of her doing, and Heraklês refuses insanely to see her side of it and the good intention behind her action. If he had, there would surely have been a reconciliation and an ending that Sophokles did not want to write. At the play's end, Sophokles is simply, and finally, emphasizing what has been his point all along: that the best of intentions is damned to defeat in the most ignominious way. It is the final nail in

Dêianeira's casket. She was always alone, always unloved, and she is so even, and most especially, in death.

But the play is not just about Dêianeira, though she may dominate it by length of role and goodness of character. It is also about Heraklês, however late he enters. Early in the play the chorus piously asserts that Zeus always cares for his children. The reference, of course, is to Heraklês who is, literally, a child of Zeus. But that piety does not materialize in regard either to Zeus' true son or to his metaphoric "daughter," the totally human Dêianeira.

But what of Sophokles' reason for omitting any mention of the traditional apotheosis of Heraklês after his suffering and death by fire? Given the implacably cruel universe that Sophokles appears to be asserting—one in which human *arête* no longer counts for anything, as it once did in *Antigonê*, and as it might still in the case of Heraklês who, for all his indifference to and final hatred of his wife, spent his life and labors in the service of good—how could the author permit even a single exception to his pessimistic view of existence by allowing whatever good Heraklês, the greatest of the Greek heroes, may have done to be rewarded in the traditional way? If we take Sophokles seriously, no such exception is possible, and he had very good reason to alter tradition, even to hope that the audience could forget it, and put in its place the philosophical view of universal evil and malignancy that he intended to show as the rationale for the action of his tragedy. If not even Heraklês, the spawn of Zeus, is spared, how could it be that a mere mortal could hope to be?

Hyllos' words that close the play are unequivocal: that all the horrors and evils that have transpired are the handiwork of Zeus.

OEDIPUS TYRANNOS

Well known as it is (perhaps, along with *Hamlet*, the Western world's best-known dramatic work), Sophokles' *Oedipus Tyrannos*, like every great play, is based on the simplest of premises, the premise of every murder mystery ever told: Who is the murderer? It is as simple as that. So simple is it that every action of the play emanates from it. In theatrical jargon it is the "through-line." *Hamlet*, for all its complexity, is every bit as simple at its root. The sentinel Bernardo, who utters the play's first line, states it as baldly as possible: "Who's there?" There is the through-line. From there on the dramatic search at its most basic level is to discover the validity of the Ghost of Hamlet's father. Faced with the Ghost, Hamlet asks: "Be thou a spirit of health or goblin damned, / Bring with thee airs from heaven or blasts from hell . . ." Everything hinges on the answer. If from heaven, the Ghost can be trusted and Hamlet can act accordingly, taking revenge on his uncle Claudius for the murder of his father; if from hell, the Ghost is demonic and out to trip up Hamlet's soul. In any event, the play's central and most basic question is made clear.

It is even more clear in Sophokles' *Oedipus Tyrannos*. From the beginning—and it is clear what the problem is from the very moment that Kreon enters the scene and delivers Apollo's message regarding how to rid Thebes of the plague—everything in the play is directed toward that end, that throughline question being: Who is the murderer of King Laïos? This does not mean that higher, more philosophical issues are not also being sought out and tested, such as Oedipus' parentage, his very identity, his tenacity in the face of adversity of the worst kind: self-incrimination for the murder of his father and marriage to his mother. Truth is the sine qua non required at every turn of Oedipus' fate. The question always facing the spectator of Oedipus' dilemma is: Will he or will he not succumb to the quite human fear of serving as his own judge and jury and executioner?

With every scene of the play, Oedipus is faced with a new, more advanced piece of information that appears to confirm his implication in the crime that Apollo says must be punished and expiated if Thebes is to be purged of the plague. At each scene's end, Oedipus, pushed to the extreme, retreats into the palace in a highly agitated state, only to return after the Chorus' thoughtful meditation on the preceding scene, calm again and determined to push on into deeper waters—which is not to imply that he does so without trepidation; if so, where would be the dramatic tension that will mount to a shattering climax?

One way of looking at the play's structure is in terms of opposites—counterpoint, a musician would call it. One note pitted against another, upward and downward musical motion simultaneously enacted. That defines precisely the progress of the *Oedipus Tyrannos*. For every notch on the scale of material consideration that Oedipus falls, he rises a notch on the scale of moral consideration. If he speaks of himself in the play's first speech as: "I, Oedipus, known to everyone," it has nothing to do with the old cliché hammered away at in too many classrooms, that Oedipus suffers from "overweening" pride, that he is haughty, that he is remote, that he is more interested in himself than he is in his people and his city. And yet these truisms are on many a student's and teacher's tongue and very difficult to shake free and into the universal recycle bin of misconceived information.

Oedipus is not extravagant in his self-praise (if indeed that is what it is). He once saved Thebes from the clutches of the Sphinx and single-handedly restored it to health. He did what no one, not even Apollo's prophet in

Thebes, Teiresias, was able to accomplish. And for that he has won the reputation with the people of Thebes of being their savior when everything else failed. He knows this. How could he not? And in the nineteen or so years since that event he has proven himself time and again as a "people's" king, one whose eye is always on the welfare of his "children," and that is what he calls them in his opening lines.

So aware is Oedipus of his mission in regard to Thebes and its citizens that he has spent sleepless nights in a state of profound anxiety, weeping for his people's pain, his thoughts groping in every direction for a cure, till finally he found one and set immediately to work. He acted. And action is at the very core of Oedipus's being. He sent Kreon to Delphi to discover from Apollo the cause of the plague and the remedy for it. Enough can never be said about action in Oedipus' modus operandi. It is so much a part of his nature that virtually his every speech is couched in the active voice. If Oedipus speaks of himself in his opening lines as "known to everyone," it is not ego, not false pride, not hubris that is being displayed (as so many have mistakenly been taught to believe), but a healthy knowledge of himself and of the position that he holds in the estimation of his people for deeds of enlightened good aimed at their well-being.

According to Nick Fisher, in his *Oxford Classical Dictionary* article on hubris, to conceive of hubris as "pride, over-confidence, or any behaviour which may offend divine powers, rests, it is now generally held, on misunderstanding of ancient texts, and concomitant and over-simplified views of Greek attitudes to the gods have lent support to many doubtful, and over-Christianizing, interpretations, above all of Greek tragedy." In Aristotle's definition of hubris, he states quite clearly that hubris gives pleasure and "the cause of the pleasure for those committing hubris is that by harming people, they think themselves superior . . ." To see the compassionate and people-directed Oedipus of the play's opening as hubristic is, therefore, seriously to misread and misinterpret the motives of a man who is justly honored as a man, not as a god by his grateful people. The old Priest of Apollo says quite clearly to Oedipus at the start that he and the people of Thebes "haven't come because we think of you as of a god; no, we know you to be a man and only a man; all of us know this, even the young, crouching here." Sophokles could not have been more explicit in his definition through action of the nature of his hero's profound humanity. According to Fisher: "Hubris is most often the insulting infliction of physical force or violence," a far cry from anything in the history of Oedipus, including his killing of Laïos, a situation, as Oedipus explains in *Oedipus at Kolonos*, that offered the prospect of kill or be killed.

Finally, in hope of hammering the ultimate nail in the coffin of this issue, we turn again to Fisher:

> Nor is it helpful to see Greek tragedy centrally concerned to display the divine punishment of hubristic heroes; tragedy focuses rather on unjust or problematic suffering, whereas full-scale acts of hubris by the powerful tend to deprive them of the human sympathy necessary for tragic victims.

How easy it would be for Oedipus, unwittingly self-condemned as he is, to put an end to the search for the murderer of Laïos and thus save himself the agony of self-incrimination and the punishment contingent upon it. Had he done so, he would indeed have been guilty of hubris for his "infliction of physical force or violence" on the plague-infested, suffering, and innocent people of Thebes by not liberating his city from it. But that is not what happens, for with every reappearance of Oedipus on the scene after a major setback of new, self-implicating information, he rises to greater and greater moral stature for not shirking his duty: to discover the truth for the good of his people: Who is the murderer of Laïos? Given the contrary-motion structure of this play, when Oedipus reaches the lowest point of his physical existence, blind, self-exiled, utterly destitute and in a state of abject misery, he at the same time reaches the epitome of implicit moral transcendence, though he may himself not realize it. He has punished himself in the most merciless way possible for the two-pronged crime of patricide and incest. So scrupulous a moralist is Oedipus when dealing with his unwitting moral infraction that rather than escape his predicament in death, he chooses, freely, to expiate crimes that he committed without knowing. If knowledge comes too late in Sophokles' tragic scheme of things, it comes to Oedipus in this play in a way so devastating that he has throughout the millennia become the tragic moral hero par excellence.

There is one further issue (and perhaps the most important) that demands comment regarding Classical Greek drama, and in particular the *Oedipus Tyrannos*, and that is the question of fate. *Oedipus Tyrannos* is widely, and mistakenly, known as "the tragedy of fate." To say the least, this is a tragedy in itself, for it unwittingly consigns one of the supreme achievements of the human mind to the trash heap of inevitability.

Perhaps more than any other, Freud's statement in his seminal work of 1900, *The Interpretation of Dreams*, stoked the fire of fate as far as the Sophoklean play is concerned. He writes: "The *Oedipus Rex* is a tragedy of fate: its tragic effect depends on the conflict between the all-powerful will of the gods and the vain efforts of human beings threatened with disaster; resignation to the divine will, and the perception of one's own impotence is the lesson which the deeply moved spectator is supposed to learn from the tragedy." And he concludes the passage by saying: "It may be that we were all destined to direct our first sexual impulses towards our mothers, and our first impulses of hatred towards our fathers; our dreams convince us that we were."

It is difficult to denigrate one of the most provocative, volatile, and contested intellectual concepts of the modern world, the Oedipus Complex, whatever one may think of it; but it is categorically reprehensible to accept Freud's dictum regarding the critical problem of fate in Sophokles' play. This is especially relevant when one considers that Freud himself made a distinction between the Sophoklean work and the myth on which it was based, for later in *The Interpretation of Dreams* he writes: "The form which it [the Oedipus myth] subsequently assumed [namely the *Oedipus Tyrannos*] was the result of an uncomprehending secondary elaboration of the material, which sought to make it serve a theological intention."

This issue of fate plays a large part in a major study of Sophokles' play by Bernard Knox, *Oedipus at Thebes*, and he expresses the problem as succinctly and brilliantly as possible when he writes:

> No amount of symbolic richness—conscious, subconscious, or unconscious—will create dramatic excitement in a play which does not possess the essential prerequisites of human free will and responsibility. The tragedy must be self-sufficient: that is, the catastrophe must be the result of the free decision and action (or inaction) of the tragic protagonist . . . If the *Oedipus Tyrannus* is a "tragedy of fate," the hero's will is not free, and the dramatic efficiency of the play is limited by that fact. The problem is insoluble; but luckily the problem does not exist to start with. For in the play which Sophocles wrote the hero's will is absolutely free and he is fully responsible for the catastrophe. Sophocles has very carefully arranged the material of the myth in such a way as to exclude the external factor in the life of Oedipus from the action of the tragedy. The action is not Oedipus' fulfillment of the prophecy, but his discovery that he has already fulfilled it. The catastrophe of Oedipus is that he discovers his own identity; and for this discovery he is first and last responsible. The main events of the play are in fact not even part of the prophecy: Apollo predicted neither the discovery of the truth, the suicide of Jocasta, nor the self-blinding of Oedipus. In the actions of Oedipus in the play "fate" plays no part at all.

ÊLEKTRA

Êlektra, like no other play by Sophokles, is an in-depth character study during the first half of which nothing Êlektra does serves to further the plot. What it does do, however, is make indelibly clear the agony her life has been since the murder of her father Agamemnon by her mother Klytaimnestra.

Perhaps the most troublesome question that the play raises is its morality. Written more than forty years after Aeschylus' *The Libation Bearers* in which Orestês murders his mother, Sophokles' play is unencumbered, contrary to that of Aeschylus, with conscience or remorse on the part of Orestês. In Aeschylus he is riddled by conscience for his matricide, and at that play's end and in the succeeding drama, *The Eumenides,* he is pursued by the avenging Furies. Though the Furies are mentioned in Sophokles' play, they nowhere materialize after the murder as forces of retribution for the murder of a mother by her son. Is morality being held in abeyance in Sophokles' play by design to emphasize its unrelenting viciousness, as, for example, having Orestês ask Apollo's oracle at Delphi not whether he should kill his mother, but how? In any event, at the play's end Orestês has done his filial duty and emerges triumphant and unconflicted, like the radiant star of fortune to which he compares himself in the prologue.

The play is replete with many startlingly theatrical moments. The scene of Klytaimnestra's off-stage murder by Orestês is one of the high points of Greek tragedy for the cruelty and viciousness of its execution. The image of Êlektra pacing the stage like a caged animal, then suddenly let loose and running up to the great doors of the palace and screaming to get on with the murder, and her screams to strike again once the first strike has been delivered are masterstrokes of stagecraft. The so-called recognition scene, when Êlektra discovers that it is really Orestês who is present and that he is not dead, is one of the transcendent moments in world theater. So high is the intensity of this moment that there is no alternative but for Êlektra and Orestês to burst into song; no mere words, however exalted, could have expressed their rapture.

A different sort of theatrical moment is the heart-wrenching scene in which Êlektra, nursing the urn in which she believes her beloved brother's ashes to be contained, addresses it and refuses to allow it to be taken from her arms by her still unrecognized brother. There is also the visceral excitement of the Tutor's narration of the supposed chariot-race accident at Delphi in which Orestês is said to have been killed. The strength of this scene resides not so much in the narration (which we know is a fiction), but in the effect that the fiction has on Êlektra. At the end of it her grasp on life is tenuous at best, so much has her hope and expectation for just revenge been demolished. And yet, so strong is Êlektra's character, which is to say her passion and her determination to survive, that she adds a new dimension to Sophokles' art.

If, as Sophokles has shown in previous plays, the human being is in possession of a divine spark (*daimon/arête*) that is nothing less than the will to see justice done, then *Êlektra* may be a preëminent example of that belief. Quite simply, *Êlektra* is *Antigonê* revisited (the plays' structures are remarkably similar). Êlektra is no less headstrong than Antigonê, no less unrelenting, nor any less determined to see justice done; she has simply suffered more, more intensely, and for an unspeakably longer time and consequently has become possessed by her mission to the point that she is close to dementia. And that difference between her and Antigonê is what places her, for all their closeness, in the final phase of Sophokles' development, a period that Whitman calls Tragic Endurance, and that informs the last three extant plays: *Êlektra, Philoktêtês,* and *Oedipus at Kolonos.* Whitman continues:

> Sophocles' last period is "purgatorial," in that it deals with the soul's use of time. The emphasis, however, is not on the purging of sin, for the characters are not sinful; the emphasis is on heroic endurance in the loneliness of heroic rightness. . . . In the *Ajax* and *Antigone* arete triumphed by a kind of phoenix death: out of the fiery ordeal arose an indestructible historic vision. In *The Trachiniae* and *Oedipus Rex,* although human virtue fulfilled its function without failure, life itself seemed an indignity no virtue could surmount. The three last works are very mysterious for all their brightness of atmosphere. Man's best has again begun to count. His inward divinity brings him closer to the gods themselves, or—since that phrase is perhaps meaningless—to a larger transcendent idea of the divine and eternal, which ratifies and seals the striving divinity of the human, or at least of the heroic sphere.

If that inward divinity of Aias and Antigonê arises out of their extinction, another major difference between them and Êlektra is that she does not have to die to have her "spirit" rise from her "ashes." Death, in Sophokles, was once a necessity; it was part of the Homeric hero/warrior ethic. Now it is metaphoric. In these last three extant plays, death is no longer a requirement for the humanistic transformation of the hero. The flame, the spirit that rises out of the ashes of Aias and Antigonê is, in Êlektra, rekindled between the conclusion of the death-narration and early in the following scene with Chrysothemis. It is in that scene that Êlektra, with no verbal but only an internal transition, announces that she will accomplish the mission on her own, with or without her sister's help. In many respects this sequence is al-chemical in its structure. In the death-narration Êlektra is plunged into the lowest, blackest depths of the *nigredo* state, which is tantamount to dissolution, and out of which "death" state there begins to emerge the spark of renewal that Whitman calls the "inward divinity . . . which ratifies and seals the striving divinity of the human . . . sphere." Structurally speaking, from that moment on everything assumes an upward curve, as opposed to the downward spiral of everything regarding Êlektra that went before.

No longer must the hero be physically destroyed to rise spiritually in triumph. It is now Sophokles' view that the hero must survive physically, but be destroyed spiritually, and out of that spiritual destruction rise triumphant. But one factor of this new equation is still missing, and that is Time.

In *Oedipus Tyrannos* (which precedes *Êlektra*), at the moment when Oedipus is in possession of all but the last bit of the truth to convict himself (the Shepherd's testimony), he experiences a transcendental insight in which he declares himself the "child of Chance." Chance is his mother, he announces, and his brothers the passing months that have seen him "great and small in Time." That moment of illumination passes as rapidly as it arrives and is not to be heard of again until the Êlektra, where it becomes a key function in Sophokles' view of existence. For Time allows for suffering, suffering for endurance, and endurance together with suffering for enlightenment, transformation, and transcendence. Although Êlektra may not be the supreme manifestation of that progress, she is a first step as far as the last three extant plays of Sophokles are concerned.

As for the climax of *Êlektra*, contrary to Aeschylus' and Euripides' versions in which it is the murder of Klytaimnestra by Orestês, in Sophokles the climax is Êlektra's victory and her release from decades of inhuman treatment by her mother and Aigisthos. The suffering she has undergone over a cruel period of time would have destroyed all but the strongest individual. But Êlektra perseveres against all odds (the first half of the play demonstrates that), and when the greatest of those odds strikes her in the form of the "death" of Orestês on whom all her hope is founded, she restructures her mental and physical universe and with no hesitation sets out to assume the burden of accomplishing the deed herself.

It is not to stretch credulity to say that by the time Orestês finally becomes known to her, his function in the operation has become virtually superfluous. Batya Laks, in a brilliant study of some of the Êlektra plays from Aeschylus to the present, suggests with considerable ingenuity that the appearance of Orestês may be seen as the visualization of Êlektra's resolve to fulfill her mission of justified vengeance herself—Peter Brook's notion of making the invisible visible. So, if Sophokles' play does not deal with the moral question of Orestês' matricide, it is because that was not his intention. It must be noted, too, that from at least as far back as Homer up to Aeschylus' *The Libation Bearers*, Orestês was portrayed as, in Whitman's words, "a stainless hero, whose act was looked upon as the deliverance of his country."

If there is any lingering doubt that Êlektra is the play's central figure (many have seen it to be Orestês), Sophokles settles it with a brilliant theatrical gesture that needs no words: Orestês and Pylades herd Aigisthos off into the palace to kill him, leaving Êlektra, of all the main characters of the play, on stage alone. As James Hogan has said: "Clearly, the revenge of Orestês is but the context for this play, not its dominant thematic or dramatic point."

PHILOKTÊTÊS

Produced at the City Dionysia in Athens in 409, *Philoktêtês* is the next to the last play written by the aged Sophokles and the last he was to see in production. It is also one of the two plays by him that can be dated with any certainty, the other being *Oedipus at Kolonos*, produced posthumously in 401, five years after his death.

These final two plays share certain attributes that distinguish them from Sophokles' other extant plays. First of all, they take place in remote regions, and there is about their setting and ambiance something that is both mysterious and sacred. The grove of the Eumenides in *Oedipus at Kolonos* is almost at once described to the blind old beggar Oedipus by his daughter Antigonê as exceedingly quiet, with laurel, olive, and vine, the only sounds the song and rushing of wings of nightingales: a sacred place. In *Philoktêtês* the area is even more remote, the island of Lemnos, uninhabited, desolate, with nothing but the waves languidly lapping the shore, birds soaring, winds rushing, rain—every page is inhabited with these images.

What has arrived in these two final dramatic works of the old playwright is Nature, and in such profusion that it threatens to overwhelm the works themselves with its power. Considering the subject matter of these two plays—time, suffering, endurance, and resolution—Nature is perhaps the only suitable setting; first, because there is nothing more basic, and second, because, as in the most profound as well as the brightest of Shakespeare's comedies, the resolution of conflict is achieved in Nature's domain without tragic loss or destruction of property or life.

New in *Philoktêtês* is the creation of a new kind of character for the

Athenian stage. In *Êlektra* Sophokles presents a profound in-depth character study, but one that is limited (if that is the proper word) by being one-directional. In Neoptolemos, however, the young son of the great Achilleus, now dead, we have a new kind of hero whose dilemma is unique in Sophoklean, indeed in Athenian, tragedy. He is a man whose situation puts him in a double-bind: allegiance to his senior officers at Troy, the Atreidai, or to his conscience. His mission is to return the abandoned, snake-bite-wounded Philoktêtês to Troy that together, as the oracle has it, and with Philoktêtês' magic bow, they may assault the walls of Troy and win the ten-year-long campaign. Odysseus, Neoptolemos' superior officer, tells him that his mission is to bring Philoktêtês back by trickery and deception, because persuasion will not work. But deception is not a part of Neoptolemos' nature, any more than it was part of his noble father's nature. Neoptolemos would rather, he says, bring Philoktêtês back by force than by deceit, especially because Philoktêtês is weakened and incapacitated by his wound and not likely to get the better of them. In Watling's words the conflict is between

> . . . physical weakness plus moral strength versus physical superiority plus moral weakness. Philoktêtês is physically at the mercy of his opponents, Neoptolemos and Odysseus, who could easily force their will upon him, and almost do so; but, as Neoptolemos well knows, might is not right, and without right (here symbolized by the bow in the hands of its rightful owner) might cannot prosper.

Neoptolemos at the start of the play, though he voices his objections to deceitful actions, is not entirely against the underhanded proposition of the wily and unscrupulous Odysseus. He does, after all, capitulate rather unnervingly too easily when Odysseus promises him two prizes if he carries through the maneuver: the reputation of courage and intelligence. "All right, I'll do it, and farewell shame," says the young man, because, as Odysseus said earlier, he can be virtuous some other day, and because the reputation of courage and intelligence are too powerful to pass by. But honor and nobility of mind are not so easily overcome in this young but noble son of Achilleus, as he discovers in the process of carrying through his deceptive maneuvers. And in the end, after mighty moral struggles and internal conflict, he places his allegiance on the side of the wronged hero Philoktêtês. Again Watling: "The sympathetic and sensitive picture of Neoptolemos gives the play an unusual charm and is one of Sophocles' highest achievements in character-drawing."

But the central character of Sophokles' play is not the fascinating Neoptolemos, it is the tragically derailed hero Philoktêtês who, ten years before, on the way to Troy, stopped off at the island of Chryse to offer prayers and sacrifices to the local deity for success in the campaign. It is there that he is unmotivatedly bitten in the foot by the guardian snake of the goddess. The wound fails to heal: it suppurates; its stench becomes unbearable. The wounded man's cries disturb the entire camp. As a result Odysseus abandons him on the desolate and uninhabited island of Lemnos. It is here, untended and in misery, that Philoktêtês remains in mortifying pain for ten years. It is only now, a decade later, that an oracle announces that Troy will be taken only by Philoktêtês and Neoptolemos, together with Philoktêtês' magically endowed bow, a gift from Heraklês, the arrows of which never miss their mark.

But for all of the interest in Neoptolemos, it is still Philoktêtês who is the central character on whom time, suffering, and endurance do their work. It is at first glance difficult to say whether this trinity of Sophoklean values weighs greater on Philoktêtês or on Êlektra. In any event, they are close, both of them outcasts, with Philoktêtês more put upon inasmuch as he is also the bearer of a near-insufferable physical infirmity, his suppurating foot which he must drag in excruciating pain from one end of the island to the other in search of sustenance—a miserable task he has had to do for ten years.

From a societal standpoint, too, Êlektra's situation is somewhat better. She has her group of women to support her, whereas Philoktêtês has no one; he is as isolated as it is possible to be, and, unlike Êlektra, for no discernable fault of his own—her "fault" being her relentless pursuit of justice, which alienates her from all but a few.

What now emerges as a central issue in *Philoktêtês* is the question of the individual and society. Society having rejected Philoktêtês in as extreme a way as possible, by abandoning him on an uninhabited island, now wants to re-claim him for its own ends, the winning of the Trojan War. But Philoktêtês, the victim of society's cruelty, now, ten years later, rejects the same society that made him an outcast. Whitman adds to this equation: "but the beggar now rejects society and is brought back into it only by his own resistance to it." And he continues:

> The problem is just such a paradox as Sophocles loved and could manipu-
> late with consummate skill; one may see at a glance that his discovery of
> truth in the utterly paradoxical—the unexpected and unexpectable—is an
> extension of his concern with the lateness of knowledge. But he is con-
> cerned now with a further ridge of knowledge, the knowledge of those who
> are already plunged in misery [unlike Aias and Dêianeira] and yet endure.
> For them [Philoktêtês and Oedipus at Kolonos] the paradox is benign, time
> fights for their dignity, and the knowledge they gain is the knowledge of a

victory implicit in a standard higher, or at least more remote, than the norm.

And by "norm" Whitman means the merely human, with no intention of a pejorative reflection on the term "merely." If the merely human were enough for the heroic nature, then, as Segal rightly puts it, the play would logically have ended with line 1408 in the Greek text, where Neoptolemos tells Philoktêtês to say his farewell to Lemnos and kiss the ground: "Both men are confirmed in the heroism of their essential natures: Neoptolemus, in his courage, compassion, and sense of honor; Philoctetes, in his ability to endure suffering, his strength of will, and his moral integrity. But the oracles have made it clear that heroism serves a larger purpose." That larger purpose being service to the societal collective as opposed to the merely personal, which at this point in the play is for both men to turn their back on society and serve their own ends.

Sophokles had been working with this idea in mind, albeit in embryo, since one of his earliest extant plays, the *Antigonê,* in which the defender of societal (and divine) justice is destroyed. In *Philoktêtês,* for the first time, he creates a situation in which a far vaster point of reference is introduced, namely to allow the hero to rise above his personal integrity, even against his own will and sense of justice, and to survive on a level of heroic endeavor that surpasses all else. And to accomplish this, Sophokles introduces one of the rare appearances of a deus ex machina in his extant work, the god from the machine. But it is not the Euripidean god who emerges at the end to unravel a plot that has become too complex for the mere mortal mind to deal with. The Heraklês who appears in the last few pages of the *Philoktêtês* is an organic plot device that serves many sublime as well as merely human purposes.

To Whitman, the appearance of Heraklês at the play's end is the visualization of Philoktêtês' heroic divinity, his *daimon,* his *arête:*

> And suddenly his victory appears to him. There are few moments in drama more breath-taking than this one. Heracles is divine, but his divinity comes from within Philoctetes. He explains this at once by comparing his own hard toils, and the "immortal arete" which rewarded them, with Philoctetes' sufferings and his glory to come. Heracles is Philoctetes' own special god who gave him his bow when he ascended to heaven. . . . He is the archetype of Philoctetes' greater self, the pattern of his glory. And what is this "immortal arete"? If it is immortal, it is because it is a god in man, the yardstick by which he measures himself against fate and circumstance. And even

the gods themselves. The whole burden of Heracles' revelation is arete. The words keep flashing out. . . .

To which Charles Segal adds that Heraklês also represents a more objective, less individually centered order, and from that, too, Philoctetes has long been estranged. Restored to that order, he will now find his proper, decisive role. His endurance on Lemnos has constituted a test of heroism as arduous as the sufferings of the Greeks on the battlefield of Troy. But heroism is not fulfilled in a vacuum (which is to say in a nonsocietal venue); it requires a context, both human and divine.

It is important to note that nothing that Heraklês says to Philoktêtês is new to him, he has heard it all before from Neoptolemos. "But now," says Whitman, "Philoctetes himself has resolved on these things, and the resolution is like a god awakening in him. It is a vision of sudden spiritual liberation which can scarcely be paralleled elsewhere." Prior to this "liberation," however, Philoktêtês rejected the gods in the form of the oracle that spelled out his divinely determined destiny, that he would overcome Troy and lead the Greeks to victory, even though acceptance meant the healing of his wound, and he did so for no less personal a reason than that it would also consist in helping his enemies, the brother generals, and Odysseus, not to mention the whole of the Greek army. Yet the acceptance of those gods is, as Segal says, "to become free of the disease." It is the sole reason for Heraklês' appearance. It is the reason that he directs Philoktêtês to exhibit piety toward the gods. The final realignment is hereby realized. Philoktêtês, by accepting, is reintegrated into both society and the order of the gods, which in turn allows him to see his destiny in the largest terms possible as opposed to the merely personal, for that is the function of the Sophoklean hero.

Philoktêtês reenters the world with a test of himself still to be realized, and perhaps the most important and difficult test of all: "to accept life and action in a world of imperfect justice." But given Philoktêtês' transformation through ten years of suffering and endurance, one is certain that this imperfect world will never be so much with him that the Odysseuses of it will ever be a threat to his new-won integrity. "The play moves," says Segal, "toward reconciliation at the end, but Sophocles does not obscure the gap that still remains between men and gods and between base men and the noble heroes whom they have victimized." That gap will be filled only in Sophokles' final play when the blind beggar Oedipus is welcomed into the company of the gods for his endurance.

OEDIPUS AT KOLONOS

The aged Sophokles chose as his valediction to the theater and to life the characters that had brought him his greatest success. *Oedipus at Kolonos* is a play that has been called apocalyptic, and so it is, if for no other reason than that the gods, who have been so elusive in the plays of Sophokles, so distant and so irrationally evil, as in the life of Oedipus, are finally humbled (if that is the word) by the tragic endurance of a man who refuses to give up against all the odds that the gods and he himself have stacked against him.

For all its length, *Oedipus at Kolonos* is an extremely simple play from a structural standpoint. The old Oedipus who has wandered aimlessly for many years in exile from Thebes and arrives at the sacred grove at Kolonos, blinded, disheveled in appearance, his clothes torn and ragged, his hair straggling, and his skin so encrusted with dirt that dirt and skin are indistinguishable from one another. His companion these many years, his daughter Antigonê, has endured a life not wholly unlike her father's.

The play has been criticized as static and lacking action, and to a superficial observer this may indeed be the case. But action in Sophoklean tragedy may atypically be defined as "the functioning of the hero's will, in whatever form," as Whitman has it. And Oedipus' will here is in constant and powerful function from the moment he learns where he has arrived and announces that he will never leave, for here is the place predicted for him by Apollo years ago: Kolonos. During his many years of wandering and depravition, Oedipus has both sunk to the lowest level of destitution and risen to a near-divine level of wisdom and spiritual enlightenment—a transcendence that has transpired in time. Time plays a major role in this play, for time alone offers the possibility of suffering, and in Sophokles' work suffering is the great purger of material concerns. "Suffering and time," says Oedipus shortly after his arrival at Kolonos, "vast time, have taught me acceptance of life's adversities, as has nobility of birth."

Acceptance, perhaps, but not forgiveness, not humility. And herein lies the source of energy that drives this final play of Sophokles to its transcendent conclusion. Time may have done its work on Oedipus, but it has not softened a nature that (to use a phrase that is uncannily apt) has been "more sinned against than sinning." Time, distance, and the razor-sharp edge of objectivity have demonstrated to Oedipus that, though he once punished himself mercilessly for the unspeakable sins of patricide and incest, he was not in any way guilty of those crimes. In some of the play's most powerful lines, Oedipus defends himself against even his former self. He killed in self-defense, he rightly affirms, when his life was threatened, and he had no way of knowing the nature of the marriage he entered into at the insistence of the people of Thebes when they offered him power and throne for his liberation of them and their city from the Sphinx. He castigates at length the aged Kreon who comes to claim him as a talisman to protect Thebes against future aggression by Athens; and he disowns his sons, one of whom, Polyneikês, has come to seek his support of a seven-pronged assault on Thebes to regain the throne from his usurping brother Eteoklês. When he needed their help, accuses the raging Oedipus, they turned their backs on him, and he curses them to suffer the consequence of mutual brother-murder.

If these tirades of the ancient Oedipus were couched purely in animosity engendered in the past, they just might be excessive. They are, on the other hand, enlivened and made volatile in the present by virtue of issues that bear immediately upon the present and that only indirectly look back to the past. Kreon appears on the scene because of the latest oracle from Delphi that Oedipus' dead body will serve Thebes as protection against future attack. Kreon insists on Oedipus' return, but will not allow him to enter the city; he must reside outside its gates, as will his eventual grave. As if this were not enough, Kreon arrives with military assistance to enforce his will and even, in fact, kidnaps one of the daughters to force the issue and threatens to take Oedipus himself prisoner if need be.

Polyneikês' arrival on the scene is prompted by his need to have Oedipus' support of his assault upon his brother Eteoklês. With Oedipus' support, the attack will succeed, and Polyneikês and his troops will win; without the support of Oedipus, the campaign will fail. This situation, too, dredges up the past for Oedipus and reminds him of his sons' failure to defend him when they had the chance. The terrible addition of the present to this long-standing situation is Oedipus' virulent curse on his two sons that not only disowns them but damns them to slay each other in the doomed encounter at Thebes.

Sophokles the playwright knew his craft and knew, like every great dramatist, that to dredge up the past can not alone be the basis for a dramatic situation. That much he had learned in *Oedipus Tyrannos,* along with the playwright's need to use the past to generate a new action in the present, an action that transpires immediately in view of the spectator. His success in that regard in *Oedipus Tyrannos* has made it one of the benchmarks of Western dramatic construction; and although *Oedipus at Kolonos* may not be as swiftly moving as the earlier play, it is made of the same fabric.

Oedipus at Kolonos is without question an old man's play, but in no way is it a tired play. Like Ibsen's *When We Dead Awaken,* it is a summation of everything that his ninety-plus years have taught him. More important, however, it adds to his achievement in a way that would be startling at any age, let alone at his.

For the decades of his wandering, the blind Oedipus took whatever was offered, took whatever begging brought him. At his end he no longer takes, he gives; and what he gives is himself. In *Oedipus Tyrannos* he declared himself the brother of the passing months that have seen him small and great in time; in this final play, in his final hours, he arrives at a status that transcends time, and it has been a long road. And that road is perhaps the steady uphill trek that this final play is also: a long haul to an end that reaches out beyond all mortal concerns. The fact that Oedipus knows in life that his dead body will be a gift beyond compare (he announces it in the opening pages) tells us without any contradiction that he has already transcended time. He is a hero, and he knows it, and this is remarkable, for heroic stature is achieved only in death. Oedipus has, quite simply, already arrived. He has achieved cult status. His road, his tragic endurance, have burned away his fallibility, and he sees for the first time with eyes freed of mortality. Everything that the earlier Oedipus play set out is here systematically put into laborious and slow-grinding reverse. In alchemical terms he has endured reduction to the *nigredo* and risen along the tortuous path of purification to arrive at the golden apex, which is the *magnum opus*—the philosopher's stone.

No sooner has the despairing and rejected Polyneikês departed, than the final movement of the play falls into gear. The gods who played so loosely and cruelly with the old man acknowledge him with the rumble of their divine thunder and the flash of Zeus' lightning: the sign that they are present, the announcement that the end is at hand and that the process of transformation/transfiguration is set in motion. All at once the formerly bent, groping, and shuffling old Oedipus stands erect, and where once he was led he now leads, where once he sought help he now gives it—a long-arriving inner vision has asserted itself. He is complete and he looks out from within Time. The gods even call to him, urging him on and sending panic through those assembled: "Oedipus! Oedipus! It's time! You stay too long!"

In this final work Sophokles not only brings his life's work to an incomparable conclusion, he also lays a blessing on the *deme* that gave him birth, Kolonos, and on the city that nurtured not only him, but, more important, a society and a government and a cultural achievement that the world has scarcely approximated since. Aias' sailors, in the play that bears his name, sing of Athens in terms that can only have come from the full heart of one of its greatest sons:

What joy is left me now,
     what joy? O if only my sails
          were set for home! Set
for Sounion's tree-topped summit
     that rears above the sea-washed rocks,
          and greet, sailing into sight,
the blessèd city,
     my holy Athens!

The tragedy is that by the time of the posthumous production of *Oedipus at Kolonos* in 401, Athens had fallen to Sparta in the Peloponnesian War, which tore Greece apart between 431 and 404, a fate that Sophokles cannot have failed to foresee as he wrote *Oedipus at Kolonos* in 406, and that must have caused him no small degree of pain and sadness.

Carl R. Mueller
Department of Theater, Film, and Television
University of California, Los Angeles

A NOTE ON THE TRANSLATION

The original texts of these plays are divided into three kinds of discourse: straight dialogue, lyrical dialogue, and the lyrical choral ode. The lyrical sections are for the most part arranged in three-stepped lines. In the choral odes, each line is meant to be spoken by an individual chorus member. This choice is based largely on that originally devised by C. K. Williams in his translation of Sophokles' *The Women of Trachis,* and later also utilized in his translation of Euripides' *The Bakkhai.* In the latter publication he summarizes his methodology.

> Essentially my ideas were based on the perception that human beings don't seem to be able to speak in real unison; we can do so only when we have music to order our voices through the abysses of time. "Choral speaking, even at its best," I said in my comments then, "always has something about it of schoolchildren reciting. There is always an imperceptible pause while the group awaits one voice to lead it out of the silence. . . . What generally happens is that a kind of sing-song rhythm is generated—the same rhythm that children give to nursery rhymes, and adults to Bible-reading." . . . Since the music of the Greek tragedies is irrecoverably lost, and since we are reluctant (rightfully so, I believe) to reconstruct or reformulate that music, I felt that perhaps the individual voices of the choruses might be organized by means of the space of the stage, rather than by time. . . . As I have rendered them, each descending line of each triplet of the choruses (or, as a possible alternative for less experienced actors, each triplet itself) would be spoken by a separate member of the Chorus, so the effect would be that of the actual speeches of the choruses being composed in their passage from one voice to another. There would then be, one would hope, a kind of musicalization of space, and of the language of the odes as they move through that space.

In the earlier statement on the issue in *The Women of Trachis,* Williams attempts "to determine what the critical difference is between poetry and music," and his deduction is that the word is the basic unit of poetry and sound that of music; and yet not sound per se, but repetition, "the repeated sound." He continues:

The repetition must occur in a pattern and this pattern can have a harmonic context, a rhythmic one: one of volume, duration, intensity, decay, etc.—or any or all of them. . . . In trying to make at least a facsimile of the basic musical experience of the chorus, I have had to violate some of the precision of grammar and image that would normally be expected, and I have taken what might at first seem to be extraordinary liberties with the literal text by using many repetitions, generally of single words, but, occasionally, of phrases and whole line units. All these repetitions, however, I have taken from the variance of complex meanings which are carried by a word from one language to another. The texture I have tried to evoke obviously does not have as its "mode" any known musical structure. The resolution, to use musical terms, can happen within a few lines or a few words, in an obvious repetition, or it can extend over almost the length of the play, following the sub-pattern of repetition that Sophocles himself used (the word "shimmering" for instance). . . . The unison-speaking problem I have tried to resolve by substituting the control of sound through time with that of sound through space. There is, strictly speaking, no unison at all. Each single, descending line, as I have rendered it, represents an individual voice, coming from a spatially distinct point on the stage. By doing this, I have hoped the audience would experience the flow of lyric meaning both visually and aurally, and thus, by involving another sense as well as by breaking down the normal expectation of meaning-unit, a more organic—i.e. musical—reaction would be evoked.

Another issue relating to the Chorus has to do with the Chorus Leader. The manuscripts of the plays that have come down to us (none of them originals) do not identify speakers, the text being simply run together without even a separation between words. Needless to say, editors must decide these matters for themselves, and, understandably, they frequently disagree. Even assuming that a Chorus Leader existed in the time of Sophokles (by no means a certainty) we would have no way of knowing which of the choral lines were spoken by him (there even being the possibility that all the chorus' lines may have been, leaving the chorus to perform its considerable choreography). Consequently, many contemporary translators have simply assumed the presence of a Chorus Leader and assigned lines accordingly. Generally speaking, in scenes where a fairly intimate conversation takes place between, say, Oedipus and the Chorus, those choral lines will be assigned to a Leader. There is, of course, no way of authenticating such a decision; it is made, wisely, in consideration of the nature of the modern stage. As late as just a few decades ago the lines now assigned to the Leader were, in production, spoken by a full Chorus—a decision that does not, and never did, recommend itself to the modern theater. In any event, a director has the freedom to reassign chorus and Chorus Leader lines at will to suit an independent view of the play.

The transliteration of Greek names has been called by Robert Fitzgerald "an uncertain and—ultimately, perhaps—subjective matter," and so it is here, if for no other reason than there is no consistency in such transliteration. The main emphasis here has been to eschew the Latinate spelling of Greek names wherever possible for the sake of greater, if not total, authenticity. Ease of reading has been the primary governing factor. We have chosen Kreon over Creon, Teiresias over Tiresias, Polyneikês over Polyneices, Iokastê over Jocasta; but have retained Oedipus over the transliterated Oidipous, Thebes over Thebai, Athens over Athenai, and Delphi over Delphoi, to name but a few. The retentions are holdovers of convenience: It seemed audacious not to use the familiar names of places like Athens and Delphi, which are visited by hundreds of thousands of travelers yearly.

Music played an enormous part in the production of Greek plays in their day, as has been discussed above, and we have made every effort to indicate very clearly where it plays its role. In addition, however, music could have been, and probably was, used almost anywhere in the course of a tragedy. It is, of course, up to the director of a production to decide whether to use the two original instruments, the aulos and lyre, or to take advantage of more modern instruments, even something as contemporary as the synthesizer. We have seen productions of several of our translations that have made startling use of the synthesizer in conjunction with other modern instruments, including a variety of percussion instruments. Perhaps the most intriguing of all was a production of the *Êlektra* with an array of only percussive instruments borrowed from various Asian theater traditions. In any event, the possibilities for music are vast, and it would be a great loss to any production choosing to do without.

It should be mentioned that the Greek originals were written not only without indication of who is speaking but without stage directions. Almost all translations, therefore, take the liberty of adding stage directions in order to make the visualization of the action easier for the reader. We have followed their lead.

The translated texts presented here are complete except for a single omission: the final choral lines at the end of *Oedipus Tyrannos*. Most editors agree that the lines are not Sophokles' but probably a later addition and that not only are they banal, but virtually senseless and are best omitted.

As for the layout of the Greek theater structure of Sophokles' time, we have adopted for the most part that advocated by David Wiles in his *Tragedy in Athens:* a simple wooden *skênê* building with a large central double door and a circular orchestra of pounded earth in front of it. A modern director must, of course, be free to make independent decisions in these regards, especially if directing on a conventional modern stage. Right and left are from the audience's standpoint.

As to text, we have been highly eclectic in our choices, using many different editions and commentaries. Needless to say, there are a lot of choices to be made in editing the frequently corrupt Greek texts of these plays. This, however, being a general and not a critical edition, we have chosen not to tabulate the source of every such textual decision.

AIAS
(ΑΙΑΣ)

CAST OF CHARACTERS

ATHÊNA

AIAS

TEKMÊSSA *captive wife of Aias*

EURYSAKES *son of Aias and Tekmêssa, about five years old*

TEÜKROS *half-brother of Aias*

ODYSSEUS

MENELAOS *king of Sparta, husband of Helen*

AGAMEMNON *king of Mykenê, commander-in-chief*

MESSENGER

CHORUS OF SAILORS FROM SALAMIS *followers of Aias*

LEADER OF THE CHORUS

SOLDIERS

SERVANTS

ATTENDANTS

The lines of the Chorus, unless otherwise indicated, are to be delivered by individual voices and varied groups of voices.

AIAS

Before dawn. The mist is heavy and visibility extremely limited. The Greek camp at Troy during the tenth year of the war. The skênê represents the tent of Aias. Large double doors leading into the tent dominate the scene. The right and left upper-side reaches of the orchestra serves as entrances, the right leading to the Greek encampment, the left to the countryside and shoreline. In the dim illumination of the pre-dawn, Odysseus is seen intently searching for footprints in the sandy soil in front of Aias' tent. Athêna is at first unseen; her voice is quiet and familiar, as if speaking to a friend, and at first seems to come from all directions. When she becomes visible, she appears in the right entrance.

ATHÊNA: Odysseus, son of Laërtês!
    I always seem to find you in hot pursuit,
    Always stalking your enemies, in hope
    Of some advantage.
    And here again, by the seaward tent of Aias,
    The last on the shore, I see you intently searching
    The sand for signs, new-made tracks, to tell you
    Is he here or somewhere else. Your keen scent
    Is like a Spartan hound's, leading you quickly
    To its goal.

    He's just gone in, his face and hands
    Sweating and bloody from his slaughtering sword.
    No need to look in now.
    But tell me, Odysseus,
    What do you think you're onto? I could help.
ODYSSEUS: Athêna's voice! Dearest of all the gods!
    Although I can't see you, I can hear you,
    And my heart leaps up as at a trumpet's call!
    Yes, and you've guessed right:
    I'm trying to sniff out Aias with his bully shield.
    No great friend of mine, to say the least.
    Yes, it's Aias I've been tracking all this time.
    He did a terrible thing to us last night—

Assuming he's the doer, nothing's certain,
We're all of us at sea over this. So, as usual,
I took it upon myself to seek out the truth.

This morning we found the cattle we'd plundered from Troy
Hacked to death, slaughtered along with their herdsmen.
It's him, all right: no question there: Aias.
He was seen last night streaking across the plain,
His sword dripping blood. Someone saw him;
And now it's for me to prove it.

These tracks here?
They're his, no doubt about it. As for the others,
They could be anybody's. What to do now?
But I'm glad you've come, lady.
You've guided my course in the past and will again;
And I'll obey.
ATHÊNA: I know, Odysseus; I hurried as fast as I could,
     Always eager to guide you in the chase.
ODYSSEUS: Do you mean, dear lady, I'm on his scent?
ATHÊNA: Indeed you are. He's your man.
ODYSSEUS: But why such senseless violence?
     What possessed him?
ATHÊNA: Raving jealousy.
     Achilleus' armor was given to *you*.
ODYSSEUS: But why take it out on the herds?
ATHÊNA: He thought the blood he was spilling was yours.
ODYSSEUS: Attacking Greeks: is that what he thought?
ATHÊNA: And would have, too, if I'd been careless.
ODYSSEUS: Imagine! How did he dare?
ATHÊNA: Night gave him cover—acting alone.
ODYSSEUS: How close did he come?
ATHÊNA: Agamemnon's and Menelaos' tents.
ODYSSEUS: What kept him from murdering them?
ATHÊNA: I did. I called up sickly delusions of triumph
     To thwart his advance and turned his rage on the droves
     Guarded by their herdsmen: sheep and cattle
     Captured from Troy and not yet even sorted.
     Attacking the horned beasts like a madman,

He cleaved their spines, hacking this way and that,
Leaving around him a widening circle of death.
At one moment he thought he held in his grip
The sons of Atreus, Agamemnon and Menelaos,
Hacking away at them single-handed;
At another, he mauled first this general then that.
I did him one better then, I pushed him headlong
Toward madness and into my trap.
When he had finished the slaughter, he bound them together,
The sheep and oxen that were still alive,
And marched them back to his tent,
Thinking they were men, and not horned creatures.
He has them inside there now, prisoners of war,
Bound and gagged, torturing them unmercifully.
But now you'll *see* the man. I'll *show* him.
Show him in all his rage, his madness.
And then you'll tell the Greeks!
Don't worry. The sight won't harm you.
I'll puzzle his eyes. He won't see you.

You there! Tormenting your prisoners' limbs!
Come out! I'm calling you, Aias!
Come out in front of your tent!
ODYSSEUS: Athêna! No! Don't call him out here!
ATHÊNA: Quiet! Are you afraid of him?
ODYSSEUS: No, but why bring him out?
ATHÊNA: What's the problem? He's only a man.
ODYSSEUS: Yes, and my enemy—still is.
ATHÊNA: Your enemy's down, Odysseus, enjoy it.
ODYSSEUS: I'd just as soon he stayed inside.
ATHÊNA: Afraid to see a madman?
ODYSSEUS: If he were sane—
ATHÊNA: He won't even see you.
ODYSSEUS: No? He still has eyes.
ATHÊNA: I'll cloud them.
ODYSSEUS: Whatever you say. Gods do what they want.
ATHÊNA: Stay right there. Not a word, now.
ODYSSEUS: I can't say I like it.
ATHÊNA: Aias! You, inside! Can't you hear?

Is this how you treat your ally?

(Aias enters through the large doors of the tent holding a bloody multi-thonged leather whip. He is covered in blood.)

AIAS: Athêna! Zeus' daughter! Welcome!

Thank you for standing by me today!

You'll have a gift of gold from my booty!

An offering for your help in this catch.

ATHÊNA: Thank you.

But tell me now, Aias:

Is your sword well-soaked in Greek blood?

AIAS: Yes, and proud of it I am, too!

ATHÊNA: Have a grand tiff with the Atreus brothers?

AIAS: They won't be slighting Aias again!

ATHÊNA: Dead, are they? Imagine that!

AIAS: Let them try to rob me *now!*

ATHÊNA: Ah, and then there's Laërtês' son.

Did he escape you?

AIAS: The cunning fox?

ATHÊNA: Yes, your rival, Odysseus.

AIAS: Hobbled inside there, dear lady!

Guest of honor, and all that!

He won't be dying anytime soon!

ATHÊNA: You're planning what? What new triumph?

AIAS: Tie him up—to the tent pole, maybe.

ATHÊNA: Ah, poor man! And then what?

AIAS: Whip him to a pulp till he dies!

ATHÊNA: Mercy, Aias! Don't torture him so!

AIAS: Your will is my command, goddess,

In all but this. He dies as I say.

ATHÊNA: Well, if it really means this much,

Do as you like, leave nothing undone.

AIAS: Good! I'm off, then!

But always stand by me,

Just as you did today.

(He enters his tent. The doors close.)

ATHÊNA: You see, Odysseus, the power of the gods?

What man was ever more farsighted

Or better skilled in timely action?

ODYSSEUS: No one I know of. He may be my enemy,

But I still have pity for him, seeing him undone
And yoked to a dreadful fate that could be mine.
We're all of us, every mortal being,
Phantoms and bodiless shadows, smoke in the wind.
ATHÊNA: You must remember your own words, Odysseus.
Never think you're better than the gods.
Never boast of strength or worldly goods.
One day can tip the scale of human events,
Up or down, whatever the gods choose.
We gods love men who think sanely
And hate evil.

(Athêna vanishes. As Odysseus turns to go off, full daylight comes on and music begins as the Chorus of Aias' Sailors from Salamis enters in groups of varying size from the right. Here as elsewhere they speak sometimes individually or in varying combinations.)

CHORUS: Son of Telamon,
      Aias,
         holder of power on
    sea-ringed Salamis,
      when your fortune is
        fair I rejoice. But
   when you are struck by
      Zeus, when slanderous
        Greeks assail you with
   rumor, then I tremble,
      fearful as a
        frightened dove.
   Now,
      as night
        fades into day, loud
  voices
     tell of our
       disgrace. My
  master, they say, under
    cover of dark,
      strode out to the
 meadows, wild with the
    play and frisking of
      horses, and

killed the herds of
    sheep and cattle,
        plunder of the
Greeks in the
    heat of battle,
        slaughtering,
ravaging with his
    blazing iron sword.
        These are the tales
Odysseus tells,
    slanders shaped by his
        devious mind,
slanders
    whispered into every man's
        ear, and every man
eager to believe,
    for the tales Odysseus
        tells are persuasive.
And each man takes more
    pleasure in the
        tale than the teller.
Take aim at a
    great man and you'll
        never miss. But
aim such tales at me
    and no one will believe.
        Men of power are a
magnet to envy. Yet
    small men without the
        great man to lead them are
no sure defense at the walls.
    Let the great man
        lead them and the
small man will
    flourish, the great
        supported
by the small. But
    how do you
        teach such things to

fools?
    They're the ones
        railing against you, and
without you I'm
    defenseless.
        Freed of your
commanding eye they
    chatter and
        screech in
flocks like angry
    starlings. But
        appear before them,
suddenly,
    and they will
        cower in terror and
silence as
    before the great
        vulture.
Tell me, great
    Rumor, mother of my
        shame, was it
Artemis, daughter of
    Zeus,
        bull-mounting
Artemis, who
    goaded you on
        to attack the
herds of all our host?
    Was it Artemis,
        avenging a
slight, a tributeless
    victory, no trove of
        arms captured, no
deer-hunt
    offering?
        Or war-god
Arês,
    bronze-clad
        Enyalios,

support in
    battle, angered at
        dishonor to his
aiding spear,
    taking night
        vengeance for
outraged
    pride?
        Never,
son of Telamon,
    never would your
        heart have so
betrayed you, to
    fall on the herds.
        Yet the gods send
madness.
    But may
        Zeus and Apollo
defend me
    against the tales the
        Greeks tell.
But if the great
    kings and that
        wicked spawn of
Sisyphos' race,
    Odysseus, lie in the
        slanderous rumor they
spread, then
    hear me, lord Aias!
        Come from your
tent! Spare me the
    evil name of
        hiding in your
tents by the
    sea!
        Spare your own
name!
(The dance gains in momentum and force.)
    Up, Aias!

Up from your
seat wherever you
brood in
embattled
leisure! Too
long! Too
long!
Making the
flame of
mischief
blaze
heaven-high! Your
enemies
rage
wild-tongued as
Bakkhants!
Insolence courses
unfettered of
fear through
breezy valleys!
Laughter!
Taunting,
mocking,
spiteful!

(Dance and music break off suddenly at their peak. The final words are spoken in unison in a mood of deep and quiet pessimism.)

How can we
bear it? Our
sorrow,
sorrow,
knows
no
end!

(Tekmêssa enters grieving and alarmed from the tent during the above, accompanied by several women Servants. The music resumes mutedly.)

TEKMÊSSA: You sailors, you of Aias' fleet,
earth-born sons of Erechtheus
sprung from Attic soil,
we who love the far-off house

                    of Telamon, his father, mourn
                        aloud here in our grief.
                 Aias our master, harsh,
                     terrible in might, lies
                         stricken, his mind muddied
                 by a storm of madness.
LEADER: What greater woe
                         has night brought with it,
                 than daylight's insult?
                     Tell us, Tekmêssa, daughter
                         of Phrygian Teleütas. Aias'
                 sword won you in battle for his
                     bed and for his love above all
                         women. You, if anyone,
                 must know. Tell us:
                     why all this?
TEKMÊSSA: How can I say it?
                 There are no words
                     terrible enough to tell this
                         tale! The disaster you will
                 hear of now is equal to death!
                     Our valorous Aias,
                         last night,
                 possessed,
                     stricken by madness, has
                         suffered outrage! See,
                 in there, see, with your own eyes,
                     the victims, butchered,
                         weltering in blood, sacrificed
                 offerings of that man that speak
                     ominously of the future.
LEADER: What you tell us of
                 our great warrior's fiery spirit
                     is unbearable and yet,
                         it cannot be escaped! The tale
                 is shouted loudly about
                     by the mighty leaders of the Danaian
                         host and swells till the camp
                 rings with the news! Omoi!

I tremble at the future
coming upon us. His fate
is sealed, his death sure,
our fiery lord, shamed before all,
dishonored in death! His hands
frenzied, his dark sword slew
both herds and herdsmen.

TEKMÊSSA: Omoiiii! So it was from there he
brought them, from there, his
captives, leading them!
Once inside,
on the tent's floor,
he cut their throats; others
he tore into many pieces, slashing
their ribs. Then seizing two
special white-footed rams,
he shears off the head of one
and its tongue-tip,
casting them from him.
The other he ties by its forelegs,
upright, to the central pole, and
catching a mighty strap
from a harness, he bends it
double, and with strokes that
whistle, he flogs the creature, uttering
curses so evil
only a god could have taught him.

LEADER: Now is the time to veil my face
and steal away quickly;
or take to the oar-bench and
pull for the open sea. No
safety anymore from the threats
hurled at me by the brother-kings,
the sons of Atreus.
I fear a violent death by stoning,
I fear to share my master's agony,
struck down with him
held in the grip
of an unapproachable
fate.

TEKMÊSSA: No, no, it's over.
                No glare of lightning flashes now.
                   Like a squall from the south,
                      its first rage spent,
                his mind is right. But now
                   another pain to bear
                      rises before him. He sees
                the weight of his own doing:
                   no hand but his, no
                      hand is responsible:
                the greatest of
                   suffering, the
                      greatest.
        (The music fades out.)
LEADER: If it's truly over, all may yet be well.
        Misfortune seems less once it is passed.
TEKMÊSSA: How would you choose, if the choice were yours—
        To give pain to others and be happy yourself;
        Or to share it equally with them?
LEADER: Two sorrows are always worse than one.
TEKMÊSSA: He may be cured, but our sickness begins.
LEADER: No, I don't understand.
TEKMÊSSA: When Aias was sick, he reveled in it,
        While we who were sane felt shame and pity, we grieved.
        He's sane again now, himself again,
        Free of the delusion, but overwhelmed
        With grief for what he did. And what of us,
        Are we any the less shamed and grieved?
        Is that a cure? Our sorrow is two, not one.
LEADER: True. This is some god's doing.
        What else could it be? His sickness ended,
        He's sane again, but less happy
        Than he was while it raged.
TEKMÊSSA: Strange, but that's how it is. Accept it.
LEADER: How did it start? How did it strike him?
        Tell us. All of us share your pain.
TEKMÊSSA: Yes, I'll tell you. We're all a part of this.
        The night was dark as pitch. Torches all out.
        Aias grabbed for his mighty war-sword

And made as if to dash off.
"Aias," I said, "what are you doing?"
I was angry. There was no reason for this.
"Where are you going? There was no call to arms,
No trumpet, the army's asleep!"
I knew what he'd say; the same old thing:
"Women are better seen than heard!"
What's the use, I thought, and kept my silence,
While he stormed off alone.

What happened out there, I can't say—
But back he came, lugging cattle
Bound like prisoners, hobbled bulls and herd dogs
And their woolly charges. Some, he lopped their heads off;
Others he turned upside down
And sliced their throats or cleft their spines;
The rest he tied and racked and attacked with a fury
You'd have thought that they were men not beasts.
Then, without warning, he darted again from the tent,
And I heard him rapping wild words
At some phantom of his brain,
Denouncing the generals Agamemnon and Menelaos
And then Odysseus— laughing, boasting
How he'd avenged them in full with the trick he'd played.
He then charged back inside,
And slowly, with great pain, regained his senses.
When he finally looked and saw the room
Littered with bloody carnage and slaughtered remains,
He beat his head and uttered a great cry
And tumbled down headlong into the ruins
Of devastated cattle and sheep and dogs
Mired in their own blood.
His hands clutching his hair,
He sat in the gore a long while in silence.

And then he spoke—no, shouted—shouted words—
Terrible words—words he threatened me with—
Demanding I tell him what horrible thing had happened
And what it would lead to now.

Friends, I was terrified!
I told him all he'd done, the best I knew.
And then he started sobbing, piteous cries,
Cries of anguish I'd never heard before—
Like a woman cries. He'd always said such cries
Were only fit for base and cowardly men—
And no shrill keening would ever come from him—
Not from a warrior; for when he grieved,
His sound was low, like a bull's deep moaning.

But now, battered by an evil fate,
Refusing food and drink, he sits there,
Unmoving, among the mangled beasts,
Planning out some new evil;
For that's what's coming,
It's what his cries and mumbled words
Can only mean.

Friends, go in, please.
Help me with him. It's why I came out.
A friendly word can work wonders.
LEADER: Tekmêssa, daughter of Teleütas,
Your news of Aias' madness is dreadful.
(Aias' voice is heard from inside.)
AIAS: Ioooooooo moiiiiii moiiiiii!!
TEKMÊSSA: He will be worse soon! Did you hear?
AIAS: Ioooooooo moiiiiii moiiiiii!
LEADER: Is it another fit? Or is he grieving
For the sight that illness created?
AIAS: Ioooooooooo! My boy, my boyyyyyyy!
TEKMÊSSA: How can I bear this?
He's calling for you, Eurysakes!
What can he want? Where are you?
AIAS: Teükros! Brother! Where is Teükros?
I sit here dying, while he's off hunting!
LEADER: He seems sane again! Open the doors!
Perhaps the sight of us will calm him.
TEKMÊSSA: I'll open it.
(Music fades in as she opens the large double doors of the tent allowing the

ekkyklêma to come forward into full view to reveal Aias sitting in blood among the slaughtered beasts.)

There. See for yourselves.

See what he's done.

The work of his hands.

See what's become of him.

AIAS: Ioooooooooo!

                       Sailors!

                           Friends!

                   My only friends! You,

                       only you, are comrades in loyalty!

                           Behold me now!

                   Behold the storm that

                       bursts upon me!

                           Wave on wave! Swirling,

                   surging round me in a

                       bloody, roiling tide!

LEADER: How true your words are, Tekmêssa!

Who can question his sick mind?

AIAS: Ioooooo!

                   Mates who sailed with me, skillful

                       mariners who plowed the sea

                           with great oars, speeding us

                   through sparkling waves! You,

                       you alone love me!

                           Save me! Help me

                   to end my misery!

                       Kill me with all these others!

LEADER: No more evil words, master!

Evil is never cured by evil!

Don't feed your pain!

AIAS: Behold the warrior!

                   The bold warrior!

                       The hero dauntless in battle!

                           Stout of heart!

                   The master now!

                       Killer of harmless beasts!

                           The shame of their laughter!

                   The mockery! Bitter,

                    bitter the outrage I suffer!
                    Bitter!
            Cruel!
            Cruel!
TEKMÊSSA: Aias, my lord, don't say such things!
AIAS: Out of my sight!
            Aiiiiiiiiiii!
            Aiiiiiiiiiiiii!
LEADER: I beg you, my lord, yield, be sensible!
AIAS: Why am I so cursed!
            How can they, accursed men,
                have slipped through my hands!
            Bastards!
            And I, slaughtering cattle, goats,
                splendid creatures, noble
                    flocks, whose blood spills
            in dark streams!
LEADER: Why grieve over what is passed?
    Things done cannot be undone.
AIAS: Iooooooo! Where are you, Odysseus?
                Son of Laërtes, where are you?
            Lynx-eyed instrument of every crime,
                foulest trickster of the army!
                    How you must be laughing at me!
            Laughing at me now!
LEADER: Laughter and grief are in god's control.
AIAS: If I could meet him now,
                broken, broken as I am!
            Aiiiii! Aiiiii! Aiiiii!
LEADER: No more boasting, Aias, my lord.
    Can't you see your miserable state?
AIAS: Zeus, father of my fathers,
                    let me kill the cunning fox
            that I detest, and the brother
                kings who command!
                    O then if I could die!
TEKMÊSSA: Then pray, pray for my own death, too.
    Why should I live when you are dead?
AIAS: Iooooooo!

O darkness!
    Darkness, my light!
Night of death, my day!
   Take me up, o take me
    into your house, your
house forever, take me,
   a man unworthy to look
    to the gods for help, a man
unworthy to look to men: things,
   creatures of a day!
    The invincible daughter of Zeus
goads me on to my end.
   How is a man to escape?
   Where shall I rest?
The man I was is dead,
   destroyed with the victims around me!
    Triumphs of a madman!
And the force, the massed
   force of the army, swords
    uplifted in both hands,
will strike me dead!

TEKMÊSSA: No, I can't hear this, I mustn't!
  How can my lord have come to this!

AIAS: Ioooooooo!
   O paths of the sounding sea!
Sea-caves, wooded pastures
   that border the lapping waters!
    You have detained me here too long,
too long beside Troy's shores.
   But you will never see me again,
    never again see me alive,
as any sane man must know.
   Waters, o waters of Skamander!
   Waters kindly to the Greeks!
You will never again see Aias, a man—
   oh, I boast a great boast!—unequaled
    in Trojan eyes by any who
sailed from Greece, though
   now he sits here
    dishonored.

(Music fades out. Aias leaves the ekkyklêma and comes forward.)

LEADER: Please, my lord, you mustn't say such things.

And yet, how can you not, mired in such misery!

AIAS: Aiii! Aiiias! My name: how it matches my fate!

Twice I cry out my misery in those few syllables,
And then a third time, so great are my sorrows.
My father once fought here at Troy,
Fought with valor and won the army's
Fairest prize, and brought home a name
Steeped in glory.
But I, his son, who came to this land,
This same land, to Troy, no less
A champion than he, no less deserving,
Am made an outcast, deprived of honor
Here among the Greeks—
To perish here.

And yet I know one thing:
If Achilleus were still alive to choose the hero
Most worthy of his armor, bravest of the Greeks,
Who else would he award it to but me?
And yet, these sons of Atreus have snatched it from me,
Pushing aside all my triumphs in battle,
And awarded it to that most unscrupulous of men!

But had my will been my own, my eyes not blinded,
My mind not led astray in futile distraction,
They'd never have lived to rig another vote,
To cheat another man as they cheated me!
Just as I raised my hand to strike the blow,
Grim-eyed Lady Athêna tripped me up,
Sending a plague of madness down upon me,
A raging illness that strapped my mind—
So now my hands are fouled with slaughtered cattle
And not the blood of those two sons of Atreus.
They're free, free and laughing, sniggering at me,
Exulting in their triumph; but the fault's not mine!
Let one of the gods do harm and even the coward
Escapes the true hero!

Well, what to do now? Hated of the gods,
Hated of the Greeks, hated of Troy,
Hated of the very plains I stand on,
Shall I turn homeward? Cross the Aigaion? Desert
These watery roadways? Leave Agamemnon and Menelaos
To their own devices, to fight without me? What?
And when I get there—home—and face my father?
How will I do it? How? How will he bear
To look at me? Stripped of honor's highest prize!
Valor's prize! A prize *he* won! And *wore!*
A crown of *fame!*
No! It can't be done!
What, then?
Suppose I go to Troy, attack the walls,
Alone in single combat against them all,
And lose my life in doing some valorous deed.
But that would be too kind to the sons of Atreus.
No, some other way, then.
Some other way to prove to my old father
That the son he bore was not a gutless coward.
Long life? Who wants it?
No warrior asks such a thing
When his nights and days are awash in endless shame.
What joy can there be in forever dodging death?
What worth is a man who lives on idle hope?
To live or die in honor is the only way.
LEADER: We know you speak for yourself, Aias;
But listen to us, listen to friends,
And give up these grim thoughts.
Give way.
TEKMÊSSA: Aias, my lord: there is no greater evil
Harder to accept than the working of fate.
My father was a freeborn man, wealthy
Beyond all other Phrygians. But what am I?
A slave. Call it, somehow, the will of the gods;
Still, it was your strong hand that did it.
But having come to share your bed, I am loyal,
Loyal to you and loyal to your best interests:
I implore you, therefore, by Zeus who guards

Our hearth, and by the marriage bed making us one,
Don't desert me to your enemies' insults
And abandon me to a stranger.

On the day you die, and, dying, leave me helpless,
On that same day, be certain that I will be seized,
Along with your boy, and dragged with force by the Greeks
To a life of slavery.
One of my masters, then,
Will say with insolent tongue:
"What have we here?
Aias' woman?
Our mightiest warrior's whore?
Fallen from a life of privilege to this!"

It's what they'll say. My fate will drive me on,
But you and all your house will suffer disgrace.
Have you the heart, my lord, to abandon your father
To a miserable old age? Have you the heart
To leave behind your mother, whose years are long,
Whose prayers, time after time, plead your return?
And your son, my lord: pity your infant son.
Why deprive him of a father's care?
Why leave him alone, why defenseless,
To be raised by guardians who will feel no love?
What evils we will suffer, the two of us,
If you should die! You are all I have, Aias,
All I can look to. Your spear ravaged my country.
My mother and father are dead: another fate
Took them off to dwell in Death's dark kingdom.
What land could I call home if I lost you?
What fortune would be mine? You, Aias:
You are all I have: my safety; all my safety.
Yes, and think of *me,* too: even me.
No *true* man forgets happiness he once knew.
Love begets love. And failure to remember
Kindness is no longer to be a noble man.
LEADER: If only you had pity in your heart,
    As I have, Aias, you'd approve her words.
AIAS: Oh, she will have my approval, be sure of that,

Once she sets her mind to do as I order.

TEKMÊSSA: Dear Aias, I'll do anything you say!

AIAS: Then bring me my son! Now! I want to see him!

TEKMÊSSA: Yes, but I sent him away. All these fears—

AIAS: When these terrible 'things' were happening, you mean?

TEKMÊSSA: I feared he might meet you, and—be killed.

AIAS: Ha, how worthy of my evil genius!

TEKMÊSSA: At least I took care to prevent *that*.

AIAS: Yes, and you did well; I credit your foresight.

TEKMÊSSA: In that case, Aias, how can I serve you?

AIAS: I want to speak to him, see his face.

TEKMÊSSA: He's very near. He's with the servants.

AIAS: Then why the delay! Why isn't he here!

(Tekmêssa goes in the direction of the tent, calling.)

TEKMÊSSA: Eurysakes! Son! Your father's calling!

(To a Servant who rushes to the door of the tent.)

Whoever has him, bring him here!

AIAS: Is he coming or not! Don't your servants obey?

(Eurysakes, about five years old, appears immediately from the tent, led by a Servant.)

TEKMÊSSA: He's coming now, the servant's bringing him.

(Aias extends his arms toward the child. Tekmêssa brings him.)

AIAS: Give him here. Give him.

No son of mine will shy away from blood,
However fresh. Not if he's truly my son.
We must break him in soon: like a young colt;
Teach him his father's ways, rough and hard
As they are; train his nature to be his father's.
Son, your father's life has not been lucky;
Be luckier than he was. But in all else
Be your father's equal and you'll be no coward.
And yet what is there I wouldn't give
To be where you are now:
Ignorant of the evil that surrounds you.

Life is sweetest when innocence is yours,
Before you know the meaning of joy and sorrow.
But once you know, then prove to your father's enemies
The man you are and the man your father was.

Till then, let light breezes nourish you,
And enjoy your young life, your mother's joy.
You may be sure no Greek will ever outrage
Or shame you, even when I am gone.
I leave Teükros behind to guard the gate,
Tireless in the care and nurture of you,
Even though just now he's far away,
Hunting down the enemy.

And you, my fellow warriors and sailors,
I urge you to join with him in this service.
Tell Teükros for me to take the child
Home to my father and mother, Eriboia,
To tend and cherish them in their old age,
Till Death takes them to the dark world below.
As for my armor, it is not to be awarded
By any judge to any of the Greeks
In competition, and least of all to my destroyer.

But now, son, take this broadshield with your name:
Eurysakes—seven layers thick
Of hardened oxhide; proof against any spear;
Hold it, wield it, here, by the well-stitched strap.
The rest of my armor will share my grave.
(To Tekmêssa.)
Take him. Here. Quickly!
Take him away!
(Tekmêssa takes Eurysakes from him.)
(To the Servant.)
Close up!
(No one moves. To Tekmêssa.)
And you, stop wailing!
What a plaintive thing woman is!

Shut it tight! Hurry!
The skilled surgeon
Never wails incantations
When the knife is needed.
(The ekkyklêma moves slowly back into the tent; the doors remain open.)

LEADER: Your sharp words frighten me, Aias.
    Why all this haste?
TEKMÊSSA: What will you do, my lord?
AIAS: You and your questions!
    You and your probing!
    Use some sense!
TEKMÊSSA: I'm frightened, Aias!
    For the gods' sake, my lord,
    And your son's,
    Don't desert us now!
AIAS: I'm *tired* of hearing you!
    I owe nothing further to the gods!
TEKMÊSSA: That's blasphemy, Aias!
AIAS: Do you think I care!
TEKMÊSSA: Why won't you *listen?*
AIAS: You've said too much already!
TEKMÊSSA: Because I'm frightened, my prince!
AIAS: Close up here! Quickly!
TEKMÊSSA: In the name of the gods, hear me!
AIAS: What a fool you are, Tekmêssa!
    The time for lessons is past.
    *(Music begins as Aias turns abruptly and enters the tent through the large
    doors that the Servant closes behind him. Tekmêssa remains with Eurysakes,
    the Servant beside her. Immediately upon Aias' turn, the Chorus assumes a
    central position in the orchestra.)*
CHORUS: Far-famed Salamis, blessèd island,
            set forever in shore-lapping waves,

            praised of all, pity us now,
            camped here on the fields of Ida,

            ground down by time, by time grown old,
            countless months, endless years,

            our only hope the evil reward
            to rest at peace in Death's dark shade.

            But Aias, Aias once your champion,
            mighty warrior sent to battle,

sits near me here, his mind cribbed
in holy madness past all cure,

pasturing his lonely thoughts,
all his splendid deeds forgotten,

spited by the hateful kings,
a heavy grief to all his friends.

His white-haired mother, heavy with years,
when she hears of Aias' ravaged mind,

will utter no dirge, no sad dirge,
not the nightingale's plaintive cry,

but drum at her breasts in wild lament,
tearing her hair with keening wail.

Far better it is that a man whose mind
wanders in darkness should go down to Death,

for Aias, noblest of warring Greeks,
no longer rules his true nature,

but has gone astray in the paths of madness.
Wretched father, how heavy the curse

of your son's sick mind will be to hear,
a disgrace which none of his name has borne.

None but he.
(The music continues as Aias enters from his tent, sword in hand.)
AIAS: Huge, immeasurable Time brings out of darkness
All things into light, and then in turn
Takes all things back to darkness.

Everything is possible. Everything changes.
Solemn oath and iron-will are vanquished.
I who once was inflexible as tempered iron

Feel my edge blunted by that woman's words.
I pity leaving her here among my enemies,
Widowed with an orphaned son.

But now I'll go down to the sea, down to the meadow
And the bathing-place to wash myself clean of disgrace,
And so free myself of the goddess' anger.
Then I'll take this sword, this hateful weapon,
And hide it in a place unknown to man
Where no one will see it. No, let Night and Death
Hold it in safekeeping! For not since Hektor,
My gravest enemy, gave it as a gift,
Have I been shown anything
But scorn and rejection by these Greeks.
The ancient proverb is true:
An enemy's gift is no gift, only trouble.

In future, then, we will know how to yield:
On the one hand: to the gods; and on the other:
Even to the sons of Atreus;
They are our kings, and we must yield to them.

Nothing in life, nothing, no matter how strong,
Can afford to defy authority. Submission is all.
Winter with his snowy mantle yields
To fruitful Summer; ominous Night gives way
For shining-steeded Dawn to brush the sky
With rosy light; the breath of violent Wind
Lulls to sleep the groaning sea; and even
Sleep, all-mastering Sleep, who takes us captive,
Loosens his bonds, not holding us prisoner for ever.

Must we, then, not learn wisdom?
Not learn discipline?
Well—I, at least, will learn.
I have learned to hate an enemy
Only so much as is due to one who in future
Will be a friend; and to serve a friend only
So much as is due to one who will not always
Be a friend.

As most men learn: friendship is a treacherous harbor.
Well, no matter: It will turn out in the end.
Go inside, Tekmêssa: pray to the gods
To bring all my heart's desire to its end.

And you, comrades in arms, do the same:
Honor my requests. When Teükros comes,
Tell him to care for me, and be loyal to you.
I'm going where I must go. Do as I ask.
You may soon hear that I have found
Safe harbor from my suffering.

*(Aias turns toward Tekmêssa and Eurysakes and with a slight motion of his
head directs them to go into the tent. The Servant follows. Aias goes off left
toward the seashore. As he turns to leave, the Chorus bursts into a joyous song
and dance.)*

CHORUS: I tremble with joy at the news!
   Soar aloft in my rapture!
    Ioo, Pan! Ioo, Pan!
     Pan! Ioo, Pan!
     Appear!
      Appear!
   Sea-roving god!
    Come, o come from your snowy peak!
     Come from rocky Kyllênê!
     Teach me!
      Teach me
       to dance!
   King Pan!
    God who makes gods
     dance to his measure!
      Untaught god!
       Teach me the wild,
        high-stepping dances
   of Knossos!
    Of Nysa!
     Come, Pan, come!
      Dance with me, dance!
       And come, Apollo!
        Delian lord!

Across Ikarian waters!
Come to me, come!
So I may know you,
shining, favoring god!
Lord, in your divinity,
appear!
I sing, I raise up my voice!
God Arês, violent god,
God Arês, destroying god,
lifts now from our eyes
his cloud of dreadful distress,
his cloud of darkness and shame!
Now, Zeus, now, once again,
your pure and perfect light
greets our sea-cleaving ships,
our swift ships with day's brilliance!
Aias' pain is past!
Again he bows to the gods!
Again he offers sacrifice!
Humble and full of reverence!
Great Time makes all things fade;
nothing is beyond belief;
for Aias, against all hope,
repents his wrath toward the Atreidai!

(The music fades out as a Greek Messenger enters, right, running and breathless.)

MESSENGER: Friends! Quick! There's news!
Teükros is back from the hills of Mysioi,
He almost can't get to the generals,
They're crowded around him so tight,
Every Greek in the army, shouting threats,
Shouting abuse, jabbing, pushing,
Calling him names:
"That maniac's brother,
Kill that traitor's brother,
Stone him, tear him to shreds!"
They drew their swords
And the worst was about to happen,
When the elders stepped in and took charge:

Words, not blood.
But where's Aias?
Aias must know of this!
He most of all!
CHORUS: Not here.
He left just now.
Something he had in mind.
Something to do.
Some new purpose.
MESSENGER: Aiiiiii!
I took too long!
Too long to get here!
They sent me too late!
CHORUS: To do what?
What haven't we done?
MESSENGER: Aias was not to go out.
Teükros said so—
Not till he arrived.
CHORUS: Yes, but he's gone.
And a good thing, too:
To make his peace with the gods.
MESSENGER: But that's nonsense
If Kalchas and his prophecy
Are to be trusted!
CHORUS: Prophecy?
What prophecy?
What do you know?
MESSENGER: Only what I saw. I was there.
Kalchas broke away from the council of leaders
To speak in private with Teükros,
Out of earshot of Agamemnon and Menelaos.
The friendly old man took Teükros' hand
And urged him to do everything humanly possible
To keep Aias in his tent the whole day,
Not let him out under any circumstance,
Not if he wished to see him alive again.
For this one day alone, this one day,
The prophet said, Athêna would pursue him
With all her anger.

"Those men," said the prophet,
"Whose lives grow overboastful, are struck by the gods
With grave misfortunes,
For they have forgotten that they were born mortal,
And presumed to think thoughts too great for man.
Yet Aias, when he first set out from home,
Proved himself foolish when his father
Spoke sensibly. 'Son,' commanded old Telamon,
'Always set out to win; but always win
With a god's help.'
But Aias, in his arrogant folly, answered:
'Father, any *nobody* can win
With the gods' help. I will win glorious fame
Without them.' So terrible was his boast.
Then a second time, when divine Athêna
Stood beside him in battle and urged him to strike
The enemy with his deadly hand, he answered
In words too terrible for human utterance:
'Goddess,' he said, 'go stand by the other Greeks.
No enemy will break a line I command.'
It was words like these, that broke all bounds of modesty
Set for man, that raised the unspeakable wrath
Of Athêna. But if he survives this one day,
Then, perhaps, with the gods' help, we may save him."

When the prophet had finished, Teükros called me to him
At once and sent me here with these orders.
But if I've come too late, and my hopes dashed,
Then Aias is dead, or Kalchas is no prophet.
CHORUS: Tekmêssa, pitiable woman, come out!
    Bad news! Come hear this man!
    This razor shaves too close for comfort.
    (*Tekmêssa, carrying Eurysakes, enters from the tent, attended by several Servants.*)
TEKMÊSSA: Why have you disturbed me?
    I had only now found peace
    From this siege of troubles.
LEADER: It was my pain called you.
    Hear what he has to say—
    About Aias.

TEKMÊSSA: Tell me!

    What are you saying?

    Are we ruined?

MESSENGER: For you, I can't say.

    For Aias, if he's left his tent,

    There's no hope left.

TEKMÊSSA: He *has* gone out, he *has!*

    Why are you torturing me?

MESSENGER: It's Teükros' orders.

    Keep him inside;

    Don't let him out alone.

TEKMÊSSA: Teükros? Where is he?

    Why does he say this?

MESSENGER: He's just returned.

    If Aias goes out there, his fate is sealed.

TEKMÊSSA: Oimoi! No!

    Who told him this?

MESSENGER: The prophet Kalchas.

    Today. Today, he said,

    Brings life or death to Aias.

TEKMÊSSA: Aiiiiii!

    O friends! Protect me

    From this threatening doom!

    Hurry, some of you,

    Run, bring Teükros!

    The rest, split up,

    East and west,

    Search each bend of the shore!

    Search out his fated steps!

    I know now I have been deceived

    By the husband who held me once in his heart

    And now banishes me!

    O child, what can I do?

    I must do *something!*

    Yes—

    I'll go—

    I'll go myself—

    As far as strength allows—

Hurry! There's no time to lose!
Not if we're to save a man
Longing to die!
LEADER: I'm with you, lady.
Deeds, not words, now.
Fast as my feet can carry me.
*(The Chorus splits into two groups. Tekmêssa, the Leader, the Messenger, all
the Servants, and both parts of the Chorus rush off through the right and left
exits, as the double doors slowly open and the ekkyklêma moves forward into
full view. The scene is now an isolated grove of trees near the seashore, rep-
resented perhaps by a single tree on the ekkyklêma on which Aias is discov-
ered crouched down, planting the haft of his sword in the earth.)*
AIAS: There—
The sacrificial slayer ready—
Just at the angle to be most cutting.
But why all the talk—less thinking—

The sword was Hektor's. A gift from him.
The man of all men that I most hated.
And there it stands.
Planted in enemy Trojan soil.
Edge new-whetted by the iron-scouring stone.
Buried with care for a kind and easy death.
There. Ready. Everything in order.
Now for my prayers.

Almighty Zeus,
I call first on you, as is only right:
Give me your protection.
I ask one small favor.
Send Teükros news of my disaster,
Let him come and be the first to find me,
And lift me from this newly bloodied sword,
And save me from some enemy casting me out,
A prey for dogs and birds.
Grant me this, great Zeus.

And you, god Hermês,
Conductor of souls to the Dark Kingdom,

Give me death without struggle;
Lay me to sleep softly when in one swift leap
I plunge the sword through to my heart.

You, too, I call as helpers, ever virgin,
Ever defenders of all suffering mortals,
The dread, long-striding Furies:
Behold my death brought on by the Atreidai:
Destroy them with deaths as vile as they are vile.
Those men, those evil men who see me fall
By my own hand, may they, too, fall
By the hands of kindred most loved.
Go, swift daughters of vengeance, dread Erinys,
Drink deep the army's blood!
Spare none of them!

And you, Hêlios, sun-god,
Whose chariot wheels course the heavens' steep slopes,
Draw up your reins of gold when you pass my land,
My native land,
And tell of my disasters and my death
To my agèd father and sorrowing mother,
The mother who nursed me once.
For when she hears of this, poor, wretched woman,
Her cry will echo through all the city.

No time for tears now.
To work. Quickly.
Death, o Death!
Come! Attend me here!
And yet, I'll greet you face to face below.
But you, o you, grand radiance!
And you, great Hêlios, charioteer!
I will not see you again!
O light of day!
O Salamis!
Land of my fathers' hearth!
Sacred soil!
And Athens! Glorious city!

Kin to my people!
Farewell!
And farewell, Troy,
Troy with your plains, your streams,
Your rivers that nourished me!
Aias greets you for the last time.
His next words will be to the dead
In the great Realm of Darkness.

(Music fades in as Aias falls on his sword and dies and the ekkyklêma slowly retreats into the skênê, now the House of Death, as the doors close behind it. Heard before they are seen, Chorus I and Chorus II rush on through both exits, still searching frantically in the orchestra, neither seeing the other.)

CHORUS I: Toil
      brings toil and
         makes only toil!
    Where!
      Where!
        Where have my steps
   not taken me!
    Where!
      Where!
   No place draws me!
    No place tells me!
      Tells me where he is!
   Where!
    What was that sound?
      Listen!
   That sound!
    Listen!
      Listen!
   There!
    There!
      Who's there?
   Who?

CHORUS II: Shipmates!
    Comrades!
   Friends!

CHORUS I: What news?

CHORUS II: We've searched the area

                              west of the ships—
CHORUS I: And?
CHORUS II: Rough going!
                   Nothing!
                       Nothing found!
                           Nothing!
CHORUS I: Nothing eastward either!
                   Nothing!
                       Nothing!
CHORUS: If only there were someone to tell me,
                   some sea toiler on his sleepless search,
              a nymph from Olympos or a wandering stream,
                   a river that flows into wide Bosporos,
              to tell me where fierce Aias wanders.
                   How hard it is to wander in vain
              and not to have found our troubled master.

(As the Chorus delivers the above facing away from the skênê, the double doors open and the ekkyklêma again moves forward into full view with the impaled body of Aias on it. At the same time, Tekmêssa, followed at a distance by a Servant carrying Eurysakes, enters, right, unseen by the Chorus, and finds the body of Aias. The Servant carrying Eurysakes, fearful for his safety, hurries out right in the direction of the Greek camp.)

TEKMÊSSA: Ioo moi moiiiiiiiiiii!
LEADER: Whose is that cry?
CHORUS: There!
                  In the grove!
TEKMÊSSA: Ioooooooooo!
CHORUS: Tekmêssa!
                  I see her!
                      His unhappy bride!
                          Lost in her grief!
TEKMÊSSA: Friends,
                  dear friends!
                      There's nothing,
                  nothing to live for now!
                      Nothing!
CHORUS: What is it?
                  Tell me!
                      Tell me!

TEKMÊSSA: Aias—
        Aias—
           dead—
              dead—
       there—
          there—
           a sword through his body—

CHORUS: Omoiiiiiii!
       No way home now—
         Omoiiiiiii!
    You have killed me, King
      Aias! Killed me, too!
        Omoiiiii!
    Your ship's companion!
      O talas!
        Miserable lady!

TEKMÊSSA: He's dead! Dead!
  Weep for him! Weep!

CHORUS: Who could have done this?
  Who? Whose hand?

TEKMÊSSA: His own. The sword—
  Here in the ground—the point upward—
  Here is the proof.

CHORUS: Omoiiiiiii!
      My blindness!
        Where were my eyes?
    What a fool I was!
      You bled alone!
        Alone! Alone!
    No friend to guard you!
      Where were my eyes?
        Where were my wits?
    Doomed Aias!
      Willful Aias!
        Where is he lying?
    Where? Where?
      Where is Aias?
        Where is he, where?
    Ill-named Aias!

TEKMÊSSA: No one must see.
    No one. We loved him.
    Who could bear it?
    Rivers of blood from his heart's core.
    Bloody gore from his nostrils.
    And here—the mouth of the wound
    Made by his own hand.
    I'll cover him, cover him, here,
    Here with this robe—
    All of him, all!
    (Tekmêssa wraps Aias' body in her cloak.)
    Ah, what can I do?
    What now?

    O Aias, Aias,
    Where is the friend
    To raise you, lift you
    In his arms?
    Where is Teükros?
    O god, let him come:
    Now, now when we need him:
    To tend him in death: his brother's body!
    O Aias, unhappy Aias,
    To have come to this.
    To see you fallen so low.
    Even your enemies would
    Weep to see you.
CHORUS: Stiff-hearted man!
        You were
           doomed!
      Doomed to
        destruction!
          Doomed from the
    start!
      Doomed by this
        terrible
    blow of
      destiny! Doomed to
        fulfill in suffering,

suffering, endless
   misery! An
      evil fate I
see now! The
   awful omen, that
      night, that
morning, of your
   groaning bitter
      wrath on the
sons of Atreus'
   house! Your
      heart
unyielding, your
   passion
      fatal,
that was the time,
   that was the start, the
      beginning of
sorrows, the
   source of
      misery, when the
golden
   prize of
      Achilleus'
armor was
   given in a
      contest of the
greatest
   prowess!

TEKMÊSSA: Ioo moi moi!

LEADER: True grief, I know,
      pierces your heart.

TEKMÊSSA: Ioo moi moi!

LEADER: I understand your cries, lady.
      Weep, then weep again,
        for you have only now lost
    one dearly loved.

TEKMÊSSA: You can only imagine my pain,
      but I must feel it—

LEADER: I know, I know—
TEKMÊSSA: Oimoiiiiiiiiiiiiii!
                    O child, child,
              what a bitter yoke
                    will bend our necks, what
                    eyes will watch us!
LEADER: The ruthless son of Atreus
                    will do unspeakable things, lady,
                        if what you said is true,
              and only add to our present misery.
                    God save you from it.
TEKMÊSSA: Only the gods
              have brought us to this!
LEADER: Yes, they have dealt us
                    a crushing blow.
TEKMÊSSA: The dreadful daughter
                    of Zeus did this; gave us this
                        pain to please Odysseus!
CHORUS: Odysseus, who
                    jeers in his
                        black heart, the
              patient much-enduring
                    hero, mocks
                        cruelly at our frenzied
              pain;
                    féu! féu!
                        and when
              they hear, the
                    twin kings will
                        join their mocking
              laughter to
                    scorn us!
       (The music fades out.)
TEKMÊSSA: Let them laugh at his ruin, let them rejoice
     At their enemy's destruction. They scorned him alive;
     Perhaps they will mourn his loss in the heat of battle
     When they most need him. Evil men never know
     The worth they hold in their hands till they've flung it away.
     His death, so bitter to me, is sweet to them,

But a great joy to him. He has it now,
The death that he so passionately longed for,
Has it, holds it to him, death by choice,
On his own terms. What right have they to laugh!
His death was due to the gods, *never* to them!

So, Odysseus, revel in your empty triumph.
Aias is dead to them now. Nothing remains.
And I am left with anguish and lamentation
(Teükros' voice is heard from the right.)
TEÜKROS: Ioo moi moiiiiiiiiii!
CHORUS: Shh! Someone coming!
It's Teükros' voice! His cry's arrow
Strikes the mark of our sorrow.
(Teükros enters right and, immediately seeing the covered body of Aias, rushes toward it uttering a long drawn-out lament.)
TEÜKROS: O Aias!
Aias, dear brother!
Is it true what they say?
LEADER: It's true, Teükros.
Aias is dead.
TEÜKROS: Aiiiiiiii!
How can I bear it!
LEADER: So it is.
TEÜKROS: O talas talas!
LEADER: We have cause to mourn.
TEÜKROS: O dreadful blow!
LEADER: Yes, Teükros.
TEÜKROS: Féu talas!
(To Tekmêssa.)
But the child! Where is the child?
Where can I find him?
LEADER: Alone by the tents.
TEÜKROS: Bring him, quickly.
They'll snatch him away like a lion's cub
Strayed from its mother, its father dead.
Hurry! Go with her! No time to waste!
Men love to gloat when the dead lie helpless.

(Tekmêssa hurries off through the right exit toward the Greek encampment with several of the Servants.)

LEADER: Well done, Teükros.
  Aias' last order
  Asked you to care for the child.

TEÜKROS: O Aias, Aias! In all my life no sight
  Has been so sad as this! No road I've traveled
  Has been more painful, dearest Aias, than this
  That led me here when I learned about your fate!
  Rumor, fanned by a god, surged through the army,
  Saying that you were dead. While still far off,
  I heard and groaned low with pain—but now,
  Now, seeing you here—my heart is broken—

  Oimoiiiiiiiiiiiiiiiiiiiiiiiii!
  Take off the cover—
  Let me see the worst.
  (An Attendant removes the covering from Aias' body.)
  Aiiiiiiiiiiii! Aiiiiiiiiiiiiiii!
  Horrible horrible sight!
  Face hard with cruelty!
  Eyes cold with courage!
  Your death has sown a bitter harvest.
  Where can I turn to now?
  Where can I go? Where?
  Where was I when you needed me?
  Anywhere but here—
  Not here—not here—

  Oh, our father Telamon, no doubt,
  Will greet me with bright smiles when I come home—
  Your father and mine—
  And you not with me.
  Be sure of that!
  The man who never smiles at good news!
  What evil will he level at me then?
  What vile names and curses?
  What will he keep back?
  "Bastard son of a slave won in battle!"

He'll cry at me: "Coward, deserter, traitor!"
For having failed to protect you, dearest Aias,
Or else through deceit to have caused your death
To take your kingship from you and your home!
This is what he will charge, the peevish old man,
Whose anger seeks out quarrels without provocation.
And then in the end he'll exile me from home,
Deny me my country, make me out a slave,
Rather than what in truth I am: a free man.

That's what I look for at home.
While here at Troy, my enemies abound
And helpers are few.
These are the benefits your death brings me.

Oimoiiiiiiiiiiiiii!
What shall I do?
O Aias, how shall I lift you,
How shall I drag your body from this cruel blade,
This gleaming spike,
The slayer, poor poor Aias,
Who took your dying breath!

Do you see now how Hektor, dead Hektor,
Was destined to destroy you in the end?
He needed only to raise his hand in death
To take your life.
The gifts you gave each other on the field of battle
When you ended your duel before the gathered armies
Were gifts of honor that turned to gifts of death.
The war-belt you gave to Trojan Hektor
Was the same belt that lashed him to Achilleus' chariot
That dragged him by his heels and mangled him
Till he breathed his last.
And Hektor's gift, this sword,
This same sword you took from him,
You fell on and died.

Two men: one fate!

Some Fury forged this sword,
And cruel Hades the belt.
The gods contrive men's lives,
The gods did this.
At least it's what I think.
Agree or not, it's no matter.
Each man thinks what he likes.

CHORUS: No time for words now, my lord.
Get him buried first.
I see the enemy coming:
Perhaps to mock at our grief,
As an evil man would.

TEÜKROS: Who is it? Someone from the army?

LEADER: Menelaos. The man we sailed here to join.

TEÜKROS: Not a man easily ignored!

(Some of the Sailors are about to lift Aias' body as Menelaos, accompanied by armed Soldiers, enters, right, from the Greek camp.)

MENELAOS: You there! Hands off that corpse!
That's an order! Leave it, I say!

TEÜKROS: Whose order?

MENELAOS: Mine. And the Supreme Commander's, my brother's!

TEÜKROS: Ah! Yes! And the reason?

MENELAOS: We brought him here,
Thinking we had a friend
And ally on our side,
But what did we find?
An enemy more terrible than any Trojan.
He plotted against us all,
The whole damn army,
Stealing out at night to lay us low
With his coward's sword!
Had some god not sat on his little ploy,
His fate would have been ours, and ours his,
With us sprawled out there dead as dogs,
And him here still alive.
Some god or other turned his rage aside
To fall on sheep and cattle.

There's your reason.

No. No grave. Not for him.
He's to be cast on the sand
Somewhere along the shore
For birds to peck at.
There's not a man alive big enough
To dig this man underground,
So don't get ideas!
He's ours now.
Maybe we couldn't control him alive;
But now he's dead; now we will;
Like it or not; *this man*
Who never once obeyed a word of mine!

It's a common man who dares defy authority
Set above him: proving himself to be evil!
No state can sail a prosperous course
Where there's no fear: no army can be disciplined
Where the bulwark of dread and reverence are lacking.
There's no man, however great in bulk,
Who must not know that he can be toppled
By the slightest mischance.
Fear and shame will be his best security.
But give men license to insult and act at will,
The ship of state, no matter how favoring the wind
May once have been, will, in the course of time,
Sink to the depths.

Where fear is proper, I say, let us establish
Fear in its proper place. Let us not think
We can take our pleasures at will and not pay for them
With our pains. These things come by turns.
(Indicating the body of Aias.)
This was a man who once flamed high with insolence,
But now it's my turn to be arrogant.
And I order you here and now not to bury him,
For in burying him you might slip and fall in yourself.
LEADER: There's wisdom in what you say,
Menelaos, just be careful.
Don't outrage the dead.

TEÜKROS: Ah, friends, friends, will I ever again be amazed
        When I see a man, a nobody in birth,
        Go wrong; when those who claim nobility of birth
        Allow themselves to utter such ignoble words?
        (To Menelaos.)
        Come! Let me hear it again. Just once more.
        You say that *you, you* brought him here from Greece?
        That *you* enlisted him to fight as an ally?
        That he did not sail to Troy on his *own,*
        His *own* master? Not of his *own* doing?

        By what right do you claim to be his commander?
        Who put you in charge of the men he brought
        From his own country?
        You came here the King of Sparta, not *our* king.
        You had no more right to discipline *him*
        Than he to discipline *you.*

        You sailed to Troy not the Supreme Commander,
        But one subject to the orders of others.
        You *never* had the right to govern Aias.
        Rule those you have a *right* to rule: lash *them*
        With your arrogant words. But as for me, I'll bury him,
        Bury him in all piety as justice demands,
        And in defiance of every prohibition
        That you or that brother-chief of yours can lay down!

        Do you think you frighten me, you and your *words?*
        Can you *really* believe he went to war for your *wife,*
        Like those drudges you lord it over?
        No!
        He sailed to honor the oath he had sworn!
        Never for you!
        He had only scorn for 'little' men.
        And when you come again,
        Bring more soldiers to back you.
        And bring the general that *counts.*
        The noise you make means nothing to me—
        Not *that*—

(He snaps his fingers in Menelaos' face.)
As long as you are what you are.
LEADER: Things are bad enough, sir,
Don't make them worse.
Harsh words, however true,
Can cut too deep.
MENELAOS: I see our 'bowman' thinks well of himself.
TEÜKROS: Archery is no contemptible art.
MENELAOS: How he would boast if he had a shield!
TEÜKROS: I'd match you fully armed with *no* shield!
MENELAOS: What courage his ferocious tongue talks!
TEÜKROS: A man in the right may boast a bit.
MENELAOS: Right to honor the man who killed me?
TEÜKROS: Killed you? And still alive? My word!
MENELAOS: Saved by a god but dead in *his* mind!
TEÜKROS: If the gods saved you, why dishonor them?
MENELAOS: Dispute the gods' laws? What are you saying!
TEÜKROS: By denying proper burial to the dead.
MENELAOS: Not to a man I'm personally at war with!
TEÜKROS: Aias openly declared war on *you?!*
MENELAOS: Our hate was double-edged, as you know.
TEÜKROS: Because you robbed him with false votes.
MENELAOS: No! It was the judges' doing!
TEÜKROS: You could even make evil look good.
MENELAOS: 'Someone' is sure to suffer for that speech.
TEÜKROS: That 'someone' won't suffer more than he gives.
MENELAOS: My word is final: He will not be buried!
TEÜKROS: Mine's final, too: He *will* be buried!
MENELAOS: I heard of a man once, a bully of a talker,
Who urged his sailors out in winter weather.
But when the storm blew up, you would hear nothing,
Not a word, coming from under his cloak,
Huddled there in the stern, where everyone trampled him.
And so, I suspect, would you and your blustering speech
Be quenched by a gale from a piddling cloud.
TEÜKROS: And I once heard of a man, one puffed with folly,
Who mocked at his neighbors' misfortunes. But another man,
Like me, who felt as I do, looked at him and said:
"Don't outrage the dead; for if you do, be certain

That you will regret it." And so, straight to his face,
He gave him warning, this—this foolish man.
And—could I be mistaken?—that man is you.
Yes, you. Or do I speak in riddles?
MENELAOS: I'm leaving now.
Why battle with words
When I have power
To force you to my will!
It's beneath my dignity!
TEÜKROS: Beneath mine, too,
To hear idle words from fools!
Get out!
(Menelaos goes off right, followed by the Soldiers.)
CHORUS: A deadly quarrel, trouble coming—
LEADER: Hurry, Teükros, find some hollow
Deep in the earth to hold his body:
A dank and moldering tomb that will rise
A signal to memory in ages to come.
(Tekmêssa enters, right, carrying Eurysakes and followed by several Attendants.)
TEÜKROS: Here they are,
His wife, his son, to help
Bury and mourn his body.
Come here, boy.
Here by your father.
Stand by him. Touch him.
Here, like a suppliant,
With your hand. You see?
He gave you life.
Kneel here now
And in supplication implore his help
With these locks of hair.
(He cuts a lock of his own hair, then Tekmêssa's, and places it in the boy's hand.)
Mine—
hers—
now yours:
A suppliant's offering.
(Pauses with the knife before cutting Eurysake's hair.)

If anyone, any man of the army,
Comes with force to wrest you away from this body,
May he die the evil death of an evil man,
His body unburied,
Cast out from his country,
The root of his race cut away,
As I now cut this lock!
(Cuts the lock and places it in Eurysakes' hand.)
Take it, boy.
Guard it.
Kneel and cling to the body.
Let no one move you from it.
(To the Chorus.)
And you, stop crouching like women!
Act like men! Defend him!
I'll dig his grave—see to it myself.
Let them try and stop me!
(Music begins as Teükros goes out left. Eurysakes remains beside the body of Aias, with Tekmêssa beside him in silent grief to the end of the play. As Teükros turns to leave, the Chorus takes up a new position in the orchestra.)

CHORUS: When will they
                 end? When, o
                       when, the interminable
              years of
                 sea-wandering?
                       When will the
              toil that never
                 ends; the endless
                       wielding of
              spears; the
                 pain and hardship of
                       battle on Troy's vast
              plain; the sorrow and
                 shame of Greece; oh,
                       when,
              when will it
                 end? If only that
                       man who taught us to
              league our lands in

warfare with hateful
    arms had plunged to the
sky, or sunk into
   all-accepting
    Hades!
Strife of our strife!
  Toil of our toil!
    Shared by all for all time!
Destroyer of men!
  Him I curse!
    Him I curse who
deprives me of
  pleasures! Who
   robs me of
garlands and elegant
  wine-cups
    filled and
overflowing! Who
  robs me of the
   sweet din of
flutes: a
  joyful noise! And
   company of
friends! Of
  blissful
   rest in the
arms of
  night! And of
   love, of
love's dear
  treasure! But
   here I lie,
alone, on my
  couch; no
   sweet companion,
untended,
  neglected! My
   hair heavy with
dew to remind me of

Troy's discomforts!

    Aias was

once my

    bulwark;

        defense against night's

fears and the enemy's

    swift shafts; but

        here he lies,

sacrifice to an

    evil fate!

        What joy is left me

now, what

    joy?

        O if only my

sails were

    set for

        home! Set for

Sounion's tree-topped

    summit that

        rears above the

sea-washed rocks, and

    greet, sailing into

        sight, the

blessèd city, my

    holy

        Athens!

(Teükros enters, left, in haste, and the music fades out.)

TEÜKROS: I ran back! Ran when I saw him!

    The general! Agamemnon! He's coming!

    He won't let us off lightly! He's raging!

    (Agamemnon enters, right, followed by Menelaos and a contingent of armed Soldiers.)

AGAMEMNON: Ah! So it's you, Teükros!

    You with your monstrous charges!

    You! You! And expecting to get away with it!

    You son of a whore of a slave!

    If you'd had a noble mother,

    You'd be blowing your horn all over the place

    And strutting around on tiptoes!

But you're a nothing, that's what you are—
A nothing defending a nobody!
We lack authority, do we?
My brother and I?
That the way it goes?
No right to lead the Greeks?
The fleet? The Army?
Not even you?
Ah, yes—
And Aias sailed here his own man,
His own command!
How dare you, a slave, spout such arrogance?

Who is this man, what is he,
That you bleat about so mightily?
Where has he been, where has he fought,
That I haven't fought as well?
Are there no other 'real' men in the army?
You were beaten, Teükros,
Beaten by a majority vote of the judges.
And yet it appears the award of Achilleus' armor
Will continue to cost us dear if we're to be always
Denounced as evil by Teükros, slouching around,
Stabbing us in the back, slandering us
With false accusations—because you disagree.
Run an army like that and you're in trouble.

Where would order be if at a whim
We place the losers first, the winners last?
Where is law in that?
No, it must end!
Brawn isn't what's called for, strong shoulders, backs.
No! We need brains, clear thinking, sanity!
Any lummox of an ox can be led down a path
With a tiny goad; and you can look forward to the same
Unless you get some sense.

The man is dead! A shadow!
And here you are, running off at the mouth,

Spouting out your arrogance as if you were privileged!
Get some sense! Think who you are! A slave's son!
If a case is what you call this, get someone else,
A freeborn man, a warrior, to plead it for you,
Because I don't understand your barbarian babble.
LEADER: All I can say is both of you
   Should listen to reason.
TEÜKROS: Ah, gratitude to the dead! How brief it is!
   How quickly it fades, Aias, turns traitor,
   If this man, for whom you risked your life
   Time and again in battle, whose shield you were,
   Can find no single word, no hint of tribute,
   To your remembrance! All forgotten now!
   Quite tossed aside!
   (To Agamemnon.)
   Just now, as you were shooting off your mouth
   In that nonsense speech of yours, did you forget
   The time when you were penned behind your barriers,
   You and your men; routed; as good as dead;
   And *he* came! *Aias* came! *Alone* he came!
   And rescued you? Had you forgotten the day
   Your ships' sterns were wrapped in flame, and Hektor
   Bounding high above the trench to reach your ships?
   Who checked *that* disaster? Wasn't it *this man?*
   Wasn't it *Aias?* Wasn't it he
   Who, as you said just now, never fought
   Where you also did not fight? Won't you allow
   He did his duty *that* day? Or that other time,
   That time he took on Hektor single-handed,
   Not by any orders you might have mouthed,
   No, but by *vote,* casting his lot in the helmet,
   No renegade lot, no lump of moistened clay
   That would sink straight to the bottom,
   But one that would leap up lightly when it was shaken,
   Straight up to the top and over the edge?

   These were the deeds he did, and I was there,
   There, there at his side, I, the 'slave,'
   Son of a barbarous mother, as you say!

Who gives you the *right* to speak of me this way?!
And while we're at it, who was your father's father?
Pelops, was it? Pelops the barbarian?
Pelops the stinking Phrygian?
And your father? Atreus?
What's he become famous for?
Stirring up a stew for his brother's feast?
Serving up the flesh of his own nephews?
Dishing out tender morsels of his brother's sons?

Ah, yes, then there's your mother. A Krêtan, I believe,
Whose father found her bedded down with some stranger,
And sent her off on a long ocean voyage
To feed the fishes—for fishes tell no tales.
If this is your family tree, then why mock mine?
My father was Telamon, my mother a princess,
Laomedon's daughter, given to him
For peerless valor in battle by Heraklês,
A gift of gifts! And you expect me to stand here
And disgrace one of my blood by letting you cast him
Out unburied? The shame is yours, not mine.

But let's get one thing straight: you cast *him* out
And you'll cast out three others:
His wife, his child, his brother;
For I would rather die here for him
In the light of day than for that woman of yours—
Ah, I beg your pardon: your brother's woman.
Take my advise. Think of yourself, not me.
Touch me and you'll find yourself regretting it.
Better a coward than be too bold with Teükros.
(Odysseus enters right.)
LEADER: You've come just in time, Odysseus.
    If you're here to help, not make things worse,
    You're welcome.
ODYSSEUS: Gentlemen, friends, what is this?
    First Menelaos, then you, Agamemnon:
    Voices raised over this valiant corpse.
    I heard it way across camp.

AGAMEMNON: Shouts, indeed, Odysseus!
    If you'd heard the foul-mouthed insults
    That man there had the nerve—
ODYSSEUS: A man who gives as good as he gets
    Is a man I understand.
    Who can blame him?
AGAMEMNON: I didn't exactly mince words!
    His behavior to me was vile!
ODYSSEUS: I see. And how had he harmed you?
AGAMEMNON: I gave specific orders
    Not to bury that body.
    He refused! Defied me!
ODYSSEUS: Aha. Well, my friend,
    May a friend give advice
    And still be partners with you?
AGAMEMNON: Feel free. I'd be a fool
    Not to listen to my greatest friend.
ODYSSEUS: All right, then, bury him.
    Use some sense. You're all in a rage,
    Not thinking straight. Don't trample Justice.
    If you cast him out unburied, that's what you're doing.
    Don't let Vengeance guide you.
    He was brave; and, yes, my hated
    And most hating enemy, as he was yours,
    The worst in the army, ever since I won
    Achilleus' armor. I loathed him
    And all he stood for.
    But how can I stand here and fail to admit
    That he was the bravest of us all,
    The bravest warrior to come to Troy,
    Except for Achilleus.
    Can I deny him that?
    Justice says no.
    Shame this man and you dishonor not him
    But the laws of the gods.
    Kicking a man who's down can never be just,
    No matter how much you hate him.
AGAMEMNON: Odysseus? Are you taking his side against me?
ODYSSEUS: Yes; but when hating was right, I hated him.

AGAMEMNON: He's dead now, why not trample his corpse?

ODYSSEUS: Don't glory, my friend, in triumphs won in dishonor.

AGAMEMNON: Piety doesn't come easy for a king.

ODYSSEUS: But he can accept a friend's good counsel.

AGAMEMNON: A loyal friend respects authority.

ODYSSEUS: Enough. There's victory in yielding to a friend.

AGAMEMNON: Do you know the man you're befriending here?

ODYSSEUS: An enemy, yes, but nonetheless noble.

AGAMEMNON: You'd honor the corpse of a hated enemy?

ODYSSEUS: His greatness weighed is more than his enmity.

AGAMEMNON: Unsteady and changeable men speak this way.

ODYSSEUS: Today a friend, tomorrow an enemy.

AGAMEMNON: I see. You approve of making such friends?

ODYSSEUS: Not of men whose minds won't bend.

AGAMEMNON: Aha, today you'd make us seem cowards.

ODYSSEUS: No. Men of justice in all Greek eyes.

AGAMEMNON: Then you recommend we allow this burial?

ODYSSEUS: I do. For one day *I'll* come to this.

AGAMEMNON: There we have it: Each man for himself.

ODYSSEUS: Who else, then, if not for myself?

AGAMEMNON: The doing of this is yours, not mine.

ODYSSEUS: Whose ever it is, your generosity is great.

AGAMEMNON: You can be sure of one thing, Odysseus:

> For you I'd do an even greater favor.
> But as for him, whether above
> Or below the earth,
> He'll be my enemy forever.
> Do whatever is needed.
> *(Agamemnon, Menelaos, and the armed Soldiers go out right.)*

LEADER: You're a wise man, Odysseus;

> Whoever denies it is a fool.

ODYSSEUS: And to you, Teükros, I have this to say:

> From this day forward I will be as great a friend
> As I was an enemy. And, with your permission,
> I'm willing to share in all the rites and duties
> Of burial due this noblest of men.

TEÜKROS: Noble Odysseus—

> What can I have but praise,
> Praise for your words?

My fears about you were groundless:
Of all the Greeks, you alone stood by him;
You who of all the Greeks were his bitterest enemy
Refused to be a part of it:
The outrage, the inhuman outrage,
What the living do to the dead!
Not like that bastard general,
The one who came here,
Demanding, demanding;
With that brother of his, loathsome brother;
Who came here with him;
The two of them; demanding—
Demanding his body—be thrown out—
To rot—his body—
Unburied—!
(Regaining his calm.)
May Zeus who rules from Olympos,
And the Furies, those avengers who never forget,
And Justice, who brings all things to completion,
Destroy those men with evil to match the evil
They sought to work in casting out this body!

Son of old Laërtes, kind Odysseus,
I hesitate to say, and yet I must,
That it would not be proper if you touched the body,
For fear it displease the dead. As for the rest,
Feel free to join with us in the burial.
And if you like, bring any man from the army,
For they are most welcome.
I'll see to the rest.
You have proven yourself to us a noble friend.
ODYSSEUS: I'd have wished to help, of course;
But in respect of your feelings, I will go now.
(Music fades in as Odysseus goes off, right, and Teükros begins preparations.)
TEÜKROS: Come; let's make an
            end; it's time.
                You, hollow a
            grave out quickly;
                you, set the cauldron

on its lofty stand,
　fire-surrounded,
　　for the ritual
　　　cleansing; and you,
　bring the armor his shield
　　protected.
　　　And now, boy, since
　he is your father,
　　with your little strength
　　　help me to lift him.
Gently,
　gently,
　　for his blood
still runs warm.
　And you who
　　count yourselves his
friends, come,
　help us bear him,
　　this excellent man,
of all men who have
　lived, the
　　noblest.

(Several Attendants quickly come forward to lift the body of Aias off the sword and raise him to shoulder level. Teükros, with Eurysakes and Tekmêssa beside him, takes up his position behind the body's head. The Chorus forms a procession, followed by Attendants and all others, and leads off right, followed by the body of Aias.)

CHORUS:　　　Man learns many things by experience.
　　　　　　　What is to come, no man knows.

ANTIGONÊ
(ΑΝΤΙΓΟΝΗ)

CAST OF CHARACTERS

ANTIGONÊ *daughter of Oedipus and Iokastê*
ISMENÊ *sister of Antigonê*
KREON *King of Thebes and uncle of Antigonê and Ismenê*
HAIMON *son of Kreon and Eurydikê*
TEIRESIAS *blind prophet*
EURYDIKÊ *wife of Kreon*
CHORUS OF OLD THEBAN CITIZENS
LEADER OF THE CHORUS
A SENTRY
A MESSENGER
A BOY *guide to Teiresias*
GUARDS
ATTENDANTS
SERVANTS

The lines of the Chorus, unless otherwise indicated, are to be delivered by individual voices and varied groups of voices.

ANTIGONÊ

Thebes. The skênê represents the royal palace of King Kreon. A large central double door dominates the façade. On either side of the circular orchestra is a passageway for entrances and exits, the right to the city, the left to the country. It is very early morning, barely dawn. The invading Argive armies have only now been driven off by the defending Theban forces. Eteoklês and Polyneikês, the sons of Oedipus, and the brothers of Antigonê and Ismenê have killed each other in battle, leaving Kreon king of Thebes. Antigonê leads Ismenê stealthily through the large double doors into the orchestra.

ANTIGONÊ: Dear Ismenê, dear sister—we are the last,
    The last in line of the house of Oedipus,
    And you would think that we had endured enough
    From the ancient curse laid down upon our father.
    Is there any suffering that Zeus
    Has not used to blight our lives as well?
    Both you and I have suffered every evil,
    Every pain, every shame, every dishonor.
    But now there's more. They say that King Kreon
    Has issued a proclamation, an emergency edict,
    To all of Thebes. Have you heard? The evil
    That fate once kept for our enemies
    Is now used to punish those we love.
ISMENÊ : Heard what, Antigonê? All I've heard,
    All I know is that two sisters lost two brothers
    On a single day at each other's hands;
    And that last night the Argive army
    Fled from Thebes. That's all, I know nothing more,
    Nothing either to cheer me or make me sad.
ANTIGONÊ: I thought as much. It's why I brought you here
    Beyond the gates, so we could talk unheard.
ISMENÊ: What is it? Trouble? I mean, the way you're acting.
ANTIGONÊ: Kreon buried only one of our brothers!
    Eteoklês went to his grave with full rites,
    And well he should, military honors and all,
    A soldier's funeral. His body lies there now,

Mounded with earth, as the law demands.
He goes down to death in a blaze of glory.
The other, Polyneikês, who died a death
As wretched, he dishonors; proclaiming in Thebes
That Polyneikês will not be given burial,
But left lying in the field, unburied, unmourned,
His body a sweet feast for birds to peck at.

It's whispered about that Kreon, worthy Kreon,
Made this proclamation for you and me.
Yes, for me! And he's coming here himself
To make it clear to anyone who may have missed it.
No, he's not taking the matter lightly.
Death is the payment, stoning in the square,
For anyone who dares to disobey.
Now it's your turn, Ismenê, to show your colors:
A loyal friend or traitor to your family.

ISMENÊ: Sister, you're mad! What can I do?
ANTIGONÊ: Decide whether you'll help me or not.
ISMENÊ: Help do what? At what risk?
ANTIGONÊ: To bury him. Help lift his body.
ISMENÊ: Bury? Against the law? Antigonê!
ANTIGONÊ: He's my brother and, yes, yours,
    However you'd deny it. But no one
    Will ever say I betrayed my brother.
ISMENÊ: How reckless you are! Defy Kreon?
ANTIGONÊ: Kreon can never make me abandon my family!
ISMENÊ: O sister! Remember how father died!
    Remember the disgrace he lived with, the hatred
    People spat at him because of the crimes
    He himself brought to light! Oh, and his eyes,
    His eyes ripped out with his own hands!
    And then mother—
    His mother and wife in one, who hanged herself
    With twisted cords once she learned the truth.
    And last, our two brothers, who killed each other
    On a single day.
    We're all alone, Ismenê, the last of our family.
    Think of the cruel death we'll die, the worst,

If we defy the law laid down by the throne,
If we question its power. We're only women,
It's not our place to fight with men. We're weak,
We're ruled by stronger hands; what can we do
But submit—not only to this, but to worse?
There's nothing I can do, my dear; I'm helpless;
And I beg the dead to forgive me if I choose
To submit to authority.

Hopeless resistance is senseless.

ANTIGONÊ: If that's the way you feel, I wouldn't want you
Now to share my labor even if you offered.
I will bury my brother; and if I die,
I will say that my crime was dear to the gods,
And death a glory.

I'll lie beside him I love, and who loved me,
For I choose to please the dead and not the living:
Their demands are longest.

Death is forever. But do as you like, if the gods'
Laws mean nothing to you.

ISMENÊ: They do! But defy the laws of the people?
I'm not that strong, Antigonê; I can't!

ANTIGONÊ: Then that's your excuse.
But I'm going now to bury the brother I love.

ISMENÊ: Oh, Antigonê! I'm so afraid for you!

ANTIGONÊ: Don't be. There's yourself to consider.

ISMENÊ: Keep it quiet, at least! Tell no one!
I'll do the same, I promise!

ANTIGONÊ: No, tell the world if you want!
I'll hate you all the more for your silence!

ISMENÊ: So fiery, when you should be numb with fear!

ANTIGONÊ: I know whom I must please the most.

ISMENÊ: If you can, yes! But you love the impossible!

ANTIGONÊ: I'll fail when I fail—and there's an end.

ISMENÊ: It makes no sense to hunt the impossible.

ANTIGONÊ: If you believe that, then I must hate you,
Hate you as our dead brother will hate you
For the dreadful things you've said.
Leave me my madness. I'm not afraid.
And if I die, I'll die with honor.

ISMENÊ: Go, if you must, but I'll say this:

    Rash as your act may be,

    You are a deathless friend to those who love you.

    (Ismenê turns to reenter the palace. Antigonê remains facing out. When Ismenê is gone, Antigonê turns to exit left, to the plain. At her turn into her exit, music fades in and the Chorus of Theban Elders enters the orchestra from the right, making a startling contrast with Antigonê. They are jubilant at yesterday's victory, exultant in the glory of the new dawn. Here, as elsewhere throughout the play, they speak sometimes together, sometimes separately in varying combinations.)

CHORUS: —Bright sun, bright

        ray, great light of

           lights, glorious,

    gleaming, eye of

        golden

           day, refulgent,

    radiant

        chariot of the sun, the

           fairest that ever

    shone on

        Thebes,

           Thebes,

    Thebes of the

        Seven

           Gates!

    You rise, you

        rise, you

           rise

    triumphant,

        triumphant,

           victorious,

    victorious over

        Dirkê's

           streams,

    out of the

        dismal barrel of

           night,

    routing,

        routing the

Argive invader, the
bronze-clad
warrior, with his
white
shield, his
silver-white
shield, with
bolts of
light, routing,
routing him in
headlong
flight
with the sharp,
piercing
bit of your
steed!

LEADER: Polyneikês' quarrel
swept him through our land,
an eagle screaming,
swooping, soaring,
diving, plunging,
his white wings
their dazzling shields,
his snowy plume
their bristling crests!

CHORUS: —Circling wide,
wide,
circling wide,
circling,
circling, he
closed on our
walls, his ravenous
maw gaping
wide, his thirsty
spears
clogging our
gates! But
before,
before,

before his
jaws could be
sated,
sated with our
blood,
blood, sated with our
blood; before,
before
before our
towers, our
circle, our
crown, our
crown of
towers could
tumble,
crumble,
fall to destruction
in clouds of
smoke from the
Fire-god's
flame, his
pine-fed
flame,
Hephaistos' torch, the
Dragon rose
up, Thebes rose
up, Thebes'
Dragon
rose with a
roar in the
din of battle,
rattling its
arms, rose
up behind,
not to be conquered,
never conquered,
not to be
vanquished,
rattling its
arms!

LEADER: Zeus who hates
                a boasting tongue,
                saw the swarms
                of Argives swagger
                in clangorous gold,
                and blasted, as he
                reached the top,
                with fiery bolt,
                the first to crow!

CHORUS: —He fell, he
                  fell in a wide
                      arc, wide,
              flame-streaming
                  torch trailing,
                    trailing, and
           struck the
                  earth, struck,
                    struck, with a
           terrible
                  noise, he who
                    breathed on us
          blazing white
                  hate like a raging
                    stormwind's
          savage
                  blast, failing,
                    failing in
        all he
                  threatened!
                    And Arês,
        god,
                  storming,
                    raging;
      Arês,
                war-god,
                  gave to each
        man, to each,
                each, a different
                  death! Arês,

Arês
gave us
victory!

LEADER: Seven invaders,
seven defenders,
seven gates,
seven tributes
of enemy arms
to Zeus of Battles;
two loathing brothers,
two hating swords,
duel to the death!

CHORUS: —Now Nike, now
Victory, now
victorious
Nike, Nike
victorious comes,
comes with the
dawn, in answer to
Thebes'
rejoicing, Thebes
of the many
chariots!
Let us raise
high,
let us raise
high our
voices,
let us raise
high our
joyous
voices, our
joyous
voices, in
praise,
praise, put
battle behind in
sweet
forgetfulness!

Let us
    lift our
        voices and
feet to the
    gods, lift
        high our
feet in
    all-night
        dancing, with
Bakkhos to
    lead us,
        Bakkhos,
Bakkhos,
    lead us in
        joy!
Let our
    stomping, our
        stomping, our
stomping
    feet
        lead us,
Bakkhos,
    lead us, and
        shake,
shake the
    earth,
        shake with
delight!
    Bakkhos!
    Bakkhos!

(Kreon enters through the double door of the palace, surrounded by a full contingent of Guards.)

LEADER: But here comes Kreon, son of Menoikeus,
    New-crowned king of Thebes, our ruler.
    What new fortunes have the gods in store?
    What has he in mind to call this assembly of elders?
    (The music fades out.)

KREON: Men of Thebes!
    Our ship of state, so tossed on turbulent seas

In recent days by the gods, has once again
Found safe harbor by the same gods' help.
I have called you here, of all the men of Thebes,
Because I know the loyalty you proved
To old King Laïos; and later to his son
King Oedipus who also steered our land;
And when he fell, you loyally upheld his sons,
The princes Polyneikês and Eteoklês.

But now, as you have heard, those two sons
Have, in one day, in a double stroke of fate,
Slain each other, each his brother's murderer,
Each polluted with his brother's blood,
On the field of battle.

I, now, as next in blood,
Have taken to myself both throne and power
In Thebes. I know too well no man is tested
Except in action, for there is no other way
To divine the soul and mind and spirit of any—
And so of me.
But I say this:
No ruler who presumes to steer the state
And fails to heed the best counsel; who fears
And fails to speak; that man, I say, that man,
That man of all men, is the most base.
This I have always believed, and believe it now.
That man who places the good of a friend
Above the good of the state is beneath contempt.

I call on Zeus, all-seeing, to witness for me:
If ever I see my country headed for destruction,
And fail to speak, I would damn myself as well.
Nor would I make a friend of a state's enemy.
The state is our ship; and when that ship sails straight
And bears us safely, and prospers, then, only then,
Can we make true friends.

These are the laws by which I govern this state;

And these are the laws that led me to issue the edict
Relating to these two brothers, the sons of Oedipus.
Eteoklês, who died as a man should die,
In defense of his land, will be buried with full honors
And every rite that follows the noblest dead.
But Polyneikês, his brother, who returned
From exile in a rage of insane desire
To waste his father's land with fire and sword,
Upturn the shrines of his gods, batten on the blood
Of his people, and lead the remnant into slavery:
To that man I say: I deny burial
And every sign of ritual lamentation.
Let him lie on the open, barren field,
A naked corpse for birds and dogs to tear at:
A sight of unspeakable shame!
These are my orders:
While I am king, the patriot will always be honored
Above the traitor; and he who is loyal to the state
Will have my praise in life as well as death.
LEADER: If this is your will, Kreon son of Menoikeus,
Touching the city's enemies and friends,
So be it. As king, the power of law is yours
To enforce upon the dead as well as the living.
KREON: See to it, then, that my will is obeyed.
LEADER: We are old, Kreon; let younger men see to it.
KREON: No, not the body; I've posted guards.
LEADER: What would you have us do?
KREON: To side with no one who breaks this law.
LEADER: Only a fool is in love with death!
KREON: And death is the answer.
Yet many a man has been ruined by hope of gain.
(*A Sentry has entered, left, during the above. When he reaches Kreon he salutes. He is a rough-hewn type, somewhat comic, and naturally direct in expressing himself.*)
SENTRY: King, I won't say I'm breathless from running.
I haven't kicked up my heels, so to speak,
To get here faster. Fact is, I didn't want to come.
I stopped on the road time and again, thinking.
Doubled back and back more than once.

"Fool!" I said to myself, "where's the fire?"
And then: "Why rush smack into the lion's den?"
And: "Who needs the trouble?"

But then I thought: "What if there's someone else?
What if someone else brings the news to Kreon?
Your neck's had it, soldier!"

Well, my head whirls that around a while.
And my pace gets slower.
A mile becomes a league. But here I am,
Like it or not. Not that there's much to tell.
But I'll tell it anyway, whatever it costs me.
I mean, well, what happens, happens. You know?
(Kreon is at first amused by the Sentry's rough manner.)
KREON: What is all this? What's the problem?
SENTRY: First let me get myself off the hook, king.
  I didn't do it and swear I don't know who did,
  So please, sir, don't take it out on me!
KREON: You set up your defenses well, soldier.
  It's clear that you have something important to say.
SENTRY: Serious matters can rattle a man's brain.
KREON: Come to the point, soldier, and get out!
SENTRY: Yes, sir! Right, sir! I sure will!
  Well, here goes!
  Just now—someone—out there—
  The dead man?—Polyneikês?—Well, I mean—
  Someone—someone buried the body—dust on it—
  Scattered—and the rites—and then was gone—
KREON: What man would dare!
SENTRY: I don't know, sir—no sign of digging—
  No shovel, no pick, the earth hard and dry,
  No cart tracks—nothing to tell who did it.
  But then at sun-up the first watch came on,
  And—well, the corporal points it out—
  We're amazed, struck with wonder! There's the body,
  You could still see it there, not buried yet,
  Not all the way, covered with dust, just enough—
  Like someone meant to lift the curse from a corpse

Left lying unburied in the field to escape pollution.
No tracks either, no dogs, wild animals,
No sign the body'd been torn—the skin—

And then it started. Words flew like stones.
"That one did it!" "No, him!" Each of us knew
It was the other, and it might have come to a fight,
Nothing to stop it, any of us could have done it,
No way to prove it! We'd each of us have picked up
Red-hot iron, walked through fire, sworn
We hadn't done it, or knew anyone who'd planned
Or done it, but there was no way out—

Then one of us said something—something—well, that—
That made us all shut up and stare in terror
At the ground. He was right, no argument there,
Not and come through it all in one piece.
Someone had to tell you, he said, report it.
So we threw the dice, and the lot fell to unlucky me,
And here I am, unwelcome as unwilling.
Bringers of bad news can't be choosy.
LEADER: Is it possible, my lord,
    The gods are involved in this?
KREON: Stop! I refuse to hear this senile drivel!
    Have you all gone mad in addition to your age!
    What can the gods care for a naked corpse?
    Would they bury him to honor his loyalty,
    His good deeds, the traitor who invaded their city,
    Who burned their pillared temples and sacred treasures,
    Savaged the land and cast its laws to the winds?
    When have you seen the gods honor traitors?
    No! Never!

    But I am aware that there are those here in Thebes
    Who have always opposed me, always opposed my authority.
    Heads together, murmuring against me,
    Refusing to keep their necks to the yoke,
    And submitting to *me,* their *king!* They're the ones
    Who have bribed my own sentries to bury that body!

Money! What will men not do for money!
What power corrupts men more? Cities fall,
Men driven out, great houses collapse,
Honest minds depraved and led into villainy!
But every man bribed to this crime may be certain
That he will pay the full price for his treachery!
(Turning on the Sentry.)
You there! Listen carefully! I swear by Zeus,
Either you bring me the man guilty of this crime,
Or I will hang you alive till you beg for death!
I think then you'll find it easier to confess
Who bribed you to this act. And in the process
You may also learn that it isn't wise
To seek profit wherever you might fancy.
The price may be too great

SENTRY: Sir, have I leave to speak?

KREON: Every word you say grates me!

SENTRY: Grates your ears or tears your heart?

KREON: By god, he's going to analyze me!

SENTRY: Words don't hurt; what's done hurts.

KREON: Doesn't anything shut you up!

SENTRY: Yes; but I did nothing wrong!

KREON: Nothing but sold your soul for silver!

SENTRY: You think you know the truth, sir,
But you're wide of the mark.

KREON: Play all you want with words! But play with this now!
Either you catch the criminals and bring them to me,
Or the bribes that bought you will bring more pain than pleasure.
(Kreon turns and enters the palace followed by his contingent of Guards. The Sentry speaks when Kreon is barely out of hearing.)

SENTRY: "Find the criminals," he says! Oh, sure!
What else! But found or not, I'm out of here!
Luck or no luck, you'll never catch *me* here again!
At least *my* neck's saved! Thank god!
(As the Sentry begins his hurried exit, left, in the direction of the plain, music begins, and at once the Chorus takes up a new position.)

CHORUS: —Many are the world's wonders,
                    but none more wondrous than man.
               He rides the storm-gray sea,

   mounting white-capped waves
in winds that surge and threaten;
   and holy Earth, the oldest
of all the gods immortal,
   he furrows with his plough,
turning her soil with the labor
   of generations of stallions.

—With excelling sharpness of mind
   he snares whole nations of birds;
takes captive tribes of wild beasts,
   and catches in woven nets
the brood of the ocean's deep.
   And with his art he masters
the lion whose lair is the mountain,
   and tames the shaggy-maned horse,
and the unbroken mountain bull,
   with the powerful yoke of his will.

—And words and wind-swift thought,
   and moods that mold a state,
and law that rules a city,
   all, all are his.
And his, too, the skill
   that shelters him from cold;
never without resource,
   except when Death appears.
And yet, from ills that baffle,
   he has devised escape.

—Intelligence of mind,
   power beyond all measure,
man's fertile skill
   leads now to good, now to evil.
When laws of man and god are kept,
   then his city stands with pride.
When man betrays both god and man,
   then his city falls in shame.
He will never share my hearth.
   He will never share my thought.

(Antigonê, led on by the Sentry, has entered left during the final section of the choral ode. The music fades out as Kreon enters from the palace.)

CHORUS: What is this! No! Not Antigonê!
    Unhappy daughter of unhappy Oedipus!
    Were you so rash as to defy the king?
SENTRY: Here she is! The one who did it!
    Caught her burying the body!
    Where's King Kreon?
LEADER: Here he is, just when you need him.
KREON: What is it? What am I just in time for?
SENTRY: I'll never swear to anything again, King:
    I might have to change my mind and look the fool.
    The last time I was here, I swore to god
    I wouldn't be caught dead scurrying back here,
    What with your threats to do me in and all.
    But luck decided, and here I am again,
    Oath or no oath. And with this girl, no less,
    Caught in the act, burying the corpse.
    No need for the dice this time to decide
    Who comes or doesn't. *This* stroke of luck was mine
    And no one else's.
    Here she is. Question her,
    Put her to the test. But at least *my* hands
    Are clean of this mess.
KREON: How and where was this prisoner taken?
SENTRY: Burying the corpse. What more is there?
KREON: Do you realize what you're saying?
SENTRY: I said she was burying the body;
    The one you said no one was to touch.
    I can't be clearer.
KREON: What was she doing?
SENTRY: Well, it was like this, you see.
    Your awful threats still ringing in our ears,
    We hurried back and swept the body clean
    Of the dust and bared the soft and slimy flesh
    That smelled to heaven! Then to escape the stink,
    We climbed a hill keeping the body downwind.
    No dozing this time. We jabbed each other hard,
    Screaming threats, in case one of us got sloppy.

Time passed.
And then at noon, when the white wheel of the sun
Whirled at midpoint, scorching everything around,
A stormwind blew up, troubling the sky
With a blanket of dust, blotting out the plain,
Ripping leaves off trees,
The air a mass of black.
We screwed our eyes tight shut against this plague
Sent by the gods, and waited. It lasted for ever,
It seemed, the whirlwind. But then when it had passed,
And we opened our eyes again, we saw the girl.
I have heard the high screech of a bird
Returning and finding its nest bare of its nestlings.
She, too, when she sees the naked corpse,
Raises a high wail and calls down bitter
Curses on the hands that did it.

All at once, without a pause,
She scoops up hands of dust,
And raising high a well-wrought urn pours out
Three dark libations for the dead.
Seeing her there, we rushed down and took her.
But she wasn't afraid. Not even when we charged her
With this and the other burial. She denied nothing.
Which pleased me, sure, but pained me, too, you know.
It's a relief to escape great danger yourself;
But to bring a friend to danger is a painful thing.
But at least I've saved my skin, and that's what counts.
KREON: You, Antigonê, head bent,
    Eyes to the ground! Look at me!
    Did you or did you not do this?
ANTIGONÊ: How can I deny what I did!
    (Kreon turns to the Sentry.)
KREON: And, you! Leave when you like.
    You're cleared of a very heavy charge.
    (As the Sentry turns to go off left, Kreon continues.)
KREON: Now tell me, and be brief.
    Did you know of my edict forbidding this?
ANTIGONÊ: How could I not? It was public.

KREON: And yet you dared defy these laws?
ANTIGONÊ: Yes, I dared. It wasn't Zeus who made them.
And Justice dwelling in the underworld
Makes no such laws for men. Your edict, Kreon,
For all its strength, is mortal and weak when measured
Against the laws of the gods, unwritten, unshakable,
Laws not meant for now, but for ever,
For no man knows their age; laws that no
Proud spirit of a man could make me break,
For one day I must answer to the gods.
I know that I will die. How could I not know?
Even without your edict.
And yet, if I die now, before my time,
How can that be a hardship?
How can one live, as I do, surrounded by evil,
And not greet Death as a friend?

My death isn't important;
And yet, to see my brother lie dead and unburied
Is an agony beyond words. But this is nothing.
If you think me foolish, Kreon, me and my acts,
Perhaps I'm judged a fool by another fool.
LEADER: Like father, like daughter,
Stubborn, unbending:
Neither learned to yield to adversity.
KREON: The strongest will breaks first. The toughest iron,
Tempered in white-hot flame, shatters first.
And wild horses are curbed by the smallest bit.
Pride in a slave? When the master is nearby?
This girl is guilty of double impertinence:
Breaking the law and then boasting of it!
If this crime goes unpunished, and she's the victor,
Who's the man here then? She or I?
No! Sister's child, or closer even
Than anyone who worships at Zeus' altar
In my own house, she and her sister will pay
For their crime with death! I hold her sister guilty
In the same degree in the plotting of this burial!
(To Attendants.)

Bring her, someone! I saw her inside just now,
Distracted and free of her wits. The mind that plots
Mischief in dark corners often betrays itself
Before the deed is done. But I hate worse
The one who acts the crime, then glories in it.

ANTIGONÊ: What more could you want than my death?

KREON: Having that, I have everything.

ANTIGONÊ: Go on, then, kill me. Your words are as hateful to me
As mine to you, and I hope they always will be.
And yet, how could I have greater praise
And glory than by giving the brother I love
A decent and honorable burial?

(To the Chorus.)

And these men agree, if only their lips
Weren't locked in fear of you. But then, of course,
Tyrants have power to do and say what they please!

KREON: You're the only one here thinks so.

ANTIGONÊ: No, they support me. Their tongues are leashed.

KREON: Aren't you ashamed to talk treason!

ANTIGONÊ: Ashamed? Me? Of loving my brother?

KREON: Wasn't Eteoklês your brother, too?

ANTIGONÊ: Yes, by the same mother and father.

KREON: Then how can you dare insult his memory?

ANTIGONÊ: Eteoklês would never say I did that.

KREON: No insult to honor the traitor?

ANTIGONÊ: He was his brother, not some slave!

KREON: He warred on his country; Eteoklês championed it!

ANTIGONÊ: Death demands equal rites for all.

KREON: Equal rites for the wicked and the just?

ANTIGONÊ: Who knows what the gods below call wicked?

KREON: A traitor is a traitor, even in death.

ANTIGONÊ: My nature is to love, not to hate.

KREON: Then share your love with the dead! Go and join them!
While I'm alive no woman rules me!

(Ismenê enters from the palace led on by Guards.)

LEADER: But here comes Ismenê, weeping hot tears
For a dear sister, her beauty clouded
By a dark grief.

KREON: Viper! Viper! You, too, Ismenê!

Lurking here in my house, sucking my blood!
Without knowing, I raised two sources of ruin
To topple my throne and power!
Come here! Tell me!
Did you share in this crime, or do you deny it?
Answer me! The burial!

ISMENÊ: I did it, yes, if she lets me say so.
I share the guilt; I share the penalty.

ANTIGONÊ: No! Justice doesn't allow this.
You wanted no part, I gave you none.

ISMENÊ: But now your ship is battered by a stormy sea,
I'm not ashamed to join in your suffering.

ANTIGONÊ: Words are all you know, Ismenê!
Death and the dead know what I did.

ISMENÊ: Please—don't deny me the right
To die with you and honor the dead!

ANTIGONÊ: Why should I share my death with someone
Who never once raised a hand to help?

ISMENÊ: But what's the use of life without you!

ANTIGONÊ: Ask Kreon. You're always quoting him!

ISMENÊ: You're laughing at me, Antigonê! Why?

ANTIGONÊ: Laughing at you? Yes. But it pains me.

ISMENÊ: I'll do anything—even now.

ANTIGONÊ: Save yourself. I won't envy you.

ISMENÊ: Ah, but why can't I share in your fate?

ANTIGONÊ: You chose life, I chose death.

ISMENÊ: Yes, but not before I warned you!

ANTIGONÊ: Some praised you, others me.

ISMENÊ: Yes, but our offense is the same!

ANTIGONÊ: Be happy, Ismenê: you're alive.
I gave my life long ago
When I joined hands to serve the dead.

(Kreon turns to the Chorus.)

KREON: Gentlemen, it occurs to me
One of these girls just lost her mind;
The other never had one.

ISMENÊ: Cruelty unhinges the soundest mind.

KREON: As yours did when you sided with evil.

ISMENÊ: What would life be worth without her?

KREON: Forget she ever lived. She's dead.

ISMENÊ: You'd actually kill your son's bride?

KREON: He'll have other fields to plough!

ISMENÊ: Yes, but what of the love they share?

KREON: My son marry a worthless woman?

ISMENÊ: Oh, Haimon, how your father wrongs you!

KREON: I've heard enough of your marriage babble!

ISMENÊ: You'd steal this girl from your own son?

KREON: No; I'll count on Death for that!

ISMENÊ: It's settled, then? Antigonê dies?

KREON: Settled? Yes! For both of us!

    Guards, take them inside! Hurry!

    They're only women; but even bold men

    Try to escape when Death closes in.

    No running loose.

    (Music begins as the Guards come forward to lead Antigonê and Ismenê into the palace. Kreon remains, as the Chorus at once takes up a new position.)

CHORUS: —Blest are they who have known no evil,
        for once the gods strike
            that house is doomed
        for ever.
    Generation after generation
        falls beneath the blow
            to the end of days,
        like the wave,
    blasting from the black northeast,
        hurling dark sand from the depths
            onto the echoing
        shore.

    —I have seen now from ancient times
        how sorrows pile on sorrows
            for the house of Labdakos
        with no relief from the gods,
    generation after generation;
        and now the last light
            is cut to the root
            by dust,
    by dust offered to the gods below,

by the folly of a passionate word,
        by frenzy at the heart.

—Zeus, what human arrogance
    can check your power, Zeus,
    whom neither sleep nor track
        of weariless months of the gods
        can master?
Ageless you reign in the glistering
    mansions of high Olympos,
        and near and far,
        past and future,
    your law is fixed forever.
            No greatness ever enters human life,
            but with it comes the curse of Zeus' heaven.

—For hope, far-ranging hope,
    is for some men a comfort,
    but for many a false lure,
    leading to giddy desires.
            And so,
innocent and unknowing,
    they wander into the flame.
        Ancient wisdom
        speaks for all.
    The man god leads to doom
            will soon say good is evil and evil good;
            for one brief moment does he breathe free of ruin.
*(Haimon has entered, right, during the last part of the ode and approaches
Kreon.)*
LEADER: But here comes Haimon, my lord,
    your youngest son.
    Is it grief for Antigonê he feels,
    or bitterness at losing his marriage?
    (The music fades out.)
KREON: We'll know soon, and will need no prophets to tell us.
    (To Haimon.)
    Do you come here, son, raging against your father
    For condemning that girl, your one-time bride-to-be?

Or do you come with love and acquiescence,
Whatever we do?
HAIMON: Father, I'm your son.
Your wisdom guides me in all things. I obey.
And no marriage means more to me than your guidance
When it is just.
KREON: There's my Haimon—my boy!
That's what sons are meant to be: subordinate
In every way to their father's will. There's not
A man alive who doesn't implore the gods
For a house of sons devoted and attentive;
Sons to avenge a father's enemies, and respect
His friends as they do him.
The man who begets useless children,
What has he fathered but endless troubles,
And howls of laughter from his enemies?
No, son, take my advice, never lose
Your head to a woman. Never, Haimon, never
Let pleasure unseat reason, pleasure that soon
Grows cold in your arms.
There's nothing worse for your house and bed
Than a woman who's evil. No wound
Cuts deeper than a dear one who turns against you.
Spit her out, spit her out as an enemy!
Let her find a husband to suit her in Hades!
She alone of all the citizens was caught
In open rebellion against my proclamation,
And I will not be known as a liar to my people!
The girl dies!

I suppose she'll plead to Zeus
Guardian of Kindred Blood, "family ties"
You call it! Let her! Let her!
But if I'm to tolerate rebellion in my family,
Well, then, what choice have I but to accept it
Outside my home as well!
No!
The man who keeps his house in order is a man
Fit to rule in public life. And yet,

There's one thing I will never tolerate,
The man who disobeys the law, or dictates
To his superiors. That man, Haimon, that man
Will have no respect from me. That man the city
Chooses to rule must be obeyed in matters
Large and small, just as well as unjust.

And I know this:
The man who knows how to obey knows also
How to give orders. He's a man you can trust,
A man who will take his stand in the storm of battle,
A man loyal and unflinching who will stand beside
His comrades-in-arms.

But anarchy—
Anarchy is an insupportable evil!
Anarchy ruins cities, destroys great houses,
Divides and scatters armies into headlong rout!
Most men, men who live decent lives,
Owe their safety strictly to obedience.
And therefore what choice is given to us,
Except that we support those disciplined lives,
Never to be seduced by a woman.
If we *must* fall, let us fall to a man,
And never be called inferior to a woman.

LEADER: Unless I've lost my wits, my lord,
    Your words make sense.

HAIMON: Father, the gods' most precious gift to man
    Is reason. Now, I know I haven't the right,
    Nor the skill, nor, god knows, do I want,
    Ever, to tell you that you have reasoned badly.
    And yet it's possible that someone else
    Might think differently and still be useful.
    I realize that, normally speaking,
    It's not for you to hear what people say,
    See what they do, learn what they feel and think.
    You terrify them; they say what you want to hear,
    Everything else they hold back.
    But I hear what they're saying, I hear their whispers,

Their muttered words in the dark,
And how they mourn the girl.
They say no woman ever deserved a fate
So evil; that no one ever died so dishonored
A death for an act so glorious.

"What's so terrible?" they ask.
"She only covered her slaughtered brother's body,
A body, naked, lying in the field,
Unburied, because she couldn't bear to see it
Torn to shreds, mangled by dogs and vultures.
A brother killed in battle! Where's the offense?
She deserves a golden prize, not our scorn!"
This is what I hear them saying out there;
Dark rumors spreading in secret.

Father, there's nothing more dear than your success.
What greater happiness can there be for a son
Than to see his father's name increase in glory,
And for a father to see his son's do the same?

I beg of you, don't make the mistake of thinking
That only you are right. The man who thinks so,
The man who believes that only he has wisdom,
That he alone has the gift of words, the power
Of Reason—that man, when you lay him open,
Is seen to be empty. There's no shame in yielding
To Reason, even for a wise man.

Trees that bend with the flooding torrent
Come through safe and sound;
But those that resist are torn out, roots and all.
The same in sailing: pull a cloth too taut,
And never slacken, you'll end bottom-side up
For the rest of the voyage. Give yourself leeway, father:
Forget your anger, allow for change.

I know I'm young,
But if I had advice to give,

I'd say that men should always be all-wise
By nature. But since that's not the way of things,
Then learn from the good advice of others.
LEADER: If what he says makes sense, my lord,
Listen to him. And you, Haimon,
Listen to Kreon. You both speak well.
KREON: What are you saying?
A man of my years lectured to by a stripling?
HAIMON: Not if I'm wrong; but if I'm right,
Then judge my words, not my age.
KREON: It's wisdom, then, to honor anarchy?
HAIMON: Not if that means honoring evil.
KREON: Ah! The very disease that grips *her!*
HAIMON: Not one Theban accepts that judgment.
KREON: And Thebes tells me now how to rule?
HAIMON: Who's the child now, father?
KREON: My voice alone rules in this city!
HAIMON: No, one voice never rules a city.
KREON: The city belongs to the king! The law!
HAIMON: Then find a deserted city to rule!
KREON: This boy's been taken in by that girl!
HAIMON: If you're a woman, I'm fighting for *you!*
KREON: For me! How dare you challenge your father!
HAIMON: Yes! When my father challenges justice!
KREON: Not "just" to stand on royal prerogative?
HAIMON: Not when it defies god's laws!
KREON: Perverted fool! Seduced by a woman!
HAIMON: I'm not taken in by anything vile!
KREON: Every word you say defends her!
HAIMON: And you, and me, and the gods below!
KREON: You'll never marry that girl alive!
HAIMON: Then her death will cause another.
KREON: Don't you threaten **me**, young man!
HAIMON: How is it possible to threaten emptiness?
KREON: It's you who are empty! And you'll regret this!
HAIMON: If you weren't my father, I'd call you perverse!
KREON: Father! Groveling slave of a woman!
HAIMON: You never want to listen, do you?
KREON: Oh, by the gods—!

This will cost you!
Enough of your taunting insults!
(To the Guards.)
You! Bring her out! That woman!
Now! Kill her here!
Let him watch! The brave bridegroom!
This is where she'll die!
HAIMON: No! Not here!
No, not beside me!
Don't fool yourself!
You'll never see my face again!
Rave till you're blue in the face, old man,
Just do it to friends, if you have any!
(Haimon rushes off left.)
LEADER: He's gone, my lord, in a bitter rage.
A young man's anger is a dangerous thing.
KREON: Let him go! Let him plan some impossible dream!
Nothing he does, nothing, can save those girls!
LEADER: Girls? You plan to kill them both?
KREON: No, you're right. Just the guilty one.
LEADER: And the other? How will she die?
KREON: I'll take her down some wild, deserted path,
And there lock her alive in a vault of stone.
She will have food enough to acquit the state
Of her death and avoid pollution to the city.
There she can worship the only god she honors:
Death, who may, god knows, reprieve her. Otherwise
She will learn, though late, how wasteful it is
To honor Death.
(Music begins as Kreon moves to another part of the orchestra, critically observing the scene as the Chorus takes up a new position.)
CHORUS: —Love unconquered in battle,
                Love that plunders the rich,
                Love that keeps its vigil
                on the soft cheek of a girl,
                      roamer of seas,
           · visitor of forest dwellings,
                none among mortals escapes you,
                nor man whose life is a moment;
                all in your grip are mad.

—You lead the just man
to ruin and injustice;
you struck the spark that ignited
the strife between father and son:
      and Love is the victor.
Triumphant and bright the desire
in the eyes of a lovely bride:
Love that reigns beside law,
merciless Aphroditê.

*(Antigonê has entered during the choral ode, led on by palace Guards. The
music changes to a lyrical lament.)*

LEADER: O child, now even I, even
        I am carried beyond the bounds
           of law, the bounds of loyalty.
How can I keep my tears from
        flowing, flowing tears that
           tear at my heart, for here is
Antigonê, passing to her grave, Death's
        bridal chamber, where all men sleep.

ANTIGONÊ: O citizens of Thebes, citizens of my
father's land, behold me on my
        journey, my final journey, for I will
           never again see the light of the
sun. Death, who invites us
        all to rest, leads me living
           to Acheron's shore, I, who had no
share in the chant that brings the bride,
        who knew no sounds of hymns,
           of wedding songs, go down
to wed the Lord of Death,
        Lord of the Dark Waters.

LEADER: It is not without praise, not without
praise and honor, not without
        glory you enter Death's dark kingdom.
        No wasting sickness, no sword
struck you; you, only you,
        of all living, will enter Death's
           domain of your own free
choice and will.

ANTIGONÊ: I have heard that in Phrygia, Niobê,
                    daughter of Tantalos, died the
            saddest of deaths on Sipylos' lofty
                heights; how stone like creeping
                    ivy bound her fast in its embrace;
            and unending rain and snow, like
                tears, never leave her, perpetual
                    tears, flooding like raging torrents,
            stream the slope of her neck, wearing
                and wasting her breast. And I
                    see in her rocky end a fate whose
            loneliness is like my own.

LEADER: And yet, she was a goddess,
                    a goddess, child of the gods; and
            we, we are mortals, mortals born to
                mortals. But think of the glory
                    a woman, a mortal woman, who
            shares the same death with a goddess,
                will have in this life and the next,
                    a fate equal to the gods.

ANTIGONÊ: Ah! Why must you mock me, why
                    mock me? In the name of our fathers'
                        gods, why mock me now? Can't you wait,
            wait till I'm gone, to hurl
                abuse at me? O city of lordly
                    sons, wealthy sons of Thebes, my
            noble Thebes, sweet springs of Dirkê,
                sacred groves, glorious for her chariots,
                    you, on you I call: bear witness and
            remember as I walk to my rocky prison,
                unwept, remember the law, the
                    unjust law, that sends me friendless there.
            Alive, I have no home, no
                home among the living; dead,
                    I am an alien without rights.

LEADER: Child, you went too far, dared
                    too much, and stumbled
                        at Justice's throne.
            I'd say that you have been caught
                in your father's dreadful fate.

ANTIGONÊ: You have touched on the bitterest
thought of all, the pain that wracks
the house of Labdakos, pitiful Oedipus
and the misery that beggars its glory. O bed,
bed where mother coupled with son and husband,
my father, my parents, scene of my making,
wretched fate, I go to them now
below, accursed, unmarried,
an exile. Ah, brother, brother that I love,
brother Polyneikês, doomed
in your own ill-fated marriage,
you now destroy my own, and
with it destroy my life. It is
you, my belovèd dead,
who cause my own death.

LEADER: To respect the dead is a virtue deserving
respect; but to challenge the power of him
who holds power is not to be
borne. It was your fury, your
passion, that brought you to destruction.

ANTIGONÊ: Unwept,
unfriended,
unmarried,
misery's child, I'm led on my
final journey. I'll never again
see the sacred eye of the blessèd
sun; no tear will be
shed for me; no friend
lament my going.

(The music fades out as Kreon comes forward.)

KREON: If dirges and mournful chants could put off death,
Men would never put an end to their wailing.
(To his Guards.)
Take her! Now! Go quickly! And when you've walled her
In the rocky tomb, as I have ordered, she can choose
To live or die. As for me, my hands are clean.
She'll be denied her alien's rights to live
Above here with us in the world of light.

ANTIGONÊ: O tomb, o bridal-chamber, vaulted grave,

My home for all eternity! I leave here
To join my own, my dear ones, that growing family
Of the dead whom Persephonê has already welcomed.
I, the last, and most evilly punished of all,
Enter among you before my days are done.
But you will smile, dear father, and you, dear mother,
And dear Eteoklês, and welcome me:
I, who washed and dressed your bodies, and poured
Wine across your tombs. And now, Polyneikês,
For tending to and burying your body,
This is my reward. But what I did
Every wise, right-thinking man must honor.

And yet, if I'd had children, or a husband,
Dead and rotting, I would never have defied the city
As I have done. What law gives me this right?
With a husband dead, I could have found another,
And borne another child with another man
If I'd lost the first. But when mother and father are gripped
In Death's embrace, there can be no other brother.
That was the law, Polyneikês, by which I honored you.
But Kreon holds it a crime, judges me guilty
Of grievous outrage. He takes me now, leads me
Out by force, I who never knew
The sound of bridal hymns, or bridal bed,
Or marriage, or the joy of raising children.
And so, alone, without friends, I go living
To the hollow caverns of Death.
What law have I transgressed, what law of the gods?
What gods can I implore and call an ally?
What gods, if those I honored
Denounce my piety as impious?
(Music fades in under Kreon's lines to accompany the lyric dialogue.)
Very well, if these things please the gods,
Once I have suffered I will come to know
Where I was wrong. And yet, if they're the wrongdoers,
I wish upon them a punishment no more evil
Than the evil they unjustly put upon me!
LEADER: The same savage blasts
                tears at her passionate heart!

KREON: Her guards will soon regret
            their slowness in taking her off!
ANTIGONÊ: That voice! The voice of Death!
KREON: You can be certain of that!
ANTIGONÊ: Thebes, city of my fathers,
            gods of my land and house!
            And you, rulers of Thebes,
            take your last look
            at the last of your royal house!
            See me, dragged away,
            see the punishment I suffer,
            and at whose hands I suffer,
            I who gave reverence for reverence!
*(Antigonê is led off left by the Guards as the Chorus begins to assemble.
Kreon remains, observing.)*
CHORUS: —Danaë, too, was locked away
            in a brass-bound prison where day's light
                  no longer shone.
            Within this bridal-chamber tomb
            her loveliness was all concealed
                  for none to see.
            Born of high estate, she treasured
            Zeus' seed within her womb,
                  a golden rain.
                  O child, child,
            dreadful the mysterious power of fate;
            neither wealth, nor war,
                  nor towered city-state,
                  nor dark sea-struck ships,
                        prevail against it!

            —Furious-tempered Lykourgos, king
                  of Edonians and son of Dryas, endured
                  containment and binding
            in a rocky prison when he taunted Dionysos,
                  and expelled the god in maddened rage.
                  But his madness draining,
            he learned to know the god he mocked,
                  the god he assaulted with feverish hate,

forcing his Bakkhai,
shouting eüoi,
to snuff the god's flame,
and enraged the Muses who love
the flute's piping!

—In the deep north, where the Dark Rocks
split the sea, are the shores of Bosporos
and Thrakian Salmydessos.
Here Arês beheld the blinding wound
dealt to Phineias' sons by his wife,
step-mother fierce in temper.
Her shuttle struck
dark eyes,
her bloody hands
bathed in gore,
blood that cried loud for vengeance!

—Imprisoned they wept their dark fate,
sealed with their mother's heavenly birth.
Descendant of ancient Erechtheus,
reared in far-distant caves by stormwinds
of Father Boreas, she raced beside stallions
over wind-scoured hills, a child
of gods. She, too,
suffered, child,
as you do now,
unspared by the Fates,
implacable ladies of darkness.

(The blind Teiresias has entered, right, during the choral ode, led on by a Boy; they slowly make their laborious way to Kreon. The music fades out.)

TEIRESIAS: Noblemen of Thebes, the prophet comes,
The blind prophet, led on by a boy,
Hand in hand, two eyes to light one road.
KREON: What news have you brought us, old Teiresias?
TEIRESIAS: I will tell you. But you must heed the prophet.
KREON: Have I ever slighted your counsel, old man?
TEIRESIAS: Ah, then you have steered the city well.
KREON: I admit my debt to you; no question.

TEIRESIAS: Beware: You stand on the razor's edge of Chance.
KREON: What does this mean? Your words make me tremble.
TEIRESIAS: Then listen to the warnings of my art!

    As I sat on my ancient seat of augury,
    Where every bird of omen gathers round me,
    I heard a strange voice from the beat of their wings
    That I had never known. A barbarous scream
    That drowned their speech in a whir of clashing wings
    As they tore each other with their bloody talons.

    In fear I approached the altar and set about
    The rite of burnt offering. But the god of fire
    Allowed no fire to catch my offerings. Instead
    Of flames from long thighbones, a slimy ooze
    Trickled out and dripped onto coals, hissing
    And sputtering in a smoky haze. And then
    The bladder puffed, and, with a burst, spattered
    Gall all about; and the fat that wrapped the thighs
    Slid off and onto the coals, splattering everywhere.
    But still no fire! This boy described the scene
    Of ruined offering; he is my eyes
    As I am yours.

    It is your counsel, Kreon,
    Your dark counsel, that brings this sickness on Thebes.
    The altars in our temples and homes are polluted
    With carrion brought in by birds and dogs,
    Ravaged from the wretched corpse of Polyneikês,
    Son of Oedipus. The gods refuse our prayers,
    Refuse our offerings, refuse the flames that consume
    The thighbones; and birds scream sounds I cannot
    Decipher, birds gorged on the greasy blood
    Of the dead.

    Think, my son, for all men are given to error.
    But the man who makes a mistake,
    And then takes steps to right the wrong, will never
    Be thought a fool or a son of Misfortune
    Because he remains unyielding. Stubbornness

Incurs the charge of folly. Yield to the dead.
Why strike a man who's down? What glory is there
In killing a dead man twice?

Listen to me.
I speak for your own good. My advice is sound.
It is good to learn from a wise counselor
If what he says is to your profit.
KREON: Old man! And that includes all of you!
You level your arrows at me as an archer
Zeroes in on his target, and now you send
Your prophets after me! You have been trying
For years to sell me short and ship me out!
If profit is what you want, then trade in the silver
Of Sardeis and the pure gold of India.
But you will never lower that body into a grave!
Not even if Zeus' eagles carried the corpse,
Stinking, bit by bit, to the throne on Olympos!
No, not even in fear of *that* pollution
Would I grant him burial! For I know well, no mortal
Can defile the gods. But even wise men fall,
Old Teiresias; but their fall is even more shameful
When they dress their shameful advise in fine words
In hope of making a profit.
TEIRESIAS: Ah, Kreon!
Is there no man left, no man who knows—
KREON: Come! Let's hear the cliché!
TEIRESIAS: —that wisdom is better than worldly wealth?
KREON: As folly is man's greatest curse.
TEIRESIAS: The same folly that afflicts you now.
KREON: I don't trade insults with prophets.
TEIRESIAS: But you have, in calling my prophesies lies.
KREON: The clan of prophets is partial to gold.
TEIRESIAS: The tribe of tyrants is partial to profit.
KREON: Don't presume. You're talking to your king!
TEIRESIAS: Yes. I helped you save this city.
KREON: You're a skilled prophet, but given to deceit.
TEIRESIAS: Don't prod me to reveal secrets I know.
KREON: Tell them! Just don't expect to profit!

TEIRESIAS: My secrets hold no profit for you.
KREON: Nor will you ever change my mind.
TEIRESIAS: Then know this, and know it well!

     The time is not far off, the sun's swift chariot
     Will not make many more courses through the sky,
     Before you pay with one born of your loins,
     A corpse in exchange for corpses—for you have cast
     A child of light into the world of darkness,
     Blasphemously lodging a living being
     In a tomb beneath the earth, and kept above
     In light what belongs to the gods below,
     A thing unburied, unhonored, unhallowed.
     Neither you, no, nor the gods above
     Have any rights in this matter, and yet you forced
     This violence upon them. Because of this,
     The avenging destroyers lie in ambush, the Erinyes
     Of Hades and the gods, to catch you up
     In the same evils you yourself devised.

     Consider, Kreon. Do I sound like a man bribed?
     Not many hours will pass before your house
     Will ring with the sounds of men and women wailing.
     All cities will rise in enmity against you,
     Cities whose mangled sons dogs or wild beasts
     Have consecrated with burial, or some winged bird
     That carried the polluting stench of carrion
     Back to their homes and the gods of their hearth.

     These are the arrows which, like an archer,
     I have aimed in anger at your heart,
     For you have rankled me and will not escape
     Their sting.
     (To the Boy.)
     Lead me home, boy.
     Let him spit his rage at younger men,
     And learn to train his tongue for gentler speech,
     And his mind to carry better sense than it does.
     (As Teiresias is led off, right, by the Boy, the Leader continues.)
LEADER: He's gone, my lord,

Leaving terrible prophecies.
But never in all my years have I known
The man to be faithless to this city.

KREON: It's true. I know. It tears at my mind.
   To yield is a terrible thing;
   And yet to resist—to damn my soul
   To destruction? That's no better.

LEADER: Take my advise, Kreon.
   There's no more time.

KREON: Tell me what I must do.

LEADER: Free Antigonê now from the rocky cavern,
   And raise a burial mound for Polyneikês.

KREON: Is this what you want? You want me to yield?

LEADER: Yes, and at once, my lord! The gods' avengers
   Are never slow to cut down misguided men.

KREON: How hard it is to resign my heart's desire!
   And yet I'll do it. How can I fight Necessity?

LEADER: Do it yourself. Now. Don't trust to others.

KREON: I'll go at once!
   Servants! All of you Go quickly!
   Take up axes! Each of you! Hurry!
   There, to the plain! My judgment overturned,
   I will be present to free the one I imprisoned!
   Ah, I fear the ancient codes are true:
   That it is best to keep the laws of the gods
   Till the day we die.

   (Music enters immediately as Kreon rushes out, left, to the plain, followed by his men. At the same time, the Chorus takes up a new position and begins a slow dance that culminates in a loud frenzy of supplication.)

LEADER: —God of many names!

CHORUS: Glory of Semelê,
                     Kadmos' daughter!
                 Son of Zeus,
                     deep-thunderer!
                        Ikaria's guardian!
                 Lord of Eleusis,
                     Dêmêter's plain,
                        where all men are
                 welcome!

Bakkhos!
  Bakkhos!
Dweller in
 Thebes,
  mother-city of
frenzied
 Bakkhants,
  on ground
sown with
 dragon's
  teeth,
beside Ismênos'
 rippling
  stream!

LEADER: —God of many names!
CHORUS: Seen suffused in
  smoky light of
flaring torches
 blazing over twin
  peaks, where
Korykian
 nymphs dance
  Bakkhic rites
beside Kastalia's
 spring!
  From Nysa's ivied
hills, shores
 green with many-clustered
  vines, come, o
come,
 Dionysos, whose
  name is sung by
more than mortal
 voices! Come
  to the streets of
Thebes!
 Come to your
  city that raises the
cry:

Eüoi!

Eüoi!

LEADER: —God of many names!

CHORUS: Of all cities you

honor Thebes

highest of all,

you and your

mother,

lightning-married

Semelê.

Come to us

now,

Dionysos!

Your land lies

sick in the grip of

plague!

Come!

Come!

On your healing

feet down

Parnassos'

slopes or over the

sighing sea!

LEADER: Dionysos!

Lord of the starry

dance of fire-breathing

constellations!

CHORUS: Lord!

Master of night's

voices!

Come!

Come!

CHORUS: O come,

son of

Zeus!

Come, lord

king, with your

train of Thyiads that

dance the

                          night in
                            frenzy!
                    Lord of Cries!
                        Iakkhos!
                          Steward!
                  Giver of all things
                          good!
                          Iakkhos!

(One of the men who went off with Kreon has entered, left, as a Messenger and approaches as the Chorus concludes and the music fades out.)

MESSENGER: Neighbors of the house of Kadmos and Amphion:
    There is no condition of human life
    That I can truly praise or blame as settled.
    Fortune raises us up and brings us down,
    Lucky and unlucky, and no prophet
    Reveals to man his fate.

    Kreon, as I see it,
    Was once a man to be envied. He saved this land
    Of Kadmos from its enemies, achieved all-powerful
    Kingship and led us well, and he was blest
    With noble children.
    But now it's past—all past.
    When a man tosses aside all his pleasures,
    He also forfeits his life: a living corpse.
    Pile riches upon riches, live like a king,
    But when joy deserts I wouldn't give the price
    Of smoke's shadow for what remains, compared
    With the value of true happiness.

LEADER: What new sorrow have you brought this house?

MESSENGER: They're dead! And the living are guilty of their deaths.

LEADER: Dead? Who? Who is the murderer?

(The central doors of the palace begin to open.)

MESSENGER: Haimon. His blood shed by the hand—

LEADER: His father's or his own?

MESSENGER: His own.
    Enraged by his father's murder of the girl.

LEADER: O prophet, how clearly, how truly you saw!

MESSENGER: These are the facts. Now do as you will.

(The double doors to the palace are now open and Eurydikê steps forward, always remaining framed in the open doorway.)

LEADER: Look, Eurydikê, Kreon's wife.

    Poor woman, she either comes by chance,

    Or has already had news of her son.

EURYDIKÊ: People of Thebes, as I was on my way

    To offer prayers at the shrine of Pallas, my hand,

    Ready to open the door, I heard news

    Of some new disaster concerning my family.

    Terror-struck, I fell back, caught by my women.

    Tell me what has happened. Tell me again,

    For I have known sorrow before: I can bear it.

MESSENGER: I was there, dear lady, I saw it all;

    I'll tell you the best I can, omitting nothing.

    Why comfort you with words, when a moment later

    I'm proven a liar? Truth is always best.

    I accompanied your husband, leading him out

    To the edge of the plain where Polyneikês lay

    Still unburied, his body savaged by dogs,

    No one to pity him.

    Praying to Hekatê, goddess of crossroads,

    And Pluto, to be merciful

    And restrain their wrath, we washed the body clean

    With lustral water; then with newly uprooted

    Bushes burned what remained and raised a mound

    Of earth from his native soil.

    We turned then

    And made our way to Antigonê's bridal chamber

    With its bed of stone, the hollowed out dwelling

    Of the bride and her husband—Death.

    Still a long way off, we heard a voice

    Grieving helplessly inside the tomb,

    Resounding in that unhallowed marriage chamber,

    And fell back to tell our master the news.

    As the king approached, the same inscrutable cry

    Of despair rang out, hovering in the air around him,

And Kreon, groaning in anguish, cried in pain:
"O god, god, am I now a prophet,
And this the gravest path I have ever followed?
My son, my son's voice! Quickly, men,
Come quickly! Hurry to the cavern! There where the stones
Have been dragged back, and look into its mouth
To see if it's Haimon's voice, or if the gods
Have horribly deceived my senses!"

We went as we had been ordered by the king,
And there, in the deepest recess of the tomb,
We saw her, hanging, a noose at her neck,
Made of fine linen, her own veil.

Haimon embraced her, arms about her waist,
Lamenting her, now with the dead below,
His father's deeds, and his own unhappy marriage.
When Kreon saw, he rushed with a terrible groan
In toward him, his voice stifled with sobs,
Calling to him: "Child, what have you done?
What possessed you—what ? What disaster
Tripped up your reason? Come out, child! Come out!
I implore you!"

But his son, whose eyes blazed wild
With hatred, spat in his face, saying nothing,
And drew his two-edged sword. His father fell back
And fled in fear as Haimon lunged and missed.
Doomed and in despair, the miserable boy
Leaned his weight into the blade and drove it,
Halfway to the hilt, into his side.
Then, with a last effort, he embraced the girl
In the crook of his failing arm, as a burst of blood
Fell on her white cheek.

He lies there now, corpse embracing corpse,
Married in death in the world below,
Witness, poor boy, that of all man's vices
Stubbornness is the most deadly.
(*Eurydikê turns slowly and reenters the palace in silence. The doors close be-*
hind her.)

LEADER: What do you make of that?
  The lady has gone in
  Without a word.
MESSENGER: Yes, it troubles me.
  And yet I hope she goes inside
  And weeps her sorrows in private
  With her women. She has discretion.
  She'll do nothing rash.
LEADER: I hope you're right.
  But I distrust silence
  No less than wild lamentation.
  (Music fades in and continues to the end of the play.)
MESSENGER: I'll go in and see what dark purpose
  She may be hiding in her heart.
  Who knows? Silence so deep
  May have its dangers, too.
  (Immediately as the Messenger turns to enter the palace, Kreon enters, right, carrying the body of Haimon, followed by Guards and Attendants. His laments are heard even before he enters.)
LEADER: Here is the king himself,
  In his arms clear proof, if I dare say it,
  Of his own madness,
  None but his own:
  The work of his erring mind.
KREON: Aiiiiiiiiiiiiiiiiiiii!
        Ah, crimes, crimes of my
            darkened soul, misguided
        mind! Ah, stubborn, obstinate
            mind, heavy with death!
            Look!
        Look on us now!
            Slayer and slain!
                Father and son!
        Aiiiiiiiiiiiiiiiiiiii!
            I curse the wretched
                blindness of my counsel!
        My son, my son,
            too young to die,
                Haimon, my son, my son!

Aiiiiiiii! Aiiiiiiii!

All my error!

All my folly!

Never your own!

Never your own!

Never!

LEADER: You have learned too late, my lord,

Learned too late what justice means.

(The Messenger enters from the palace and approaches Kreon.)

KREON: Oimoiiiiii!

I know now, now I

know, now I have

learned the bitter lesson!

Oimoiiiii!

What god was it, what god

sent down the weight of heaven

to crush me with its burden,

and drove me a barbaric way

to trample down my joy?

Féu!

Féu!

Weep,

weep, o weep,

weep for the sorrows of men!

MESSENGER: My lord, the sorrow you bear

In your arms is only one.

This sorrow of your doing

You bring yourself. But soon

You will look on others

Inside your house.

(The doors to the palace begin to open and slowly during the following the ekkyklêma is rolled forward into full view to reveal the dead body of Eurydikê beside the altar of Zeus Herkeios which is awash with her blood.)

KREON: Can greater evil

Follow such evil?

MESSENGER: The queen is dead;

That boy's true mother.

Unhappy lady! Her wounds

Still run with her blood.

KREON: Aiiiiiiiiiiiiiiiiii!
                   Aiiiiiiiiiiiiiiiiii!
                         Death, insatiable harbor,
                   death, devourer of all, what
                         further ruin can I suffer?
                               Messenger of evil tidings, what
                   more, what more can I suffer?
                         Aiiiiiiiii!
                               I was dead,
                   dead!
                         I am killed a second time!
                               What are you saying, boy?
                   What new message—
                         aiiiiiiii! aiiiiiiii!—
                               of my wife's death?
                   Slaughter!
                         Slaughter heaped on
                               slaughter!

LEADER: See for yourself, Kreon,
       Nothing is hidden now.

(Kreon turns to view the sight and begins to stagger under the weight of the body he is carrying. Attendants come forward to take it from his arms but at first he refuses to relinquish it.)

KREON: Aiiiiiiiiiiiiiiiiiiiii!
                   Aiiiiiiiiiiiiiiiiiiiii!
                         What new, what
                   second disaster must I
                         see? What more, what
                               further fate must I bear?
                   Just now, here, in my
                         arms, my son, my
                               son, I held him; and
                   there, my wife,
                         dead!
                               Féu!
                   Féu!
                         Miserable, wretched mother!
                               O my child!

MESSENGER: There, at the altar,

A sharp knife entering her side,
She closed her darkening eyes,
And raised a cry, mourning her son
Megareus who died earlier,
And Haimon.
And as Death took her,
She called down every evil upon you,
The slayer of your son.

KREON: Aiiiiiiiii!

          Aiiiiiiiii!

             My mind leaps in fear!

       Will no one strike me, strike me
         down, kill me, no
            sword to the heart?

      Aiiiiiiiiii!

        I twist, I twist in
          anguish!

MESSENGER: She who lies there dead
   Cursed you and held you guilty
For the deaths of them all.

KREON: How did she come
   To her bloody end?

MESSENGER: Hearing the pitiable fate
Of Haimon, her son,
She struck home to the heart
With her own hand.

KREON: Aiiiiiiiii! Aiiiiiiiii!

        I alone, only I,

          I am guilty here! I,

       I alone, only I,

         must bear the guilt!

        I killed you, I,

      I own to the truth.

(To his Servants.)

        Lead me away,

          quickly, lead me

      away! I am nothing,

        less than nothing!

        Nothing!

LEADER: Good advice,
    If there is good in suffering.
    Quickest is best when
    Evil blocks the way.
KREON: Let it come,
          o let it come,
              the best of fates,
      that brings my final day,
          best fate of all!
            Let it come quickly,
      quickly, come
          quickly, I must not
            see another day!
LEADER: All of that is for the future.
    Now the present claims our thoughts.
    The future is cared for by those responsible.
KREON: All my desire
    Was in that prayer.
LEADER: Pray no more.
    Man's fate is sealed.
    *(The ekkyklêma moves slowly back into the palace during the following, the
    doors remaining open.)*
KREON: Lead me away,
          lead me,
             lead me,
      foolish, rash, imprudent man!
          I killed you, son;
             not willingly, no,
    not with thought;
          and you, my wife!
            Ah, wretched, wretched,
    wretched man,
        where shall I look,
          where shall I look for
    comfort?
        All that my hands touch
          goes awry!
    An unspeakable fate leaps on my head,
        crushes me,
          crushes me!

(Kreon is led into the palace by his Attendants. The doors close behind them.)

LEADER: There is no happiness without wisdom,
    And wisdom comes in submission to gods.
    Boasting words reap violent harvests;
    Great words teach wisdom to men of experience.
    (The music fades out as the Chorus and others go off.)
    (Darkness.)

THE WOMEN OF TRACHIS
(TPAXINIAI)

CAST OF CHARACTERS

HERAKLÊS *son of Zeus and Alkmênê*
DÊIANEIRA *wife of Heraklês*
HYLLOS *son of Heraklês and Dêianeira*
NURSE
LICHAS *herald*
MESSENGER
OLD DOCTOR
CHORUS OF YOUNG TRACHIAN WOMEN
LEADER OF THE CHORUS
WOMEN CAPTIVES *from Oichalia*
IOLÊ *one of the captive women, daughter of Eurytos*
BEARERS
SERVANTS
ATTENDANTS

The lines of the Chorus, unless otherwise indicated, are to be delivered by individual voices and varied groups of voices.

THE WOMEN OF TRACHIS

Dawn. Trachis in southern Thessaly. The skênê represents the façade of a regal house where Heraklês and his exiled family have been living as the guests of King Keyx. It is dominated by a large double door. The circular orchestra is flanked on either side by an entrance, the left to the country, the right to the city. A statue of Zeus is situated in the orchestra. Dêianeira, alone, enters through the doors.

DÊIANEIRA: Men have been saying since time began:
  Think no one happy or unhappy
  Till death comes calling.
  And yet, as for my life,
  Well, I don't need death to tell me how heavy
  And piteous it's been, even as a girl
  At home with my father Oineüs, in Pleuron,
  Where I was more terrified of marriage
  Than any girl in Aitolia ever was.
  A river god came one day, named Acheloös,
  To ask for my hand in marriage.
  A thing like that—
  Each time a different shape—
  Approaching my father!
  Once as the roaring torrent of a bull!
  Then as a snake with coils that writhed and shimmered!
  And then, once, oh, yes! in a *man's* body!
  With the head of an *ox!*
  And bursts of river cascading from his shaggy beard!
  With this to look forward to, this suitor!
  I longed for death, poor creature,
  Rather than share a bed with a thing like *him!*

  But then, at last! oh, then! Heraklês came!
  Famous Heraklês! Son of Alkmênê and Zeus!
  And my spirit danced!
  He closed with that *thing* in combat, and I was saved!
  How the struggle went, I don't know.

Only one who watched
Without my fear and dread that my own beauty
Would bring me bitter pain could speak of that.
But Zeus Arbiter of Contests brought it to good.
If good is what this is—

Since chosen by him,
By Heraklês, sharing his bed,
I've known nothing but fear after fear,
Haunting me, on his account,
Each night's troubles turning the last night's out.

And then we had children.
Children whom he sees seldom enough.
As a farmer sees his outlying fields:
At sowing and at harvest.
That's what his life has been:
Home, then away, home, then away again;
Slaving for *him!* his *master!*

But now it's over, these labors; he's free;
And my anxieties are worse than ever.
Since he slew the mighty Iphitos,
We, his family, have been uprooted, exiles
Here in Trachis, guests of a great foreign lord;
And where *he* is, Heraklês, no one knows.
All *I* know is that he is away again,
And my heart is torn for him again!
I'm almost certain he's caught in some dreadful mishap!
No short time has passed,
Ten months, no, *not* ten! add another *five!*
And still no word!

What trouble is it now
That plagues his life? This tablet he left behind
When he set out assures me of something terrible.
So I pray the gods it not be another source
Of suffering for me.
(The Nurse enters silently and unknown to Dêianeira through the doors of

the house during the last few sentences, closing the doors behind her. She waits till Dêianeira has finished before approaching and embracing her solicitously.)

NURSE: Dear mistress. Dear Dêianeira.
How many times I've watched you weep bitter tears
For Heraklês' absence and said nothing.
True, you are the mistress, I the slave.
And yet, if a slave may advise her freeborn lady,
Listen to what I suggest.
Of all your sons,
You have never sent one, not one,
To search for your husband! Why not Hyllos?
He's the logical choice. Or doesn't he care
For his father's safety?
(Hyllos enters, right, on his way from early-morning exercise. Seeing his mother and the Nurse, he approaches them.)
But look, here he comes, bounding homeward.
Unless you think my words out of place,
Use them, and your son along with them.

DÊIANEIRA: Dear, dear Hyllos! Dear son!
Good advice, it seems, may spring from anyone.
This woman, my slave, has spoken like a free man.

HYLLOS: What did she say, mother? May I hear?

DÊIANEIRA: That you should be ashamed, in all this time,
Never to have tried to find your father.

HYLLOS: But I *know* where he is, if rumors can be trusted.

DÊIANEIRA: And where do these rumors say he is?

HYLLOS: Last year, they say, he lived in Lydia,
Enslaved to some woman—a barbarian.

DÊIANEIRA: Well, if he's borne *that,* then anything's possible.

HYLLOS: He's free of that now, from what I hear.

DÊIANEIRA: Yes, but where is he? Alive or dead?

HYLLOS: I've heard he's either warring or planning a war—
Against Euboia, King Eurytos' city.

DÊIANEIRA: Did you know, Hyllos, he left me certain prophecies?
About that place, I mean.

HYLLOS: Prophecies, Mother? No, I've never heard.

DÊIANEIRA: They say that either he dies, or, if he survives,
His labors will be ended, and he will live out

The rest of his days in peace and contentment.
Go to him, Hyllos; his life hangs in the balance!
Go to him! Help him! If *he* lives, *we* live!
But if he dies, then we will all die with him.

HYLLOS: Of course I'll go, Mother. If I'd known,
I'd have been there long ago. But father's
Luck has never given me cause to worry.
But now I won't rest till I've learned the truth.

DÊIANEIRA: Go, then, Hyllos. Good news is always welcome
No matter how late.

(Music fades in as the Nurse turns to enter the house with Dêianeira, and Hyllos goes out left. At the same time, the Chorus of Trachian Women enters dancing from the right. Here as elsewhere they speak individually or in varying combinations.)

CHORUS: Night,
                    shimmering in starry splendor,
            goes to her grave
            as she gives you birth,
                    despoiled,
                    destroyed
                    in blazing light,
            and then at evening
            folds you again,
            dying torch,
                    in her darkening womb,
            shuddering blast of
            fiery might.

            Sun,
                    great Hêlios,
                    lord of light,
            tell me where he is,
                    tell me,
                    Alkmênê's child,
                    where is he,
                    tell me,
            tell me with flaring lightning flame.

            Does he sail the narrow

straits of the east?
>Does he rest on the double
>pillars of the west?
Tell me,
>great radiance,
>>where Heraklês bides.
>>Tell me,
>>tell me,
>>great lord of sight.

Speak to me,
>all-seeing eye of the firmament.
For Dêianeira, or so I've
>heard, forever suffers
>longing.
>>The woman once fought for, now
cries out her sorrow like the
>hapless, longing bird
>>bereft of its mate, her eyes
never dry on her manless
>bed; abandoned,
>grieving, never
>>sleeping,
>fear-obsessed for her
wandering man;
doom-ridden,
>consumed by terrible expectation.
>>And just as the sea,
>>blown by tireless
blasts from the north,
blasts from the south,
>is roiled to its depths,
>wave after wave,
>wave upon wave,
endless coming,
endless going,
>so Heraklês, seed of
>>Kadmeian Thebes,
>lives out his

Krêtan sea of life,
                    one moment
          nestled in a sheltering trough,
          the next
                    high on the cresting wave;
          always
     a god to save him from
                    Death's door.

(Dêianeira has entered through the doors of the house during the last lines.
The Chorus turns to face her.)

LEADER: With all respect, lady,
                  respect yet with reproof,
                       I cannot praise your actions.
               You must not ever lose hope,
                  not hope, lady. God,
                       son of Kronos, decrees
               for no man a life free of pain;
                  but joy and sorrow circle,
                       like the Great Bear in the heavens,
               and come around to us all,
                  each in turn,
                       endlessly.

CHORUS: Nothing lasts, nothing
                  abides, not
                       starry
               night, not
                  pain, not
                       wealth,
               not for
               man.
                       Tomorrow it's
               gone,
                  disappeared, the
                       pain, the
               joy, and
                  lights on
                       another, the
               joy, the
                  deprivation,

in turn.
Lady,
do not lose
hope;
keep
hope
ever.
Zeus,
Father,
cares for his
children.
When has it
not been so?

(The music fades out.)

DÊIANEIRA: I assume you have heard of my suffering,
And that has brought you. But you have never known
The anguish I suffer, and I hope you never will.

Youth pastures and grazes in its own good place,
Unvexed by the sun's heat, or wind, or rain,
A pleasant, happy time, free of troubles.
Until the maid becomes a wife,
And then anxiety comes,
And trembling at night for husband or for children.
Only she who has suffered what I have
Can know what my life is.
Yet for all my weeping, there is a grief now,
Sharper than all the rest, that I'll tell you of.

When Heraklês left home on his latest journey,
He left me an ancient tablet
Inscribed with unknown characters.
Never before, though he had set out on many
Ordeals, had he ever explained them to me.
He'd always gone off to conquer, not to die.
And yet, this time, he seemed a doomed man.
He told me clearly what property I should expect
To get from our marriage,
And which of his lands should go to which of his sons.

He also fixed a time.
If a year and three months passed without his return,
He would be dead; or, if he survived,
From that day forward his life would be free of pain.
(A Messenger, an old man, enters, left, and begins his approach.)
That, he said, would be the end of his labors,
Ordained so long ago by the gods
At Dodona's ancient oak,
Spoken by the twin dove-priestesses,
The Peleiades.
And now that time is come,
That moment of fulfillment. And that is why,
Dear friends, I wake suddenly from sweet sleep
And tremble with fear that I've lost
The greatest of men.
LEADER: Hush, lady, no more doom-filled words.
Here comes a man with a wreath.
A sign of good news.
MESSENGER: Queen Dêianeira. Let me be the first
To free you from your fear. Heraklês lives
And returns victorious with the spoils of battle for the gods.
DÊIANEIRA: What is this news you've told me, old man?
MESSENGER: That your much admired husband will be here soon,
Radiant in the glory of his victory.
DÊIANEIRA: Who told you this? A citizen? Some foreigner?
MESSENGER: Lichas the herald, lady. Down in the meadow
Where they pasture the oxen in summer.
He's telling the crowd assembled there.
When I heard, I hurried to be the first to tell you,
And perhaps to win a reward and your gratitude.
DÊIANEIRA: With such good news, why isn't he here?
MESSENGER: It isn't easy for him, lady. The crowds
Won't let him move. Everyone has a question.
He'd be here, but he can't. He'll be here soon.
You'll see him for yourself.
DÊIANEIRA: O Zeus! Master of Oïtê's unreaped fields!
However late your news, it has *come!*
(To the women of the Chorus.)
Women, *in* the house and *out!*

Raise your voices! *Shout!*
Like heaven's eye, glorious in its radiance,
Dawning on me, the word has come
That lifts me up in joy!
(Music enters immediately as the Chorus raises high its arms in an attitude of joyous exaltation and simultaneously breaks into jubilant song and dancing.)

CHORUS: Shout!
        Shout for the
           house!
      Shout the
        song!
          Shout!
      Shout at the
        hearth! Hearth
           altar of the house
    hungry for
      husbands!
        Let it
rise!
    Voices!
      Men!
Sing!
    To Apollo!
      Sing!
Lord of the
    feathered
      arrow!
Apollo!
    Defender!
      Voices!
Shout!
    Praise the Healer!
      Raise his song!
Men of the house!
    Virgins!
      As one!
And to
    Artemis!

Sister!
Twin of the
flaming
torches!
Raise a song!
Deer-hunting goddess!
Raise a song!
for Ortygian Artemis
and her
neighboring
nymphs!

(As the dance and song grow increasingly more ecstatic, Lichas enters, left, with the Captive Women, among them Iolê, none of them noticed by the frenzied Chorus.)

You have me!
Have me now!
I give myself to you,
lord of enchantment!
Frenzy's lord!
Lord of the dark fluting night!
Winding with ivy!
Heart's tyrant!
I feel you!
On me!
In me!
Heart soars!
Soars!
Soaring!
Where am I?
Spinning!
Whirling!
Dying!
Master!
Ioooooooo!
Iooooooo!
Apollo
Healer!

(Having just returned to the praise of Apollo, they catch sight of Lichas and the Captive Women and rush to Dêianeira, speaking rapidly.)

Lady!
    Lady!
        Lady!
What's
    here? Look
        there!
Good
    news! Good
        news!
There!
    Now!
        Before your
eyes!
    Look!
    Look!
(The music fades out.)
DÊIANEIRA: Dear friends, here they are!
    My keen eyes have not failed
    To see these women's approach.
    (Approaching Lichas who comes forward to meet her.)
    Welcome, Lichas! It took you long enough
    For someone with good news, if such it is!
LICHAS: We are pleased to be back, lady,
    And pleased with your greeting, which fits the deed
    Accomplished. When a man is triumphant,
    He must profit from words of praise.
DÊIANEIRA: Dear, good friend,
    Tell me first what I *must* know.
    Will I have Heraklês back? Alive?
LICHAS: Not only alive, I assure you.
    I left him in the best of health and strength,
    Untroubled by illness.
DÊIANEIRA: Where? Abroad or here at home?
LICHAS: No, in Euboia, lady. There, on a promontory,
    He's consecrating altars and offering tribute
    Of first-fruits to Zeus Kênion.
DÊIANEIRA: To fulfill a vow or because of some prophecy?
LICHAS: A vow he made before he destroyed the land
    Of the captive women you see here.

DÊIANEIRA: Who are they? Whose daughters? Poor things!
    Prisoners? How pitiable they are,
    Unless I'm deceived.
LICHAS: After he had leveled Eurytos' city,
    Heraklês chose these women for himself
    As gifts worthy of the gods.
DÊIANEIRA: The war that kept him from me all that time,
    Those endless days and nights?
LICHAS: No, he was in Lydia most of the time—
    A captive, against his will, as he says,
    Sold into slavery.
    Don't take offense at the word, lady,
    For Zeus himself was author of *that* deed.
    As for Heraklês,
    He was sold into bondage to Omphalê,
    A barbarian queen, and spent a whole year serving her.
    He told us himself. But the insult so much offended him,
    That he swore to avenge the man responsible,
    Along with his wife and child, and make them slaves.
    He meant it, too. For once free and absolved,
    He raised an army and marched on Eurytos' city,
    Against that only man who had ever shamed him.

    It happened that once when Heraklês visited his friend—
    As he had done often before, they were old friends—
    Eurytos turned against him in a rage,
    Denouncing him with terrible, insulting words,
    Saying that, though his arrows from Apollo
    Were charmed and destined never to miss their mark,
    His sons, Eurytos' sons, were superior archers
    When matched in a fair contest.
    He called him a slave, then,
    And a broken-down freeman's toady.

    Later, at dinner, when Heraklês was drunk,
    He kicked him from his doors. That galled Heraklês.
    And so, when one of Eurytos' sons, Iphitos,
    Came to the hill of Tiryns tracking stray horses,
    And found himself distracted by some event,

Heraklês took advantage of the moment
And cast him from the fortress' high rampart.

This angered Zeus Olympios, Father of all,
And he sold him into slavery. For Heraklês,
For the first time in his life, had killed by treachery,
And Zeus could not forgive him.
If he had fought him openly in a fair fight,
Zeus would have accepted and pardoned his victory.
The gods favor insolence no more than we.
But all those braggarts who slandered Heraklês
Are in Hades now, and their city is enslaved,
The same as these women, whose lives were once
Filled with favor, but now are unenviable,
As your husband wished. I've followed his orders faithfully.
As for Heraklês himself, he'll be here soon,
Once he's finished sacrificing to Zeus.
Of all my happy news, this is the sweetest.
LEADER: Your joy will soon be complete, dear lady,
    Both with what you have now
    And what is promised.
DÊIANEIRA: Of course. Haven't I every right
    To rejoice at my husband's success?
    My joy must keep pace with his triumph.
    And yet, when you think about it carefully,
    You tremble that one who has had such success
    Will one day be swept to his knees.

    Dear friends,
    Some terrible pity grips me to see these women:
    Unhappy, homeless, fatherless, in a foreign land;
    Once, perhaps, daughters of free-born citizens,
    Now doomed to slavery.

    Zeus Arbiter of Battles,
    Never treat my children in such a way.
    Or if you must, not while I'm alive,
    For that is what I fear when I see them.
    (*She approaches Iolê among the other Women Captives.*)

You, poor woman, who are you?
Are you married? Are you a mother?
No. Your looks tell me you have never known
Such treatment, but are born of a noble house.

Lichas, whose daughter is she?
Her father? Her mother? Tell me.
For, seeing her, I feel more deeply
Than for all the others. She alone appears
To know the heavy weight of what is to come.

LICHAS: You're asking the wrong person, lady.

She may not be from the lowliest of families.

DÊIANEIRA: Is she a noble? Did Eurytos have a daughter?

LICHAS: I don't know. I didn't ask many questions.

DÊIANEIRA: Not even her name? Didn't you hear them talking?

LICHAS: No, I did not! I worked in silence.

DÊIANEIRA: Poor girl!

(To Iolê.)

At least tell *me* who you are.

It would be a pity not to know you.

LICHAS: She hasn't said a word on the whole trip;

To hear her speak now would greatly surprise me.

All I've heard since leaving her windswept land

Is weeping and moaning in terrible pain, poor creature.

Her fortune hasn't been good; she deserves understanding.

DÊIANEIRA: We'll spare her, then. Let her come in with us.

She has enough pain. Let's not give her more.

But now let's go inside.

That way you may leave whenever you're ready,

And I'll set about putting my house in order.

(Dêianeira is about to lead Lichas, Iolê, and the Women Captives into the house when the Messenger who has become part of the crowd during the preceding scene comes forward, disturbed, and urgently enlists her attention. He leads Dêianeira forward in the orchestra while the others enter the house.)

MESSENGER: Your pardon, lady; a word with you alone!

There are things that you must know about these captives.

Things that only I know.

DÊIANEIRA: What is this? Why have you stopped me?

MESSENGER: Wait! Listen to me! What I say now

Is even more important than my earlier message.
DÊIANEIRA: Shall I call the others back, or will you speak
    To me and to these women?
MESSENGER: Yes, to you and them, not the others.
DÊIANEIRA: Very well, they're gone. You were saying?
MESSENGER: That man Lichas, either he lied just now,
    Or he lied in his first report.
DÊIANEIRA: What are you saying? I don't understand these riddles.
    Explain yourself.
MESSENGER: I heard him say—as did many others—
    That Heraklês destroyed King Eurytos
    And high-towered Oichalia all for that girl.
    Of all the gods, Love alone seduced him
    To carry out this slaughter,
    And not his year-long slavery to Omphalê,
    Nor the murder of Iphitos. But now he tells
    A different story in which Love is pushed aside.

    It appears that when your husband failed to convince
    Her father to contribute his daughter for his whore,
    He grabs at any petty pretext he can
    To war against her country, where Eurytos—
    That's her father, remember—is king, kills him,
    And sacks the city.

    Now he comes home,
    Sending her on ahead with all due ceremony,
    And not as a slave. Why do such a thing? Oh, no!
    Especially seeing he's head over heels in love with her!

    I thought I had no choice but to tell you, my lady,
    Tell you everything I heard. And not just me;
    Many men of Trachis heard it, too,
    Out there in the public square. They'll tell you the same.
    And if my words offend you, I apologize;
    But at least I've spoken the truth.
DÊIANEIRA: O god! What have I done?
    What disaster have I welcomed into my house?
    A girl with no name, as her escort swore,
    But as brilliant in her looks as in her birth!

MESSENGER: Eurytos' daughter, once known as Iolê.

But *he* couldn't tell you that! He never asked!

LEADER: The evilest of the evil is the crafty liar!

DÊIANEIRA: Friends, what am I to do?

This man's story has left me stunned.

LEADER: Speak to Lichas.

Perhaps if you insist, he'll tell the truth.

DÊIANEIRA: Yes, of course. You're right. I'll go.

(As she turns to go in, Lichas enters from the house.)

MESSENGER: Am I to stay, my lady? What's your wish?

DÊIANEIRA: Yes. Stay. He's coming without being summoned.

LICHAS: Is there a message for Heraklês, lady?

I'm leaving now.

DÊIANEIRA: But you've hardly arrived,

And that took long enough; and now you're off,

With no further chance to talk!

LICHAS: Ask what you like. I'm at your service.

DÊIANEIRA: Yes, but will you tell the truth?

LICHAS: Zeus as my witness! All I know.

DÊIANEIRA: Who is the girl you brought to my house?

LICHAS: A Euboian. Her parents I don't know.

MESSENGER: You! Who do you think you're talking to?

LICHAS: And who are *you* to ask me that?

MESSENGER: You'll answer if you have any sense!

LICHAS: I'm speaking to Dêianeira, daughter of Oineüs,

Wife of Heraklês, and, unless I'm deceived,

My queen!

MESSENGER: Ah! Just what I wanted! Your queen!

LICHAS: Her dutied servant! Yes!

MESSENGER: And if you fail in your duty to her?

What then? What should your punishment be?

LICHAS: Fail in my duty? Is this some trick?

MESSENGER: No trick—except the one you're playing!

LICHAS: I'm off! I've had enough of this!

MESSENGER: Not before you answer one question.

LICHAS: Then ask! You're certainly not short on words!

MESSENGER: The captive you brought—you know who I mean?

LICHAS: Yes. Why do you ask?

MESSENGER: You claim to know nothing about her,

Yet earlier you said her name was Iolê,
Daughter of Eurytos.
LICHAS: Said? To whom? Where?
Show me *one man, one,* who heard me say it!
MESSENGER: Many heard you, many in the town square,
In Trachis—a whole crowd of witnesses.
LICHAS: *Thought* they heard it, is what! An opinion's an opinion!
Not my actual words!
MESSENGER: Actual words! Didn't you swear under oath
That the girl you brought was a bride for Heraklês?
LICHAS: Bride for Heraklês? Me? For god's sake, lady,
Who is this stranger!
MESSENGER: One who heard from your own mouth
That the city was destroyed because of desire
For that girl—Heraklês' desire—
And nothing to do with the Lydian affair—
Just overwhelming passion!
LICHAS: Send this man away, my lady!
Sane men don't trade words with lunatics!
DÊIANEIRA: By Zeus whose lightning strikes the high glens
Of Oïtê, don't cheat me of the truth!
I'm not an evil woman.
I know how easily men's hearts can change,
That one day's joy is not another's.
And I know how insane it is to contest
With Love and trade him blow for blow.
And even the gods are ruled by him as he wills.
So why not me? And why not another woman
No different from me?
I would be mad beyond redemption to blame
My husband, struck as he is with this illness for the girl.
Or the girl. What shameful thing is she guilty of?
What harm has she done me?
No, it's impossible.
But if Heraklês taught you to lie,
You've learned a mean lesson.
Or if the lesson is yours, to keep from hurting me,
You are lower still, for you wound me all the more deeply.
Come, tell me the truth. To be branded a liar

Brings dishonor on the freeborn man.
And if you think you can hide it,
There are too many men you've spoken to
Already who will confirm it for me.

Are you afraid? Afraid of hurting me?
Not knowing hurts me. To know can never hurt me.
How is knowing so terrible?
Heraklês has had more women than can be counted,
And not one of them has had an evil word
Or reproach from me. Nor will she,
Even though all her being is absorbed in his passion.
I pitied her deeply when I saw her,
Knowing that her beauty had destroyed her life,
And that, unknown to herself, poor creature,
She had laid waste her native city and delivered it
To slavery.

But let be what will be,
And hear me when I tell you: Lie to others,
But to me tell the truth!
LEADER: Her advice is good. Do as she says.
    You won't regret it. You'll also earn my thanks.
LICHAS: Well, dear lady, seeing you are not unreasonable,
    But, being human, allow for human weakness,
    I'll tell you the whole truth and hold back nothing.

It's just as that man says.
One day, run through with passion for the girl,
Heraklês leveled Oichalia with war's devastation—
And all because of her—her unfortunate home.
In fairness to him, he hid none of this,
Nor asked me to do so.
To cause you no pain,
My queen, I did as I did, and doing so,
Did wrong, if wrong you call it.

Now that you know,
For your sake and his, bear with the girl,

And keep with the kind words you spoke to her.
For Heraklês, who has conquered all obstacles,
Has, in his love for this girl, been totally vanquished.
DÊIANEIRA: I agree, and I'll do as you say;
Why add to my afflictions by struggling with gods?
But now let's go inside. I have messages for you
To take to him, and gifts, gifts to match
The many gifts you brought. It would never do
To return empty-handed, having come
With so well-stocked a train.
(Music enters as Dêianeira, Lichas and the Messenger go into the house. At the same time, the Chorus comes forward.)
CHORUS: Great is her
  power,
   great the
 power of
  Aphroditê, great
   Love goddess,
 Love,
  Kyprian,
   never
 defeated
  in love's
   war!
I will
 pass over the
  stories, stories
told of the
 gods:
  how
Love tricked
 Zeus,
  beguiled him,
Zeus
 son of
  Kronos, and
Death,
 lord of
  darkness,

Death, and
　　Poseidon who
　　　　makes the
earth
　　tremble.
LEADER:　　　Who was it, then,
who, who, when our
　　mistress was
　　　　sought by
men,
　　sought in
　　　　courtship,
what
　　heroes, what
　　　　two mighty
rivals
　　struggled,
　　　　struggled to
win her hand,
　　win her in
　　　　contest,
struggled,
　　blow against
　　　　blow,
fearful,
　　fearful struggle, in
　　　　blinding dust?
CHORUS:　　One was Acheloös,
　　Acheloös of
　　　　Oinaidai's tribe,
Acheloös,
　　river-god,
　　　　mighty,
monstrous,
　　four-footed bull,
　　　　horns held high,
brute force.
　　The other,
　　　　Zeus' son from

Thebes,
 Thebes,
  favored city of
Bakkhos,
 Heraklês,
  Heraklês, his
curved bow
 brandished,
  spears and club.
Heavy with
 desire to
  bed her as
bride, they
 clashed,
  clashed in a
fury,
 clashed, only
  Kypris,
Love,
 goddess of
  wedded
bliss,
 Love's goddess,
  beautiful Aphroditê,
was there with them,
 there in the center,
  there in their midst,
referee,
 judge,
  to choose.

LEADER: Then the
CHORUS: noise,
LEADER: clatter of
CHORUS: fists,
LEADER: twang of
CHORUS: bow,
LEADER: bull's horns
CHORUS: clashing,
LEADER: bodies

```
                        grappling,
CHORUS:             grappling,
LEADER:                 waists
CHORUS:     wound
LEADER:         round
CHORUS:             with
LEADER:     legs,
CHORUS:         twisting,
LEADER:             bodies groaning,
CHORUS:     groaning,
LEADER:         deadly
CHORUS:             blows
LEADER:     raining
CHORUS:         down,
LEADER:             raining
CHORUS:     down,
LEADER:         foreheads
                    butting,
                aiming to
                    kill,
CHORUS:             aiming to kill,
LEADER:     bodies,
CHORUS:         twisting,
LEADER:             strangled
CHORUS:     sounds!
    (Pause.)
LEADER:             And she,
                        delicate beauty,
                sat far off
                    on a high hill,
                        awaiting,
CHORUS:     awaiting the
                husband,
                    chosen
LEADER:     by Love's wand.
CHORUS:         The battle
                    rages, the
                bride,
                    prize
                        of the
```

                contest
                    watches, anxious to
                        see its
                    end.
LEADER: And then,
                    as a calf,
                as a calf torn,
CHORUS: torn from its
                    mother's
                side,
                    she is
LEADER: gone.

(Well before the Chorus has ended its dance and disperses, Dêianeira, carry-
ing a richly encrusted and sealed casket, enters from the house.)

DÊIANEIRA: Friends, while our visitor is inside,
    Saying goodbye to the strangers, I have stolen
    Out here to you. I want to tell you, partly,
    What my hands have devised, and partly to have
    Your sympathy in my sorrow.

    A virgin, or no, no virgin! some outrageous baggage!
    Has entered my house as freight comes to a mariner,
    To shipwreck my peace! We two, beneath one blanket,
    Waiting to share his embrace!

    This is my reward
    For all the weary years I've guarded his home,
    Heraklês,
    Whom I called true and loyal, my honest love!
    Angry? How can I be angry?
    He's suffered the same disease often enough.
    But to live in one house, we two together,
    Wife and mistress, to share one marriage?
    What woman could countenance that?
    Her flower
    Is coming to bloom, mine fading. Men's eyes
    Adore plucking a youthful blossom,
    But turn away when it withers.
    What do I fear, then?

That I will call him husband,
But she will share his bed.
She's the younger. But as I've said: anger
Is not for the wife; not a wife of good judgment.
And now I'll tell you how I will find relief.

While still a girl, I had a gift, kept hidden
In a bronze urn, from a fabled monster, Nessos,
The shaggy-breasted Centaur, while he lay dying.
He gave me the blood from his wound. The same Nessos
Who for a fee ferried men in his arms
Across the Evenos without oar or sail.
I, too, was carried on his shoulder
When my father first sent me off with Heraklês
As Heraklês' bride. And then, in mid-stream,
His hands, the monster's, touched me, as they should not have,
And I screamed.
Hearing, Heraklês turned and shot
A feathered arrow that pierced the monster's breast,
Hissing into the lung. As he died,
He said to me: "Daughter of Oineüs,
Since you are the last I'll ferry across these waters,
Listen, and you will profit from my words.
Take with your hands the blood that clots my wound
Around the arrow dipped in the Hydra's black bile:
A love-charm to keep the heart of Heraklês
From loving any woman more dearly than you."
It was this I thought of just now.
For after he died, I did as the monster said:
Locked it away; kept it, in a secret place;
And now I have smeared the salve on this robe—
(Indicating the casket in her hands.)
Doing all that the monster advised before he died.
It's finished now.

I am no friend to evil,
Nor do I care to know or learn anything of it.
I detest women who do.
And yet, if there is some charm, some spell to use

On Heraklês, to regain his love, to defeat

This girl, then I am ready. Unless, of course,

You think me rash. Do you?

If so, I'll do nothing.

LEADER: No, if you think it will work,

You've done nothing wrong.

DÊIANEIRA: I think it might, but I've never tested it.

LEADER: The proof's in the doing.

How else will you know?

(Lichas enters from the house and approaches Dêianeira.)

DÊIANEIRA: We'll know soon enough. He's coming.

He'll be on his way soon. Just don't betray me.

Shameful deeds done in darkness,

Kept hidden, bring no disgrace.

LICHAS: What are your instructions, my lady?

I've stayed too long.

DÊIANEIRA: While you were inside, Lichas,

Talking to the foreign women,

I prepared this for you to take to my husband.

A long, fine-woven robe made by me.

A gift for him, my absent husband. Tell him

That he alone must be the first to wear it,

And never to let the light of the sun or the flame

From the holy precinct or a hearth strike it.

Not till he reveals it to all eyes,

Both gods' and men's, on the day the oxen are sacrificed.

I vowed to myself once that, when I saw him,

Or knew he was coming, I would wrap him in this robe,

To appear new-clad to offer the gods new sacrifice.

(Showing him the seal on the casket.)

You will carry this with you as proof, this token:

My sign in the circle of this seal. He'll recognize it.

Now go. Go. And remember: A messenger

Never interferes with his mission.

Do well, and you will have not only his praise,

But mine as well, doubling our gratitude.

LICHAS: Believe me, lady, as a messenger guided by Hermes,

I won't be tripped up, but deliver the casket

And your message as you yourself would.

DÊIANEIRA: Go at once. You know how things are here.

LICHAS: I do. That everything is well in hand.

DÊIANEIRA: And that I received the foreign girl
　　With friendly kindness. You saw it yourself.

LICHAS: Kindness that amazed and moved me.

DÊIANEIRA: What else could you tell him, then?
　　It's really too soon to speak of my love for him;
　　Not knowing his love for me.
　　(Music begins as Lichas turns to go out, left, carrying the sealed casket and
　　Dêianeira returns to the house. At the same time, the Chorus comes forward
　　and begins a flowing dance.)

CHORUS:　　You who dwell where warm springs
　　　　　　gush from rocks at the narrow pass;

　　　　　　who dwell on the heights of Oïtê's peak,
　　　　　　by the shore of the landlocked Mêlidian bay,

　　　　　　by the shore beloved of the virgin goddess,
　　　　　　Artemis, armed with golden shafts,

　　　　　　where the Greeks meet at the Gates in council;
　　　　　　soon, soon the flute's lovely voice

　　　　　　will sound again with no harsh strain
　　　　　　of tears and lament, but like the lyre's

　　　　　　soft strings, music pleasing to the gods!
　　　　　　For Zeus's and Alkmênê's son,

　　　　　　Heraklês, son of god, comes home,
　　　　　　bearing trophies of battles won.

　　　　　　Lost to me, lost to my land,
　　　　　　on sea, a wanderer, for twelve long months

　　　　　　no news, and his suffering, miserable wife,
　　　　　　loving wife, wept tears. But now

　　　　　　Arês, war-god, roused to fury,
　　　　　　frees her from her days of sorrow.

Let him come! Let him come! Let no rest detain him!
Let his many-oared vessel carry him homeward;

carry him to me from the high island altar!
Let him come to her steeped in the love of the charm,

steeped in the salve to turn his love round,
the robe of persuasion to melt his mind!
(Dêianeira has entered from the house during the last third of the ode and approaches the women of the Chorus.)
DÊIANEIRA: O dear friends! I'm afraid!
Have I gone too far in my action?
LEADER: What is it? Tell me!
DÊIANEIRA: I don't know. But I have serious misgivings
That some disaster will come of my good intentions.
LEADER: Surely not your gift to Heraklês?
DÊIANEIRA: Oh, yes, yes, and now I know never to act blindly
When the consequence can't be foreseen.
LEADER: Tell us, lady, what makes you afraid?
DÊIANEIRA: Something has happened, friends,
That when I tell you, you'll think it truly incredible!
The tuft of sheep's wool
That I used to anoint the robe I sent to Heraklês
Has vanished, disappeared, consumed by nothing,
Nothing in the house—
But by itself—
Eaten from within and crumbling to dust.
But wait, I'll tell you everything, just as it happened.

All that the monster told me as he lay there
With the death-dealing arrow in his side
Was graved on my brain as on a bronze tablet,
And I left out nothing. I did as I was ordered.
I kept the drug in a dark, safe place,
Away from fire and the sun's hot rays,
Till the moment I came to apply it.
I did all that. And when it came time to act,
I did so in secret, deep inside the house.
I had plucked a handful of fleece from one of our sheep

And spread it with the mixture, and then applied it
To the robe, folded the gift, and laid it untouched
By sunlight into the casket, as you have seen.

Then, just as I'm leaving to go out,
I see a sight beyond words that staggers belief!
Somehow I'd thrown the tuft of wool on the floor
In a patch of sunlight; and as it warmed it shriveled,
Crumbled to powder, like sawdust at a logger's feet.
It lies there where it fell. But from the ground
Beneath it, clots of foam boil up, as when
The blue-green juice of Bakkhos' vine
Is poured on the earth.

Ah, what am I to think?
This terrible thing I've done! Why should that dying
Monster do me a kindness? I? The cause
Of his death? Impossible! No! He beguiled me!
Using *me* to pay back that man who shot him!
But now I know, now it's too late.
For I know now, unless my judgment betrays me,
That I alone, dear god! will kill my husband!
I know that the very arrow that made the wound
Also wounded Cheiron, and he was a god:
It kills every beast it touches.
How can the venom,
The same poison that mixed with the blood of Nessos,
Not kill Heraklês? It can't. It will, it will,
I know it. At least I've made up my mind:
If he dies, I die, too, at the same time.
How can a woman who believed her life honorable
Continue living with a name stained with evil?
LEADER: However dreadful what you expect may be,
　　Never lose hope before it happens.
DÊIANEIRA: When a plan is ill-advised from the start?
LEADER: Unintended wrong is always forgivable.
DÊIANEIRA: That's easy for the innocent to say;
　　But not so simple when you share in the evil
　　(Hyllos has entered, left, during the above and approaches them.)

LEADER: Hyllos is back from searching for his father.
　　　Unless you want him to know, you'd best keep silent.
HYLLOS: Mother, I wish either that you were dead,
　　　Or someone else's mother, not mine!
　　　Or another person with a better heart!
　　　Any of these would do!
DÊIANEIRA: Oh, son, what have I done to make you hate me?
HYLLOS: I'll tell you what you've done!
　　　You've murdered your husband, my father!
DÊIANEIRA: Hyllos! What are you saying?
HYLLOS: The truth, Mother! What's done cannot be undone.
DÊIANEIRA: How can you say such things! By what authority
　　　Do you accuse me of something so monstrous?
HYLLOS: I saw my father fall with these two eyes!
　　　No one told me!
DÊIANEIRA: Where did you find him?
　　　Where did it happen? Were you with him?
HYLLOS: If you must know, I'll tell you, but I'll hold back nothing.
　　　Once he had sacked Eurytos' famed city,
　　　He went with trophies and the first-fruits won in battle
　　　To a point washed by the sea called Cape Kênaion.
　　　There he erected and dedicated altars
　　　And a grove of trees to Zeus his father.
　　　It was there I first saw him,
　　　And my heart leapt with joy.
　　　He was set to begin the great sacrificial slaughter
　　　When Lichas, his herald, appeared bringing from home
　　　Your gift, the fatal robe.
　　　He put it on,
　　　As you had instructed, and began the sacrifice.
　　　Twelve bulls, unblemished victims,
　　　The pick of the lot, he slaughtered first;
　　　And then a herd of cattle, large and small,
　　　Together numbering a hundred.
　　　He was so serene as he prayed.
　　　Suspecting nothing. His spirit buoyed
　　　By the handsomeness of the robe.
　　　But then, as the bloody flame leapt high with fat
　　　And resin-rich pine, a sweat bubbled out of his body

Making the robe cling at every joint,
Glued to his skin, as if the work of a sculptor.
Pain in spasmed waves bit into his bones,
And then the venom, as if from some deadly viper,
Began to devour him.
Next he shouted for Lichas,
Poor man, who was innocent of your crime,
Asking what treason provoked him to bring that robe.
But Lichas knew nothing. All he could say
Was what you had told him:
That the robe was a gift from you, just as you sent it.

When Heraklês heard these words, and a piercing spasm
Gripped his lungs, he seized Lichas by the foot,
Where the ankle turns in the socket,
And cast him against a rock that juts from the sea
So his white brain oozed through his hair
As his skull shattered into pieces on the bloody rock.

Everyone there raised a cry of horror
At the sight of one man in a frenzy,
The other slaughtered, and no one dared
Approach the raging man, who, in his pain,
Dashed himself to the earth, then, screaming in agony,
Flung himself into the air, till the rocks resounded
From Lokris to the cliffs of Euboia.

But when he could no longer move,
Exhausted with throwing himself to the ground,
Lying there groaning and cursing
His misbegotten marriage to your bed,
His deadly agreement with Oineüs for your hand
That brought him to destruction!
Cursing your vileness!
Only then, lifting his head from the shrouds
Of altar smoke, did his eyes, wild in their sockets,
See me weeping in the crowd.
He called to me:
"Son! Come closer! Don't run from me in my agony!

Not even if it means your death!
Take me to a place where I won't be seen.
If you have any pity, at least take me
Out of this country. Don't let me die here."

As he commanded, we placed him aboard, midship,
And brought him here, groaning in his torment,
No easy task. You'll see him soon.
Alive or dead, I don't know.

These are the things you've done, Mother.
And I pray that avenging Justice and the Furies
Hound you down and punish you!
If right permits a son to curse his mother,
Then I curse you, for you gave me that right
By killing the noblest man of all.
A man whose like you will never see again.
(Dêianeira moves in the direction of the house.)
LEADER: My dear, why are you leaving so quietly?
Your silence only pleads his case.
(Dêianeira goes into the house.)
HYLLOS: Let her go! It's a fair wind
That blows her out of my sight!
Why should she be dignified with the name
Of mother when nothing she does is motherly!
Let her go! Good riddance! And let her share
In the joy she brought my father!
(Music fades in as Hyllos enters the house after her. During this, the Chorus comes forward and bonds tightly together, its laments strangely restrained yet filled with fear and foreboding. A slow dance takes shape out of the huddle and builds to a terrifying climax.)
CHORUS: Children!
                 Children!
                     Look!
             Look,
                 children! How
                     quickly, how
             quickly it
                 comes, the

                    word, the
        word of old
             prophecy,
                  prophecy
        heralding the
             time when
                  twelve
        plowings,
             twelve years'
                  labor, had
        reached its
             end, an
                  end would
        come, an
             end to the
                  labors of
        him,
             Zeus' own
                  son,
        Heraklês!
             And it is fulfilled!
                  Fulfilled! The time, the
        time come
             round, the
                  time, for how,
        how could he,
             he whose eye is
                  pale, whose
        sight
             broken,
                  broken, toil in
        servitude when life is
             fled? How,
                  with a cloud of
        death around him,
             caught in the
                  Centaur's crafty
        doom that
             clings to his

sides, clings,
clings, devouring
    flesh,
       venom,
venom born of
    death, of
       death and
swift shining
    serpent,
       clasped,
clasped in
    Hydra's
       terrible
embrace,
    how shall he
       see,
how,
    how know, another
       dawn enflame the
east, while
    black-haired
       Nessos
mounts his
    victim,
       goads his frenzy,
burning,
    boiling, brutal
       merger, meshing
monstrous, flesh in
    flesh, bone in
       bone, blood in
blood, poison
    flowing, obscure
       fusion, cruel
confusion, beast and
    man, one
       being, one
being, one,
    degrading

madness?
Pity, o pity the
     woman, the
          wife.
She foresaw
     nothing. Not this
          tragedy. Nothing.
No calamity.
     Nothing.
          Seeing only
misfortune enter,
     enter her house, in the
          new bride's
coming, new bride's
     coming, coming,
          and applied the
remedy herself,
     not
          knowing, not
knowing.
     The end, oh,
          the end was
not her
     doing, not her
          doing, but the
monster's
     counsel, the
          fatal
meeting,
     fatal,
          fatal.
And now in
     tears, in
          tears, tears in
wretched
     lament, she
          dissolves in
tears, and the
     coming of Atê's

doom
foreshadows
ruin,
ruin,
ruin from
treachery and
great disaster.
Hot tears
flood me.
Hot tears for
agonies
suffered by
him, by
him, greater than
any hands,
greater,
greater than any
enemy's hands ever
brought him,
glorious Heraklês, pity
greater than any yet gave,
Heraklês,
master!
O black-pointed spear,
goring spear,
spear victorious, that
led in battle, that
led the bride
swiftly from Oichalia's
heights, where are you
now, we
mourn you,
mourn you, and
see that silent
Aphroditê,
Kyprian goddess, has
made this work!

*(The low, extended, guttural moan of Hyllos is heard from inside the house
during the last several lines. At the sound, the members of the Chorus scatter*

agitatedly throughout the orchestra, their whispered words at times wildly overlapping.)

     Am I deceived?
      What is that
       cry? That
   cry! What is that
    cry I hear?
      What is the
  grief,
    grief, what is the
     grief inside the house?
   What?
    What?
     What has
  happened?
    What?
     A new
  wave of
   anguish!
     Another!
  Another new
   misery for the house!

(The Chorus sees the Nurse emerge from the house and gathers around her in agitation after scattering wildly again.)

     The nurse!
   There! She's
    coming!
     Look at her!
   The old woman!
    Look at her
     face! Look!
   How she
    frowns. Coming
     toward me. To
  tell me, to
   tell me,
    what? Tell me
  what?

NURSE: Children, the gift to Heraklês!

	What evil it has loosed
	no one can measure!
LEADER:	Old woman, tell me!
	What new calamity has
	stricken the house?
NURSE:	Dêianeira, our lady, has
	gone her last journey,
	with no step taken!
LEADER:	Surely not dead!
NURSE:	You've heard all there is.
LEADER:	Dead!
	Poor woman!
NURSE:	You hear it again.

(The Chorus, in shock, begins a low lament, muttering and whispering among its members, occasionally reiterating words heard in the discussion.)

LEADER:	Poor lady—
	lost—
	How?
NURSE:	Horrible, too horrible—
	the telling of it.
LEADER:	Tell me, woman, how she
	met her doom.
NURSE:	Destroyed herself—
LEADER:	What frenzy pushed her?
	What passion?
NURSE:	A blade—
	a point—
	two edges—
LEADER:	Death upon death.
	Alone. All alone.
NURSE:	A swift blade's thrust.
LEADER:	And, helpless, you
	saw her terrible act?
NURSE:	I saw it—
	watching—
	near her—
	there—
LEADER:	Tell me.
	How?

NURSE:	Her own mind's
	work. Her own
	hand's doing.
LEADER:	How can you say it?
NURSE:	The truth.
LEADER:	The first-born,
	the first-born
	of the new-come bride
	has birthed a mighty
	Fury for this
	house!

(The music breaks off suddenly as the Chorus disperses.)

NURSE: True! If you had been there to see,
 Your pity would be even greater.
LEADER: Can a woman's hands dare such a thing?
NURSE: They could! And it was terrible! Listen;
 I'll tell you; then you can bear me witness.

 She went into the house—went in alone—
 And there in the courtyard saw her son prepare
 A litter to carry his father back.
 She hid herself then where no one could see,
 And threw herself at the altars, moaning her grief
 That soon those altars would be abandoned.
 And anything she touched that once she'd used,
 Some domestic piece, or, rushing through the house,
 Saw a much-loved servant, she would cry,
 Poor creature, howl at her fate and the fate
 Of her house, that they would have no more children.
 Then stopping suddenly, she rushes into his room,
 The room that she had shared with Heraklês,
 And unseen by her, I watch from a hidden place.
 She makes his bed, her husband's bed, casting
 Coverings over it, and then leaps into its middle
 And dissolves in a flood of hot tears, saying:
 "Dear bed, dear bed of love, goodbye forever!
 You'll never again hold me as a wife!"

She was quiet then. But all at once,
With a violent sweep, she tears open her robe,
Held at her breast by a golden brooch, baring
Her whole left side and arm.
As fast as I could,
I ran to tell her son of what she planned,
But time ran out, and when we returned she'd thrust
A two-edged sword deep in her side and heart.
Her son shrieked at the sight. He knew, poor child,
That his rage had driven her to this; he learned too late
From the house's servants that she had acted in innocence,
Prompted by the monster's words.
Howling his anguish,
The poor boy knelt and rained kisses on her lips,
Stretched out beside her, weeping bitter tears
That he'd killed her with his anger and slanderous words,
And now had to live an orphan—fatherless—motherless.
(Music begins softly as a transition leading into the choral ode.)
That's how things are inside this house.
Only a fool counts on the future
Before we've passed today unharmed!
(During her final lines, the Nurse moves toward the house and goes off. At the same time the Chorus takes up a new position in the orchestra and begins a dance of lamentation.)

CHORUS: Whom shall I
                moan for
                    first? Whose
            misfortune is more
                grievous?
                    Ah, misery!
            I cannot
                tell, cannot
                    judge!
            One sorrow we can
                see in the house,
                    the other is
            expected;
                pain and suspense:
                    there is no difference.

Where,
    where is the
        breeze to
blow me away,
    blast me from this
        house, from its
hearth, to
    save me from
        dying of terror,
terror, terror
    at the
        sight, the mere
sight of him,
    Zeus' son,
        Heraklês, mighty
Heraklês,
    coming, coming
        in pain,
pain unstoppable,
    a sight of
        unutterable
sorrow!

(The procession enters left preceded by Servants carrying the unmoving Heraklês on a litter. The procession's progress is exceedingly slow.)

When I
    mourned for him
like the shrill-voiced
    nightingale, it was for
        what was near, not
far, not
    far, for here are
        strangers approaching,
strangers from
    far away! How,
        how are they
bringing him?
    How?
        In sorrow,
as if for a

friend; in
         silence, with a
heavy tread.
         Aiiiiiiiiiiiiii!
            Aiiiiiiiiiiiiii!
As they
         carry him, he says
               nothing. Is he
dead?
         Is he
               sleeping?

(Hyllos, followed by an Old Doctor, enters last, at the end of the procession, after the litter bearing Heraklês has been set down in front of the palace. The Chorus reacts to the scene.)

HYLLOS: Oimoiiiiii!
                  Father!
                     O sorrow sorrow!
                  What can I do?
                     How can I help?
                        Oimoiiiiii!

OLD DOCTOR: Hush, son, hush, don't,
                     waken his wild pain;
                        it turns him savage!
                  He is alive,
                     though his life is fading.
                        Bite your lip, son,
                  control yourself!

HYLLOS: What are you
                     saying, old man?
                  Is he alive?

OLD DOCTOR: Let him sleep.
                     Don't waken the
                  ever-recurring fury
                     that wracks his body!
                        Let him sleep, son!

HYLLOS: My grief, old man,
                     my grief weighs me
                        down! Old man,
                  I'll go mad!

(Heraklês wakes on the litter and attempts to raise himself but cannot. He catches sight of Zeus' statue.)

HERAKLÊS: O Zeus!
                            God!
                   Father!
                         What is this place?
                               What people are these,
                   watching my agonies?
                         Oimoi moiiiiiiiiiii!
                               No! It
                   gnaws me again,
                         gnaws me,
                               gnaws me!
                   Féu!
                         Féu!

OLD DOCTOR: See what you've done?
                   I told you silence!
                         You've swept away sleep,
                               sleep from his head,
                   sleep from his eyes!

HYLLOS: How can I bear to
                         watch such misery?
                   How?

HERAKLÊS: Ah, Kênaion!
                         Rock where I raised my
                   altars in sacrifice; and you,
                         Zeus, you, is this your
                               thanks, this torture,
                   this outrage? If only I had
                         never seen that place, never
                               seen that place of my destruction!
                   Never known, never, this
                         incurable flower, this flower of
                               madness, that blossoms inside me!
                   Where is the healer, where the
                         singer of charms, the surgeon's
                               hands, where, where,
                   save Zeus alone,
                         to calm my agony?

Oh, to see him!
Only to see him
would be a miracle!
É!
É!
Let me be!
O let me sleep! Man of misery!
My last sleep!
(The Old Doctor moves to raise Heraklês to a sitting position.)
Ah, why are you touching me?
Why moving me?
You're killing me!
Killing me!
Waking the demon
that was lulled to rest!
It has me again!
Tototoi!
Has me! Gnawing!
Gnawing! Where are you
from, you who call yourselves
Greeks! Most unrighteous,
ungrateful of men!
For you I destroyed my
life, for you! Cleared
monsters from your seas and
forests! But now, now, when
pain tears me, will no one
plunge his sword deep in my
side? No one bring
merciful fire to end my
agony?
É!
É!
Will no one come
to hack the head
from my loathsome body!
Féu!
Féu!
(The Old Doctor is unable to restrain Heraklês.)

OLD DOCTOR: O son, son,
I can't anymore!
No more strength
left to my age!
Help me here!
Your hands are strong
to bring him comfort!
(Hyllos has put his arms around the thrashing Heraklês.)
HYLLOS: My hands are doing all they
can, but no one, not I, not
anyone, can make his life
forget its misery! His fate
is the will of Zeus!
HERAKLÊS: É!
É!
Son,
son!
Where are you?
Where?
Raise me!
Hold me!
Here! Here!
É!
É!
Iooooooo!
Daimôn!
What is this fate? What?
It comes again!
Leaps at me!
Evil, evil thing!
Tears me! Again!
Again! Destroying!
O god! The pain!
Unspeakable!
Ah, savage fury!
O Pallas!
Goddess!
Sister!
Again the outrage!

Again!
Have pity, son!
Pity for your father!
Strike with your sword!
Strike! Here in my chest!
No one will blame you!
Heal the pain your godless
mother brought down on me!
O god, to see her suffer as I do!
The same! The same!
The same pain! The same
destruction!
Aiiiiiiii!
Aiiiiiiiiiii!
Sweet Lord of
Death, Zeus' brother,
give me
rest, give me
sleep, let my
doom
be
swift—

(The music fades out.)

LEADER: Dear friends, I tremble to hear our master's pain.
How can a great man suffer so terribly?

HERAKLÊS: Even to speak of the burdens this back has borne,
The pain these hands have labored through, is a torment!
Not even Zeus' wife or the loathsome Eurystheus
Laid on me such torments as the two-faced
Daughter of Oineüs.
It was she who threw across my shoulders
This net woven by Furies that now destroys me!
Glued to my sides, it gnaws at my inner flesh!
It lives inside me and sucks the breath from my lungs.
It has drunk my blood, wasted my body,
Conquered me by this unspeakable bondage!
No warrior's spear, no horde of earth-born Giants,
No savage beast, no Greek, no barbarian land
That I purged of evil ever did such a thing!

But a woman, an unmanly woman, did this to me,
Alone, unarmed, destroyed me!

Hyllos, son, prove that you're truly my son!
Never honor your mother's name above mine.
Bring her to me, here, with your own hands,
That woman who bore you, and show whom you pity most:
Me, here, in my wretched agony,
Or her, when she suffers the pain she deserves.
Go, my boy. Be brave now. Pity me,
As I am pitiful to many others,
Weeping here like a weak-willed girl.
A sight no man can claim ever to have seen.
I never complained, wherever my fortune took me,
However evil. But look at him now! The hero!
A woman to the core!
                              Come closer. Here.
Stand by your father. Look! At the misery he endures!
Look! Under the coverings. All of you. Look!
This body! Agonized! This wretched, sight!
Aiiiiiiiiiiii!
              Aiiiiiiiiiiii!
                              O talas! Aiiiiiiiiiiii!
                                            Aiiiiiiiiiiii!

It comes again, the burning,
Burning, stabbing, stabbing,
Stabbing my sides, again,
Again! I must fight it,
Fight it, eating,
Inside me!

O Lord of the Dark Regions,
Take me! Zeus!
Your fire, quickly,
Strike!
          King!
                    Father!
Blast me with your bolt!
It tears me again,

Eating me,
Blossoms into searing flame!

O hands, hands, shoulders, chest, my arms—
(A pause. The pain recedes, leaving him more control.)
Can I believe your former feats of glory?
It was *you* by force of strength subdued
And killed the man-eating Nemean lion,
The scourge of flocks and herdsmen that none could approach!
You that rid the land of the Lernian Hydra,
And of that monstrous union, man and steed,
Strong beyond believing, violent, lawless!
And the Erymanthian boar! And the three-headed hound
From Death's dark kingdom under earth,
Invincible creature, born of the dread Echidna!
And the dragon that guarded the golden apples
At the farthest reaches of earth's domain!
These few, and countless others, mine, all mine,
Toil on toil on toil,
And no one took the spoil from these hands!
But now, broken, torn, my body wasted,
I lie here miserable prey to unseen disaster!
I, called the son of the noblest mother!
I, called the son of Zeus himself,
Lord of the starry heavens!
But though I am nothing,
Nothing that even can crawl,
Bring her to me, I say, bring her to me,
Who did these things!
And these hands, these *hands*
Will teach her to tell to the world
That in death as in life I punished evildoers!
LEADER: Greece! Unhappy land! What will you do,
If death deprives you of him!
HYLLOS: Father, since your silence permits me to speak,
However great your pain, listen to me.
I ask nothing more from you than is right.
Control your anger, Father, or you won't understand
How useless your vengeance is, how misdirected.

HERAKLÊS: Say what you have to say. My pain
    Is too great for your riddling words.
HYLLOS: It's my mother. I've come to tell you what happened,
    And how she never meant to harm you.
HERAKLÊS: Traitor! How dare you utter her name!
    The very mother who killed your father!
HYLLOS: I have to speak—to tell you of her.
HERAKLÊS: Yes, of all the wrongs in her past!
HYLLOS: No, of what she did today.
HERAKLÊS: Yes, go on—just don't betray me.
HYLLOS: All right, then, here it is—she's dead.
HERAKLÊS: Who did it? What disastrous good news!
HYLLOS: She did—no one but her own hand.
HERAKLÊS: Ah, it should have been *these* hands killed her!
HYLLOS: You wouldn't rage if you knew the truth.
HERAKLÊS: A strange beginning, but don't stop there.
HYLLOS: She intended good, but it all went wrong.
HERAKLÊS: Killing your father—a good deed?
HYLLOS: When she saw your new bride in her house,
    She tried to work a love-charm on you,
    And it all went wrong.
HERAKLÊS: What Trachian makes such potent drugs?
HYLLOS: Long ago Nessos the Centaur
    Told her the charm would kindle your love.
HERAKLÊS: Ah! Ah! I'm dead! Dead!
    No more light for me now, only doom!
    Son, your father is no more.
    Call your brothers, and my mother, Alkmênê,
    The luckless bedmate of Zeus.
    My last words will be of the prophecies
    The oracles have told of my life.
HYLLOS: Your mother lives by the sea at Tiryns
    With some of your children, the others at Thebes.
    But those of us here will do what must be done.
HERAKLÊS: Then listen to the task you have in store!
    The time has come to prove yourself my son.

    Zeus my father told me long ago
    That no living thing would ever kill me,

But that I would die at the hands of one
Who lived with the dead in Hades. And so it is:
The dead killing the living; the divine prophecy
Fulfilled by the brute Centaur. But recent prophecies
Agree with the old.

When I was in the mountains
Among the Selloi who sleep on the bare earth,
I wrote them down from my father's sacred oak
That speaks in many tongues.
It said that when the present time came round
I would be released of all my labors.
I thought it meant I'd lead a happy life;
But now I know it means that I will die.
The dead alone are free of labors, son;
It's all so clear now; so you must help,
Stand by me to the end and never hesitate
And make me use harsh words. Accept with grace
The help I seek, and learn that the greatest law
Is obedience to the father.

HYLLOS: Father, it frightens me what you'll say next;
    But I'll do whatever you ask.
HERAKLÊS: First put your right hand in mine.
HYLLOS: Is this really necessary?
HERAKLÊS: Your hand! Don't disobey!
HYLLOS: There, my hand. Whatever you say.
HERAKLÊS: Swear by the head of Zeus my Father!
HYLLOS: What must I swear to? Tell me that!
HERAKLÊS: Whatever I ask, whatever task!
HYLLOS: I will. I swear in Zeus' name.
HERAKLÊS: Under pain if you violate it!
HYLLOS: Violate? No. I'll keep my oath.
HERAKLÊS: Do you know the mountain sacred to Zeus—Oïtê?
HYLLOS: Yes, I've often sacrificed there.
HERAKLÊS: You must carry me there with your own hands
    And with the help of whatever friends you need.
    And when you have cut down many deep-rooted oaks,
    And sturdy, gnarled branches of wild olive,
    Pile them up, and lay me on them,

And fire it with a flaming torch of pine.
Do this for me if you are truly my son!
But not with tears or laments, no weeping or moaning,
Or I will curse you from the grave forever.

HYLLOS: Ah! Father! What are you saying?

HERAKLÊS: I'm saying what you must do! If not,
Forget that I'm your father! Get another one!

HYLLOS: No, Father, you can't mean it!
I? Your murderer? Your blood on my hands?

HERAKLÊS: Murderer? No, not murderer! Healer!
My healer! The only physician to cure
This misery that torments me!

HYLLOS: Heal your body by burning? How?

HERAKLÊS: If this is too much, then do the rest.

HYLLOS: I'll carry you there. I can do that much.

HERAKLÊS: And heap the pyre high, as I've asked?

HYLLOS: With my own hands? I could never touch it!
Everything else you ask, I'll do.

HERAKLÊS: That's good enough. Just one thing more.
One small service more.

HYLLOS: Yes, no matter how large, I'll do it.

HERAKLÊS: You know the girl? Eurytos' daughter?

HYLLOS: Iolê. Yes?

HERAKLÊS: You know her, then. Do this for me, son.
Once I'm dead, if you care to honor your oaths,
Then marry her. Don't refuse. She's lain beside me,
So no other man must have her. Promise me!
Fail in this small matter and you lose my thanks!

HYLLOS: How to argue with a man in pain!
But how can I hear this and say nothing?

HERAKLÊS: What does this mean? You refuse?

HYLLOS: I can't help it! *She* caused my mother's death
And brought you to *this!*
Only a man driven mad by avenging fiends
Would make such a choice! I'd rather die
Than marry my bitterest enemy!

HERAKLÊS: Disobey me? My dying wish?
The avenging gods will chase you down!

HYLLOS: This is your sickness talking, Father!

HERAKLÊS: My sickness slept until you woke it!
HYLLOS: Gods, I'm helpless wherever I turn!
HERAKLÊS: Yes, because you refuse your father!
HYLLOS: You'd have me do an impious act?
HERAKLÊS: Impious if it gives me joy?
HYLLOS: Is this your order? This my duty?
HERAKLÊS: Yes! And let the gods bear witness!
HYLLOS: I'll do it —with the gods to witness.
    Can it be wrong to obey a father?
HERAKLÊS: There's my son, at last.
    Now turn words into deed.
    Take me to the pyre and lay me
    High on the branches before my pain
    Comes again to tear and sting me!

    Come. Lift me. Quickly.
    Labors' end.
    The end of all my miseries.
    The end of Heraklês.
HYLLOS: Nothing prevents your will's fulfillment, Father.
    It is your command moves us. We have no choice.
    (Music fades in.)
HERAKLÊS: Come, then, my stubborn soul, be hard,
    let not my sickness be roused again.
    Fix a brace of steel to my lips,
    like stone against stone, to curb my cry.
    Make an end of Heraklês,
    and welcome the unwelcome task.
    (The Servants lift the litter as Hyllos speaks and begin the procession toward the left.)
HYLLOS: Lift him, men, and forgive what I do.
    But mark the gods' indifference,
    for this is their doing, their cruelty.
    They spawn children, call themselves father,
    and then sit back and watch them suffer.
    (Chanting.)

            None sees the future,
            but now is the present,
            and what we see

is pitiful for us,
shame for the gods,
and for him who endures,
pain, pain.

(To the Leader.)

Come, girl,
leave this house.
The death, the agonies
you've seen today,
many and terrible,
are nothing,
nothing,
but Zeus.

(Hyllos goes off, left, following the Servants bearing the litter. The Chorus follows in procession.)
(The music dies away.)
(Darkness.)

OEDIPUS TYRANNOS
(ΟΙΔΙΠΟΥΣ ΤΥΡΑΝΝΟΣ)

CAST OF CHARACTERS

OEDIPUS *King of Thebes*
A PRIEST
KREON *brother of Iokastê*
TEIRESIAS *blind prophet*
IOKASTÊ *queen and wife of Oedipus*
KORINTHIAN MESSENGER
SHEPHERD
PALACE MESSENGER
ANTIGONÊ *daughter of Oedipus and Iokastê*
ISMENÊ *daughter of Oedipus and Iokastê*
CHORUS OF THEBAN CITIZENS
LEADER OF THE CHORUS
SUPPLIANTS
GUARDS
ATTENDANTS
PRIESTS

The lines of the Chorus, unless otherwise indicated, are to be delivered by individual voices and varied groups of voices.

OEDIPUS TYRANNOS

Dawn. Thebes. The skênê represents the palace of King Oedipus. A large double door dominates the façade. On either side of the circular orchestra is an entrance, the right leading to the city, the left to the country. In the center of the orchestra stands a smoking, carved stone altar. A large, slow procession of Priests and Suppliants enters praying and moaning; they carry branches wound in wool which they place on and around the altar. The doors open and Oedipus, walking with a noticeable limp, enters.

OEDIPUS: Children, why have you come, why are you here,
    Suppliants, bearing branches wound with wool,
    Crouching at my altars? I look around,
    I see our city heavy with clouds of incense;
    I hear cries and groans to Apollo Healer,
    Prayers, rumors of disaster. But no news,
    No messenger's news can tell me what I need
    To know, so I have come myself, I, Oedipus,
    Known to everyone.
    (Helping an old Priest to his feet.)
    Come, old man, old priest of Zeus, stand up,
    Speak for them all, your age gives you that right.
    I know, I see, their hearts are heavy with fear;
    It's why I have come, for there's nothing I won't do,
    Nothing to help them. My heart isn't made of stone
    And proof against pity. How could it be? These are mine,
    My people, groaning, suffering, here at my feet.
PRIEST: Oedipus, ruler of Thebes, you see before you,
    Prostrate at your altars, men of all ages.
    Boys not strong enough to fly the nest;
    Others, old men weighted with years, priests
    Like me, the priest of Zeus; and here, youths
    Chosen from those not married, our dearest treasure.
    But we are not all, my lord, there are many more,
    Crowding the city square with wreathed branches,
    Praying before the twin temples of Athêna,
    And the prophetic ashes of Ismênos.

You have only to look, my lord, to see your city
Awash on a stormy sea, tossed by a current
That will not let it raise its head from the depths!
Billows of red death! Our trees are blighted
In the bud, herds of cattle, sheep and goats,
Wither, collapse in the fields, our women give birth
To stillborn things, and we, we stagger and stumble,
Weak with hunger, gasping for air, for breath,
While the cruel god of fever, searing fever,
Swoops down upon us, cutting, slashing, seizing
Our city, emptying houses, hateful Plague!
Draining the house of Kadmos to its dregs,
While Death, Black Death battens on our miseries!

My King, we haven't come because we think
Of you as of a god; no, we know you
To be a man and only a man; all of us
Know this, even the young, crouching here.
We know you as the first and noblest of men;
A man well practiced in the ways of life
And living, as well as wise in the ways of god.
You freed us from that harsh singer the Sphinx
And cut the cord that bound us to the tribute
We paid to her. Not one of us gave you advice
Or instructed you or helped in any way.
And yet you triumphed; a god was with you, they say;
We all know that: you saved our lives that day.

So now, Oedipus, we turn again to you,
We, kneeling here, for only the greatest of men
Can lead us to a cure. It's not important
Where the advice comes from, god or man,
We trust you to know what is needed. So help us now:
You, a man tested by experience,
A man who wields power: fuse action and thought
And make us well! Raise up suffering Thebes!
This land that calls you savior for what you did
Long ago must never be remembered
As one who lifted us once, then let us fall.
Raise us to our feet again, Oedipus!

Raise our city high as you did once!
Signs were good that day you brought us luck!
Be that man again! You have the power
Of wisdom to rule the land; but what use
Is a land of barren waste: rule a land
Of men, a land where men live and work
In harmony of mind and spirit! What use
Is a towered city or a ship when empty of men
Striving in powerful union?
OEDIPUS: Children! How I pity you! I know
The need that brings you here! Believe me, I know
How sick you are; and yet, of all of you,
Not one is sicker than I. The pain you suffer
Strikes each of you alone; and yet, my heart
Grieves for each of you, and for myself,
And for the city.
No, you haven't roused me,
Not wakened me from sleep, for I have wept
Bitter tears through many anxious nights;
My thoughts have groped and stumbled down many paths,
Till finally I have come to see the cure
That I have acted on. I have sent Kreon,
My wife's brother, to Apollo's shrine at Delphi,
Instructing him to learn from the Pythian oracle
What prayers or rituals I can offer to help me
Save Thebes from certain destruction and death.
(Kreon, a wreath of laurel on his head, enters, left, unseen by Oedipus. He
is accompanied by several Attendants.)
What can be keeping him? Where can he be?
He has been gone too long by now. It troubles me.
But once he arrives, I would be a traitor
If I failed to carry out what the god reveals.
PRIEST: Well spoken, and just in time!
He's here!
OEDIPUS: Lord Apollo, let him come with news
As bright as the gleam in his eyes!
PRIEST: The news is good!
His head is crowned with laurel
Heavy with berries.

OEDIPUS: We will know soon enough;
    He can hear us now.
    Kreon, what news has Apollo sent us?
KREON: News that we should find hopeful.
    Troubles hard to bear, he says, are bearable
    If all goes well!
OEDIPUS: Yes, but I don't understand.
    What does it mean? I have heard riddles.
    What do we do?
KREON: In front of these people? Now?
    We can go inside.
OEDIPUS: No, let the city hear!
    I pity my people their agony!
    My people mean more than my life!
KREON: Then here are the god's words, clear beyond doubt.
    Apollo commands that we are to drive from Thebes
    The ancient pollution that stains everything and everyone,
    A pollution that we have nourished for many years,
    That eats at our very core! We must purge it away,
    Root it out of our soil before its evil
    Spreads beyond any hope of effecting a cure.
OEDIPUS: Pollution? What are you saying?
    How can we purify Thebes?
KREON: Banishment or blood. Blood for blood.
    For bloodshed sent this plague-storm on our city.
OEDIPUS: Who is this man the god condemns?
KREON: Before you arrived and set our city on course
    And took up power, Laïos ruled in Thebes.
OEDIPUS: I know. I have heard. I never saw him.
KREON: Laïos was murdered. Apollo commands us now—
    And very clearly, too—to avenge those men.
    Whoever they are.
OEDIPUS: But where? Where are they?
    How do we to find clues to so old a crime?
KREON: Apollo says here in Thebes.
    What we pursue will be caught;
    What not, slips past.
OEDIPUS: Where was Laïos murdered?
    In his palace? Out of the country?

KREON: He said he was going to Delphi.

He never returned.

OEDIPUS: Was no one with him? No messenger?

No one to tell what happened?

No witness?

KREON: All but one were killed, and he fled in panic.

He remembered only one thing for certain.

OEDIPUS: And? One clue can lead to others.

KREON: He said that he was killed not by one man,

But a marauding horde of bandits.

OEDIPUS: Bandit? Kill a king? How would he dare!

Unless he was paid in Theban gold.

KREON: We suspected as much. But Laïos was dead;

We had no king to help us in our distress.

OEDIPUS: Your king killed, your throne empty,

And you failed to uncover every shred of evidence?

KREON: The riddling song of the Sphinx persuaded us otherwise.

It seemed to tell us to deal not with the past,

But with the present, with our more immediate troubles.

OEDIPUS: Then I will begin again and bring truth to light.

It was good of the god and of you, Kreon,

To rise again in defense of the dead man.

You will find in me a strong ally in fighting

His cause and in avenging the city and Apollo.

And yet, in purging Thebes, I won't be acting

To defend some distant friend, but for my sake;

For whatever man killed him, killed Laïos, might turn

His hand against me. In defending Laïos,

I defend myself.

(To the Priests and Suppliants.)

Quickly, children, up from these steps,

And take up your suppliants' boughs!

(To the Guards.)

Call the people of Thebes to assembly!

Tell them that I will do everything possible to help;

And if the god wills, luck will triumph;

If not, then we are doomed.

(Music begins as several Guards hurry off and Oedipus and Kreon turn to begin their entrance into the palace, followed by the remaining Guards. At

the same time the Priest turns to address the Suppliants, rousing them and urging them to pick up their branches and leave the altar.)

PRIEST: Rise, children! We have what we came for:

Our King's promise to act!

(He turns to the altar.)

May Apollo who sent these oracles come himself

To deliver us from this plague!

(The Suppliants rise and pick up their wound branches from the altar and disperse around the orchestra in various combinations. At the same time, the Chorus of Theban Citizens enters right. Here, as elsewhere throughout the play, they speak sometimes together, sometimes separately in varying combinations.)

LEADER: How sweet is the message of Zeus!

What word do you bring me from Delphi?

From Pytho's gold-rich temple?

What word do you bring here to Thebes?

To Thebes, my glorious city?

Healer of Delos, I tremble!

God of the rapturous cry,

my heart is shaken with terror!

Reveal to me, god, your demands!

CHORUS: What do you ask me?

What is your will?

What new doom

do you bring upon me?

Or is it renewed

with the circling years?

CHORUS:

Raise up your voice, immortal daughter!

Child of Golden Hope, give us hope!

LEADER: Athêna, first I summon you;

daughter of Zeus; eternal maiden!

And then your sister, throned in the market;

splendid Artemis, land's guardian!

And Apollo, archer of the unfailing aim!

Triple defenders against doom, appear!

Rise before me! Let me see you!

You who shielded me once!

CHORUS: Appear!

LEADER: You who averted my ruin!
CHORUS: Appear!
LEADER: You who defended my city!
CHORUS: Appear!
LEADER: Gods who banished the fires of doom!
CHORUS: Hear me!
LEADER: You the triple defenders of Thebes!
CHORUS: Help me!
LEADER: Unnumbered the miseries that beat me down;
                unnumbered the lives Plague drags into darkness.
                Where is the sword of the mind to protect me?
                My glorious fields are barren of fruit;
                my women in labor cannot give birth.
CHORUS: Lives take wing like
                   birds in flight:
                   sparks that rise
                   when fire rages;
                   hastening into
                   darkening death.

(The Chorus' tone grows hushed, ominous, and its ranks begin to disintegrate as one member after another darts with increasing speed from one area of the orchestra to another in a frenzied choreography, their voices gradually rising to a frantic pitch at the end, and their phrases wildly overlapping.)

CHORUS: —The city wavers,
                   stumbles,
                      falls!
                Unnumbered
                   dead, graveless
                      bodies, heavy with
                death,
                   unmourned! Young
                      wives, ancient
                mothers,
                   herd around
                      steps of
                altars from all
                   directions!
                         Grieving!
                Raising

prayers to
Apollo! Cries!
Laments! Golden
child of
Zeus,
Athêna, send
lovely Strength!
Arês, fire-raging
god! Arês,
god of
war,
storms among us!
Fever-bringing,
feverous god!
Unarmored he comes!
Unshielded he comes!
He burns me!
Burns me!
Bruiting his
clamorous song!
Drive him,
drive him
back from my
borders! Cast him
out into the vast
sea of Amphitritê!
Or into the turbulent
harbor of Thrake!
If tonight I
escape him, the
fiery god, the
god of
death, his
fever
returns with the
sun, and I
die!
—Zeus!
Father!

Ruler of
    stormwind! Whose
bolts are
    lightning!
        Destroy!
Destroy the
    invader!
        Crush him with the
thunder of your
    brow!
        —Apollo Lykêios!
Lord of
    light! Be my
        defender! String your
bow with the
    sun's golden
        threads!
Shoot with unerring
    aim against my
        enemy! Let your
arrows stand
    guard before Thebes!
        —And, Artemis, you,
racing with fiery
    torches over
        Lykêian hills!
Drive harsh
    death from our land!
        —And I call
now upon
    you,
        Bakkhos!
Bakkhos!
    God of
        wine-dark
eyes!
    Hair bound
        back with
golden

band! Who
bears our city's
name!
Master of
maenads who cry
eüoi!
Descend with your
torch upon
Arês! The
fiery god! The
feverous god!
God of
death!
Burn him!
Burn him!
Burn him whom
all the
gods
hate!

(The Chorus' frenzy suddenly freezes into icy silence. The music then faintly reasserts itself as Oedipus enters through the large doors of the palace and addresses the Theban Elders. The music fades out.)

OEDIPUS: My people, listen to me. I have heard your prayers
And supplications, and I am moved by your plight.
Now here is an answer; but you must do your part, too.
Help me to your cure, do as required,
And soon you will be relieved of all your pains.

Until today, I knew nothing of this tale.
How could I have known of Laïos' death,
Or of the murder, without some link with you?
How could I have tracked the murderer
Without a clue? I was a stranger here,
A stranger to the crime as to the city,
Arriving only after your king's death,
Made a Theban only then.

But hear me out.
There is one among you knows who killed King Laïos,

Son of Labdakos; one among you
Who knows the man whose hand did the deed,
Who held the instrument. Who is he? I ask you
To tell me now. I command you by my authority,
Step forward and speak. And fear is no excuse.
Even if he incriminates himself,
Let him speak and clear himself of the charge.
I assure him that he will not be harmed,
He will not go stumbling into exile,
But leave the land in good and proper health.
(Silence: no response.)
If anyone knows the murderer to be a stranger,
A foreigner from an alien land, let him speak,
For he will have a reward as well as my gratitude.
(Silence: no response.)
If, however, you keep your silence, refusing
To speak in hope of shielding yourself or a friend
Or loved one from my edict, then hear this:
I command every citizen of the land
Where I hold throne and power to give no shelter
Or word to him, whoever he may be!
Shut your doors against him! Deny him place
In your prayers and sacrifices and lustrations!
Drive him from every hearth, from every house,
Drive him out of Thebes, out of the land,
For he is our pollution, our corruption,
Our disease, as the god's Pythian Oracle,
God's word of prophecy, has revealed to me!
And I, as god's own ally, Apollo's warrior,
Take up arms now in defense of the dead man.

As for the murderer, whether he acted alone,
A single man and unknown, or one of many,
I pray that his evil life be ground down
To miserable and wretched days!

As for me,
If I have given shelter and shared my hearth,
Knowingly, with that man, may the same curse

Turn back to haunt me. These are my orders:
Do it for me, do it for Apollo,
Do it for the land that withers barren
Under pitiless heavens. Even had the gods
Never thrown you into such misery,
You should never have given up your search
To seek out the culprit and wipe the land
Free of the stain. He was your king who died,
First among men! But now, holding the power
That he once held, holding his marital bed
And wife, the wife who now bears me children
That might have been his had Chance not denied him a son,
A son who would have been my children's brother,
Sharing blood between us: I say now:
I will take up his cause as son to father,
And vow not to give up the fight till the hand
That murdered Laïos son of Labdakos,
Sprung from Polydoros and Kadmos before him
And from Agenoros long ago,
Is brought to light!
And to those who will not listen,
Who refuse to help, may the gods blight your fields
Till you die of hunger, and may they infect the wombs
Of your wives with stony barrenness! May you perish
Of the plague that ravages us now, or one more terrible!

As for you men of Thebes, loyal citizens
Of Kadmos' city who support me in this, may Justice,
Our ally, and all the gods stand by and protect us
In the battle still to come!
LEADER: In light of your curse, my lord, I can only say
That I am not the murderer, nor can I point
To the one who is. Apollo ordered the search,
Apollo should properly tell us where to find him.
OEDIPUS: A man force a god to speak?
LEADER: Then may I suggest the next best thing?
OEDIPUS: Even if it is a third, let us hear it.
(Teiresias, an aged, blind prophet, enters, right, from the city, led by a Boy

along with Attendants. Because of the prophet's age their progress in the cross is slow and tortuous.)

LEADER: The prophet Teiresias, sir.
　　Next to Apollo, he has the keenest sight
　　Where truth is concerned.
　　We could learn from him.

OEDIPUS: Teiresias, yes! On Kreon's advice,
　　I have sent for him already. Twice, in fact.
　　Where could he be?

LEADER: Except for him, there are only rumors.

OEDIPUS: Such as? I will consider everything.

LEADER: That Laïos was killed by bandits.

OEDIPUS: I've heard; but where is the murderer now?

LEADER: If he has any fear in him,
　　And has heard your curses,
　　He's not in Thebes now.

OEDIPUS: Words won't frighten a killer of kings!

LEADER: Here is the only man who knows:
　　The holy, inspired prophet. God's truth
　　Lives bright as day in his dark eyes.

OEDIPUS: Teiresias, seer who knows all things,
　　Master of omens earthly and divine,
　　Of things that can be learned, and things mysterious:
　　Though your eyes are blind, you see and know
　　The plague that sears our city. You alone, my lord,
　　Can save us from this destruction. You may have heard;
　　If not, then I will tell you.

　　Apollo has sent us word through his Pythian oracle,
　　That if Thebes is ever to raise its head from this pestilence,
　　We must first find the murderers of Laïos,
　　And then either kill them or send then into exile.
　　Share your gifts now, old man, your powers
　　Of divination; read the flights of birds,
　　Or else use other means, but spare us nothing—
　　Nothing. Pull us from danger. Care for yourself,
　　Care for your city, for me; rescue us
　　From the vile pollution the dead man brings upon us.
　　There can be no nobler act for a man
　　Than to use every means in helping others.

TEIRESIAS: How terrible truth can be when all it brings
To the one who knows is pain! I knew this once,
I knew it well, but I drove it out. I forgot.
No, I should never have come.
OEDIPUS: Never have come?
Why so bleak, so despairing?
TEIRESIAS: Let me go home!
You bear your fate, I will bear mine;
It is better this way.
OEDIPUS: Who are you to say such things to Thebes
That gave you life! Tell us what you know!
TEIRESIAS: Be careful: your own words
Are not as well-aimed as you may think.
I won't have the same be said of mine.
OEDIPUS: We beg you in the god's name!
Tell us what you see!
TEIRESIAS: You're blind—all of you;
You know nothing. Leave me my sorrow;
I will leave you yours!
OEDIPUS: Know and not tell?
Are you set on betraying Thebes?
Destroying your city?
TEIRESIAS: Why grieve myself or you?
Why insist? I will tell you nothing!
OEDIPUS: Despicable, villainous old man!
You could inflame a stone to anger!
Won't talk, eh? Well, I say *talk!*
TEIRESIAS: You rant against *my* temper?
You don't know the one *you* live with!
OEDIPUS: Who could listen to your insults and not be angry!
You shame your city!
TEIRESIAS: Speech or silence, what will be will be.
OEDIPUS: If what will be will be, then tell me!
TEIRESIAS: No! Nothing! Rage on!
I have nothing to say!
OEDIPUS: And rage I will! For I *will* speak!
Yes, and in anger, too! All I suspect!
Hear me now!
I say that *you* helped plot the death of Laïos!

Plotted it in every way you could,
Even though your hand never struck a blow!
Oh, and if you had eyes, I would even say
You did that, too!

TEIRESIAS: Aha!
Then take responsibility for your own words
And carry out your edict to the letter:
Never to speak another word to me
Or to anyone here in Thebes: for you yourself
Are this land's curse, you are this land's corruption!
You! The plague is you!

OEDIPUS: And you really think to get by with this?

TEIRESIAS: I have already. My strength is truth.

OEDIPUS: Who taught you this? Your prophet's craft?

TEIRESIAS: You! In forcing me to speak.

OEDIPUS: Then say it again so I will understand!

TEIRESIAS: Did I make no sense? Are you testing me now?

OEDIPUS: Not so I know it clearly! Again!

TEIRESIAS: You—you are the murderer you're hunting.

OEDIPUS: Say that once more and see what happens!

TEIRESIAS: Do you want more to fan your anger?

OEDIPUS: Say what you will! Your words are worthless!

TEIRESIAS: I say that you are living a life of shame
With those who are closest to you,
And yet you know nothing, blind to the evil!

OEDIPUS: You'll pay for this, old man.

TEIRESIAS: Not while there is strength in truth.

OEDIPUS: There is, just not in yours—you,
Blind in your ears, your mind, your eyes!

TEIRESIAS: It is you who are blind, and all men
Will soon curse you, as you curse me.

OEDIPUS: Protected by darkness, you could never harm me
Or any other man with sight.

TEIRESIAS: It is not for me to take you down;
Apollo has that well in hand.

OEDIPUS: Are these inventions Kreon's or yours?

TEIRESIAS: Kreon's no threat. Your doom is yourself.

OEDIPUS: Ah, wealth! Ah, kingship! Skill excelling skill
In life's great contests! What envy is stored up

Against you here, if Kreon, loyal Kreon,
Trusted friend, plots in secret to steal
My throne, a throne not sought by me but offered
By Thebes in gratitude, and brings in tow
This charlatan, conniving beggar-priest,
Whose eyes are blind to prophecy, but keen
In seeking profit!

Tell me, *friend* Teiresias:
When was your skill as prophet ever proved?
Not when that raucous singer chanted her spells
Of death and destruction!
Why were you silent then?
Where were your words to liberate this city?
Her riddle wasn't meant to be resolved
By any passer-by, but by prophecy!
Where were you and your birds of augury?
Where were the gods, for all that?

Then I came along!
I! Poor ignorant Oedipus! No birds
To give my wisdom flight—only thought!
And this is the man you seek to overthrow!
To stand secure beside King Kreon's throne!
But you, you and this scheme's plotter, will regret
This witch-hunt! Oh, if you were not senile,
I would have made you pay for your plot by now!
LEADER: My lord, he spoke in anger,
        As you did, and that we don't need.
        Our task is how to fulfill the god's oracle.
TEIRESIAS: You may be king, Oedipus, but I'm your equal
        In one respect at least: the right to speak,
        And now I will claim that right. I'm not your slave,
        Nor do I need Kreon to speak for me.
        I belong to Apollo and say what I please.

        You mocked me, mocked my blindness, slandered me,
        So now I say to you who still have eyes,
        Eyes that are blind to the wretchedness of your life,

That you do not know in whose house it is you live;
That you do not know with whom you share that house;
That you do not know your origins! Who are your parents?
Do you know? Do you know the evil you have done
To your own, done to your family, not just here
In the light of the sun, but in the world below?
The two-pronged curse of your father and your mother
Will one day whip you, whip you out of this land,
Whip you and stalk you down with its deadly stride,
Whip you out of Thebes!

Ah! And your eyes!
Your eyes, that now see day, will stare into darkness,
Stare into endless night; and your cries,
Terrible in their sound will echo and re-echo
From every valley, from every gully and stone,
From every blind path on Kithairon,
And shake them with the sound when you have learned the meaning
Of your marriage, and the favoring wind that swept you
To that calamitous harbor!

Nor can you see
The multitude of sorrows that will pursue you,
And cut you down, and strip you of your pride—
Wipe you clear of the earth's face, and level you,
And show you who you are to your own children!

Vilify me, then, curse my words,
Words that stream from Apollo; insult Kreon;
But no man will ever know greater sorrow,
Greater pain and defeat, and be ground down
To common dust as will you!
OEDIPUS: I won't hear this! Not from this man! Damn you!
Out of my sight! Leave my palace! Now!
Back where you came from!
TEIRESIAS: Would I be here if you hadn't asked me?
OEDIPUS: Had I known you would talk such fool's drivel,
I would never have brought you here!
TEIRESIAS: A fool to you, perhaps, but not to your parents.

OEDIPUS: Parents? Wait! Stop! Who are my parents?

TEIRESIAS: Today you were born, today will destroy you.

OEDIPUS: Damn your riddles! Are they your wisdom?

TEIRESIAS: Ah, but aren't you the master of riddles?

OEDIPUS: Mock me! You will soon discover it is true!

TEIRESIAS: The same luck has brought your ruin.

OEDIPUS: If it saved the city, then I don't care!

TEIRESIAS: I will leave you, then. Lead me home, boy.

OEDIPUS: Yes, lead him home, boy!

> Underfoot you're only a nuisance!
>
> Go! Good riddance!
>
> *(Oedipus turns in anger and, unknown to Teiresias, begins his entry into the palace.)*

TEIRESIAS: I will go, once I have said what I came to say,

> And no scowls or threats of yours will frighten me.
>
> You are not the one to bring me down,
>
> So listen closely, for this is how things stand.
>
> The man that you have looked for all this time,
>
> The man that you have cursed and threatened with death,
>
> The murderer of Laïos—that man is here—
>
> Here in Thebes. Thought to be a resident alien,
>
> Time will show that he was Theban born,
>
> And he will take no joy in that relation.
>
> *(Oedipus storms into the palace.)*
>
> He who now has eyes will be blind,
>
> He who now has wealth will be a beggar;
>
> He will go tapping his stick with every step
>
> Along foreign roads, knowing himself brother
>
> To his own children, husband and son to her
>
> Who gave him birth: sower of the field
>
> His father plowed: his own father's murderer.
>
> *(Music begins as a transition into the ode.)*
>
> Go inside now and think it out;
>
> And if you find that I have lied, then say
>
> That the blind old prophet has no understanding!
>
> *(As Teiresias turns and is led off by the Boy, Attendants following, the Chorus immediately takes up a new position.)*

CHORUS: —Who is he?

Who is the man?
Who is the man denounced
        by prophetic stones of rocky Delphi?
Who is the man?
        Who is he?
Who is he whose hands
        are stained with blood of unspeakable horror?
Let him flee!
        Let him run!
Let him escape with feet
        fleet as horses of raging stormwind!
For now son of Zeus,
        Apollo, armed for charge,
            wielding father's fire,
leaps and mounts his prey,
        plunges fiery bolt,
                god of unerring aim!
And in his wake relentless fate pursues!

—In blast of light
        Parnassos' peak
streams forth Apollo's word!
        Hunt down, hunt down the unknown man!
Man who wanders
        in forest gloom!
In caves, in rocky clefts!
        Wild bull wandering hills, alone!
Unguided foot!
        Fleeing far
from Delphi's sacred stone!
        Ancient omphalos! Earth's navel!
Racing from god's own word!
        Prophetic word of god!
            Echo off jagged hills!
Soaring birds of augury!
        Wings that whip in pursuit!
        God's undying demands!
Relentless fate that cannot know defeat!

—Terrible! Terrible!
> Fear gone wild!
Born of prophet's words!
> Confusion mounting high in my heart!
I ponder. I question.
> Filled with doubt.
His words: Can I believe them?
> Can I deny them? Can I approve them?
I hover on wings.
> No place to light.
Blind to past and future.
> What quarrel arose in Labdakos' house?
What strife between Laïos and Polybos' son?
> I have no knowledge. Nor do I know now.
> Where is the touchstone? Where is the proof?
How can I stand against my king?
> Oedipus, famed throughout the land!
> Can Laïos' blood stain Oedipus' hand?
No man ever brought such word before.

—Zeus and Apollo
> know all things mortal.
But can a blind prophet,
> a man with eyes sheathed in night,
know more of truth
> than I, a man?
There is no test, no proof;
> yet a man may surpass another's wisdom.
But not till I see,
> not till I know,
not till the finger of proof
> points at my king, will I believe.
I saw him when the winged maiden
> stood before him taunting, daring.
> I saw then his heroic temper;
saw him prove his power of mind.
> That was his test; that was his skill.
> He raised us up and we adored him.
Never in mind or heart will I condemn him.

(Kreon has entered during the final section of the ode and approaches. Finished, the Chorus disperses to listen to Kreon's speech as the music fades out.)

KREON: Men of Thebes—I have heard the accusation
    King Oedipus makes against me, and I have come
    In haste, because I'm not a man to endure
    Such indignity!

    If, in the present crisis,
    He believes that I in any way
    Intended harm to him in word or deed,
    Then I would never choose a long life,
    For a life without honor is no life.
    This outrage to my name is no small matter.
    There is no more grievous charge, none
    More heinous than this: to be damned by my own city,
    By you, and those closest to me, as a traitor.

LEADER: He spoke in anger, not from careful thought.

KREON: And said that I persuaded the prophet to lie?

LEADER: Yes, but why, I don't know.

KREON: Did he look you straight in the eye?
    Was his mind steady?

LEADER: I can't say.
    I don't judge the deeds of great men.
    (Oedipus enters from the palace.)
    But here he is now.

OEDIPUS: You, Kreon! You! You have the gall
    To come here! You! You have the audacity
    To approach this house! You who openly plotted
    Its master's murder! You who sought to steal
    My throne, steal my power, like a bandit!
    O by the gods, Kreon, were you so stupid
    To think me a coward, a fool, blind to your plot
    Against me? Did you think I had no eyes
    To see your stealthy moves; that I would not
    Without one moment's pause take arms against them
    In my own defense? What a fool you are, Kreon!
    What a fool! To set out hunting for throne
    And power when throne and power need friends and funds;

When power and throne are caught with wealth and armies!

KREON: Finished? Then listen to me, I have listened to you,
    And judge on the facts!

OEDIPUS: Ah, Kreon, you have a way with words,
    But how do I listen to a known enemy?

KREON: First things first: listen for a change!

OEDIPUS: First things first, deny that you are a traitor!

KREON: If you think stubborn unreason a virtue,
    Then you are a man who has lost his balance!

OEDIPUS: If you think you can wrong a kinsman
    And escape the penalty, then I tell you
    That *you* are a man who has lost his balance!

KREON: All right! There I agree! Only tell me
    What this wrong is you say that I have done you?

OEDIPUS: Did you or did you not convince me to send
    For that pious fraud of a prophet?

KREON: I did, yes, and I would do it again.

OEDIPUS: How long ago was it that Laïos—

KREON: That Laïos what? I don't understand.

OEDIPUS: Vanished, struck down in his tracks, murdered!

KREON: Years—many long years ago—

OEDIPUS: This prophet—was he practicing then?

KREON: Yes, with the same skill and honor.

OEDIPUS: And what did he say about me at the time?

KREON: Nothing—not while I was about.

OEDIPUS: And you never hunted the king's killer?

KREON: We did, but came away with nothing.

OEDIPUS: Why didn't your prophet accuse me then?

KREON: When I don't know, I prefer to keep silent.

OEDIPUS: But *this* you'd tell, if you were honest.

KREON: What would that be? If I know, I'll tell.

OEDIPUS: If you and he hadn't schemed together,
    He would never have said I murdered Laïos.

KREON: If this is what he said, well then—
    who would know better than you?
    But now it is my turn to question.

OEDIPUS: Ask away. But I'm not a murderer.

KREON: Very well.—Is my sister your wife?

OEDIPUS: Now there's a fact I can't deny.

KREON: And you rule together, equal in power?

OEDIPUS: Everything she wants, she has.

KREON: And I'm the third? We're all of us equal?

OEDIPUS: And that is where you are proven a traitorous friend!

KREON: Not if you see it as I do, rationally.

Why would a man in his right mind ever choose
The distressing cares of kingship over untroubled sleep,
Especially if he has equal power and rank?
Certainly not I. I have never longed to wield
Royal power. Why should I? I live like a king.
Any man with reason would choose as I have.
As it is, I have everything from you.
My life is free. I live unburdened by the demands
Put upon kingship.
But if I were king,
I should be bound to act as a king must act:
Against his will and pleasure. So what could kingship
Give me that I don't have: unruffled power
And influence, without the care, without
The pain, without the threat.
I'm not so insane
Yet to seek out other honors than those
That bring advantage. I'm welcome everywhere.
And those who court your favor, curry mine:
Their success depends on me.
Why give up comfort for worry?
No sane mind is treasonous.
No. I have no leanings in that direction,
And I would never deal with a man who did.
Test me, why don't you? Go to the Pythia at Delphi.
Ask the goddess if I reported correctly.
And if I didn't, if I'm found to be in league
With the prophet, plotting treason, then have me executed!
But not on your vote only; on mine as well:
A double charge. Just don't convict without proof,
on a mere guess.

It is just as wrong to think a bad man good,
As it is a good man bad.

To reject a loyal friend is to tear life
Out of your own breast: there is nothing more precious!
Only time will tell, and time will tell
For certain who is just and who is not;
The traitor is easily spotted.

LEADER: Good advice for a careful man.
Hasty judgment is often dangerous.

OEDIPUS: Hasty conspiracy is hastily met.
If I delay, he wins, I lose.

KREON: What do you want? Say it! Banishment?

OEDIPUS: Banishment? No! It is your head I want!

KREON: You refuse to believe! You refuse to yield!

(*Iokastê enters from the palace with a woman Attendant and approaches them.*)

OEDIPUS: You don't persuade me you're worthy of belief!

KREON: Quite frankly, I think you've lost your wits!

OEDIPUS: In *my* interest, yes!

KREON: And what about mine?

OEDIPUS: But you're a traitor!

KREON: What if you're wrong?

OEDIPUS: But I *must* rule!

KREON: When your rule is evil?

OEDIPUS: Think of the city!

KREON: It is *my* city, too!

LEADER: Please, my lords, no more!
Look, Iokastê, just in time!
Let her end this.

IOKASTÊ: Senseless fools! What's all this quarreling in public!
Aren't you ashamed, stirring up private matters
When Thebes is sick to the death!
(*To Oedipus.*)
Come inside, now.
And you, Kreon, go home.
Why make something out of nothing?

KREON: Nothing?
Sister, your husband plans one of two things:
Either to exile me or to have my head!

OEDIPUS: It's true! I caught him plotting against me!

KREON: No, if I am guilty of anything,

I will die accursed and consider it a blessing!
(Music fades in to accompany the lyric dialogue.)
IOKASTÊ: Oedipus, I beg of you, believe him!
    In the gods' name, respect his oath,
    Respect me, respect your people!
LEADER: I beg you,
        my king,
           be guided,
    consent!
OEDIPUS: Concede?
        And if I do,
    what?
LEADER: He was never a
        man to be
    despised. He is
        strong in his
           oath.
    You should
        respect him.
OEDIPUS: Do you
    know what you're
    asking?
LEADER: I know.
OEDIPUS: Then tell me.
LEADER: A friend who
        binds himself with a
    curse should
        never be
           charged without
    proof.
OEDIPUS: In asking this you
        ask my death or
    exile from Thebes.
CHORUS: No, by the
        god of the
    Sun, by the
        god
           Apollo!
    Destroy me,

> friendless,
>> wretched,
> forsaken by the
>> gods, forsaken by
>>> friends!
> Give me the
>> worst of
>>> deaths,
> if ever I
>> thought such a
>>> thought!
> The land is
>> wracked,
>>> wasted, a
> torture, a
>> pain to my
>>> soul! Don't
> add to my
>> misery troubles that
>>> spring from you two!

(The music fades out.)

OEDIPUS: He's free, then! Free! And if I must,
Let me die or end my life dishonored,
Exiled far from Thebes!
(To the Chorus.)
Your pitiful words move me, not him!
He'll take my hatred with him wherever he goes!

KREON: Ah, you yield as fiercely as you rage!
Natures like yours torment themselves most.

OEDIPUS: Leave me! Get out!

KREON: Yes, I'll go.
But you know nothing—nothing!
These men saved me!
(As Kreon turns and begins his entrance into the palace, music fades in to accompany the lyric dialogue.)

CHORUS: Lady, why do you
> hesitate? Lead him
>> back to the palace.

IOKASTÊ: Yes, but tell me

first what happened.
CHORUS: Words were
spoken, unproven
    words; but
        unproven words
have as
    sharp a bite.
IOKASTÊ: Words on both sides?
CHORUS: Yes.
IOKASTÊ: Tell me.
CHORUS: This land has
suffered enough.
    End it where they
      left it.
OEDIPUS: Here is where your
    thoughts have led.
      You're wise; and yet
you persuade me to
    blunt my anger.
CHORUS: Oedipus,
king, I have
    said not
      once, but
many times, and
    say it
      again:
I'd be a mad and
    reckless fool to
      abandon you
who saved
    my city.
    You took
command and
    steered our ship
      to a safe
harbor.
    Take the
      helm and
lead us once

again from
misfortune.

(The Chorus gradually retreats to another part of the stage, except for the Leader who is about to leave but is held back by Oedipus. The music fades out.)

IOKASTÊ: Oedipus, my lord, please, tell me, what is it?
　　Whatever can have put you in such a rage?

OEDIPUS: Yes, I'll tell you, Iokastê, because I trust you
　　More than I trust those men. It is Kreon—
　　Kreon who raises plots against me!

IOKASTÊ: Then tell me how it started, and be clear.

OEDIPUS: He tells me to my face that I murdered Laïos!
　　That's it!

IOKASTÊ: And how does he know this?
　　Does he have facts, or is it hearsay?

OEDIPUS: Oh, no! He sends in against me
　　That damnable prophet! Kreon's lips are clear
　　Of *that* indictment, be sure!

IOKASTÊ: Let's have no more of this. Forget it now;
　　Listen to me. No man born of woman
　　Has ever possessed the art of prophesy!
　　And I can prove it by means of an experience.

　　Long ago an oracle came to Laïos,
　　Not from Apollo himself, but from his priests.
　　It said that he, Laïos, would meet his fate
　　At the hands of a son yet to be born to us—
　　His flesh and mine. And yet, it is said, Laïos
　　Met his death at the hands of foreign bandits,
　　Where three roads meet.

　　As for the son I bore,
　　That poor child, not three days had passed
　　When Laïos pierced his ankles, bound them together,
　　And had him thrown onto a trackless mountain.
　　So it wasn't Apollo
　　Made the child kill his father; nor was it Laïos'
　　Fate to be killed by the son he so dreadfully feared.
　　So much for prophets and their prophecies!

Forget them! Whatever it is the god wants
He will look for and reveal in his own good time.

OEDIPUS: Ah, Iokastê! Just now, now, as you spoke,
Some terrible, shadowy memory chilled my heart!

IOKASTÊ: Why do you say that?

OEDIPUS: I thought I heard you say that Laïos was killed
At the place where three roads meet.

IOKASTÊ: They said so then, they say so still.

OEDIPUS: Where did this disaster happen?

IOKASTÊ: In Phokis. There is a two-forked road
Comes in from Delphi and Daulia.

OEDIPUS: When? How long ago?

IOKASTÊ: Shortly before you arrived in Thebes
And were offered the throne.

OEDIPUS: Aiiiiiiiii!
Ah, Zeus, what terrible design have you plotted for me?

IOKASTÊ: What torments you so, my lord? Tell me.

OEDIPUS: No, not yet!
Tell me about Laïos first.
How old he was, what he looked like.

IOKASTÊ: Dark, his temples beginning to gray,
His figure—not unlike yours.

OEDIPUS: O god, without knowing, I have cursed myself!

IOKASTÊ: You frighten me when you say such things!

OEDIPUS: I fear the blind old prophet sees!
Help me! Tell me one thing more.

IOKASTÊ: Oh but, my dear, I'm so frightened.
But do, yes, ask me, I'll answer.

OEDIPUS: How did he travel—Laïos—a light escort,
Or many guards, as befits a king?

IOKASTÊ: Five in all—one was a herald.
Laïos rode in a single wagon.

OEDIPUS: Aiiiiiiiiii!
It's all so clear! So suddenly!
How do you know this? Who told you?

IOKASTÊ: A servant—the only survivor.

OEDIPUS: And is this servant still with us?

IOKASTÊ: No. When he returned and saw you in power,
And Laïos murdered, he knelt and touched my hand,

And begged to be sent far from the city, to the country
Where shepherds tend our flocks. He was a slave,
But I thought that he had earned this of me—and more.
OEDIPUS: Can he be brought back quickly?
IOKASTÊ: Of course. Easily. Why?
OEDIPUS: Dear Iokastê, I'm afraid I may have said
Too much already. I must see him.
IOKASTÊ: He'll come. But now, my dear,
Haven't I the right to know what troubles you?
OEDIPUS: Every right, and so you shall.
Now that I have scaled this pitch
Of wild foreboding, why should I keep it from you,
This fierce omen that Chance stirs in me?

My father was Polybos of Korinth;
My mother, Meropê, a Dorian.
I was seen as the first among men at home
In Korinth, prince of the city, when out of nowhere
A strange thing happened. Strange, but scarcely worth
The passion it caused in me.

During a banquet,
A man who had drunk more than his fill shouted
That I was not my father's son. This hurt me,
Hurt me deeply, and all the rest of that day
I was hard put to temper my anxiety.
Then, the next day, I questioned my parents.
They were both enraged at the man who had dared
To level such a dreadful insult against me,
And they saw that he paid dearly for it, too.
I was satisfied, and yet that lie kept gnawing,
Gnawing at me, and rumor spread, till one day,
Unknown to my parents, I went alone to Delphi.
But Apollo refused to hear; he cheated me.
Instead, he flung such detestable horrors at me,
Such hideous filth, saying that I was doomed
To know my mother's bed, to breed children
That no man could bear to look at, and murder my father,
The father who gave me life!

Hearing this, I fled from Korinth, swearing
Never again to return, and knew its position
Only by the stars. I fled to a land
Where I would never see the horrors foretold
By the despicable song of the oracle;
And in my flight I arrived at the very place
Where, as you say, the great King Laïos was murdered.

All right, then, Iokastê, here is the truth.
As I was walking one day, I came to a place
Where three roads meet. Approaching me was a herald
Driving a colt-drawn chariot with an old man,
As you describe, seated inside on a bench.
The driver tried first to force me off the road
With brute strength and I struck back in anger,
Struck him hard, and then, as I passed the wagon,
The old man struck at my head with a two-pronged goad!
I hit him back, hit him so hard
With the staff in my hand that he tumbled down backward
And lay face-up in the road! I killed him then.
I killed them all.

Ah, Iokastê,
If this stranger has any tie with Laïos,
What man is more miserable than I,
More hated by the gods? No man, no citizen
Or alien resident, may speak with me again,
Or give me shelter, but shut his door against me,
And shun me like the plague! And who, who
But I alone laid these curses on myself!

These, these hands have touched you, you, his wife,
Made love to you, the same hands that killed Laïos,
Bloodied hands, hands defiling his marriage.

Am I not a seed of evil?
Am I not the most unclean of men!
I who must be exiled from Thebes,
And in my exile never see my parents,

Never set foot on native soil,
Or else be doomed to sleep with my mother,
And kill my father who gave me life,
The father who raised me,
Polybos!
If I was born the victim of some savage god,
Then who could deny the evil of Divinity itself!
Ah, pure and holy gods, let it not be!
Let me not see that day! Let me perish
From the race of men before I witness the evil
That is my fate!

LEADER: Dreadful as this is, my lord,
Don't lose hope; wait to hear the man
Who saw the murder.

OEDIPUS: Yes, my only hope: waiting;
Waiting with hope to hear the shepherd!

IOKASTÊ: What do you hope to hear when he arrives?

OEDIPUS: If his story and yours agree, why, then,
I will have escaped disaster

IOKASTÊ: Why do you say that?

OEDIPUS: You said he used the word 'bandits': Laïos
Was killed by bandits. If he still holds to bandits,
Several, why, then, I'm not the one who killed him.
How can one man amount to many?
But if he says one *single* man, single-handed,
The full weight of evidence falls on me.

IOKASTÊ: Believe me, my dear, it's what he said.
How can he go back on his word now?
There's not a man in Thebes who didn't hear him.
And even if he changes some part of his story,
The murder of Laïos can never be forced to fit
The god's prophecy. Apollo said quite plainly
That Laïos would die at the hand of my son.
And he, poor miserable creature, died before Laïos.
So much for prophecy! I will never again
Turn right or left in fear of prophecy or prophets!

OEDIPUS: Yes; but even so, send for the shepherd.

IOKASTÊ: I'll do it at once.
Come. Let's go in.

How could I deny you anything?
(Music begins as Oedipus and Iokastê turn and begin their entry into the palace. Immediately upon their turn, the Chorus takes up a central position in the orchestra.)
CHORUS:

      —May Destiny lead me always in purity of word and deed,
          whose laws are given birth and tread the lofty heaven,
    exalted upper region, brightest vault of light,
          Olympos their only father! No mortal could sow the seed,
    memory never will fail, nor drowsy oblivion lull them!
          God in essence is in them! God who never grows old!

      —The will to violation sows the seed of the tyrant!
          Pride that gorges itself and knows no even measure!
    Pride swollen with folly that claws its way to the summit,
          then plunges into the abyss where no footing serves!
    I pray the god to protect the man who wrestles for good;
          that god is my protector; in him I place my faith.

      —If a man can dare to sneak with disdain
    into vile deeds of hand or mouth,
    fearless of Justice, no reverence for shrines:
          —Let Retribution strike him down!
          Punish his calamitous pride!—
    —If a man can seek dishonorable gain,
    scornful of piety and holy things,
    clinging foolishly to the untouchable:
          —Can such a man truly believe
          to escape the gods' fiery arrows?—
    —If honor now accompanies such deeds,
    why should I bend to join the sacred dance?

      —I will never again visit Delphi's shrine.
    Never again Apollo's at Abai;
    or Zeus' fiery oracle at Elis:
          —Unless prophecies are proven true,
          and manifest for all to see.—
    —Zeus, if you are god indeed;
    deathless god, prove your might.

This blasphemy must not escape you:
—The prophecies to Laïos fade.
The minds of men have turned aside.—
—Where is reverence to Apollo now?
Love and faith in the gods have died away.
(Before completion of the ode, Iokastê enters from the palace with several fe-
male Servants bearing incense and suppliants' wreaths on their way to the
altar. When finished, the Chorus disperses diversely across the playing area
and the music fades out.)
IOKASTÊ: Lords of the land, the time seemed right for me
To visit the sacred altars of our gods,
Bringing in their honor these suppliant's wreaths
And fragrant incense.
Our king is not himself.
Oedipus no longer thinks like a rational man,
But believes every tale of horror, unable
To judge present prophecies by the hollow
Prophecies of the past.

Since my advice is wasted,
(Turning to the altar of Apollo Lykêion.)
I turn to you, Apollo Lykêion,
For you are nearest!
(A Korinthian Messenger, an old shepherd, enters, left, and makes his way
forward simultaneously as she speaks the invocation.)
Receive my suppliant's prayers and offerings,
And deliver us from pollution,
For when we look at him, at Oedipus,
Our hearts quake with fear: we are like sailors
Lost at sea when their helmsman loses control.
(Iokastê places her offerings on the altar and kneels before it as the
Korinthian Messenger completes his approach. He is a near-comic figure who
tends to speak in circles. The Chorus is amused.)
KORINTHIAN: Friends, excuse me, could you help?
I'm looking for the king's palace—
Oedipus it is I mean;
Or even better, the king himself.
LEADER: In that case, you have arrived, stranger.
The king is inside; but here is his wife,

Mother of his children.

(Iokastê rises from the altar and turns to him. She is also amused.)

KORINTHIAN: I wish her well,

And wish the same to her household,

For she is your queen.

IOKASTÊ: The same to you for your courtesy, sir.

But why have you come? What's your news?

KORINTHIAN: Good news for your house and husband.

IOKASTÊ: Tell me, and tell me who sent you.

KORINTHIAN: I come from Korinth.

As for the news, it will give pleasure,

But maybe some pain.

IOKASTÊ: Two-pronged news?

What could that be?

KORINTHIAN: The people of Korinth are saying

They want to make Oedipus their king.

I heard it myself.

IOKASTÊ: But Polybos?

Has he lost his throne?

KORINTHIAN: Oh, that he has!

Death holds him in his grip!

IOKASTÊ: Dead? Dead? The father of Oedipus?

KORINTHIAN: If I'm lying, death take me, too!

IOKASTÊ: *(To a Servant near the doors.)* Hurry! Go in, go in!

Tell your master!

(The Servant hurries off.)

Prophecies of the gods, where are you now!

· Polybos, the man that Oedipus fled

Long ago in terror that he would kill him!

That same Polybos is now destroyed by Chance,

And not by him—not by Oedipus!

(Oedipus enters from the palace and speaks as he approaches her.)

OEDIPUS: Iokastê, dearest wife, why have you called me?

IOKASTÊ: Listen to this man, Oedipus,

Then tell me what's become of Apollo's prophecies!

OEDIPUS: Where is he from?

What has he said?

IOKASTÊ: Korinth, with news of your father.

News that Polybos is dead!

Your father is dead!

OEDIPUS: What is this, stranger?

Tell me yourself.

KORINTHIAN: If this is the news you want first,

Then rest assured: he's dead; dead

As dead can be, and that's a fact.

OEDIPUS: Treachery?

Or did sickness kill him?

KORINTHIAN: A tip of the scales does an old man in.

OEDIPUS: He died of illness.

Ah, poor man!

KORINTHIAN: Yes, to be sure; and the weight of his years.

OEDIPUS: Ah! So there we are, Iokastê!

To think we ever trembled at Pytho's oracles,

Or at the racket-raising birds above us,

That led me to believe that my father's death

Would be at my hand! But he lies there,

Secure in his grave, deep in the earth at Korinth,

And here am I, who never touched a sword!

Unless, of course, he died of longing for me,

The only way I could have caused his death.

But Polybos lies there, and with him he took

Deep into Hades the worthless oracles!

IOKASTÊ: Haven't I said this all along?

OEDIPUS: Yes, but I was crippled with fear.

IOKASTÊ: You needn't think of this ever again!

OEDIPUS: Not fear my mother?

My mother's bed?

IOKASTÊ: Fear! Why should a man fear? Why?

When life is ruled by Chance? There's nothing sure.

Nothing! Foresight is guesswork, nothing more;

Live however you choose! Why be afraid of marriage

With your mother! Many men have slept with their mothers

In dreams. Life should be easy. Don't trouble your mind.

OEDIPUS: Your words are well taken, Iokastê, except

My mother still *lives;* and since she lives, I'm bound

To fear, and your fine words are useless to me.

IOKASTÊ: Your father's death brings great joy!

OEDIPUS: Great—yet I fear the living woman.

KORINTHIAN: Who is this woman, this wife you fear?

OEDIPUS: Meropê, old man, the wife of Polybos.

KORINTHIAN: Meropê? Hm! What's to fear there?

OEDIPUS: A dreadful prophecy from the gods, stranger.

KORINTHIAN: Can you tell it; or is it unlawful?

OEDIPUS: No. No reason not.

> Long ago the prophecy came
> That I would sleep with my mother,
> And shed my father's blood with these hands.
> This is why I left Korinth long ago,
> Avoiding it all these years. And Chance has been good.
> And yet there is no sweeter thing in life
> Than to see the kindly faces of one's parents.

KORINTHIAN: And this is why you fled the city?

OEDIPUS: To escape killing my father, old man.

KORINTHIAN: Well, then, king, I'll save you from that.

> After all, I've come in friendship
> To do you service.

OEDIPUS: And what a reward you would have, old man!

KORINTHIAN: Of course, yes, exactly, my very reason!

> I mean, for a generous reward
> Once you've come back home to Korinth!

OEDIPUS: I will never go near my parents' house!

KORINTHIAN: Child, you don't know what you're doing—

OEDIPUS: I don't understand. Say what you mean.

KORINTHIAN: —if fears like these keep you away.

OEDIPUS: Apollo's oracle keeps me away.

KORINTHIAN: Afraid of your father's blood on your hands?

OEDIPUS: Yes, old man, it terrifies me.

KORINTHIAN: But don't you see? Your fears are groundless.

OEDIPUS: Groundless? When I was born their son?

KORINTHIAN: Polybos was no relation to you.

OEDIPUS: What are you—? Polybos not my father?

KORINTHIAN: No more than me—in that we're equals.

OEDIPUS: You're nothing to me—how can my father—?

KORINTHIAN: He no more sired you than I did!

OEDIPUS: Then why did he call me son? Why?

KORINTHIAN: He got you once as a gift—from me.

OEDIPUS: And loved me so dearly? From another's hands?

KORINTHIAN: His life was childless; he turned to you.

OEDIPUS: You bought me? Found me? What? Tell me.

KORINTHIAN: I found you on the slopes of Kithairon.

OEDIPUS: Why were you there? What took you to those—?

KORINTHIAN: Shepherding, tending my flocks in the mountains.

OEDIPUS: A wandering shepherd. You worked for hire?

KORINTHIAN: I was your savior *that* day, child!

OEDIPUS: What did you save me from—that day?

KORINTHIAN: Your ankles could tell the tale of that.

OEDIPUS: Dear god! Why mention that ancient anguish?

KORINTHIAN: When I freed your feet, your ankles were pierced.

OEDIPUS: The shameful mark I had from my cradle!

KORINTHIAN: The very thing that gave you your name.

OEDIPUS: Who did this to me? Mother? Father?

KORINTHIAN: Can't say—the man who gave you knew more.

OEDIPUS: It wasn't you who found me? Who, then?

KORINTHIAN: Not me, child; another shepherd.

OEDIPUS: Who? Do you know? Describe him to me!

KORINTHIAN: One of Laïos' men, I think.

OEDIPUS: The king who ruled here long ago?

KORINTHIAN: Yes, he did shepherding for him.

OEDIPUS: Is he alive? I have to see him!

KORINTHIAN: It is these men here would know that best.

OEDIPUS: Does anyone know the shepherd that he means?

    Has he been seen in the city, in the fields?

    Tell me if you have. The time is come

    That all things in this matter be brought to light.

LEADER: He's the shepherd you asked to see.

    The Queen would know that best.

OEDIPUS: The man we have sent for, lady,

    Is he the shepherd the old man speaks of?

IOKASTÊ: *(Distraught.)* The shepherd? What? No—

    Forget him, don't even ask!

    His words mean nothing!

OEDIPUS: Give up? How can you—? A clue like this?

    Not throw light on the mystery of my birth?

IOKASTÊ: For god's love, no, don't do it,

    Don't do it, Oedipus, if you care for your life!

    Don't, don't! Give up the search!

My anguish is enough!

OEDIPUS: Come, come, be brave, Iokastê!

Even if I were born a slave of slaves,

your honor would never be tainted!

IOKASTÊ: Listen! Please! Don't do this thing!

OEDIPUS: No! I *will* know! You will never persuade me!

IOKASTÊ: Oedipus, my thoughts are always for you!

OEDIPUS: Your thoughts have tormented me long enough!

IOKASTÊ: You're doomed! You must never know who you are!

OEDIPUS: Go, one of you, bring the shepherd!

The queen will bask in her honorable birth!

IOKASTÊ: Aiiiiiiiiii! Aiiiiiiiiii!

Poor miserable man!

What more can I say?

Nothing—nothing—

Ever—ever—

(Iokastê rushes off into the palace in silence.)

LEADER: Why has she run off so, Oedipus,

In such bitter pain? Something terrible

May burst from this silence.

OEDIPUS: Then let it burst! Let it come!

However base my birth, I'm bound to see it

Face-to-face! As for her, my queen,

She who has more pride than woman has right to—

She feels herself soiled in my birth!

But I,

I am the child of Chance, giver of good,

I cannot be dishonored! Chance is my mother,

The passing months my brothers, and they have seen me

Small and great in time!

I will never be other than I am

And fail to seek out the truth of my birth!

(Oedipus remains. Music enters as the Chorus takes up a new position.)

CHORUS: If I have prophetic

power, skillful and

sound in

knowing, then

by the

skies of
Olympos, when
tomorrow's
moon
rises, you will
know, Kithairon, how
Oedipus honors you
who gave him
life and your breast!
For we will
celebrate your
gentle care with
dance and song!
And you,
Apollo,
lord,
god,
let our
rejoicing give you
pleasure!
Oedipus,
child, what
long-living nymph
lent you her
womb? To
whom did she
bear you?
Had she
lain with Pan the
mountain
wanderer? Or was it
Apollo, ranger of
pastures high in the
hills? Or
Hermês? Or
god of the
Bakkhic feast,
god
Dionysos,

frenzied god of the

peaks? Was it

he who

received you from a

nymph on

Helikon, a

gift to the

god of

dancing and

darkness?

(As Oedipus becomes aware of the old Shepherd who enters, right, accompanied by Attendants, the Chorus disperses itself around the orchestra and the music fades out.)

OEDIPUS: Although I have never met the man coming toward us,

My guess would be that he is the one we sent for.

His age and this old man's agree,

And the men bringing him are my servants.

But you would know best if you ever saw him.

LEADER: Yes, I know him. Laïos' man.

The best servant a man could have.

OEDIPUS: Let me ask you first, Korinthian.

Is this the man you spoke of?

KORINTHIAN: The same.

OEDIPUS: You, old man, come here!

(The Shepherd, frightened, reticent, looks at the ground.)

No, look at me! There. Answer me.

Were you once a servant of Laïos?

SHEPHERD: Yes, but born in the palace, not bought.

OEDIPUS: And what kind of work did you do?

SHEPHERD: Most of my life, tending sheep.

OEDIPUS: And where did you pasture your herd?

SHEPHERD: Kithairon, or the hills near by.

OEDIPUS: Did you ever see this man out there?

SHEPHERD: What was his job? What man is that?

OEDIPUS: That man there. Have you ever met him?

SHEPHERD: Me? Him? Not that I can—

KORINTHIAN: No surprise there, my lord;

But let me goad his memory a bit

And he'll remember. He'll remember Kithairon

And his two herds, and me with only one.
We spent six months together in the hills,
Three whole seasons, spring to autumn when red
Arktouros rises in Boötês. And winters
He'd take his herds back to Laïos' fold,
And I, mine, back to Korinth.
Isn't that so?

SHEPHERD: True—ah—but such a long time—
KORINTHIAN: Right enough! And you gave me a child—
A boy child to raise as my own.
SHEPHERD: And if I did? Why are you asking this?
KORINTHIAN: That child is this man here.

(The Shepherd raises his staff to strike.)

SHEPHERD: Damn you! Can't you hold your tongue!
OEDIPUS: Stop this, old man! Do you hear me?
It is you deserve to be struck, not him!
SHEPHERD: Noble master, what have I done?
OEDIPUS: You refuse to answer about the boy!
SHEPHERD: He knows nothing! He's wasting words!
OEDIPUS: You will answer willingly or else by force!
SHEPHERD: No, don't torture an old man!
OEDIPUS: One of you! Pin his arms behind him!

(An Attendant does as ordered.)

SHEPHERD: Ah! But why? What do you want?
OEDIPUS: The child—did you give it to him?
SHEPHERD: I did—I wish I had died that day!
OEDIPUS: You will, if you don't tell the truth!
SHEPHERD: Yes, and my death will be worse if I tell!
OEDIPUS: I'd say this man is playing for time.
SHEPHERD: No, no! Please! I gave the child!
OEDIPUS: Where did you find it? Yours? Another's?
SHEPHERD: No, not mine—given to me.
OEDIPUS: A citizen's child? From which house?
SHEPHERD: Master, no more questions, I beg you!
OEDIPUS: You're dead meat if I ask again!
SHEPHERD: The child was from the—the house of Laïos.
OEDIPUS: Slave-born or one of his own?
SHEPHERD: Aiiii! I'm on the verge of dreadful speech!
OEDIPUS: And I of dreadful hearing! Say it!

SHEPHERD: The child was said—to be Laïos' child.

> Your wife knows best how it happened.

OEDIPUS: She gave it to you?

SHEPHERD: My lord, she did.

OEDIPUS: Why? Her reason?

SHEPHERD: To—to kill it.

OEDIPUS: A mother could do—?

SHEPHERD: There were prophecies.

OEDIPUS: What?

SHEPHERD: That he would kill his parents.

OEDIPUS: Why did you give him to this old man?

SHEPHERD: Pity for it, my lord! Pity!

> I thought he would take him away,
>
> Far away to some other place,
>
> His own country!
>
> But what a fate he saved him for!
>
> Ah, if you are the man he says,
>
> You are the most miserable of men!

OEDIPUS: Aiiiiiiiiiiiiii!

> It is all come true! All the prophecies! All!
>
> In a burst of radiance!
>
> > > O light—
> >
> > > > o light of day—
>
> Let me see you this last time!
>
> > > > I!
> >
> > > > Oedipus!
>
> Damned!
>
> > Damned in my birth!
> >
> > > > Damned in my marriage!
>
> Damned in the blood I shed with my own hand!

(Music begins as Oedipus rushes into the palace. At the same time, the Korinthian Messenger goes off, left, while the Shepherd and the Attendants go off right. Simultaneously the Chorus reassembles.)

CHORUS: O generations of

> > men, how fragile, how
> >
> > > frail your lives,
> >
> shadows only,
>
> > nothing,
> >
> > > nothing!

Is there a man,
  who grasps at
    happiness, but to
see it sink,
  dream,
    illusion,
ephemeral moment?
  I take as my
    model you,
Oedipus, most
  wretched of
    men, the luck that
fate has
  dealt you, and see that
    no man is
blest.
  But it was he,
    Oedipus, whose
unerring mind
  shot its arrow!
    It was he,
Lord Zeus, who
  ascended to radiant
    prosperity when he
leveled the riddling
  Sphinx, that
    hook-taloned
virgin,
  chanter of
    evil, and
rose in the face of
  Death, a
    tower, a
bulwark to
  save me and my
    city! That
deed made you
  king, great ruler,
    wielder of power so

great that no
     prince of Thebes of the
          Seven Gates ever
held its like!
     Noble Oedipus,
          man of wisdom and grace!
But now, of all men
     living, whose
          life is more to be
pitied, whose
     fortune more
          changed, more
wretched?
     Golden
          Oedipus,
both of you,
     son and father, dropped
          anchor in the same harbor;
both content with a
     single haven.
          O calamity,
how could the
     furrow your father
          plowed have
served as your own
     refuge and borne it so
          long in silence?
How?
     But
          Time that sees all
things, all-seeing
     Time has
          found you out
unaware, and
     sits in judgment
          on the
monstrous marriage,
     marriage that is no
          marriage, where

                    father and son,
                         begetter and
                              begotten as well, have
                    long been one!
                         O son of Laïos, if
                              only my eyes had
                    never seen you, for
                         now I pour a
                              dirge from my lips!
                    But to say it
                         justly, it was
                              you who once
                    restored me to
                         life; it is
                              you
                    now who
                         close my eyes
                              in death.

(The Chorus disperses around the orchestra as a Messenger enters from the palace and the music fades out.)

MESSENGER: Elders, most honored men of Thebes,
   If you are still true to your birth and revere
   The royal house of Labdakos, prepare to hear
   And see such horrors whose weight will pull you down
   With grief!
   Not all the vast waters of Istros
   And Phasis can wash clean the corruption concealed
   In this house, corruption that soon must be seen.
   Horrors willed, not unwilled!
   Our greatest griefs are those we bring on ourselves.

LEADER: Haven't we enough of grief,
   Enough of pain? What more can you add?

MESSENGER: Our royal lady the queen is dead.

LEADER: Oh, unhappy lady! How?

MESSENGER: She killed herself.
   How fortunate you are you didn't see it,
   That dreadful sight; but I saw, and I will tell you
   As best my memory serves me of the suffering
   Of that pitiable woman.

Having left us, she passed through the palace gates
And rushed in a frenzy of passion straight to her rooms,
Tearing at her hair with both hands.
Slamming the doors behind her, she lay on her bed,
The marriage-bed, and called on Laïos her husband,
Dead so long, remembering the sowing of that son,
That fatal son who would kill his father;
Then cursed the double shame of her loins:
Husband of husband, children of her child.

I can't say for certain just how she died,
For at that moment Oedipus burst in a rage
On the room with a terrible cry, and all we could see
Was him, ranging the floor, accosting each of us,
Demanding a sword, spitting out curses on her,
Curses on the wife who was no wife,
Calling for the double mother-whore
Who had reaped two crops, him and his children!

Then, in a storm of passion, led by some god,
He found his own way, none of us helping.
A great shout rose up from inside him,
And with a great lunge, as if urged
By some unknown guide, he thrust his body
At the double doors, making them bulge inwards
And burst with a crack!

There we saw her—hanging,
Swaying in a mass of twisted cords;
And seeing this, a roar rose from his breast
That broke our hearts; and then he slipped the noose
From around her neck and in his arms lowered
Her body to the floor; and when, poor woman,
She lay on the ground, so terrible a scene was played,
I wish I didn't remember!

He tore the two gold pins that fastened her dress,
And seeing her there, raised high the pins,
One in each hand, and plunged them deep into his eyes,

Crying that they would never again see
The misery of his fate, the horrors of his deeds,
Eyes that from here onward, in the dark,
Must look on those that they should never have seen,
And never again see those they long to see.
And as his chanting soared, his hands brought down
Grief after grief on his eyes, strike upon strike,
Opening wide his lids to welcome more,
Till his whole face streamed not with drops,
But with dark currents of gore that pulsed from his eyes.

This evil sprang from the unhappiness of both,
A curse on the man and the woman alike.
Prosperity once reigned in this house.
Happiness, success, were truly theirs.
And yet today, on this day,
Mourning, ruin, death, disgrace,
All, every evil, has come
To dwell in these walls.

LEADER: Is there any rest for him now?

MESSENGER: He's shouting to open the gates so all of Thebes
Can see him as he is, his father's murderer,
His mother's—no, I can't, I can't say it,
The unholy word! He will then leave ThebesH

That done, he will take himself
Away from Thebes to wander in self-exile,
And doing so to purge the house of the curse
That he himself laid on it.

He's weak, though, and needs a guide,
Someone to lead and help him
Endure his terrible sickness.
(Music begins as the palace doors begin to open.)
But look! The gates! Now you will see a sight
To make his enemies weep.
*(The ekkyklêma is rolled forward into full view to reveal the blind Oedipus,
the sockets of whose eyes still ooze gore. He is propped on the floor by both
arms. Once he rises, he wanders aimlessly, staggering, his arms outstretched.*

At sight of him the Chorus at first reacts in horror, dashing individually and in small groups in various directions around the orchestra as if trying to avoid proximity as well as sight. Eventually they subside and draw close to him in pity.)

CHORUS: Terrible sight! Dreadful,
      horrible, most
        horrible! What
    man has seen a
      sight so fearful?
        Oedipus! What
    unknown guide
      possessed you? What
        madness sent from
    god, more
      terrible than
        mind can
    know,
      leapt upon you?
        leapt!
    leapt beyond
      bounds to
        crush you!
    Ah!
      Féu!
        Féu!
    Pitiful man, most
      miserable, how can I
        look at you? And
    yet, there are so
      many
        questions, so
    many, so
      much to
        know, so
    much.
      Pitiful,
        pitiful man, you
    make me
      shudder!

OEDIPUS: Aiaiiiiiiii!
Aaiaiiiiiii!
     I am a man of
          misery! Where have you
     brought me, god?
          I stumble in
               darkness! My voice
     wings away into
          nothingness!
               Daimôn!
     Dark divinity!
          How far have you
               leapt?

CHORUS: To a place
          unspeakable!
               Terrible to
     say or
          see!

OEDIPUS: Dark cloud!
     Dark cloud!
          Cloud of night!
               Unreasoning cloud
     enshrouding me, always
          with me, always,
               always!
     unspeakable!
          invincible!
               sped by an evil wind!
     Oimoiiiiiiiiiiiiiiiiiiiiiiiiiiiiiiiiiiiiiiiii!
          Oimoiiiiiii!
               Again!
     Again!
          The pain!
               The pins, two
     prongs where I once
          saw, memory of
               evils, both at
     once, your
          shafts, never

ended, never,
never!

CHORUS: Your pain, sir, your
pain, I understand!
One grief
rises from your
body's wrench, the
other from your
mind!

OEDIPUS: Still there, old friend, still
there with the
blind man! Only
you to protect me!
Still caring!
Féu! Féu!
You are here, you are
here, I know, and
I am dark!
Your voice I
know so clear, so
clear! I feel its
comfort,
though I am
dark!

CHORUS: What deed have you
done, lord, what
deed, Oedipus, have you
done, to make your
eyes
wither? What
divinity, what
dark
divinity
raised your
hands to strike?

OEDIPUS: Apollo!
Apollo!
Destroyer!
Apollo, dear children,

Apollo led me to
pain, to
pain, to these
evils! But I, only I,
I only, with my
own hands
raised the
double pins to
fall, to
plunge in my
eyes!
How could I
see, how could I
bear to see, when
everywhere was horror?

CHORUS: Horror.
Yes. Too true.

OEDIPUS: Why then should I
wish, why wish to
see, why hear,
what could
never bring me
joy, my friends?
Take me away, friends,
take me, quickly, no
delay! A man
destroyed!
utterly! most
cursed of men, most
loathed of the gods!

CHORUS: Wretched in
knowledge, wretched in
fortune; my
friend, I wish I had
never known you!

OEDIPUS: Curse him, curse the
man, damn him,
whoever he was, who
unpinned my feet,

                    there on the
            wild pastures!
                There!
                    There! On
            Kithairon! That
                man who saved me from
                    death will have no
            thanks of me!
                I wish I had
                    died,
            died that day,
                died never to have
                    dragged myself and all my
            loved ones down,
                down into
                    misery!
CHORUS: I, too, Oedipus,
                would have
                    wished the same.
OEDIPUS: Then never, never,
                never would I have
                    been my father's
            murderer! Never be
                known to Thebes as my
                    mother's husband! Never be
            abandoned by the
                gods, a son of
                    shame, polluter of my
            mother in my
                father's bed that
                    birthed me in
            misery! What
                evil is
                    greater than the
            evil that
                lighted on
                    Oedipus?
(The Chorus disperses around the orchestra as the Chorus Leader approaches
Oedipus and the music fades out.)

LEADER: How can I say that you were well counseled?
    Better to be dead than blind and living.
OEDIPUS: No more counsel! No more! The punishment
    I laid on myself was just: it could not be better!
    How could I have made my way down
    To Death's Dark Kingdom and borne the sight of my father,
    The sight of my mother? Not even hanging could atone
    For the terrible deeds I did to these two.

    My children—
    How could seeing them, born as they were born,
    Bring me happiness? No! Not with these eyes!
    And not this city, not her high walls,
    Not her holy temples, and sacred statues.
    No! I, Oedipus—
    Once the noblest of all men in Thebes—
    Now the most wretched—damned myself
    Never to know these things again, condemned
    Myself with my own voice, refusing shelter
    To the great polluter, god-pronounced defiler
    Of the house of Laïos, ah! and son of Laïos!
    And once I had declared the stain as mine,
    How could I have looked with a clear eye
    At these faces?
    No! If I could have stifled the source of my hearing,
    Confined this pitiable body
    To a prison beyond the reach of hearing and sight,
    I would have done so! How sweet it is to live
    With thoughts outside the reach of sorrow!

    O Kithairon!
    Why did you shelter me?
    Why did you not kill me?
    For then I would never have shown to all the world
    My evil birth!
            O Polybos!
                 O Korinth!
    My ancestral home! Or so I believed!
    What a fair child you raised, never knowing

The fester beneath the skin; for I am evil,
Evil in my origins; evil in my being!
O three roads!
          Dark ravine!
               Oak grove
And narrow pass where three roads meet!
You drank my father's blood,
My blood,
From these hands!
Do you remember?
Remember the evil I did there?
And the evil I did when I came here!
O marriage, marriage, you gave me birth,
And then devoured the sperm of your own progeny,
To grow again, mingling fathers, brothers,
Sons, the same blood, brides and wives
And mothers! No evil more horrid!
No evil more vile!
          Unspeakable!
              Unspeakable!
I'll say no more.

By all the gods, take me away from Thebes,
Far from Thebes, hide me, kill me, throw me
Into the deep where you will never see me again.

Come—
        Come—
             You mustn't fear to touch me.
Don't let my misery frighten you. I alone,
Of all men, can bear the weight of my evil.
(Kreon enters from the palace with Guards and approaches Oedipus.)
LEADER: Kreon is your successor in Thebes;
    He should be the one to advise
    And act on your request.
    He's here.
OEDIPUS: Ah! How can I speak to him now?
    How do I dare? By what right?
    How can he ever trust me? I have
    Wronged him deeply; I see that now.

KREON: I'm not here to mock you, Oedipus,
    Or to condemn whatever wrong you have done.
    But if you no longer respect the race of men,
    At least respect the Sun that nourishes life!
    Hide your vile pollution,
    An offense to sacred earth and rain and light!
    (To Attendants.)
    Take him inside! Piety demands
    That only kinsmen witness a kinsman's sufferings.
OEDIPUS: I beg you, Kreon, in the god's name,
    Since you have dealt me better and with nobler heart
    Than this vile wretch expected, do as I ask.
    I speak not for my good, but for yours.
KREON: What is this favor?
OEDIPUS: Drive me away from Thebes, Kreon!
    Out of sight where no human voice
    Will ever reach me!
    Cast me out now!
KREON: I would have done just that already,
    But first I must know the god's will.
OEDIPUS: He couldn't be clearer. Destroy, he said,
    Destroy the father-killer! Destroy
    The evil one! Destroy Oedipus!
KREON: So they said. And yet, it is better to learn
    Precisely what the god desires.
OEDIPUS: You would trouble the god over this wretch?
KREON: I'd say you're ready now to obey the god!
OEDIPUS: Ready? Yes! And I hope, Kreon,
    That you will be just and see that woman in there
    Is given proper burial, for she is your sister.
    As for me:
    Thebes must never give me shelter—
    Not while I'm alive. Let me live
    In the mountains, on Kithairon—Kithairon
    Whose name and mine are so famously joined!
    That rock chosen by my mother and my father,
    To be my tomb! Let me die in the place
    Where they would have had me die, those who set out
    Once to kill me.

And yet, I know this much:
I know that death would never have come from sickness
Or anything else. I would not have been spared
The first time had fate not put me aside
And saved me for some unthinkable end.
Let fate lead where it will.

As for my children, don't worry about my sons;
They're males; and wherever their lives may lead,
They can see to themselves.

Ah, but my girls,
Poor pitiable daughters, who have shared my table,
Never apart from their father: look after them, Kreon,
Look after them for me! Ah, and if you would,
Let me touch them, my girls, with my own hands,
And weep for my sorrows.
Oh, come, my lord, come,
Your heart is true and noble! If I could touch them
With my hands, only once, I would think I held them
Again as when I had eyes!
(*Two very young children, Antigonê and Ismenê, are lead on from the palace by an Attendant.*)
What am I saying? O gods! Is it my dear ones?
My dear ones weeping? Has Kreon taken pity
And sent to me here the dearest of my children?
Has he?
KREON: I have; knowing the joy they give you,
 I asked that they be brought.
OEDIPUS: Thank you, Kreon! Bless you!
 May the god guard you better on your road
 Than he did on mine!

 Children? Where are you?
                              Come!
                                        Come to my hands!
A brother's hands that made your father's eyes
See as now he sees: once bright and clear,
Now dark! He, my children, saw nothing,

Asked nothing, that time he planted the seed
Where he was sown.

I weep for you now, who cannot see you,
Thinking of the bitter life of sorrow
That men will force on you. What assemblies
Of citizens will you not join: what Theban festivals
Will you not attend, except to turn back,
To return home in tears, instead of enjoying
The celebration?

And when it is time to marry,
What man will risk the burden of infamy
That will haunt you because you are my children?
What evil won't you know?
Your father killed his father,
Seeded the womb that bore him,
The same womb that bore you.
These are the insults you will have to bear.
Who will marry you then? No one, my children.
You will wither away, unmarried, barren fields—
Without children.
(To Kreon.)
Son of Menoikeus! You are the only father
My dear ones have, since those who gave them birth
Are both destroyed. Don't let them wander about
In beggary, without husbands; they are your blood.
You mustn't let them suffer for my wrongs.
Take pity on them now, so young, deserted
By all the world. They have no one but you.
Promise me. Touch my hand as consent.

Children! If only you could understand,
If only you were old enough to know,
I would have so much to tell you. As it is,
This is the prayer that I would have you pray:
To find a place to live and have a life
Better than your poor father ever knew.
KREON: You have shed enough tears.

Go inside, now.

OEDIPUS: I will, yes, though not with pleasure.

KREON: All things have their time and place.

OEDIPUS: I will go on one condition.

KREON: And that is?

OEDIPUS: That you send me from Thebes.

KREON: If only I could!

OEDIPUS: The gods detest me!

KREON: Then you will have your wish!

OEDIPUS: You consent, then?

KREON: I don't waste words.

OEDIPUS: Take me away!

KREON: Let go of the children.

OEDIPUS: No, don't take them from me!

KREON: Still playing the king?

Don't presume!

What you achieved in life is over.

Your power is dead.

(Kreon turns to the Guards and indicates for them to take charge of the children in Oedipus' arms. He then indicates to other Guards to disperse the Suppliants scattered around the orchestra. The Guards approach Oedipus, pull them from him, and, at a sign from Kreon, lead them into the palace. Kreon, with great authority, surveys the scene, turns, and silently strides into the palace after them. The doors close behind him with a dull-heavy thud. Oedipus is left alone in the center of the orchestra. The Chorus and the others, except for the Leader, slowly turn from him and go off variously, in silence, to the right. Slowly and silently the Leader approaches Oedipus from the edge of the orchestra. Oedipus hears the scraping of the Leader's sandals on the earth and apprehensively, with quick movements of his upward-tilted head, like one attempting to assess the direction of a sound, he utters scarcely-heard mutterings of fear. The Leader gently puts his hand on Oedipus' shoulder causing the blind man to start, then grab at the hand and recognize it. The Leader helps Oedipus to his feet, slowly turns him in the direction of the palace and leads him to the doors and into the palace. The sole sound is the scraping of their sandals on the ground.)

(Silence.)

(Darkness.)

ÊLEKTRA
(ΗΛΕΚΤΡΑ)

CAST OF CHARACTERS

ÊLEKTRA *daughter of Agamemnon and Klytaimnêstra*
ORESTÊS *son of Agamemnon and Klytaimnêstra*
KLYTAIMNÊSTRA *widow of Agamemnon and wife of Aigisthos*
CHRYSOTHEMIS *sister of Êlektra and Orestês*
TUTOR *old servant of Orestês*
AIGISTHOS *current King of Mykenê*
PYLADES *a friend of Orestês*
CHORUS OF THEBAN WOMEN
LEADER OF THE CHORUS
WOMAN ATTENDANT OF KLYTAIMNÊSTRA
MALE ATTENDANTS OF ORESTÊS
MALE ATTENDANTS OF AIGISTHOS

The lines of the Chorus, unless otherwise indicated, are to be delivered by individual voices and varied groups of voices.

ÊLEKTRA

*Before dawn. Mykenê. The skênê represents the royal palace of Agamemnon,
a citadel situated on a commanding height overlooking the Argive plain. A
large double door dominates the façade. A carved stone altar stands in the
middle of the circular orchestra. Elsewhere are statues of Zeus, Hermês, and
Apollo among others. Right and left of the orchestra is an entrance, the left
leading to the country, the right to the city. The Tutor, Orestês, and Pylades
enter left. They come far forward in the orchestra from which place they look
out over the plains of Argos below.*

TUTOR: Here you are, Orestês, son of Agamemnon,
  Son of the great leader of the Greeks at Troy:
  Here you are at last; here the sight
  Your heart so longed to see.

  Below us there, the ancient Argive plain
  You often dreamed of. And there, the grove where Io,
  The river-god's daughter, Inachos' poor child,
  Was stung to madness.

  And there, Orestês, see?
  The Lykêion of Apollo, wolf-killing god,
  Now a market place. And there to the left,
  The temple of Hera, famed throughout the land.

  But here, here where we have come to now,
  Here you see Mykenê radiant with gold;
  And here the blood-stained palace of ancient Pelops
  So often touched by crime.
  It was from there,
  Your father murdered, I carried you away,
  Charged by your sister to save your life and raise you
  To manhood to avenge your slaughtered father.

  But now, Orestês, and you, faithful Pylades,
  Must make your decisions quickly. The sun's bright glare

Already rouses the morning song of birds,
And night's stars fade with the dawning day.
Make your decisions before men rise from their beds.
No delay now:
Time has come for action.
ORESTÊS: Dear old friend, who could doubt your loyalty!
It's quite the same with a noble horse, a thoroughbred.
Old as he is, like you he thrives on danger,
Pricking up his ears, urging us on,
Always the first to follow us into action.
All right, then, here's my plan. Pay keen attention.
And if I miss the mark, I want correction.

When I went to the god's oracle at Delphi
To learn how to avenge my father's murder,
Apollo gave this advice: "Go alone,
Unaided by arms or soldiers, and snatch by stealth
The lawful vengeance that is yours."
This is what he said, the god's words.

Our plan, old friend, is for you to enter the palace
At the first chance, learn all there is to know,
And bring us word.
Don't worry,
They'll never know you after all these years,
Especially now your hair's gone gray.
They'll never suspect.

Now, then, here's your story:
Tell them you're from Phokis; a stranger here;
Sent by their greatest ally, Phanoteüs.
Swear an oath that Orestês was thrown from his chariot
And killed in the Pythian Games.
Orestês is dead.
Have you got that?
And while you're busy with that, Pylades and I
Will visit my father's tomb to pour libations
And leave a lock of hair as the god requires.

When we come back we'll bring the bronze urn
We hid in the bushes earlier and trick them
With the happy tale of my death and my body's ashes
Resting in that jar. No harm in that.
Not as long as my death is only a tale,
And I'm alive and safe and out to win
Vengeance for my father and my own glory.
What harm can words do if I profit from them?

I've heard how clever men have played at death,
Only to return home again, alive,
In higher esteem that ever.
From this I conclude that, from my rumored death,
I will rise from the gloom a radiant star
To dazzle my enemies!
(At the central stone altar.)
Land of my fathers, Argos,
And you my country's gods,
Bless my journey here and its mission!
House of my fathers,
I have come at the gods' calling
To purify your halls.
Do not turn me away,
Dishonored, out of this land,
For I bring you back your greatness
And reclaim my ancestral right!

Enough of words.
You know your task, old friend.
Pylades and I will leave here now.
The time is right, and time well chosen
Dictates all success.
(Êlektra's cries are heard from inside the palace)
ÊLEKTRA: Ioo moi moiiiiiiiiii!
TUTOR: Orestês, listen!
Inside the palace!
An unhappy slave girl most likely!
ORESTÊS: Is it Êlektra?
Poor creature!
Shall we stay and listen?

TUTOR: No. Apollo first.
> Libations at your father's tomb
> Puts victory in our grasp.
> *(As Orestês and Pylades go off right and the Tutor goes left, music fades in
> and Êlektra enters through the doors of the palace. She is raggedly dressed,
> unkempt, and barefoot.)*

ÊLEKTRA: O holy light,
>   o air embracing the
>   earth's broad
> frame! How many
>   laments, how many wild
>   blows to my bleeding
> breast have you
>   witnessed when night's dark
>   gloom recedes?
> How many
>   nights has my hated
>   bed borne my
> despair in this house,
>   keening dirges for father, not
>   slaughtered in battle by
> Arês on foreign shores, but
>   felled like an oak by my
>   mother and her
> bedmate, Aigisthos, like
>   woodcutters:
>   head cleft with an ax,
> murderous blow upon blow!
>   But where, where are the
>   laments, where are the
> sounds of sorrowing in this
>   house for you, father?
>   None to lament the
> dishonor, none to
>   keen the disgrace
>   of a death so cruel, so
> piteous!
>   None, only
>   mine,

mine!
    As long as stars
        tremble in glory, as
long as light dawns into
    day, that long will the
        agony of my pain,
like the nightingale
    torn from her young,
        here, at my father's
door, wail my
    sorrow and loss for
        all the world to hear!

(Making her way to the altar in the center of the orchestra, she faces out-
ward, her arms raised in supplication.)
    House of the God of Death and Persephonê!
    Chthonian Hermês! Holy Curse!
    Furies, Dread Daughters, Erinyës who see
    and curse the wasters of life in violence!
    Who see and curse the polluters of beds!
    Come, o come, and lend your aid!
    Gods, avenge our father's murder!
    O send him to me, gods: my brother!
    My strength is gone, my burden bows me,
    grief defeats me, I am nothing alone!

(During the above invocation, the Chorus of the Women of Mykenê enters
the orchestra through both exits. Here as elsewhere the Chorus speaks indi-
vidually and in varying combinations.)
CHORUS: O child,
        child, Êlektra,
            daughter of a
    wretched mother,
        why are you
            always lamenting
    for a father
        dead so long? For
            Agamemnon, godlessly
    snared by your
        mother's net of
            deceit,

delivered to
   death by her
      evil? I
pray the end of
   him who
      dared such a
deed be
   evil, if I may
      pray such a prayer!

ÊLEKTRA: Daughters of noble fathers,
   your kindness touches my
      heart. You come to
console my distress,
   but I will not end my
      mourning, I will not
leave undone the
   task of lamenting my father.
      Women, you whose
love matches mine in
   every mood, leave me my
      grief, I beg of you!

CHORUS: No degree of
   sorrow, no
      level of
lamentation will
   raise your loved
      father from the
Lake of the
   Dead into which
      all descend. The
course of your
   grief is
      fatal; it knows no
cure; forever
   breaking the bounds of
      measure. This way
knows no
   deliverance from
      evil. Why is your

heart set on sorrow?

ÊLEKTRA: Foolish, foolish the
        child that turns
memory away
    from a parent's piteous
      death! But dearer to my
heart is the mourner
    forever lamenting for Itys,
      Itys, bird maddened with
grief, messenger of Zeus!
    And you, Niobê, you
      who mourn eternally in your
rocky tomb,
    you are blest!

CHORUS: You are not the
only one, child, that
    great sorrow has
      visited. Your
grief is far greater than
    any other of your kin:
      your own sisters,
Chrysothemis and Iphianassa;
    and Orestês, whose
      fortunate youth is
nurtured far from this
    terrible sorrow;
      whom one day
famed Mykenê will
    welcome to his father's
      throne as savior, if
Zeus will be kind.

ÊLEKTRA: I wait and I wait,
      weary with longing,
childless, unwed! With
    tearful eyes I
      endure the suffering that
never ends, no
    end to evil!
      He has forgotten

all he endured,
              all he was taught! What
                          word have I had, what
news has he sent, what
              word that does not
                          mock the result? He
yearns to come,
              or so he says,
                          yet never comes!

CHORUS: Child, have faith!
                  Zeus is powerful!
                              He sees all, he
governs all!
                  Leave your bitter
                          quarrel to him.
Remember your
                  foes, but don't be
                              destroyed by too much
wrath. Time is a
                  kindly god, a
                          god who brings
relief. Neither
                  he who dwells in Krisa,
                          the shore where cattle graze,
Agamemnon's son,
                  nor the god of
                          Acheron's waters, is
heedless of Time's resolution.

ÊLEKTRA: Ah, no!
                  Most of my life has
passed me by without hope!
                  I have no strength left,
                          wasting away without
children, no loving
                  husband to protect me!
                              But like some honorless alien
I serve in my father's
                  chambers daily
                          in these ugly rags,

standing at a bare table!

CHORUS: The cry heard at your
        father's return was piteous!
Piteous, too, was the
    cry when he saw,
      lying there on his couch,
the blade of the brazen
    ax sink swiftly to his
      skull in murderous
deadly flight!
    Guile led the way,
      lechery did the deed!
Together they birthed a
    dreadful Shape,
      dreadful whether of
man or god.

ÊLEKTRA: Ah, the bitterness, the
      bitterness of that day,
bitterest of all the
    days I have known!
    Oh, that night!
Unspeakable banquet of
    horror and shame!
    And the dreadful death my
father tasted at the
    hands of those two!
    The hands that took my life
captive!
    Treasonous hands!
    My life in ruins!
God, in your greatness,
    Olympian god,
      give them suffering to
match their deed!
    Give them no joy in the
      splendors they've won!

CHORUS: Say no more, child!
    Think of the miseries your
      actions have brought you!

Your load of
  suffering is weighted,
    weighted by
forever breeding
  war in your soul!
    You cannot,
cannot fight such
  battles with powerful
    princes!

ÊLEKTRA: I was forced to it,
    forced by terrible
      events! I know my
passion, I know it well,
  but with such deeds of
    horror around me, I
refuse to curb this
  passionate frenzy while
    life is in me!
Who, dear friends,
  who that thinks right
    could ever believe that there are
words of comfort to
  soothe me?
    Give up your mission,
dearest comforters! I know no
  comfort, my ills are cureless, my
    sorrows endless, my
complaints uncountable!

CHORUS: I speak in love,
    like a faithful
mother. You mustn't
  add to your
    miseries, child.

ÊLEKTRA: What is the measure
  for my misery? Is it
    honorable to neglect the dead?
Was such impiety ever
  born in man? If so, I'll
    never seek his respect,

never! If ever comfort
　　comes, I will never
　　　　live at ease by
　　restraining the wings of
　　　　shrill lamentation to my father's
　　　　　　shame. For if he who
　　lies in earth is
　　　　nothing, mere
　　　　　　dust, wretched man, and
　　those who slew him
　　　　know no justice,
　　　　　　death for death,
　　where, then, is piety?
　　　　Where is shame?
　　　　　　Dead,
　　vanished,
　　　　gone,
　　　　　　gone from the earth!
(The Chorus disperses as the music fades out.)
LEADER: Dear child, I came with as much concern for you
　　As for myself. But if there is no way to help,
　　Then have your own way. I'll stand by you.
ÊLEKTRA: Friends, dear friends, it shames me if you think
　　I mourn too much; if I am too impatient
　　With my endless tears and complaints.
　　Forgive me. What can I do?
　　But how could any woman of noble birth
　　Do otherwise if she saw wrongs committed
　　Day and night against her father's memory;
　　Yes, as I see them here, wrongs that grow
　　Incessantly, without check?

　　First: my mother: the mother who gave me birth:
　　I find in her the deepest cause for hatred.
　　And then I live in my own home with them:
　　My father's murderers: king and queen now;
　　Subject to them, my rulers; for them to decide
　　What to give and what to withhold.
　　What do you think my days are like, watching

Aigisthos sitting on my father's throne,
Wearing my father's robes, pouring libations
At the same hearth where he slew him?
And then the gravest outrage of all: seeing him,
My father's butcher, lounging in his bed,
My father's bed, with the wretch that is my mother,
If mother I can call her—*his* lover, *his!*—
So hardened now she cohabits with that polluter,
Fearing no avenging Fury.
No!
She laughs, she gloats, she chooses that day she murdered him,
Murdered him with treachery, to celebrate
With dancing and hymns and monthly ritual sacrifice
Of cattle to the gods who saved her skin.

And what of me? What am I to do
But mourn my loss with miserable tears
When I see that abomination of a feast
Named for my father's death, forced to grieve
Not as my heart would wish but in seclusion.

For this, this woman, known to all as Majesty,
Berates me with evil insults: "Impious, hateful
Creature," she screams, "are you the only daughter
Who ever lost a father? Are there no other
Mourners in the world? Damn your life!
May the gods below give you no end of weeping!"

These are her insults—
Except when there are rumors Orestês is coming.
Then she comes at me raging: "I owe this to you!
You who stole Orestês out of my arms!
Took him off in secret to 'save' him from danger!
Yes—and I'll see you pay the penalty in full!"

These are the barks she makes, the mother-bitch,
Yapping away, while her noble bridegroom stands by,
Urging her on in the same tune, Aigisthos,
This coward, this plague, this warrior who fights his battles
From under a woman's skirt.

And I wait, here, always for Orestês' coming;
Orestês who will free us from these miseries.
But little by little my life here rots away.
He's always coming. Always about to do something.

What hopes I cherished, all, are frazzled away.
This is no time, my friends, for moderation,
No time for or piety.
Surrounded by evil, evil is all I can do.
LEADER: Where is Aigisthos? Here or away?
ÊLEKTRA: Away, of course. In the country.
If he were near, I would have kept inside.
LEADER: I'll speak freely, then.
ÊLEKTRA: Yes, say what you like.
LEADER: It's your brother Orestês.
We were wondering—is he coming or isn't he?
ÊLEKTRA: He promises, yes; but he never arrives.
LEADER: A terrible task. Any man would hesitate.
ÊLEKTRA: I didn't hesitate when I saved *him!*
LEADER: His is a noble nature. He'll come.
ÊLEKTRA: Without that hope I'd have died long ago.
(Chrysothemis, carrying grave offerings, enters from the palace.)
LEADER: Say no more.
Here's your sister Chrysothemis,
With offerings to the dead below.
CHRYSOTHEMIS: Sister, what are you doing outside the palace?
Why must you always speak where all Argos can hear?
Haven't you learned in all this time
Not to give way to this useless display of anger?
I share your grief. You know that.
If I had the strength, I would have made it clear
Exactly what I think of them. But I don't dare.
In times like these it's best to bend to the storm,
Rather than *seem* to be doing but have no power.
I advise you to do the same.
And yet, the weight of Justice is on your side,
Not on mine. But if I am to live free,
Then I must bow to those in power.
ÊLEKTRA: How can you, the daughter of Agamemnon,

Forget him and put your mother first.
All these lectures you throw at me are hers,
Not yours. You have to choose, Chrysothemis, choose,
Whether to be correct—a fool, like me—
Or be mistaken and betray those you love best.

You said just now that if you had the strength,
That if you *dared,* you'd show just how much you hate them.
And yet, when I give my all to avenge my father,
You do nothing. You struggle to drive me off course.
Why add to your disgrace by being a coward?

Tell me, then, or no, let me tell *you,*
How would I profit by giving up my mourning?
Do I not live? Yes, miserably, I know;
But well enough for me. And when I vex *them,*
That honors the dead, if indeed the dead
Know anything of pleasure in their world.
But you who hate them, or so you say, hate only
In *words,* while in *deed* you are on *their* side,
The side of your father's butchers. I would *never,*
Not for all the privileges they've given you,
That you so pride yourself in, *never* yield to them!
Have all the well-spread tables and luxury you want.
All I want for myself is peace of mind.
I don't choose to enjoy the honors you do.
Nor would you, were you wise.
You might have called yourself Agamemnon's daughter,
Daughter of the noblest of fathers;
But you choose to be called your mother's daughter,
Daughter of Klytaimnestra, known to most
As the vile traitor to your dead father and your loved ones!
LEADER: No, my dears, don't quarrel;
What good can come of it?
There's good in both your arguments;
Learn from each other.
CHRYSOTHEMIS: I know all her arguments by now.
I'd never have brought this up if I hadn't heard
Of some dreadful disaster coming to end her complaints.

ÊLEKTRA: Dreadful disaster? Tell me.
　　If it's any worse than what I suffer now
　　I'll say no more.
CHRYSOTHEMIS: I'll tell you all I know.
　　They've said that either you stop this public mourning,
　　Or they'll send you to a place beyond the border
　　Where you can wail your griefs in a living grave
　　And never see daylight again.
　　Listen to me, please!
　　Be sensible while there's time.
　　And don't be blaming me when its too late.
ÊLEKTRA: Aha, so that's what they plan.
CHRYSOTHEMIS: Yes, when Aigisthos returns.
ÊLEKTRA: Then let him hurry back!
CHRYSOTHEMIS: Poor Êlektra! What are you saying!
ÊLEKTRA: That he should come quickly if he'll do what you say.
CHRYSOTHEMIS: So you can suffer? Have you lost your senses?
ÊLEKTRA: Yes, to escape from all of you.
CHRYSOTHEMIS: Are you so eager to give up your life?
ÊLEKTRA: My wonderful miracle of a life!
CHRYSOTHEMIS: It could be if you used some sense.
ÊLEKTRA: Don't teach me to betray my loved ones!
CHRYSOTHEMIS: I'm not! Only to yield to power!
ÊLEKTRA: Yield all you want! Not me!
CHRYSOTHEMIS: There's no honor in being destroyed by folly.
ÊLEKTRA: If I fall, I'll fall honoring my father.
CHRYSOTHEMIS: My father won't blame me. He'll understand.
ÊLEKTRA: Only cowards think such thoughts!
CHRYSOTHEMIS: You refuse to listen; refuse my advice.
ÊLEKTRA: Yes. I'm not that foolish yet.
CHRYSOTHEMIS: Yes, all right then, I'll go.
ÊLEKTRA: To do what? What offerings are these?
CHRYSOTHEMIS: Libations for father's grave. From mother.
ÊLEKTRA: Offerings to the man she hated?
CHRYSOTHEMIS: To the man she killed is what you mean.
ÊLEKTRA: Whose idea was this? Who persuaded her?
CHRYSOTHEMIS: It was some nightmare terrorized her.
ÊLEKTRA: Gods of my father, stand by me at last!
CHRYSOTHEMIS: You're saying that her fear gives you hope?

ÊLEKTRA: Tell me her dream. Then I'll answer.
CHRYSOTHEMIS: What can I say? I know so little.
ÊLEKTRA: Tell what you know. A single word
　　Seals a man's fate.
CHRYSOTHEMIS: All I know is that she saw my father—
　　Our father, I mean—come back to life
　　And stand there in front of her holding the scepter
　　That once was his but now Aigisthos holds.
　　He planted it beside the hearth; and that scepter
　　Sprouted upward and into a leafy bough
　　That shaded all of Mykenê.
　　I heard it from a slave who was at her side
　　When she told the dream to the Sun. That's all I know—
　　Except that she sends me because she's terrified.

　　By the gods of our house, Êlektra, listen, please!
　　Don't destroy yourself by being foolish!
　　Refuse, and you'll be needing my help later,
　　When things get worse.
ÊLEKTRA: Sister, these gifts must never touch his tomb!
　　No law divine or human allows such offerings
　　To my dead father, not from his hating wife,
　　His enemy wife! Scatter them to the winds!
　　Bury them deep in the earth where none of them
　　Will ever come near his tomb, so when she dies
　　She'll find them stored up below,
　　To remind her of what she did.

　　She's hard, our mother. The hardest of women.
　　Who else could have sent these enemy offerings
　　To pour over the tomb of the man she killed?
　　How could he welcome gifts from someone who treated
　　His corpse as an enemy, without honor, mutilating him,
　　And then wipe the bloodstains off in his hair!
　　Do you think these gifts absolve her of the murder?
　　No! Throw them out! Now!

　　Take him an offering cut from your hair, a lock
　　From the fringe, there, and from mine—

Mine so plain and dull, a scant gift,
But all I have.
And take this, too, this belt, this plain cloth belt.
Then fall to your knees and pray him to come in kindness
From deep in the earth to help us against our enemies, ·
Pray that Orestês comes to fight his foes
And set his foot in victory on his enemies' heads!
Then, then, we will deck his tomb with gifts
Far richer then these!

I believe, o I believe, it was he who sent
This dream to terrify that woman!
Do this for me, sister!
Dear sister, do it!
For your sake and for mine! And for his,
Dearest of men, in the world below!
LEADER: What she says, my dear,
Is said from the heart.
Be wise; do as she says.
CHRYSOTHEMIS: I will, yes, at once.
I have a duty that can't be argued.
But you must help with your silence, friends.
If our mother hears, I'll regret my daring action.
(As Chrysothemis goes off, right, music fades in and immediately the Chorus takes up a new position in the orchestra. Êlektra remains.)
CHORUS: If I am not deceived,
                  my mind
                        maddened with prophecy,
                  failing in wisdom, then
                        Justice, who presages the
                              coming event, will
                  appear, bearing in her
                        hands the righteous
                              triumph of revenge.
                  My heart rises in
                        courage; new hope
                              wakes in my breast,
                  when I hear the
                        word of the dream, the

               dream that
comforts.
       He hasn't forgotten you,
           child, the hero who
led the Hellenes,
       king of the Greeks,
           your father. Nor has the
ax forgotten, forged in
       bronze,
           double-edged,
made to
       slay him in an act of
           foul cruelty.
Many-footed,
       many-handed,
           out of ambush Erinys will
come! Erinys, never
       tiring in her
           dread pursuit,
marching like a
       host of brazen-footed
           warriors! Wicked,
wicked their ruinous
       lust that led to an illicit
           bed! Evil, accursed
liaison, blood-stained
       marriage! And so,
           I know the dark night's
portent cannot come to them
       without great misery,
           doers of the deed,
partners in crime!
       Man will know no
           danger from evil
dreams and oracles
       if this night's dark vision
           brings no fulfillment in its
wake!
       O chariot-race of Pelops

in days long gone, how
heavy the disaster you have
brought this land!
From the day when Myrtilos
plunged into the sea,
hurled to his destruction
from the golden chariot,
this house has known no
freedom, none, from
misery and violence!

(During the conclusion of the ode, Klytaimnêstra, dressed in her finery, in great contrast to Êlektra, enters from the great doors of the palace accompanied by a woman Servant who carries offerings for the dead. The Chorus disperses around the orchestra in various combinations.)

KLYTAIMNÊSTRA: Loose again, are you?
Prowling the grounds with impunity
While Aigisthos is out of the palace?
At least he kept you from ranging beyond the gates,
Disgracing your family in public.
But now, with him gone, you ignore me.
I who, according to you—
Oh, you've spread it around, far and wide!—
Am an arrogant, ruthless tyrant who abuses you!
Insolent you call me?
No. I merely return in kind
The evil taunts you always level against me.
Your father—this is your pretext, never off it!—
Was killed by me. Oh, and how right you are.
I glory in it. Justice at my side.
Justice's hand and mine brought down the ax.

And you, if you knew where your duty lay, would have helped.
This 'father' you're always moaning and groaning over,
Alone among the Greeks, was brute enough
To sacrifice your sister to the gods;
That 'father' who knew nothing of the pangs
I suffered in giving her birth.

Tell me this: Why did he sacrifice her?

Who was he trying to please?
The Greeks, you'll say.
But what right had they to slay my child?
Or was it for his brother Menelaos?
For his sake my child died?
If so, then Justice demands he pay the price.
And Menelaos: what of his two children?
Shouldn't they have been first in line for sacrifice,
Considering their mother and father were the cause
That sent the Greeks to set their sails for Troy?
Or had the God of Death a taste more suited
To my offspring than hers?
Or that 'father' of yours, curse him, curse him!
Had he no love for the children of my womb,
And loved his more? Menelaos' more?
Callous, perverse excuse for a father!
Or so I see it. Whatever you may think!
And so would my dead child if she could speak.

What I have done was done without regret.
But if you call me evil, first make certain
Your own judgment is sound before you condemn.
ÊLEKTRA: This time it's not for you to say I started it;
No provocation on my part for your words.
But allow me to speak, and I will lay out the truth
As it concerns my dead father and my sister.
KLYTAIMNÊSTRA: Say it. You have my permission.
If you had always addressed me in that tone,
I'd not have been pained.
ÊLEKTRA: Well then, I'll speak.—
You killed my father, you say.
What word could bring you greater shame than that,
Whether you did it justly or unjustly?

I maintain that your deed was not just;
That you were seduced to it by the wooing
Of the evil man whose bed you now share.

Ask goddess Artemis what sin she punished

When she held back the frequent winds at Aulis.
Or, no, better yet, I'll tell you:
It isn't right we learn from her.

As I hear it, my father, one day,
Hunting in the goddess' sacred preserve,
Startled with his footstep an antlered stag.
He shot it, and then boasted at the kill,
Angering the goddess, daughter of Lête,
Who, in turn, stayed the winds at Aulis,
Detaining the Greeks, and, demanding in balance,
The sacrifice of his own daughter for the slaughtered beast.

And so it happened; no other solution forthcoming:
The fleet could sail neither homeward nor to Ilion
Without a wind.
And he had no easy time of it,
Struggling with himself.
And so he killed her.
And *not* for Menelaos!

And even if he had, and here I plead
Your own argument, sought to aid his brother,
Does that justify his murder at your hands?
By what law?

Take care in setting out such laws for men;
You may be sowing pain and repentance for yourself.
If blood could pay for blood, you'd be the first
To pay the price, if Justice had her say.

But consider, now.
Isn't this pose of yours without foundation?
Tell me you are not committing the most shameful of acts:
Cohabiting with him whose hands are blood-stained
With my father's murder,
With whom you first laid plans to kill my father,
And breed with him children you cherish more
Than the lawful children you bore in lawful marriage,
Whom now you cast off from your love.

How is this just?
Or is it, as you will say,
Still revenge for your daughter? For if so,
What you are doing is shameful.
One doesn't marry the enemy for the sake of a daughter.
Where is honor in that?
But I haven't even the right to rebuke you.
You'd shriek I'm reviling my mother.
Mother!
You're no mother!
You're a jailer who makes my life wretched
With all the miseries you cast at me,
You and your bedmate in crime!

And then there's the other,
Who escaped by the skin of his teeth,
Wretched Orestês, whose life wears away
In misery and exile.
You have often charged
I reared him to avenge your crime.
And I would have, too, believe me I would,
If I had had the power.
For that matter, denounce me all you like:
Evil call me! Insolent! Impudent!
If I have any 'natural' skill in these 'arts,'
At least I don't shame the mother who gave me birth!

LEADER: She's furious, too furious to know
   Whether what she says makes sense.

KLYTAIMNÊSTRA: But *I* know!
   Why should I care for the creature!
   Insulting her mother! And at *her* age!
   She'll stop at nothing! Nothing!
   She has no shame!

ÊLEKTRA: No shame? Oh, I have shame,
   Whatever you choose to think.
   I know I'm insolent.
   I know that my behavior does me no credit.
   But your hatred of me, your ill-treatment,
   Force me to act as I do.

Ugly acts engender ugly acts.
I learned that from you.
KLYTAIMNÊSTRA: Shameless, impudent creature!
How right you are!
You talk entirely too much
Of what I do and say!
ÊLEKTRA: No, mother,
Your actions speak for themselves.
KLYTAIMNÊSTRA: By Artemis, I swear
You'll pay for your insolence when Aigisthos returns!
ÊLEKTRA: There, you see?
You tell me to have my say;
And when I do, you're outraged
And refuse to listen.
KLYTAIMNÊSTRA: Give me some peace, won't you,
And allow me to sacrifice?
I let you say freely what you had to say.
ÊLEKTRA: Make your sacrifice.
My lips won't be to blame.
I'll say no more.
KLYTAIMNÊSTRA: Slave, bring the offerings to Lord Apollo.
I'll pray and ask him to free me from these fears.
(The Servant approaches with the offerings. Klytaimnestra kneels.)
Apollo! Protector! Hear and answer my prayers.
I am not among friends and cannot speak my heart,
Cannot unfold the secret prayers that lie there,
Not while she is here, whose malicious tongue
Would wag with vicious rumor all my thoughts
Through all the city. Hear me as I would be heard.

The dreams I dreamt last night, Lykêian king:
If they were good, turn them to my advantage;
If bad, turn them against my enemies.
If there are those who plot to cast me out
From my high estate and wealth, frustrate their schemes.
Let me live as I live now! Safely!
Ruling the House of the Atreidai and the throne.
Spending happy days with friends I have,
And those of my children who do not hate or resent me!

Apollo Lykêios, be gracious, hear my prayers.
Grant them to us all, even as we ask.
And for all I do not say, I know you know,
For children of Zeus see all things.
(Finishing her speech, she takes the offerings from the hands of the Servant and places them on the altar, then kneels again. During this, the Tutor enters left, pretending not to know his way.)
TUTOR: Ladies—excuse me.
A stranger here, I'm looking for the palace
Of King Aigisthos.
LEADER: You've found it, then, sir.
This is it—you've guessed right.
TUTOR: And the lady there—is that his wife?
She has a queenly bearing.
LEADER: Right again, sir.
You're in her presence.
(Klytaimnestra rises from the altar as the Tutor approaches her.)
TUTOR: Greetings, royal lady!
I bring news for you and Aigisthos—
Good news that should please you—
From a friend.
KLYTAIMNÊSTRA: A welcome omen, then.
I accept. Who is this friend?
TUTOR: Phanoteüs of Phokis.
And news that concerns you deeply.
KLYTAIMNÊSTRA: A good friend, yes.
What is it? Coming from him
It must be good.
TUTOR: Orestês is dead.
That's it.
ÊLEKTRA: O god! Orestês!
I can't bear this!
KLYTAIMNÊSTRA: Tell me again! Again!
Ignore her! Again!
TUTOR: He's dead—Orestês is dead.
ÊLEKTRA: O god, god, kill me too!
KLYTAIMNÊSTRA: You! Mind your business!
—All right, sir, the truth now.
How did he die?

TUTOR: Yes, my lady, it's why I was sent.
  I'll tell you—tell you all.
  He made his way to Delphi to enter the games
  That are the most highly praised of all in Hellas.
  When he heard the herald call runners to the footrace,
  The first event scheduled, he strode on the field,
  His gleaming body the joy of all who saw him,
  And finished the course in form as fine as his looks,
  Winning the victor's prize.

  After that—well, to cut it short,
  There wasn't a man to match him in achievement:
  He bore away every prize in every footrace,
  And the crowd went wild with cheers each time his name
  Was called: "Orestês of Argos, son of Agamemnon,
  Son of the great general who commanded Greece."

  So far, so good. But when a god does mischief,
  Not even beauty and strength can save a man.
  The day finally arrived for the chariot race,
  A fast event that he and many others
  Entered at sunrise; ten in all in the lists.
  An Achaian, a Spartan, two other teams from Libya,
  And Orestês fifth, driving Thessalian mares.
  An Aitolian was sixth with a team of chestnut colts.
  Seventh, a Magnesian; eighth, with white horses,
  An Ainian; the ninth from god-built Athens; and finally,
  A Boiotian. Ten teams in all.

  Taking the places assigned to them by lot,
  The race began at the blast of a bronze trumpet,
  Each man shouting at his horses, shaking the reins;
  And the entire course roared with the rattle of cars
  As dust rose up in clouds.

  Drivers raced in confusion, sparing no goads
  To push their steeds beyond the axle and the horses
  Snorting in front of their own. Both their backs
  And the wheels below were flecked with the foaming breath
  Of the snorting teams.

Driving near the pillar at each turn,
Orestês lightly grazed the wheel of his chariot,
Loosening rein on the trace horse to his right,
Checking the inner horse. Up to then
No chariot had been injured; but all at once
The Ainian's colts bolted, swerving aside
As they passed on from the sixth to the seventh lap,
And plunged headlong into the Barkaian's car.
In quick succession, team after team crashed
And overran each other till the plain of Krisa
Was a mass of wrecked chariots.

The clever Athenian saw the danger coming
And pulled his team aside, reining them in,
Allowing the confusion of chariots in mid-course
To pass him by.
Orestês came up last,
Holding his horses in check,
Trusting his team for the finish.
But when he saw the Athenian alone remained,
He sent a shrill cry through his fine colts' ears
And gave chase. Team raced level beside team,
First one then the other pushing his horses' heads
Into the lead. To the last lap ill-fated Orestês
Made all the turns safely, standing steady
On his steady car. But then at the final turn,
He loosed the rein on the left and, unaware,
Struck the pillar's edge, breaking in two
The axle, and falling headlong from the chariot,
Over the rail, tangled in the reins.
And as he fell, the colts bolted madly
To the center of the course.

When the crowd saw he'd fallen from the chariot,
A cry of pity went up for the beautiful youth
They'd seen carry off so many triumphs
Come to so terrible an end, dragged along,
His body smashed to the ground, then tossed in the air,
Till charioteers halted his horses and freed him,

So covered in blood that none of his friends recognized
The pitiable, mangled corpse.

They burned it then, the body, on a pyre,
Without delay, and chosen men of Phokis
Are carrying here the dust of his mighty form
In a small bronze urn, for burial in his father's land.

There's my story; a story as painful to tell
As any ever was; but for us who saw it,
The most dreadful disaster our eyes have ever seen.
(The Chorus has begun a low keening under the final part of the Tutor's speech and continues it under the following.)

LEADER: Our royal house,
  Our ancient masters,
  Destroyed root and branch!

KLYTAIMNÊSTRA: O god, what is this news?
  Good or terrible? It sets me free.
  My good is served. But it is bitter
  To preserve my life when my own loss
  Is the price for living.

TUTOR: Why does this news distress you, lady?

KLYTAIMNÊSTRA: There's a strange power in motherhood.
  No wrong can make a mother hate her child.

TUTOR: My journey was wasted, then.

KLYTAIMNÊSTRA: Wasted? No, not wasted! How wasted?
  You brought me proof of his death, clear proof,
  My son, my own son, born of my body,
  Who tore himself from my breast and his mother's nurture,
  To become an exile, a stranger, in a foreign land.
  From that day to this he never saw me,
  But held me guilty for the murder of his father;
  Swearing vengeance that robbed me of my sleep
  Night and day, no shelter of sweet peace.
  From moment to moment, I lived in fear of death.
  But now, today, I'm free!
  Free of my fear of her and of him!
  But mostly of her, who lived beneath my roof,
  The greater evil, draining my life's blood.

From this time on I can live my life in peace,
Free of her threats.

ÊLEKTRA: O my dear dear Orestês!
To suffer, to die as you did,
And now to have your mother mock you,
For all your misery!
(To Klytaimnêstra.)
Are you content?

KLYTAIMNÊSTRA: No, not with you!
But where he is, there's content.

ÊLEKTRA: Let divine Vengeance hear what she says
Of the man just dead!

KLYTAIMNÊSTRA: She has heard what she should have heard
And acted well.

ÊLEKTRA: Insult us, yes! Enjoy your victory!

KLYTAIMNÊSTRA: Will you and Orestês put a stop to this?

ÊLEKTRA: It's we who are stopped!
How could we stop you?

KLYTAIMNÊSTRA: Your journey here, my friend,
Deserves a reward.
You've stopped her yappings.

TUTOR: I've no more to say.
May I go?

KLYTAIMNÊSTRA: Go? Certainly not!
Your welcome, then, would be unworthy of me
And of him who sent you. Into the palace!
Come!

As for her, leave her here to yowl
Laments for herself and her loved ones!
(Klytaimnêstra and the Tutor enter the palace.)

ÊLEKTRA: Did you see the pain she suffered,
The grief she suffered,
The mother shedding tears of anguish for a son
Whose death report you heard?
No, she laughed.
Left here laughing.

O Orestês! Dearest Orestês!
Your death has brought my own!

You've torn from my heart
The last shred of hope:
That you would come, someday,
To avenge our father and my wretched self.

Where can I turn?
Where? All alone now.
No brother. No father.
(To the women of the Chorus.)
Back to slaving for those I most despise.
Those who slew my father.
Can I live with this?
No! I will never again enter that house
To live where they live!
I will lie here by the gates, alone,
Till my life withers away.
If anyone inside there is angry,
Let them kill me.
Death is a grace.
Life is grief.
Why should I want to live?
(Music fades in for the lyric dialogue.)

CHORUS: Zeus, Zeus,
   where are your
    thunderbolts?
   Where is the all-seeing
    Sun? How can you
     see and hide this?
   How can you
    hold your
     peace?

ÊLEKTRA: Ah!
   Ah!
    Aiiiiii!
  Aiiiiiiiiiiii!

LEADER: Why are you weeping, child?

ÊLEKTRA: Aiiiii!

LEADER: Don't cry so!

ÊLEKTRA: You're destroying me!

LEADER: But how?
ÊLEKTRA: By planting hope,
                    where hope is dead!
                         They're dead,
                  dead! Why
                       beat me down?
LEADER: But King Amphiareös
                  died for a chain,
                       a chain of gold caught
                            in a wife's net; and now
                  he sits beneath the earth—
ÊLEKTRA: Ah!
                         Ah!
LEADER: —and reigns among the dead.
ÊLEKTRA: No!
                         No!
LEADER: Yes, for she who
                       Killed—
ÊLEKTRA: —was killed!
LEADER: Yes!
ÊLEKTRA: I know, I know!
                         A champion came to
                  avenge the dead! For me
                       there's no one! He who
                            was is
                  torn from me!
LEADER: Misery strikes
                       hard on misery.
ÊLEKTRA: I know, I know!
                    I know too well!
                         A torrent of horrors,
                  dreadful, dark, what
                       else is my life, month after
                            month, never
                  an end!
LEADER: I see your pain;
                         I understand.
ÊLEKTRA: Don't deceive me or
                    lead me astray

	where, where—
LEADER:	What are you saying?
ÊLEKTRA:	—where there is no hope for
	help from a brother,
	son of my father, no
	hope, no hope—
LEADER:	All men must die.
ÊLEKTRA:	But to die as he did,
	wretched Orestês,
	dragged along in a
	whirl of hooves, his body
	cut by tangled reins!
LEADER:	A cruel death, too
	terrible to think of.
ÊLEKTRA:	I know; in a
	foreign land; without my
	touch—
CHORUS:	Aiiiiiiiiii!
ÊLEKTRA:	—buried, buried, his
	grave untended, no
	keening, no
	mourning laments!

(Chrysothemis, excited and out of breath, has entered, right, before the end of the above. The music fades out.)

CHRYSOTHEMIS: Dear sister! Dear Êlektra! I'm so happy!
  I ran all the way, never thinking how it might look!
  I have news for you! News! Wonderful news!
  An end to your suffering!
ÊLEKTRA: Where would you find an end to my suffering?
  My suffering has no cure.
CHRYSOTHEMIS: He's here!
  Orestês is here! Near us now!
  As surely as I stand here in front of you!
ÊLEKTRA: Poor girl, have you lost your mind?
  Laughing at your own sorrows and mine?
CHRYSOTHEMIS: No, I'm not mocking,
  I swear by our father's hearth!
  He's here! Here with us now!
  Among us now!

ÊLEKTRA: Who told you this?
　　And you believed him!
CHRYSOTHEMIS: I know what I saw!
　　My own eyes! I've seen all the proof I need!
ÊLEKTRA: Proof? What proof?
　　What set you into this feverish whirl?
CHRYSOTHEMIS: Êlektra! Listen! Please!
　　And when you've heard, then tell me I'm insane.
ÊLEKTRA: Tell me, if it gives you pleasure.
CHRYSOTHEMIS: I'll tell you all I saw.
　　When I reached father's grave with the offerings I brought,
　　I saw it running with a newly-poured milk-gift,
　　And flowers, fresh-cut flowers of all kinds,
　　Circling the tomb. Amazed, I looked around
　　For someone nearby. But everything was still.
　　So I crept to the tomb, and there on its edge I saw
　　A lock of newly-cut hair, and all at once
　　My mind flooded with thoughts of him, of Orestês,
　　Dearest of men, for I knew that there, on that stone,
　　Lay a token of him!

　　I took it in my hands, unable to speak,
　　Tears flooding my eyes. For I knew then,
　　As I know now, that only you or I
　　Could have done such a thing, and I knew it wasn't you,
　　Forbidden as you are from leaving the house
　　Even to worship the gods, except at your peril;
　　And I knew it wasn't I. Nor was it mother;
　　She doesn't like such things; and it could never
　　Have happened without our knowing.
　　It can only have been Orestês!
　　Be brave, my dear! No one's life is fixed
　　By unchanging fortune; and ours has seen bad days.
　　But perhaps today will lead to a better life.
ÊLEKTRA: Ah, what a fool you are! I pity you.
CHRYSOTHEMIS: What are you saying, Êlektra?
　　How can this not please you?
ÊLEKTRA: You know nothing.
　　You're lost in some dream-world.

CHRYSOTHEMIS: Dream-world? I know what I saw!
ÊLEKTRA: He's dead, poor girl. Orestês is dead.
> Your hopes in *that* deliverer are dashed.
> No use looking to him for help.
CHRYSOTHEMIS: Who told you such a thing?
ÊLEKTRA: A man—
> A man who was there when he died.
CHRYSOTHEMIS: I don't believe it!
> Where is he? Where?
ÊLEKTRA: There. In the palace.
> A welcome guest for our mother.
CHRYSOTHEMIS: Oh, no. But the offerings
> —On the grave—where did they come from?
ÊLEKTRA: From someone to honor Orestês' death.
CHRYSOTHEMIS: Dear god will this never end?
> I ran here bursting with joy at my news,
> Knowing nothing, nothing, of what has happened,
> Only to find new sorrows.
ÊLEKTRA: Now you understand.
> Just do as I say and we can lighten
> This load of sorrows.
CHRYSOTHEMIS: Bring the dead to life?
> But how is that possible?
ÊLEKTRA: That's not what I said.
> I'm not a fool.
CHRYSOTHEMIS: If I have the strength, I'll do it.
ÊLEKTRA: Then have the courage to do as I say.
CHRYSOTHEMIS: I'll do anything I can to help.
ÊLEKTRA: Just be prepared for a hard fight.
CHRYSOTHEMIS: I know. I'll do all I can.
ÊLEKTRA: All right, then, here's my plan.
> As you know, we haven't a friend left here,
> None to stand by, to help us, everyone dead.
> We're alone now, sister, just the two of us.
> As long as I knew Orestês was still alive,
> I cherished the hope that he would return to Argos
> To avenge our father's murder.
> But now Orestês is dead.

I now turn to you for help, Chrysothemis,
To help your sister slay our father's murderer:
To slay Aigisthos.
There. No more secrets.

But what must it take, what, to make you act
Before you stop doing nothing? Hope is dead.
What hope can you still cling to? All that's left
Is grief for a lost treasure, grief for years
Wasted without a husband, no marriage, no bridal songs,
Nor any prospect, ever, to get these things.
Aigisthos is no fool. Can you imagine
He'd ever allow children of yours or mine
To grow to strength and threaten his precious safety?

But do as I say, my dear, and you'll have the thanks
Of the dead below the earth, our father and brother.
You'll be free, free as you once were born,
Free to marry nobly. Don't you see?
You'd win respect for yourself, for me, if only
You'll do as I say.

What citizen of Argos, what stranger,
Will see us and not greet us with words of praise?
"Here, friends," they'll say, "here are two sisters
Who rescued their father's royal house!
They faced a triumphant enemy, they risked their lives,
They avenged bloody injustice! They deserve our love,
Deserve our respect. Let them be honored at festivals
And public assemblies for their great heart and courage."
That's what they'll say, and in life and death our fame
Will never fade.

Dear sister, listen to me!
Take up our father's cause!
Take up our brother's!
Share their pain!
Free me! Free yourself!
Free us of this disgrace!
A life of dishonor dishonors the noble mind!

LEADER: Be careful, my dears.
   Caution is best: both for those
   Who speak and those who listen.
CHRYSOTHEMIS: Caution? Yes.
   She'd have done well to do so.
   But she's out of her mind:
   Arming herself in rashness
   And calling on me to help.

   You're a woman, Êlektra. You're weak.
   You don't have the strength to fight your enemies.
   Their fortune grows daily by leaps and bounds,
   While ours fails, withering away to nothing.
   Who could plot to kill a man like Aigisthos
   And escape unscathed? He'll punish us with miseries
   Worse than we suffer already if we're discovered.
   What good is fame and honor if we end up dead?
   But worse even than that is to long for death
   And not be allowed to die.

   Please, Êlektra, before we destroy ourselves
   And our whole family, rein in your anger.
   Everything you've said I'll keep a secret
   As though you never spoke it. You must learn,
   However late, to yield to those in power
   When you are helpless.
LEADER: Do as she says.
   Caution and common sense
   Are the best life offers.
ÊLEKTRA: I can't say I'm surprised.
   I knew you'd refuse. All right.
   I'll do it alone. It can't be left untried.
CHRYSOTHEMIS: O god, if only your mind had been so set
   On the day father was murdered!
   But you did nothing!
ÊLEKTRA: The will was there, just not the understanding.
CHRYSOTHEMIS: Then keep that understanding all your life.
ÊLEKTRA: This lecture of yours tells me you refuse to help.
CHRYSOTHEMIS: Yes, because to act is to court disaster!

ÊLEKTRA: I envy your caution; it's your cowardice I hate!

CHRYSOTHEMIS: The day will come, when you'll see I was right.

ÊLEKTRA: No, sister, that day will never come.

CHRYSOTHEMIS: The future's a long time; we'll wait and see.

ÊLEKTRA: Get out of here! Out! You're useless to me!

CHRYSOTHEMIS: I could be useful, but you refuse to learn.

ÊLEKTRA: Go on, then, go! Go tell it to your mother!

CHRYSOTHEMIS: No, my dear, how could I hate you so!

ÊLEKTRA: Then think of the hurt you're doing me, the dishonor!

CHRYSOTHEMIS: Hurt? Dishonor? I'm trying to save you.

ÊLEKTRA: To be saved, must I accept your view of justice?

CHRYSOTHEMIS: Yes, till you've come to your senses.

ÊLEKTRA: How clever you are, and to be so wrong.

CHRYSOTHEMIS: Yes, you describe your problem exactly.

ÊLEKTRA: Are you saying I don't have right on my side?

CHRYSOTHEMIS: Being right can sometimes bring disaster.

ÊLEKTRA: No, I refuse to live by laws like that!

CHRYSOTHEMIS: If you do this thing, you'll see I was right.

ÊLEKTRA: I *will*, I *will* do it! You can't frighten me!

CHRYSOTHEMIS: You can't be stopped, then? Nothing will change you?

ÊLEKTRA: No! There's nothing worse than wrong thinking!

CHRYSOTHEMIS: Nothing I say makes any impression on you.

ÊLEKTRA: I made up my mind on this long ago.

CHRYSOTHEMIS: What more can I say? I'll go.

> You refuse to listen, and I can't accept
> Your choice of action.

ÊLEKTRA: Then go. I won't come

> Trailing after you,
> However much you wish it.
> You're chasing illusions;
> What can be more foolish?

CHRYSOTHEMIS: Think yourself right, if you must.

> When trouble come, you'll think back on my words—
> But too late.

> *(As Chrysothemis turns to enter the palace, music fades in and the Chorus takes up a dominant position in the orchestra.)*

CHORUS: Why, like
>   birds of the
>   air who tend with

filial love to those who
     gave them life,
          do we not do the same?
By Zeus' lightning flash,
     by Themis dwelling in
          heaven, such sin will
not go unpunished, and
     leave us to suffer disgrace.
          O Voice that reaches the
dead under Earth,
     cry a cry to Atreus' son, a
          joyless message of dishonor!
Tell him his house's
     fortunes are ill!
          Tell him his children are
locked in strife! No
     harmony of former days!
          Êlektra,
betrayed,
     forsaken, braves the
          storm alone.
A nightingale,
     alone,
          lamenting,
unafraid of death,
     she moans her father's loss,
          ready to leave the light
if she can
     quell those two Furies.
          Brave child of a
noble father,
     no one nobly born will
          choose to live with evil,
shaming a good name.
     But you, child, o
          child, you chose
honor over all, to
     live in eternal lament,
          winning a two-fold praise,

                    wisest and best of
                        all daughters!
                            I pray now to
                    see your life
                        raised as high in
                            wealth and power
                    above your foes as
                        now you lie
                            low beneath their
                    hands, for I
                        find you here in
                            distress. And yet,
                    because you
                        honor both
                            bounteous nature's
                    greatest laws and
                        bend in
                            piety to
                    Zeus,
                        your name soars
                            high over all!

(Before the Chorus has ended its dance, Orestês disguised as a Phokian coun-
tryman enters left accompanied by Pylades who carries a small funeral urn.
Finished, the Chorus disperses across the stage embracing Êlektra among
them. The scene opens with a light banter, and the music fades out.)

ORESTÊS: Ladies—excuse me—I wonder,

　　　Were we advised correctly?

　　　Are we on the right road?

LEADER: What road would that be, sir?

　　　(She turns with an amused smile to the Chorus, which in turn giggles.)

　　　What are you after?

ORESTÊS: It's Aigisthos' house I'm after.

　　　We've been looking all over.

LEADER: Then you can't blame your guide.

　　　(The Chorus giggles more loudly.)

　　　This is it.

ORESTÊS: Would one of you tell those inside

　　　That those long awaited have arrived?

　　　(The Leader turns toward Êlektra unseen among the women.)

LEADER: This lady is nearest in blood.

She'll do it.

(Êlektra emerges a step or two from among the women.)

ORESTÊS: Dear lady, if you'd be so kind,

Go tell Aigisthos he has visitors from Phokis with news.

(Êlektra catches sight of the urn.)

ÊLEKTRA: O god, no! What are you bringing?

Proof of the story we've just heard?

ORESTÊS: What story would that be?

Old Strophios sent me with news of Orestês.

ÊLEKTRA: What news? Dear god, I'm so afraid!

ORESTÊS: He's dead. There. You see?

The urn he's carrying?

That urn holds all there is.

ÊLEKTRA: Oh, no! Then it's true!

I see in those hands

The weight of all my misery!

ORESTÊS: If your tears are for Orestês,

All that's left of him is in this urn.

ÊLEKTRA: Oh, sir—give them to me—please—

His ashes—let me hold them—

If he's really here—let me weep my lament—

For him, for me, for my whole family!

ORESTÊS: Bring it to her, Pylades. Let her hold it.

Whoever she is, she once loved him;

A friend or relative.

(Pylades brings the urn and hands it to Êlektra who keens for a long while before speaking to it. The Chorus joins in her keening.)

ÊLEKTRA: Memorial of him whom I loved best;

Dearest of men, Orestês! See what is left of you

Now. Only this. How different from him

I once sent away in hope do I receive you:

This nothingness in my hands; you who once

Were full of bright promise when I sent you off.

I wish I had breathed my last before sending you out,

Away to a foreign land, these hands stealing you

From death, so you could have died on that very day

Your father died and shared your portion of his grave.

But now, an exile far from home and country,
You suffered a miserable death, without a sister
To wash and anoint your body with loving hands
And lift you from the flames as custom demands.
Poor, unfortunate child, tended by hands
Of strangers, now come home, a tiny weight
Of dust in a tiny vessel.

Aiiiiiiiiiiiiiiiii!

Orestês!

All the days I nursed you with loving toil,
In vain, all, all wasted. You who were never
Your mother's darling quite as much as mine.
Only I alone in all the house
Nursed you day after day.
You called me "sister."
But now all that is vanished in a day,
For you are dead, and your death, like a whirlwind,
Sweeps all before it.
Father is in his grave;
And I am dead in you;
And you are dead.

Yes, and our foes exult.
That mother who is no mother
Rages in mad rejoicing; the one you often
Sent me secret messages about
That you would come one day and avenge.
But evil fortune, yours and mine together,
Has stolen it all away, and sent you to me
Not in the form I loved, but only ashes,
Dust and a powerless shadow.
(Music fades in as Êlektra raises her arms in an attitude of lament and breaks into an intense ritual incantation somewhere between song and declamation, the urn never leaving her hands.)
Oimoi moiiiiiiiiii!
O ravaged form!

Ah, dreadful, dreadful the
road you traveled!
Ah, dearest Orestês,
you have undone me,
undone by your
death, dearest,
dearest brother!

(The music fades out as the Chorus disperses.)

Take me with you—take me into this shelter.
I who am nothing. Nothing into nothingness.
To live beside you in the world below forever.
In life we shared equal fortune; in death the same.
Not to be parted. Sharing one grave.
I know now the dead are free of pain.

LEADER: Dear Êlektra, your father was only human,
And, being human, mortal, as was Orestês.
You really must grieve less. Death is a debt
That all must pay.

ORESTÊS: Pylades—o god, what can I say!
There are no words! But how can I not speak?

ÊLEKTRA: What is it, sir? I don't understand.

ORESTÊS: Is this—this—the noble Êlektra I see?

ÊLEKTRA: It is—it is—and a pitiable sight, too.

ORESTÊS: O god, can misery be so great?

ÊLEKTRA: Who are you sorry for, sir? For me?

ORESTÊS: So cruelly dishonored—so abused by the gods—

ÊLEKTRA: Your blasphemy describes me well.

ORESTÊS: A life of misery, no husband, a slave.

ÊLEKTRA: Why are you staring? Why this pity?

ORESTÊS: How ignorant I've been of my own misery!

ÊLEKTRA: What have I said to make you see this?

ORESTÊS: Seeing you clothed in so much sorrow.

ÊLEKTRA: You see only the fringes of my misery.

ORESTÊS: Can there be worse than what I see?

ÊLEKTRA: Living there in the house with the murderers!

ORESTÊS: What murderers? Who was murdered?

ÊLEKTRA: My father—my father's murderers, made me their slave.

ORESTÊS: Who forced you to this?

ÊLEKTRA: They call her my mother; but no mother to me!

ORESTÊS: How does she treat you? Violence? Hardship?

ÊLEKTRA: Violence, hardship, every evil.

ORESTÊS: And there's no one to help? No one to stop her?

ÊLEKTRA: No one now. You've brought me his ashes.

ORESTÊS: Poor, poor girl! How I pity you—

ÊLEKTRA: Pity? Then you're the only one.

ORESTÊS: Yes, yes, to share your pain—

ÊLEKTRA: Surely you can't be a distant relative?

ORESTÊS: Are these women loyal? If so, I can speak.

ÊLEKTRA: Loyal? Oh, yes! No betrayal here.

ORESTÊS: Give me the urn; I'll tell you everything.

ÊLEKTRA: No, no, please; I beg of you, don't!

ORESTÊS: Do as I ask. It's all for the best!

ÊLEKTRA: No! Don't take it! It's all I love!

ORESTÊS: Listen to me, no, I can't let you keep it.

ÊLEKTRA: Ah, Orestês! Orestês! Cheated of burial!

ORESTÊS: You mustn't say that! You've no reason to mourn him!

ÊLEKTRA: My brother? Dead? No reason to mourn him?

ORESTÊS: No need to speak of him that way.

ÊLEKTRA: Does even my dead brother dishonor me?

ORESTÊS: Dishonor? No. Mourning's not for you.

ÊLEKTRA: It is! Oh, it is! His body! His ashes!

ORESTÊS: No. Not his ashes. A lie.

(He gently takes the urn from her.)

ÊLEKTRA: Where is he buried, my poor Orestês?

ORESTÊS: Buried? Nowhere. We don't bury the living.

ÊLEKTRA: Oh, dear boy, what are you saying?

ORESTÊS: Only the truth.

ÊLEKTRA: Alive? He's alive?

ORESTÊS: As surely as I am.

ÊLEKTRA: You—? Is it you—?

ORESTÊS: Look, Êlektra! Father's ring and seal!

ÊLEKTRA: O my dear! My light! My darling!

ORESTÊS: My dear! My sister!

ÊLEKTRA: Dear, dear voice!

You've come home to me!

ORESTÊS: Home? Yes!

ÊLEKTRA: O let me hold you!

ORESTÊS: Forever!

(They embrace in long, unmoving silence.)

ÊLEKTRA: Dearest, dearest women!
Women of Argos!
Here is Orestês!
His death was a trick, a trick!
And now that trick gives him life!

LEADER: We see him, child, and tears of joy
stream from our eyes at your happiness!

(Music begins for the lyric dialogue.)

ÊLEKTRA: Child! Child of the
father I loved above
all! You have
come! Come here!
Now! You have
found her,
seen her your
heart so
longed for!

ORESTÊS: I'm here, but you must say nothing,
You must wait.

ÊLEKTRA: Why?
Why?

ORESTÊS: No one inside must hear.

ÊLEKTRA: By Artemis Virgin, no,
I will never
stoop, never
again fear the
women, useless,
in there, burdens
to the earth!

ORESTÊS: Women have warlike spirits, too,
As you should know.

ÊLEKTRA: Ottotoi!
Ottotoi!
Again!
Again! Your words! Your
words! My evil sorrow
cannot be hidden, not
washed away, never
forgotten!

ORESTÊS: I know, but we must act
    When the time is right.
ÊLEKTRA: Time, all time, each
                moment of time, is right to
                    cry out my complaint! For
                        now, only now,
                    is my tongue set free!
ORESTÊS: And you must guard that freedom.
ÊLEKTRA: Guard it?
                        How?
ORESTÊS: Not speak till the time is right.
ÊLEKTRA: But you are here, now,
                    returned! How can I not
                        speak, shout, now,
                when beyond all hope, all
                    thought, I see you,
                        see you, here, here!
ORESTÊS: I came with the god's direction.
ÊLEKTRA: If a god led you
                    home, that is a grace
                        greater than the first, greater
                than all you said before!
                    I see in this the
                        work of a god!
ORESTÊS: Dear sister, there's danger in too much joy.
ÊLEKTRA: Ioo! Dearest Orestês, dearest
                    brother, returned to me
                        now, after all the years, at
                last, at last, my blessing, my
                    joy! Now that you have
                        seen my sorrow, do not,
                do not—
ORESTÊS: What should I not?
ÊLEKTRA: —rob me of comfort, the
                    sight of you, of your dear face!
ORESTÊS: I'll kill the man who dares!
ÊLEKTRA: You will?
ORESTÊS: I will!
ÊLEKTRA: Women!

Friends!
Oh, I have heard,
I have heard a voice I never
hoped to hear! No
silence could have
held my joy!
How could I
hear and not rejoice!
But I *have* you now,
I *have* you,
sweet, sweet face of light,
face never forgotten
even in sorrow!

(She strides to Orestês and embraces him as the music fades out.)

ORESTÊS: No more words now, Êlektra. Later
Is time enough to tell me of mother's crimes,
Or of how Aigisthos drains us dry,
Squanders our father's wealth with wild extravagance.
There's too much to tell; time is running out;
We have to act, and fast.
Tell me what I need to know:
Are we to lie in ambush or attack openly
Those mocking enemies in there?
Once Pylades and I have gone inside,
It's for you to deceive our mother, hide your smiles,
Or she'll suspect what we're up to. Weep hot tears
Of mourning for my death, as though it were true.
The time for smiles will come when we're the victors.

ÊLEKTRA: Dear Orestês, I'll do anything you say.
You've brought me all the happiness I know.
I would never hurt you, not for all the world.
Why insult the god who's with us now?

You know how matters stand.
Aigisthos is out, mother's there inside;
And, no, she'll never see a smile on my face;
My hatred of her is steeped in me too deeply.
But the tears in my eyes that will never stop are tears
Of joy at seeing you. How could they stop,

When in a single hour you've come home twice:
First dead, then alive!
Orestês, it's all so strange!
If father appeared alive, just now, in front of me,
I'd never question that he was really here,
And not a ghost. But now that you have come,
I'll do anything you say. If I were alone now,
I would have won one of two things:
A noble defense for myself, or a noble death.
ORESTÊS: Shh! Someone's coming!
　　There at the door!
　　(Êlektra pretends Orestês and Pylades are strangers.)
ÊLEKTRA: Gentlemen, in with you!
　　Into the house! What you bring
　　Is not a gift they will welcome,
　　Yet they can't refuse it.
　　(The Tutor enters from the palace.)
TUTOR: Silly fools! Imbeciles! Are you mad?
　　Are you so tired of living, or have you lost
　　What little sense you had? You're not on the brink
　　Of danger, lads, you're in it up to your necks!
　　If I hadn't guarded the door, all your plans
　　Would be in there now, and you still out here!
　　Thank me for that! And stop all this speech-making,
　　These cries and shouts, and get inside, now!
　　Delay at a time like this is fatal!
　　Now's the time! Act! Get a move on!
ORESTÊS: What will I find inside there?
TUTOR: It's safe. No one will recognize you.
ORESTÊS: You've told them I'm dead?
TUTOR: To them you're dead and gone.
ORESTÊS: Are they pleased? What are they saying?
TUTOR: That can wait. As for now,
　　Things are as good—or bad—
　　As they need be.
ÊLEKTRA: Orestês, who is this man?
ORESTÊS: Don't you know?
ÊLEKTRA: I can't even guess.
ORESTÊS: The man you once gave me to?

ÊLEKTRA: What man? What are you saying?
ORESTÊS: The man who long ago
 Took me to Phokis—to safety—
 As you planned?
ÊLEKTRA: This? The only friend I had?
 The only being I trusted when father was murdered?
ORESTÊS: The same; no more questions now.
ÊLEKTRA: O dearest day, dearest, dearest of men!
 Dear and only preserver of our father's house!
 Have you come back at last? You? You
 Who have delivered him and me from all our troubles?
 (Taking his hands in hers.)
 Dear, dear hands, dear feet, the help they gave us!
 Oh, to have been here so long and not have told me!
 And me not know, not to have recognized you!
 Your story, your dreadful false story, broke my heart
 And almost killed me, while all along in your heart,
 Your dear, true heart, you brought me what I most wanted,
 Most longed to hear!

 Dear father, welcome, father!
 For that's how I see you!
 Welcome! Welcome! You are the man of all men
 Whom I most hated and loved on a single day!
TUTOR: This no time for words, Êlektra, not now.
 There will be many days and nights to come
 For you to hear the story of all that's happened.
 (To Orestês and Pylades.)
 But now, Orestês, and you, Pylades,
 The time has come to act. The queen is alone,
 None of her soldiers near her, and if you delay,
 There'll be an army of guards for you to fight,
 More numerous and more clever.
ORESTÊS: No time for talk or planning now, Pylades.
 Time to go in. And as we go, let us honor
 The gods of my father's house whose altars these are.
 (Orestês and Pylades approach each altar and do obeisance, then enter the palace through the large doors, followed by the Tutor. Êlektra approaches the altar of Apollo and kneels.)

ÊLEKTRA: Apollo! Lord! Hear what these men ask.
And hear me, too, who have often come to your shrine
With gifts from the little I had, but with fervent hands.
Apollo Lykêios:
With such vows as I can make now,
I pray you, I entreat you, I implore you,
Here on my knees, lend your kind support
To our undertaking, and prove to all how impiety
Is rewarded by the gods!

(Music fades in as she enters the palace. The Chorus of women gradually gathers together in a tight knot as they intone their ode.)

CHORUS:　　　Blood-breathing Arês,
　　　　　　god invincible,
　　　　　　　　moves with
　　　　　purpose to the
　　　　　　fatal feud.
　　　　　　　Beneath the roof now
　　　　hounds advance,
　　　　　pursuers of
　　　　　　guilt that
　　　none may flee.
　　　　　Soon, soon my
　　　　　　soul's
　　　vision that
　　　　hangs suspended will
　　　　　find fulfillment. With
　　foot led on by
　　　stealth he
　　　　comes, crafty
　　champion of the
　　　dead, to Agamemnon's
　　　　gold-rich palace.
　　In his hands a
　　　sword new-whetted.
　　　　Hermês leads him,
　　Maia's son,
　　　shrouder of guile. The
　　　　end is near.

(Êlektra, moving noiselessly, enters from the palace. The women disperse in

little clusters to various parts of the orchestra, crouching as though against a
storm. Êlektra speaks in an intense whisper.)

ÊLEKTRA: Women!
                        Listen!
                              The men will do it,
                        will finish their work
                              soon!
                                    Silence!
                        Silence—
                              Shh—
LEADER: What are they doing?
ÊLEKTRA: She's preparing the urn,
                        crowning it, the
                              two beside her,
                        Orestês, Pylades—
LEADER: Why have you hurried here?
ÊLEKTRA: To watch for Aigisthos,
                        keep him away,
                              away from the house.

(A long, tense silence that is almost palpable ensues. Then the voice of
Klytaimnêstra is heard screaming from the palace.)

KLYTAIMNÊSTRA: Aiiiiiiiiiiiii!
                        Aiiiiiiiiiiiii!
                              Iooooooooooooo!
                                    Where are friends?
                        Friends of this house?
                              Murderers, all,
                                    all murderers!

(Several of the clusters of women band tightly together, repeatedly uttering
strong, sharp cries of fear and terror.)

ÊLEKTRA: Inside!
                        Inside!
                              A cry!
                        Friends!
                              Do you hear?
LEADER: Terrible sound!
                        Terrible!
                              I shudder to hear it!
KLYTAIMNÊSTRA: Oimoiiiiiiiiiii!

Aigisthos!

        Where are you?

        Where?

ÊLEKTRA: The cry! The cry!

        Again!

(The remaining clusters of women join the larger group with rapid, furtive movements and cries.)

KLYTAIMNÊSTRA: Child, o child,

        pity your mother!

          Pity—

(Êlektra runs to the palace doors, beating on them, screaming.)

ÊLEKTRA: Where was yours for him?

        Where was yours for father?

CHORUS: O city, city,

          wretched house,

      your terrible fate,

          dying at last—

KLYTAIMNÊSTRA: Omoiiiiiiiiii!

        I am struck!

ÊLEKTRA: Strike her again!

         Again!

      Again!

KLYTAIMNÊSTRA: Omoiiiiiiiiii!

        Again, again—

ÊLEKTRA: The same for Aigisthos!

        The same!

        The same!

CHORUS: The curses are at work—

        the dead come alive—

         now the killers'

      blood flows—

        the dead drink

         deeply the slayers'

      blood—

(Orestês and Pylades enter from the palace with swords drawn, their clothes stained with blood.)

CHORUS: Look!

        There!

      Look!

His hand!
　　Blood! Blood!
　Blood!
　　Dripping!
　　　Sacrifice to Arês!
　Arês war-god!
　　Arês!
　　　Who can blame them?
　Not I—
　　not I—
ÊLEKTRA:　　　Orestês, Orestês, tell me—
ORESTÊS:　The house is in order
　　　if Apollo prophesied well!
ÊLEKTRA:　　　Is she dead?
　Is the wretch dead?
ORESTÊS:　　Your mother's arrogance
　　　will never dishonor you!
(The Leader sees Aigisthos approaching in the distance from the left.)
LEADER:　　Stop!
　　I see Aigisthos!
ÊLEKTRA:　　　Back!
　Go back! Hurry!
(Orestês and Pylades draw back and Êlektra rushes to the left entrance.)
ORESTÊS:　　Where do you see him?
ÊLEKTRA:　　　Coming down the street,
　puffed with pride—
LEADER:　　　Hurry, hurry, into the house!
　　　Let one success
　lead to the next!
ORESTÊS:　　Trust us!
　　We're ready!
ÊLEKTRA:　　Go!
　　Hurry!
ORESTÊS:　　　We're going!
(Orestês and Pylades rush back into the palace. Êlektra comes farther into the orchestra.)
ÊLEKTRA:　Leave all the rest to me.
LEADER:　　Greet him gently; soft
　　　words in his ear;

                    lure him, lure him,
                         without his knowing,
                              to his contest
                    with Justice.
        (During the above dialogue Aigisthos enters, left, attended by several of his
        Bodyguards. The music fades out.)
AIGISTHOS: Where are these strangers from Phokis?
        I'm told they've come with news of Orestês' death
        In the wreck of his chariot.
        (Silence.)
        You! Êlektra! I'm asking you! Yes, you!
        Where's the old boldness now!
        I think it's you this news mostly affects.
        Your brother? Hm? You're likeliest to know?
        Then tell me!
ÊLEKTRA: Yes, I know only too well.
        How could I not? My brother?
        The one I love most in all the world?
AIGISTHOS: Then answer me. Where are these strangers?
ÊLEKTRA: Inside—where they have disarmed their hostess.
AIGISTHOS: And their story? Is it true? Is he dead?
ÊLEKTRA: They've brought it, the proof; not only hearsay.
AIGISTHOS: I can see the corpse, then? With my own eyes?
ÊLEKTRA: See it? Yes. Not a pretty sight.
AIGISTHOS: Words from you at last that give me pleasure!
ÊLEKTRA: Feel all the pleasure you like, if it pleases you.
AIGISTHOS: Silence! Open the doors!
        Let all the men of Mykenê and Argos see!
        (The great doors of the palace are opened as Aigisthos continues and the
        ekkyklêma is rolled forward into full view to reveal the covered bloody body
        of Klytaimnêstra with Orestês and Pylades on either side of it with swords
        drawn.)
        And if there are any fools among the lot of you,
        Buoyed up by empty hopes regarding this man,
        The sight of his corpse will teach them to take my bit,
        Accept my yoke, and forestall the need for a whip!
ÊLEKTRA: My lesson learned, I need no teaching to tell me
        Not to fight against what I cannot change.
AIGISTHOS: The wrath of the gods, no other, destroyed this thing

With righteous retribution. Uncover the face.
This was a kinsman: I must honor my dead.
ORESTÊS: Lift the veil yourself. It's not for me,
But you, to show these signs of love and duty.
AIGISTHOS: Yes, you're right, I will.
(To Êlektra.)
You—call Klytaimnêstra if she's in the palace.
ORESTÊS: She's near you now. No need to look.
(Aigisthos uncovers the body.)
AIGISTHOS: Aiiiiii! What is this sight!
ORESTÊS: Afraid? Take a good look!
AIGISTHOS: You! Who are you?
What is this trap I've fallen into?
ORESTÊS: The one you thought dead is alive again.
AIGISTHOS: Orestês?—Orestês! I understand!
ORESTÊS: So good at guessing, deceived so long!
AIGISTHOS: My death is near. Let me say one word.
ÊLEKTRA: No! Not a word! No, brother! No more talking!
What use is time to a man on the verge of death?
Kill him! *Now!* Throw him out to the beasts
Who will give a man like him proper burial,
Out of our sight! Only that will release me
From all the evil pain and misery I've suffered!
ORESTÊS: Inside! Now!
The time for words is past!
Only your death can settle
The account between us!
AIGISTHOS: Why inside?
If this deed of yours is just,
Why hide it in the dark?
Kill me here!
ORESTÊS: Don't order me!
You'll go in there and die in the same place
You killed my father!
AIGISTHOS: Is it the fate of this ancient house of Pelops
To see its sorrows repeated to the end of time?
ORESTÊS: It will see yours at least.
In that I'm a prophet.
AIGISTHOS: This skill you boast of wasn't your father's strength.

ORESTÊS: All you do is talk. Go in. It's time.

AIGISTHOS: After you!

ORESTÊS: You first!

AIGISTHOS: In case I escape?

ORESTÊS: No. So you don't choose an easier death.

   I intend to see you suffer a bitter end.

   If the same fate fell on all such men

   Who rise above the law: death with justice;

   there would be less evil in the world.

   (Orestês and Pylades drive Aigisthos into the palace. The doors to the palace close loudly. Êlektra runs up the palace doors as music enters and the Chorus begins its exit to the right.)

CHORUS: Children of Atreus, how many pains

              you suffered before freedom dawned,

                 crowning the day's events with peace.

   (Êlektra, triumphant, stands framed against the palace doors, then after a long moment opens the doors and enters.)

PHILOKTÊTÊS
(ΦΙΛΟΚΤΗΤΗΣ)

CAST OF CHARACTERS

PHILOKTÊTÊS
ODYSSEUS
NEOPTOLEMOS *Son of Achilleus and Prince of Skyros*
HERAKLÊS
MERCHANT CAPTAIN *follower of Odysseus in disguise*
CHORUS OF OLDER SAILORS *under Neoptolemos' command*
LEADER OF THE CHORUS

The lines of the Chorus, unless otherwise indicated, are to be delivered by individual voices and varied groups of voices.

PHILOKTÊTÊS

Dawn. The orchestra is a desolate, craggy precipice on the deserted island of Lemnos. The upper part of the skênê door represents a cave mouth led up to by a steep rocky path. Right and left of the upper side reaches of the orchestra is an entrance, the left leading to the island wilderness, the right to the bay and Neoptolemos' ship. Odysseus, Neoptolemos and a Sailor from Neoptolemos' ship enter left.

ODYSSEUS: This is it. This is the spot. Lemnos.
    Desolate. Uninhabited. Unexplored.
    An island in the middle of an empty sea.
    Here we are, then, Neoptolemos,
    Son of Achilleus, the noblest of all us Greeks.

    I had a job to do once, long ago;
    Orders right from the top. I left him here,
    'Exposed' is a better word, I guess, the Melian,
    Son of Poias, his foot a running sore,
    Eaten right through.
    But like I said, Neoptolemos,
    Orders. What could we do?
    I'll never forget the racket that Melian made.
    We couldn't sacrifice, couldn't pour libations,
    Not with his ill-omened cries and shrieks
    That roared through the camp.
    He never stopped. Never. Day or night.
    But why talk of that?
    Now's no time for long-winded conversation.
    We'll have to hurry. If he finds me out, my plans
    To carry him off are dashed.

    All right, now, let's get going; no time to waste.
    First, search me out a cave with two mouths:
    One that allows for sun all day in winter,
    And a funnel that brings cool breezes to sleep by in summer.
    (Neoptolemos starts off.)

Oh, and to the left and down, you'll find

A spring to drink at; that is, if it hasn't run dry.

Be quiet, whatever you do.

Find out if he's still there or if he's moved.

When you know, give a signal.

I'll fill you in on what we'll do next,

And we'll set to work together.

(Neoptolemos climbs with difficulty up the path, and stops halfway.)

NEOPTOLEMOS: Odysseus, sir!

Quick work! Nothing to it!

There's a cave up there, I think!

Just like you said!

ODYSSEUS: Above or below? I don't see it.

NEOPTOLEMOS: Higher. No sound of movement anywhere.

ODYSSEUS: Look inside; he may be asleep.

(Neoptolemos climbs higher but still not all the way.)

NEOPTOLEMOS: I can see in now. No one there.

ODYSSEUS: No sign of an occupant?

(Neoptolemos climbs almost to the cave's mouth and looks in.)

NEOPTOLEMOS: A bed of leaves pressed flat—for sleeping.

ODYSSEUS: Otherwise nothing? Nothing inside?

NEOPTOLEMOS: A cup carved from a block of wood.

Clumsy work! And a pile of kindling.

ODYSSEUS: That sounds like his place, all right.

NEOPTOLEMOS: Oh, god, no! What's that!

Phew! Ugh! Rags in the sun!

Left to dry! Stained with the filthy

Pus of some sore!

(Neoptolemos starts back down.)

ODYSSEUS: That's our man! Still here, then!

Probably out scouting some food or herbs

He's found to ease his pain.

Put your man on guard.

(While Neoptolemos approaches the Sailor and sends him off right.)

God knows, I don't want him coming on me

Unexpected. He'd rather take me

Than any of all us Greeks at Troy.

NEOPTOLEMOS: Done. The path is guarded. What next?

ODYSSEUS: What's next, son of Achilleus, is your mission.

I need you to prove your nobility not only in body
But in mind. Whatever you're told, no matter how strange,
It's up to you to obey. You're here to help.
NEOPTOLEMOS: What are your orders, sir?
ODYSSEUS: I want Philoktêtês, and I want him taken by you.
Snared with words, not force. He'll ask who you are,
Where you're from. "Achilleus' son," tell him,
"Neoptolemos." No hedging there. You're sailing
Home from Troy; deserting the Greeks; leaving them
All behind. You've a mighty grudge against them;
Hate them, in fact. They begged and implored you to leave
Your home, to come to Troy; said they'd never
Take the citadel without you; you were the man
They needed; and on and on. But when you got there,
Arrived at Troy, you asked for your father's armor,
Achilleus' arms, and god knows you had the right!
But they denied them.
Unworthy, they said;
And handed them over to—yes, to Odysseus!

Say what you like, boy!
Say whatever comes to mind about me,
No matter how rough! Don't worry, you can't hurt me;
But you'll hurt the Greeks if you fail to bring back that bow;
Hurt them deeply. For without it you'll never take Troy:
No victory, no triumph.

In case you're wondering why it's you he'll trust,
And not me, it's because you're a free man.
You sailed to Troy not out of obligation,
No oath sworn, not part of the first expedition,
But of your own free choice.
None of which *I* can say.
And if he comes wielding his bow,
I'm as good as dead and so are you.
To avoid which we'll have to devise a plot
To steal that weapon by hook or crook.

I realize, boy, how alien this is to you;

That you don't by nature take to treachery and lying.
But consider how sweet the victory will be!
Take the dare, boy!
We'll prove just and honest some other day!
Give me your mind and heart and let me persuade you
Only for this one day,
This one short shameless day,
And serve just me!
Then all your other days can be as just
And right as you like, the noblest of all men!

NEOPTOLEMOS: Odysseus, sir, just listening to your words
Pains me more than you know;
To act them out, well, it's—it's impossible,
Doing a thing like this. I just can't;
Deception isn't part of me. Nor, so I've heard,
Was it part of my father's nature.
By the same token, though, I will use force
To take this man off Lemnos, but never trickery.
A man with only one foot doesn't win fights—
Not against all of *us*.
I was sent here, sir, to obey your orders.
If I don't, well, then I'm guilty of mutiny.
And I don't like that.
But, Odysseus, sir,
I'd rather fail with honor than win by treachery.

ODYSSEUS: Like father, like son!
Good for you, boy!
Once, when I was young, I thought like you.
Quick to act, but slow, so slow with words.
But now I'm older, I realize that words
Have a far greater power than mere blows.

NEOPTOLEMOS: Then what are your orders—except to lie, sir?
ODYSSEUS: I'm saying, take Philoktêtês with deceit.
NEOPTOLEMOS: Deceit? Why? Why not persuasion?
ODYSSEUS: Persuasion won't work. Neither will force.
NEOPTOLEMOS: What is this power he claims, sir?
ODYSSEUS: Arrows that hit their mark—they don't miss.
NEOPTOLEMOS: Then even approaching him is dangerous?
ODYSSEUS: Of course—unless you use deceit.

NEOPTOLEMOS: But lying, sir—you approve of that?

ODYSSEUS: Yes, if that lie brings us safety.

NEOPTOLEMOS: How can I look at a man and lie?

ODYSSEUS: When it's your gain, hesitation's a crime.

NEOPTOLEMOS: What's the gain if he goes back to Troy?

ODYSSEUS: Without the arrows Troy won't be conquered.

NEOPTOLEMOS: But the oracle said that I'd conquer Troy.

ODYSSEUS: You *and* the arrows; not one or the other.

NEOPTOLEMOS: Then there's no choice: we have to take them.

ODYSSEUS: Do this and you'll have a double prize.

NEOPTOLEMOS: What? Tell me—and I might not refuse.

ODYSSEUS: Intelligence and courage. It's what they'll say.

NEOPTOLEMOS: All right. I'll do it. And farewell shame!

ODYSSEUS: Good! You know what you have to do.

NEOPTOLEMOS: I do, now that I've made up my mind!

ODYSSEUS: All right. You wait here.

> I'll keep out of sight so he doesn't see me,
> And you send your scout on back to the ship.
> If it seems you're taking too long, I'll send him back
> Disguised as a merchant captain to aid the deception.
> However strange his tale, boy, go along with it,
> And take your cue from him.

> I'll be going back to the ship now.
> You know your charge.
> May Hermês, god of tricksters, guide us,
> And Athêna, Goddess of Victory,
> My protector.

(Music fades in as Odysseus goes out, right, toward the bay and ship. The Chorus of Sailors under Neoptolemos' command, but generally older than he, is heard before they enter from the same direction. When they finally enter it is in groups of varying size, they appear confounded and unsure of themselves, expressing their fear in a cautious dance movement. Here as elsewhere they speak individually or in varying combinations.)

CHORUS: Young master, I'm a
                    stranger in a
                         strange land!
              What should I
                    hide, what should I

           say to that
      man who'll be
        swift to suspect?
        Show me the
    way, master! No
      skill is greater than
        that of the prince, no
    wisdom is equal to
      his wisdom, the
        prince whose hands
    wield the divine
      scepter given by
        Zeus.
    To you, my son, this
      ancient power has
        descended from the
    dawn of time.
      Tell me
        how to
    serve you!

(The Chorus has now fully entered.)

NEOPTOLEMOS: Don't be frightened. He's
        away just now. His
      cave at the island's
        edge is empty. It's
          safe. Look around.
      But when the
        outlaw returns, who
          knows what terrible
    thing he may do?
        Stand close, and when I
          signal, be ready with the
    help I may need.

(Neoptolemos carefully makes his way up the path to the cave as the Chorus watches.)

CHORUS: I'll keep an
        eye out,
      prince. You know
        me. Always

have. Your
   safety comes
      first with me, sir. But
         tell me, where does he
live? Where is his
   home? Maybe he's
      hiding, waiting to
spring at me unawares
   out of nowhere.
      Where has he
wandered to?
   Shouldn't I
      know to be
safe, sir? Is he
   gone? Is he
      home? Is he
resting?

NEOPTOLEMOS: Here's his house.
      This cave with walls of
rock, and a mouth with
   two openings.
      Come see.

(The Leader begins to climb the path, urging others to follow, a few of whom do.)

LEADER: Poor creature,
      where can he be?

NEOPTOLEMOS: Somewhere near, I'd say.
Hunting food. Where
   else could he be, poor
      man? Dragging his
foot on some trail. It's
   how he lives. His deadly
      arrows killing his
prey. Always in
   pain; no one to
      cure him.

CHORUS: How I pity him!
      Pity the man! Poor
         man! How does he

live like this,
    alone! No one to
        care for him! Always
racked with pain,
    pain forever
        eating at him, eating,
eating! No friendly
    face to greet him! No
        smile! Suffering!
Suffering!
    Bewildered by each
        need as it comes! No
end to his
    pains!
        How can he
bear them?
    How?
        His misery!
How?
    Oh, the gods' dark
        dealings are
full of mystery for
    man! I pity the
        race! Pity the
man whose life's
    misery is greater than
        any should bear!
What was his birth?
    What was his house?
        Great in dignity,
a noble race,
    rich man's son,
        second to none? Yet
here he lies,
    bereft of all life's
        gifts! Cast out;
alone;
    beasts, dappled and
        shaggy his only

                    companions! Hungry,
                         tormented! Anguish
                              clawing his mind! No
                    peace for his
                         thoughts! No
                              cure for his fear! Only
                    Echo babbling some
                         distant reply from the
                              hills to his endless
                    round of cries!
                         Pity him!
                              Pity!
                    Pity!

NEOPTOLEMOS   Nothing to wonder at here.
                         Gods are at work, if
                    I'm any judge. His first
                         suffering came from
                              Chrysis whose ruthless
                    anger torments him. But
                         what he suffers now, with
                              no one to tend him, was
                    sent by some god. Some
                         power has willed that his
                              god-given bow, whose
                    arrows never miss their
                         mark, must not be bent on
                              Troy before the time is ripe.
                    For this weapon, they say,
                         brings Troy to its knees.

(A man's voice is heard from some distance groaning in pain.)

LEADER: Hush, boy!

NEOPTOLEMOS: What is it?

(Another groan is heard.)

LEADER: A sound like a
                         groan from a
                    man in pain! Over
                         there!

(Trying to locate the sound, they dart in various directions. The sound continues and grows louder as though amplified through a long tunnel.)

CHORUS:	No, there!
	There! It came from
	there! No!
	Here!
LEADER:	It strikes me,
	strikes my ear!
CHORUS:	The voice of a
	man in
	pain—
LEADER:	dragging himself—
	there—
CHORUS:	Again—some
	suffering
	creature—

(The Leader rushes to the right followed by several others, still trying to locate the sound's direction.)

LEADER:	I hear it coming!
CHORUS:	The anguish!
LEADER:	Anguish!
CHORUS:	No mistaking it!

(The groaning comes increasingly closer, growing in its urgency and volume till it threatens to engulf the scene.)

LEADER:	It's all too plain!
CHORUS:	Too plain!
LEADER:	Listen to me, son!
NEOPTOLEMOS:	What!
LEADER:	To new advice!
	He's almost here! Hurry!
	This is no shepherd
	piping his Pan-pipes
	in the meadow, pasturing
	his flocks, but a man in
	agony, moaning,
	howling as he
	stumbles from his terrible
	pain, or scanning the
	harbor with no
	ship in sight!
CHORUS:	His cries are

loud,
loud and
terrible,
terrible!

(Philoktêtês shuffles into view through the cave-mouth above, a ragged, pitiable, but nonetheless commanding figure of a man, carrying his bow and arrows, and with his foot wrapped in ragged bandages. He is exhausted, in pain, and breathless. The music fades out.)

PHILOKTÊTÊS: You! Strangers! Who are you?

Where do you come from?

Why have you come here?

This island with no harbor?

Desolate.

(He begins his slow, painful descent, stopping several times because of pain.)

What is your country? Your race?

Your clothes tell me you are Greek.

The most welcome sight of all to me!

If only I could hear you speak!

Dearest of sounds!

Don't let my looks frighten you off.

Wild beast of a man I look, I know.

(When the others appear about to retreat in fear.)

Don't leave. I won't hurt you.

It's a man behind this savage; a man

Who asks your pity.

Alone. Friendless.

A man who has suffered much.

If you come as friends,

Speak to me, oh, speak!

The least we can do is talk to each other.

(He arrives at ground level.)

NEOPTOLEMOS: To answer your question first, we are Greek.

PHILOKTÊTÊS: O dearest of sounds!

From my own country!

Just to be greeted by you—

A man like you—

After so long!

Why have you come, my boy?

Oh, my dear, dear son, what is it you want?

What friendliest of winds have made you land here?
Tell me who you are. Tell me. I must know.
NEOPTOLEMOS: My home, sir, is the wave-washed island of Skyros.
I'm sailing there now. And my father was Achilleus.
My name is Neoptolemos. Now you know all.
PHILOKTÊTÊS: Oh, son, son of a father I dearly loved,
And of a land I cherished!
And your foster-father, old Lykomêdês!
But what has brought you here?
Where did you sail from?
NEOPTOLEMOS: Just now from Troy.
PHILOKTÊTÊS: I don't understand. You weren't with us then,
Not on that first expedition, years ago.
(Neoptolemos pretends astonishment.)
NEOPTOLEMOS: What! You were a part of that?
PHILOKTÊTÊS: Can it be, my boy, can it be
You don't know who I am?
NEOPTOLEMOS: How can I know someone I never saw?
PHILOKTÊTÊS: Never heard my name? Never a rumor
Of the evil fate that keeps me here in suffering?
NEOPTOLEMOS: I'm sorry, but I don't know what you're talking about.
PHILOKTÊTÊS: How vile I must be to the gods if no word
Of my wretched existence has made its way back home
Or to any of the Greek lands!

Those men who cast me out so infamously
Now mock me in silence, while my sickness flourishes,
Worse each day!
Oh, son of Achilleus, have you ever heard
Of the master of the bow of Heraklês?
I am that man.
I am Philoktêtês.
Son of Poias.
I was stranded here, cast ashore
By the generals Agamemnon and Menelaos,
And that Kephallênian Odysseus. Cast ashore
On this lonely place. Banished in an act of cruelty,
Shameless cruelty. My body gnawed away
By a vicious illness. Staked out for death by the poison

Of a venomous serpent's tooth.
Left here.
That plague my sole companion.
Left here. Alone. Discarded.
They sailed away then.
The fleet that brought me here had sailed from Chrysê,
The sea-washed island.
Oh, and how glad they were when they saw me dead
Asleep on the shore, exhausted by the crossing,
The endless tossing of waves, and sheltered me
In an overhanging lee of rock with a handful
Of rags and bits of food.

God damn their evil hearts and give them the same!
Can you imagine, son, the misery I woke to?
The tears I shed? The dread that filled my heart?
The bay empty, deserted!
The ships I'd sailed with, gone!
No man left behind to support me!
To relieve my pain! O god, all I found
On looking was anguish! Anguish upon anguish!
Enough to gorge on!
Time and time and time marched on,
Season after season after season.
And what was I to do, alone, here,
In this narrow shelter, master and slave in one,
Who scratches a life from adversity with this bow?

To ease my stomach's needs I shot down doves
In flight, and when I saw them fall, I dragged
My pain-wracked body and wounded foot,
Useless now, to fetch my kill.
Or if I needed water to drink,
And the pool was frozen,
As happens often in winter,
And kindling had to be broken,
I did it myself, dragging myself in pain.
But where was fire?
I learned to rub stone on stone
To coax out the spark that kept me in life.

What more do I need?
A roof to guard my head;
A fire to keep me warm: everything I need—
Except a cure!

But now, dear boy, let me tell you about this island.
No sailor of his own choice ever comes here.
There's no harbor, no landing site, no market
For trade, and certainly no welcome. The man's a fool
Who sails this way. And yet it does happen
A ship is forced in to shore. It's not unknown
In the course of time. And so these visitors—
Well, they show me compassion, and, moved by pity,
They leave behind a bite or two of food
And a few cast off garments.
But mention rescue?
A ride home from this place?
They're off like the wind!
For ten years now, ten long years,
I've glutted this disease
With misery, pain and hunger!

Now you see what those two grand Greek generals,
Agamemnon and Menelaos,
Yes, and Odysseus, too,
Proud and mighty Odysseus, have done to me!
May the gods that guide our fates return to them,
Agony for agony, what I've suffered!
LEADER: I'm sorry for you, Philoktêtês;
    As sorry as all the others who have come here.
NEOPTOLEMOS: And I'm your witness.
    Every word is true, Philoktêtês.
    I, too, was wronged by these generals,
    Wronged by Odysseus.
    They're all criminals.
PHILOKTÊTÊS: A score to settle?
    You, too, son?
    Against these evil men?
    These sons of Atreus?

NEOPTOLEMOS: Oh, I have that, all right.
   And someday I'll prove to Mykenê,
   And Sparta, too, that Skyros
   Is also the mother of warriors!
PHILOKTÊTÊS: Good, boy, good!
   I honor such anger. But tell me, son:
   How have they hurt you
   To deserve your anger against them?
NEOPTOLEMOS: I'll tell you, Philoktêtês,
   Though it won't be easy—
   The insults they hurled at me—
   The indignity.
   When, as fate decreed, Achilleus died—
PHILOKTÊTÊS: Oh, no, son, no! Not Achilleus!
   Not Achilleus dead? What are you saying?
   Your father—dead? Tell me,
   Oh, tell me what happened.
NEOPTOLEMOS: Dead, yes, but no mortal hand did it.
   It's said the archer god Apollo killed him.
PHILOKTÊTÊS: The slain was no less noble than the slayer.
   You make it difficult, boy—
   What should I do:
   Ask you about the wrong the generals did you,
   Or mourn for my friend?
NEOPTOLEMOS: Your own suffering is great enough, poor man,
   Not to have to mourn for those of others.
PHILOKTÊTÊS: Yes. I know. You're right.
   Go on with your story.
   The generals and Odysseus insulted you—
NEOPTOLEMOS: The great Odysseus and my father's tutor, Phoinix,
   Came to get me at Skyros in a great ship
   Decked out in many flags—to bring me back
   To Troy, where they said—true or not, I don't know—
   That now my father is dead, I alone—
   Or so said the gods—can win the war at Troy.

   Well, I don't hesitate. I hoist sail.
   I want to see my father before his burial.
   I'd never seen him before. But I'm also lured

And flattered by the promise that I'm the one
To capture Troy. Two days, sped on by winds
And sailors' oars, I arrive at Sigeion,
That place of bitter memories!

As I walk ashore, the entire army crowds round me,
Shouting greetings, and words like: "Achilleus is back!
Achilleus is back from the dead!"
But, no, Achilleus is dead. Laid out for burial.
I mourn, as custom requires,
Then go off to the Atreidai,
Thinking them friends, or so I'm led to believe,
And ask for my father's arms and all his possessions.
And to their shame they answer: "Son of Achilleus,
Take everything else, everything but his arms,
For they are now the property of Odysseus,
Son of Laërtes." Rage fills me then.
Tears flood my eyes and I shout: "Bastards!
How dare you! How dare you give away his arms,
My father's arms to another without my knowing!"
Then Odysseus, who happens to be near by,
Says: "They were right, son, to do what they did.
I was there when your father Achilleus was killed.
I won his arms justly when I saved his body."

My rage breaks then! I call down every curse on his head!
Spare him nothing! "How dare you steal my arms?"
And Odysseus, stung by my abuse, Odysseus,
Who never loses control, answers me:
"You were never a part of this expedition!
Never once did you fight with us in battle,
As was your duty! And let me assure you of one thing—
You who talk so recklessly!—you will never,
Never, when you sail back to Skyros, take with you
Achilleus' arms!"

His taunts and insults ringing in my ears,
I set sail for Skyros, where I'm headed now,
Headed home, robbed of my ancestral right

By the lowest scum of earth, vile, scheming Odysseus!
And yet, he's less to blame than his commanders.
An army, like a city, is ruled by its leaders.
Men who act lawlessly imitate their leaders
Who teach them corruption.

All right, I've had my say.
But one thing for sure:
Any man who hates the twin leaders,
Agamemnon and Menelaos, is a friend of mine,
And also, I hope, of the gods.
(Music fades in as the Chorus takes up a new position in the orchestra.)
CHORUS: Goddess of
       hills!
          Goddess of
   earth!
      Goddess
        mother of
  Zeus on high!
    Ruler of
      Paktolos'
  stream of
    golden sands!
       All-nourishing
 goddess who
   reigns over all, I
     prayed to you
  then, that
    day when the
      generals and crafty
 Odysseus
   leveled their
     scorn, insulted my
 leader, giving away his
   father's
     arms, matchless
arms, to
   Laërtes' son,
     wily Odysseus!

I pray to you
                now, as I prayed
                    then, to
        witness once
            more, most
                blessèd
        goddess, supreme
                goddess throned on the
                    bull-devouring
        lion, how they
            gave his arms, his
                father's
        arms, a world's
            wonder, to
                deceitful
        Odysseus!
            Bear us
                witness!

(The music fades out as the Chorus disperses.)

PHILOKTÊTÊS: Ah, Neoptolemos, you and your friends
    Have sailed here with a tale of lies and deceits
    That matches mine. In every word I hear,
    I see the devious work of the brother generals
    And wily Odysseus. Oh, how well I know him.
    He'll lend his tongue to the basest of all pretexts,
    Lying his way through any wicked scheme
    To gain his evil end. And yet, I wonder,
    How could the greater Aias have witnessed this
    And done nothing?
NEOPTOLEMOS: Aias was dead, my friend.
    Had he not been, I'd have been spared
    This theft of my rights.
PHILOKTÊTÊS: What? Aias dead?
NEOPTOLEMOS: Yes, in the underworld now.
PHILOKTÊTÊS: O no, no!
    And those who should never have lived
    Are alive and well: Diomêdes and Odysseus!
    Why do *they* live?
NEOPTOLEMOS: Not only live, but thrive!
    The glory of the Greek army!

PHILOKTÊTÊS: And Nestor? My old friend?
>Trusted Nestor? Alive?
>Their evil never deceived him.
>He could check it in mid-course with good advice.
NEOPTOLEMOS: Alive but not doing well.
>Not since he lost his son Antilochos,
>Who sailed with him to Troy.
PHILOKTÊTÊS: Ah! Antilochos!
>Antilochos and Aias! Two men!
>Two men whose deaths almost destroy me!
>What's to be done? These men dead,
>While Odysseus lives!
>His should have been the body lying there!
NEOPTOLEMOS: He's a clever wrestler, Odysseus;
>But even the cleverest are sometimes tripped up.
PHILOKTÊTÊS: Ah, but there was Patroklos!
>Where was he when you needed his help?
>Your father's most loved friend?
NEOPTOLEMOS: Dead, too, Philoktêtês.
>War never takes the wicked, except by chance.
>Only good men die.
PHILOKTÊTÊS: I know—I know.
>But there was one, I *must* ask, a villainous creature
>With the tongue of a snake in argument—
NEOPTOLEMOS: You mean Odysseus.
PHILOKTÊTÊS: Ah, there's another!
>But, no, I meant Thersitês!
>He never knew when to stop talking!
>Is he alive?
NEOPTOLEMOS: I never met him.
>But, yes, I think so.
PHILOKTÊTÊS: Of course! Why not!
>The gods protect all that is evil;
>Shield them from death; deny them the Dark Kingdom
>Where only good men go. What's to be done?
>How can I praise gods who act unjustly?
NEOPTOLEMOS: I assure you, Philoktêtês, I'm through with this.
>I'll watch the Trojan War and the brother generals
>From as far away as distance can carry me.

I want no part of a place where evil reigns
And cowards outdistance men of noble natures.
No, I'll go back home to rocky Skyros
And live a happy life.

It's time I go to my ship now, Philoktêtês.
Goodbye! Good luck!
I pray along with you that the blessèd gods
Relieve you of your suffering, and soon.
(To the Chorus of sailors.)
Come, men, let's weigh anchor and wait for a wind
Whenever the gods see fit to send it to us!
PHILOKTÊTÊS: Are you going? Now? So soon?
NEOPTOLEMOS: I have no choice, my friend.
We must be ready to sail when the winds are right.
PHILOKTÊTÊS: Son, I beg of you, in your father's name,
Your father's and your mother's, in all at home
That you hold most dear: Don't leave me here, I implore you,
A suppliant, abandoned, a man of misery,
Living a miserable life! Give me at least
A passing thought! Take me with you! I know
That I'm no easy freight on board, but do it, son,
Do it! Bear with me. A noble nature scorns
An evil act and delights in good.
If you leave me here you will be dishonored.
But if you help, if you take me with you,
Take me home to Oïtê,
Your life will be crowned with honor.

Do it, dear boy! Do it!
What can it mean? One day!
Not even that!
Put me anywhere: the bow, the stern, the hold,
Wherever I will least disturb the crew.
I beg you, son, here on my knees, a suppliant,
A poor lame wretch, a cripple: don't desert me!

Say you'll do it! Don't leave me to this loneliness!
I pray you by Zeus who pities distressed souls!
Take me with you, take me to your home;

Or to Euboia; as far as the plains of Chalkodon.
From there it's no long journey to my country,
To the hills of Trachis and the quiet-flowing Spercheios,
Where I will see my father, if he's still alive.
I've sent word so often by passing sailors,
Praying him to send a ship or come himself
To take me home. But he never came.
Either he's dead or the messengers—
And this I think more likely—
Ignored my pleas and hurried home.

But here you are, my rescuer and messenger in one.
Save me, for pity's sake! Think how our lives
Teeter on the razor's edge of chance:
Good fortune quickly followed by an evil fate.
When life runs smoothly, look out for disaster,
For ruin may lie in ambush.
(Music fades in.)
CHORUS: Have pity on him,
                    master! He can't
                        bear much
                 more! I wouldn't
                   wish such
                        suffering on any
                 friend of mine! And
                     if, as you say, you
                        hate the hateful
                 sons of Atreus,
                     use that
                        hate and their
                 evil to justify
                     taking him
                        home.
                 They did him
                     wrong, master.
                        You can put it
                 right.
                     Take Philoktêtês
                        aboard, sir.

Let your
swift ship
carry him to the
home he
longs for.
The gods are
watching, sir. Don't
risk their
anger.

(The music fades out as the Chorus disperses around the orchestra.)

NEOPTOLEMOS: To pity him now is easy, but what of the voyage,
When you've had your fill of the stench and sound of his illness?
Will you change your mind? Will you stand by him then?

LEADER: Yes, sir, we know all that.
We'll stand by him.

NEOPTOLEMOS: At least no one can say I was less ready
Than you to help a friend. If you agree,
We sail. But see he hurries.

We're taking you with us, Philoktêtês.
Get on board as fast as you're able.
And may the gods guard our voyage
Wherever it takes us!

PHILOKTÊTÊS: O blessèd, blessèd day!
O dear, dear boy, dear friend, dearest of men!
And you, all of you, friends! If only, somehow,
I could show the love and gratitude I owe you!
Come, let us go.
But first, dear boy, let us kiss this place goodbye,
This dreadful, dismal place I once called home!
Home? How did I bear it? How?
Come inside; see the misery I lived with,
And be amazed I survived, my spirit intact.
Is there another man who could have endured this?
Necessity alone taught me patience.

(Philoktêtês moves to begin the ascent to his cave, followed by Neoptolemos.)

CHORUS: Sir! Wait! Look!
Two men from the ship!
One's a sailor, the other a stranger.

Let's hear what they have to say;
We can go in later.
(A sailor of middle-age, disguised as a Merchant Captain, enters left, ac-
companied by a Sailor from the ship. The Merchant Captain is somewhat
garrulous.)
MERCHANT: Son of Achilleus! I asked my friend here,
One of two other men guarding your ship,
Well, I asked him where I could find you. I mean,
Just by accident, here we are,
Anchored off the same coast, both of us.

Well, as it happens, I'm on a mission from Troy,
You know? Merchant ship? Sailing home
To Peparêthos? Island of grapes? Well,
When I heard that all these men were your crew,
I mean, I couldn't very well set sail,
Now could I, without first telling you the news.
I mean, who knows? It might be worth something to you!

Well, anyway, there's things going on between you
And the Greeks you probably know nothing about,
And not just plans either, actions, you know?
No time wasted *there*.
NEOPTOLEMOS: Thanks for your interest, sir.
I'm grateful! I won't forget it.
But what are these Greeks up to now?
MERCHANT: Out to hunt you down is what they are.
A squadron of ships.
Old Phoinix and Theseus' sons.
NEOPTOLEMOS: To bring me back by force or persuasion?
MERCHANT: Don't know, sir;
Just reporting what I heard.
NEOPTOLEMOS: Phoinix and Theseus' sons—I see.
Are they so eager to please the sons of Atreus?
MERCHANT: Listen, they're on their way, sir!
No time wasted there!
NEOPTOLEMOS: Odysseus—where was he?
Scared to volunteer?
Afraid to bring the message himself?

MERCHANT: Odysseus? No. He'd set sail
   With Diomêdes before I left,
   On the trail of another man.
NEOPTOLEMOS: And who was this 'other man'?
MERCHANT: A man called—
   *(Pulling Neoptolemos aside and speaking softly after pretending to see
   Philoktêtês for the first time.)*
   —Careful, sir, speak soft! Who's that?
NEOPTOLEMOS: That? Why, that's the famous Philoktêtês!
MERCHANT: Ask me no more questions, sir!
   Just get on board as soon as you can,
   And sail away as far as you can!
   (Philoktêtês has dragged himself closer to Neoptolemos.)
PHILOKTÊTÊS: What is it with him, son?
   What's he driving at behind my back?
NEOPTOLEMOS: I don't know; but whatever it is,
   He'll have to say it so we both hear—out loud.
MERCHANT: Son of Achilleus, I'm a poor man!
   I trade with the army! They reward me!
   Don't turn me in to the generals
   For telling what I shouldn't have told!
NEOPTOLEMOS: I hate the sons of Atreus. They're my enemies.
   And because this man hates them, too, he's my friend.
   You say you come as a friend. All right, then,
   Tell us everything you've heard; keep nothing back.
MERCHANT: Careful what you're doing, sir!
NEOPTOLEMOS: I *know* what I'm doing.
MERCHANT: The responsibility's yours.
NEOPTOLEMOS: Done. Just tell me.
MERCHANT: All right. Well! It's like I said.
   The men I mentioned?
   Diomêdes and the great Odysseus?
   It's him they're after. Philoktêtês.
   Swore to the army to bring him back
   With persuasion or brute force.
   And they all heard him say it—Odysseus.
   He was more cocksure of himself than the other.
NEOPTOLEMOS: After all these years, they suddenly want him back!
   The man they threw away on this island like garbage!

Why? What have these generals got in their heads?
Or is it the gods? Taking their revenge on wickedness?
MERCHANT: I can tell that, sir!
Guess you haven't heard. Well!
There was this noble prophet?
Helenos? Prince of Troy?
King Priam's son?
So anyway, one dark night, Odysseus,
Who nobody ever says anything good about—
Mighty Odysseus!—sets out to capture this Helenos,
Single-handed, by trickery, you know?
And shows him off, his prisoner, to the whole Greek army!
In chains, no less!
His proudest prize!

Well, this Helenos starts in prophesying,
Telling them Troy would never fall to the Greeks
Till they brought this man, this Philoktêtês, back,
Of his own free will, by persuasion, he said,
From the island he lives on now.

Well, when Odysseus hears *this,* he ups and boasts,
Saying *he's* the man for the job, that *he'll* bring him back,
This Philoktêtês, back for all the army to see,
A prize catch! "Most likely," he says, "he'll come
A willing captive, if not, I'll bring him by force."
And then he adds: "If I don't, my head is yours!
Cut it off in front of the whole crowd!"

So there you have it, my boy.
But take my advice: leave here now!
You and anyone you care about!
PHILOKTÊTÊS: So he'll take me back, will he?
That evil man, that plague of Greece,
Persuade me back to the Greeks!
He'd just as soon persuade me back from the grave!
MERCHANT: You'd know better than me, friend.
But I'll be going back to my ship now.
Good luck to you both!
(He goes off right accompanied by the Sailor.)

PHILOKTÊTÊS: Can you believe this, son? Believe this Odysseus?
  Who does he think I am, that he can lure me
  Onto his ship with his slippery words
  And parade me in front of the Greeks at Troy!
  I'd easier listen to my deadliest enemy,
  The serpent that took my foot, than his sly words!
  But there's nothing he wouldn't say,
  Nothing he wouldn't dare and do,
  And I know he'll come, that he'll come here, here!
  Hurry, Neoptolemos! Hurry, hurry, dear boy!
  We have a whole ocean to put between us,
  A vast stretch of sea between us and him!
  Let's go, son! Delay is a terrible thing,
  When the time is right to act; act in time,
  And we rest easy when it's done.
NEOPTOLEMOS: We'll wait till the wind's gone fair;
  It's head-on now.
PHILOKTÊTÊS: All winds are fair when you're running from evil.
NEOPTOLEMOS: True, but this wind is against them, too.
PHILOKTÊTÊS: Give a pirate a chance to loot and plunder,
  And no wind's an unfair wind.
NEOPTOLEMOS: All right, we'll go, then.
  But take what you need from the cave.
PHILOKTÊTÊS: I haven't much;
  But I'll need a few things.
NEOPTOLEMOS: Things? But the ship's well stocked.
PHILOKTÊTÊS: Leaves to ease the pain of my wound.
NEOPTOLEMOS: All right then, get them.
  What else do you need?
PHILOKTÊTÊS: Arrows I might have dropped.
  They mustn't be left for others to find.
NEOPTOLEMOS: And that in your hand?
  Is that the famous bow?
PHILOKTÊTÊS: Yes, the bow.
  The bow of Heraklês.
  (Neoptolemos looks in awe at the bow.)
NEOPTOLEMOS: Could I—could I see it up close—
  (Slowly approaching the bow.)
  The piece is like a god—holy—
  To be honored—

PHILOKTÊTÊS: Whatever you ask, son;
Anything to please you.
NEOPTOLEMOS: Anything to—
I'd really like to hold it, Philoktêtês,
But only if it's allowed—
No sacred law broken.
If not, it's all right.
PHILOKTÊTÊS: No law broken, son. It's allowed.
It's you, son, you who gave me life,
Gave me back to life, the light of my life.
You fed me with the hope of seeing my country,
Of seeing my father, my friends. You alone, boy,
Pulled me out from under the heel of my enemies;
Raised me above their reach. You, of all men,
You alone, have earned the right to touch
Philoktêtês' bow.
Here—touch it—hold it—
(Philoktêtês slowly, with both hands, has raised the bow to a position above
his head and between them. Neoptolemos, in awe, lifts his hands slowly and
gently puts them on the bow, which Philoktêtês never completely releases.
Together, they hold it aloft in silence. Nothing moves. Then Philoktêtês
slowly lets go and lowers his arms.)
Now give it back—
(Neoptolemos does so, slowly lowering the bow to Philoktêtês' arms.)
From this day on, dear son, you may say to the world
That you, you alone of all men,
You, Neoptolemos, touched Heraklês' bow.
And you deserved that right for the kindness you did me.
I won it myself for doing him a kindness.
NEOPTOLEMOS: I'm glad I met you, dear friend.
A man who knows how to give kindness for kindness
Is a friend beyond price. Go inside now.
PHILOKTÊTÊS: You with me.
(He leans heavily on Neoptolemos' arm as they make their way up to and
into the cave.)
My sickness needs your help.
(As music fades in the Chorus takes up a new position in the orchestra.)
CHORUS: I have heard it told,
              but have not seen, how he

who once came near the bed
of Zeus—his marriage bed—
was bound to a fiery wheel—
a wheel forever turning—
by the almighty son of Kronos.
But none other among mortals
have I ever heard of or seen,
who have suffered a fate more dreadful
than Philoktêtês—a man
who harmed no one by force
or fraud, but lived a just man
among just men—now left
to perish so cruelly. I marvel
how this man, alone,
in his solitude by the sea,
with only the sea's surge
to speak to him in his misery,
and his silent converse with rocks;
how, how has this man
endured, with no one to hear
his shrieks of pain; no one
to help him walk; to tend
the flow from his wound; the blood
that wells up from the flesh
gnawed by the plague that eats him;
no gentle hands, with herbs
gathered from the earth's floor,
to soothe his feverish anguish!
But when Pain's jaw widens
and pulls its teeth from his wound,
he moves from place to place,
dragging himself down paths,
or tottering like a child
without its nurse; searching
not for food that the womb
of earth bears in plenty
where men furrow the soil,
but the targets of his winged arrows
that fall from the sky. This,

this was the food that sustained him;
and never a drop of wine,
in ten long years, moistened
his thirsting mouth; but only
the stagnant pool that by bending
low to the earth he drinks from.

But now he has met the son of Achilleus.
Now he has met Neoptolemos, son
of many kings, and king himself,
who will carry him far over foaming depths
in a sea-plowing ship; a man no longer
beset with evil, but destined for greatness
and a happy fate; carry him home
to the banks of Spercheios, where Melian nymphs
haunt the waters; and to the heights
of Oïtê where the lord of the brazen shield
ascended on high, divine Heraklês,
ablaze in glory, rose to the gods,
a god himself, clothed in the splendor
of his father's holy fire!

(Even before the ode is completed and the Chorus has dispersed, Neoptolemos emerges from the cave followed more slowly by Philoktêtês who drags his foot in pain as they begin their descent. Halfway down, Philoktêtês stops suddenly, transfixed with an overwhelming pain. The music fades out.)

NEOPTOLEMOS: Come on, we have to hurry.

(He turns to see Philoktêtês stock-still.)

Philoktêtês! What is it?

Why are you standing there?

Is it the pain?

Why don't you say something?

(Philoktêtês emits sharp stabs of excruciating pain)

PHILOKTÊTÊS: á! á! á! á!

NEOPTOLEMOS: Tell me!

PHILOKTÊTÊS: Nothing—no—go on, boy—keep going—

(He forces himself to continue the descent.)

NEOPTOLEMOS: It's your wound, isn't it?

The old pain, back again—

PHILOKTÊTÊS: No—no, it's better now—

It's—it's all right—o god o god—

NEOPTOLEMOS: Then why call on the gods?

PHILOKTÊTÊS: —to come—

Come with their power—heal me—

To be kind—

(They stop again.)

PHILOKTÊTÊS: á! á! á! á!

NEOPTOLEMOS: The pain must be terrible!

Tell me what's wrong! Don't hide it!

(They reach ground level and Philoktêtês collapses in agony. The Chorus reacts to Philoktêtês' pain.)

PHILOKTÊTÊS: It's killing me, boy—killing me—

Killing me killing me—can't hide it can't hide it

Can't hide it—attataiiiiii!—the pain the pain—

Like a knife—o talas!—right through right

Through—papai! apappapaiiiiii!

Papapapapapapapapaiiiiiiiiiiiiiiiiiiii!

—It eats me—I can't—can't—

The painpainpain eats me—alive—alive—

O god! if you have a knife, son,

I beg you by all the gods—I beg you

Beg you beg you cut it off—

The foot—cut it off—your sword—cut it there—

There—oh there—forget my life—

Hurry—oh be quick son be quick be quick be quick—!

(Neoptolemos has been simultaneously astonished and revolted by the display of Philoktêtês' pain, trying to help but backing off in consternation.)

NEOPTOLEMOS: What is this? All at once, so suddenly,

No warning, nothing! Tell me, Philoktêtês! What!

PHILOKTÊTÊS: You know, son—

NEOPTOLEMOS: Know what?

PHILOKTÊTÊS: My boy, you *know*—

NEOPTOLEMOS: Tell me!

I *don't* know!

PHILOKTÊTÊS: How could you *not!*

Aiiiiiiiiiiiiiii!

NEOPTOLEMOS: I see how it tortures you.

The pain must be terrible—

PHILOKTÊTÊS: Terrible—terrible—no words—oh pity me—

NEOPTOLEMOS: What can I do?

PHILOKTÊTÊS: Don't leave me—

Don't—stay with me—don't be afraid—

It comes like this—settles in—

Weary perhaps of wandering elsewhere—

NEOPTOLEMOS: How I pity you, Philoktêtês.

All this misery. Will you lean on me?

Can I help, poor man?

(Philoktêtês shrinks back in fear of greater pain from the touch.)

PHILOKTÊTÊS: No—no—don't—don't—don't touch me!

(After a pause to recover himself.)

But take the bow. Take it. You asked earlier.

Take it till the pain leaves. Guard it till then.

When the pain passes, I sleep.

The torment stops only then, so let me sleep—

Don't wake me. And if *they* come—those men—

While I am asleep—Odysseus—the others—

By the gods and all things sacred, Neoptolemos,

You must never let this bow leave your hands!

Never let them take it no matter how!

If—if you do—it's death for both of us—

For me who am your suppliant—and yourself.

NEOPTOLEMOS: Trust me, Philoktêtês. No other hand

But yours and mine will touch it. Give it here now.

And good luck come with it.

PHILOKTÊTÊS: Take it, child. And pray the jealous gods

Don't punish you with pain, as they punished me,

And Heraklês who had it before me.

(Philoktêtês hands the bow to Neoptolemos.)

NEOPTOLEMOS: God grant your prayer and mine, Philoktêtês:

A safe and prosperous voyage to the place

Where the gods will us to go and our mission intends.

(Philoktêtês is again seized by the pain.)

PHILOKTÊTÊS: á! á! á! á!

Oh, child—no—no—your prayer is wasted on me—

Look—look—o look—

The blood—again—again—gushing—

Gushing—from deep inside—

There will be more to come—

Papai! féu!
Papaiiiiiiiiiiiiiiiiiiiiiiiiiiiiiiiiiiiii!
—More from this cursed foot—
It's coming—coming—oimoi moi talas!
—You understand now, boy,
You understand—don't leave me now—
Don't leave—attataiiii!
—Oh, evil, evil Odysseus, if only you
Were pierced like me to the heart—
(Groaning. Screaming.)
Féu! Papaiiiiiiiiiiiiiii!
Papai mala authis!
—And you, Agamemnon, you, Menelaos,
Oh you, you, you generals of the Greeks—
If only *you* could suffer the agony that tears me—
Tears me! tears me! tears me!
—Suffer as long as I have suffered!
Suffered! suffered the agony—suffered—
Omoi moiiiiiiiiiiiiiiiiiiiiiiiiiiiiiiiiiiiiiiiiiiiii!
O Death—Death—why are you deaf to my call—
Day after day after day—
But you never come—boy—come—
Neoptolemos—dear dear son—
Dear dear friend—noble child—
Come—come—take me up there—
(Feebly indicating the volcano that tops the island. The pain appears to recede.)
To the mountain, the famous fire that lights all Lemnos,
And burn me, burn me, cast me deep into the pit,
As I once cast in Heraklês
Who begged me for that act of kindness—
Begged me, and gave me the bow you're guarding
As my reward, for I knew it was right, that kindness—
(Pause.)
Neoptolemos—answer—
Neoptolemos—
(Pause.)
Why so silent?
(Pause.)

Where are you?

NEOPTOLEMOS: Suffering your suffering, Philoktêtês—

Overwhelmed with pity for your suffering—

PHILOKTÊTÊS: Don't be worried. The pain comes fast and furious,

But leaves as fast as it came. Whatever you do,

Don't leave me alone.

NEOPTOLEMOS: Trust me; we're staying.

PHILOKTÊTÊS: You *will* stay, then?

NEOPTOLEMOS: Don't be afraid.

PHILOKTÊTÊS: Swear it to me—

But no, no oath.

It wouldn't be right.

NEOPTOLEMOS: There's no way I can leave without you.

PHILOKTÊTÊS: Give me your hand.

(Neoptolemos takes Philoktêtês' hand in silence and keeps hold of it.)

NEOPTOLEMOS: I'm staying, Philoktêtês.

(Philoktêtês begins to experience another attack and uses Neoptolemos' hand for support.)

PHILOKTÊTÊS: Take me up—up—

NEOPTOLEMOS: Where?

PHILOKTÊTÊS: —there—up—

(Neoptolemos refuses to let go of Philoktêtês' hand as Philoktêtês tries to wrest himself free of his grip.)

NEOPTOLEMOS: The sky is all that's up there!

You're raving again.

PHILOKTÊTÊS: —let me go—

Let me go—

NEOPTOLEMOS: Go where?

PHILOKTÊTÊS: —let me go—can't you hear—

NEOPTOLEMOS: I won't let you!

PHILOKTÊTÊS: —it's killing me—killing me—your touch—

NEOPTOLEMOS: All right! I'll let go! I'll let go! There!

You're sane now—

(Philoktêtês sinks helpless to the ground and begins to fall into a deep sleep.)

PHILOKTÊTÊS: O Earth, take me in, take me—

I'm dying—can't even—stand—on you—

(Music fades in.)

NEOPTOLEMOS: He'll sleep soon. His head is sinking.

His body drenched with sweat.

Streams of dark blood gushing from his heel.
Let him sleep now, friends.
Let him have his peace.
Let him rest.
(The Chorus has taken up a new position in the orchestra.)

CHORUS: Come, sweet Sleep!
Sleep beyond pain,
    o come!
Come, sweet Sleep!
Sleep beyond sorrow,
    come!
Wrap him round
with your soothing breath,
and wrap us round
with your favoring winds!
    Come, o come,
sweet smiling Sleep!
Let dream's soft radiance
hover about him
and heal his pain!

LEADER: Take care, son, take
    care where you stand, take
    care where you'll go, what
course you'll take.
    Why are we waiting, doing
    nothing? The man's
asleep. Seize your
    chance and win! It's
    time to act!
It's time!

NEOPTOLEMOS: We could sail off right now,
Steal away with only the bow.
He's asleep; he can't hear us.
But what good would that do?
Without him, we have nothing.
The crown of victory at Troy is his;
The gods have said so;
He must be brought.
We can't leave it here, half done,
And that half done with lies!

CHORUS: Some god will
                    see to that, son.
                        But when you
                speak, speak softly,
                    softly, for
                        suffering makes men
                keen. The sleep they
                    sleep is no sleep, but
                        quick to
                waken. But
                    now you must
                        act, son,
                do what you
                    must—do it,
                        do it, that
                thing—do it in
                    secret, while he's
                        asleep! I
                know you
                    know what I'm
                        saying! The
                plan you're
                    planning won't
                        work. It will
                fail, and
                    failing, bring us
                        mischief.
LEADER: The wind sits fair now, son; a
                    favoring wind in the sails;
                        and there he lies sightless—
CHORUS: —sightless, no one to
                    help him,
                        helpless, stretched
                out in night's
                    darkness,
                        soundly asleep in the
                sun, no
                    muscle moving; no
                        hand, no

                    foot, stripped of
                         all his
                              powers, like the
                    dead that
                         slumber in
                              death.
                    Look to it, boy!
                         See if what you
                              say is
                    seasonable! As
                         I see it, son—
                              as far as my
                    mind can
                         grasp—trouble
                              taken without
                    fear is best!

(The music fades out as the Chorus disperses.)

NEOPTOLEMOS: Shh! Careful! His eyes moved.
    He's lifting his head.
    *(Philoktêtês wakens slowly, still dazed from his earlier pain. He shades his
    eyes against the brilliance of the sun.)*

PHILOKTÊTÊS: O light—o blessèd light—after sleep—
And you—friends—I never hoped—
To see you here still watching over me!

Oh, son! You stayed! You pitied me,
Bore with my pain and suffering—
Beside me here—helped relieve me.
Not even the sons of Atreus, our brave generals,
Had the courage to stay it out!
Not like you, dear boy:
Noble son of a noble father!
You bore it all so lightly,
The stench, the roars, the groans—

But now, boy, help me up—only you—
Peace has come again, a little while;
The pain, away, for a bit. Help me stand—
Back on the old feet again—

When this weariness leaves me,
We'll set off for your ship
And sail without delay!
NEOPTOLEMOS: I'm happy to see you alive, Philoktêtês,
Alive beyond hope, living and breathing,
And free of pain. I almost thought
You had died of your torment.

All right now, try to stand—
Or would you rather my men carry you?
They won't mind the trouble,
Since you and I agree on our plan of action.
PHILOKTÊTÊS: Thank you, son. Yes, lift me, lift me,
Since it was your thought.
I wouldn't want to trouble them too soon.
They'll have enough of my stench once we're on board.
NEOPTOLEMOS: Whatever you say.
Stand up. Here—my arm—
(*Neoptolemos extends his hand to Philoktêtês, pauses for a moment, then pulls the man to his feet.*)
PHILOKTÊTÊS: Don't be afraid. Habit gets me up—
(*Neoptolemos breaks down in a sudden rush of anguish, their hands still touching.*)
NEOPTOLEMOS: O god, what do I do now?
PHILOKTÊTÊS: What is it, son? What are you saying?
NEOPTOLEMOS: How can I tell you—there are no words—
PHILOKTÊTÊS: Tell me what, boy? What do you mean?
NEOPTOLEMOS: I don't know how—how to explain.
PHILOKTÊTÊS: My disease? Is that it? The corruption too much?
Changed your mind about taking me?
NEOPTOLEMOS: The corruption is here inside me.
I rebelled against my nature. I chose to do wrong.
PHILOKTÊTÊS: Wrong? When all you've said, all you've done,
To help a needy friend is true to your nature,
And to your noble father's?
NEOPTOLEMOS: I'll be known as a traitor! And that torments me!
PHILOKTÊTÊS: It's not what you've done, it's your words that frighten me.
NEOPTOLEMOS: Great Zeus, what shall I do?
Be a traitor twice, twice guilty?
Not speak and hide it, or tell more lies?

PHILOKTÊTÊS: Am I wrong to think this man is about to betray me,
    Sail away, leaving me behind?
NEOPTOLEMOS: Sail? Yes! But not without you, Philoktêtês.
    That's my torment. That's the truth.
    The journey will be a great grief to you.
PHILOKTÊTÊS: Son, what do you mean?
    I don't understand.
NEOPTOLEMOS: All right, then, here it is plain.
    You're sailing to Troy,
    To the generals Agamemnon and Menelaos,
    And the Greek army.
PHILOKTÊTÊS: No, it's not true, you're lying!
NEOPTOLEMOS: Yes; just listen, I'll explain.
PHILOKTÊTÊS: Explain what?
    What are you going to do with me?
NEOPTOLEMOS: Free you, first, from this misery of yours,
    And then together we'll level the walls of Troy.
PHILOKTÊTÊS: That's why you came? That's your plan?
NEOPTOLEMOS: Forgive me, Philoktêtês; I have no choice.
PHILOKTÊTÊS: Then I'm lost, betrayed!
    And by you! Why?
    I want my bow! *Now!*
NEOPTOLEMOS: I can't and do my duty. I have orders.
PHILOKTÊTÊS: Despicable! villainous! monstrous! treacherous destroyer!
    I'd sooner trust myself to fire than to you!
    What have you done to me! How have you deceived me!
    How do you dare to look at me who begged you,
    Who crawled to you on his knees in search of pity!
    Is your heart made of stone? In taking my bow
    You steal my life! Give it back! Oh, give it back, son!
    I'll do anything you ask! Anything!
    But give it back! By your father's gods, I beg you,
    Don't rob me of my life!

    No. Nothing. No answer. He looks away.
    He'll never give it back.

    O seas and rocky cliffs, lairs and headlands,
    Wild creatures of the hills, my only companions,

I turn to you to hear what this son of Achilleus
Has done to me! He swears he'll take me home,
Then takes me to Troy! He swears with his hand in mine,
Then takes my bow—the sacred bow of Heraklês
Son of Zeus—to brandish it before the Greeks
And boast of the fight he fought to subdue my strength
And drag me off by force! Is he so blind,
So blind as not to see the truth of me?
A corpse: a wisp of smoke: a mere nothing!
In my former strength he would never have taken me.
And even so, he took me only by trickery.
Betrayed and beaten down, what's left for me!

Oh, son, please give it back, give it back, child;
Be true to yourself, to your father. Give back the bow.

Nothing. Silence.
Is that your answer?
That's it?
Death.
I'm nothing.

And so I come back to you, my home in the rock—
My tunnel home—come back again to you—
Come back unarmed—no means to live.
In there, alone, I'll wither and die.
The birds of the air, the beasts that roam the hills,
Are safe from my arrow now.
And I will be the prey to those I preyed on,
A feast for those on whom I feasted;
My life's blood will repay the blood I shed,
Sentenced by a man who seemed so innocent
Of any evil.
(To Neoptolemos.)
Die, curse you, die!
But no, not yet!
Not before I see if you'll change and pity me!
No? Then die the death of a miserable traitor!
LEADER: What do we do now, sir?

It's up to you. Do we sail

Or yield to this man's prayers?

(Neoptolemos is in a state of total distraction.)

NEOPTOLEMOS: Pity for him has torn my heart from the first.

PHILOKTÊTÊS: Then let pity show itself!

Don't be scorned by men because you deceived me!

NEOPTOLEMOS: O god! What do I do?

Why did I leave Skyros to fall in this trap!

PHILOKTÊTÊS: You're not wicked, boy.

You were taught wickedness by wicked men.

Leave it to them, son; it suits them.

Now give me my bow and let's set sail.

(Neoptolemos turns slowly toward Philoktêtês and begins a slow but delib-
erate move in his direction; his hands, holding the bow, begin to extend as if
to relinquish it; his speech to the Leader is as much to himself as to anyone
else.)

NEOPTOLEMOS: Friend, what do I do now?

(Odysseus, enraged, suddenly appears from the right accompanied by several
Sailors.)

ODYSSEUS: Traitor! What are you doing! Get back!

Give me that bow!

PHILOKTÊTÊS: Whose voice is that! Odysseus?

ODYSSEUS: Yes, Odysseus, as you can very well see!

PHILOKTÊTÊS: O god! Sold out! Betrayed!

You were the one, all your doing, Odysseus!

This trick, plotting my capture, to steal my bow!

ODYSSEUS: Guilty on all counts! I admit to everything!

PHILOKTÊTÊS: Give it to me, son! Quick! The bow!

ODYSSEUS: No, not likely, not even if he wanted to!

And you, Philoktêtês, you and your precious bow

Are going with us, even if we have to drag you!

PHILOKTÊTÊS: Vile, evil man! Take me by force, will you!

These men of yours!

ODYSSEUS: If that's what's needed.

(Neoptolemos, still holding the bow, silently witnesses the scene that follows
with bewilderment and shame.)

PHILOKTÊTÊS: O Lemnos, land of my exile, my island home,

And Hephaistos, lord of the fire-breathing mountain,

Must I endure being dragged from you by force?

ODYSSEUS: Zeus is the power here; Zeus decided this.
  And mine is the hand that serves his will.
PHILOKTÊTÊS: You! Every word you say is a lie!
  You hide behind the gods! You make them liars!
ODYSSEUS: Liars? No. Truth-tellers!
  Now to the journey.
PHILOKTÊTÊS: No!
ODYSSEUS: You have no choice!
PHILOKTÊTÊS: O god, was I born for this—
  Philoktêtês, son of Poias—to be a slave?
ODYSSEUS: No. But to be an equal among brave men,
  And together with them tear down the walls of Troy!
PHILOKTÊTÊS: No! Never! I'd rather suffer the worst!
  I always have this cliff—this precipice—this headland—
ODYSSEUS: To do what?
PHILOKTÊTÊS: To throw myself from—
  Shatter my head on the rocks below—
  (He rushes awkwardly to the downstage edge of the precipice.)
ODYSSEUS: Hold him! Don't let him jump!
  (Two of the Sailors seize Philoktêtês and overpower him following a struggle.)
PHILOKTÊTÊS: What are you now, hands, without the bow
  You loved so dearly? What but Odysseus' prisoners!
  What have you ever known, Odysseus, what,
  But deceit and depravity?
  You stalked me, stalked me again, like a thief in the night,
  And not for the first time, snared me,
  Using this boy as decoy, this boy as your bait—
  This boy I never knew, a stranger to me—
  But too good for you and your men!
  He's like me, he has honor!
  What does he know except to follow your orders?
  Look at him, agonized for what he's done,
  For what I've been made to suffer!
  But you, Odysseus, you with your shabby soul,
  Lurking in shadows, turned his unsuspecting innocence
  Into your implement for evil!

  And now you've come for *me!*

To truss me up like an animal and cart me off
Where years ago you discarded me, alone,
Without a friend, without a city, helpless,
A living corpse!

May the gods damn you to perdition, Odysseus!
But they never do! For here you are, alive,
Happy, content, while I grovel in the misery
And pain I've wished on you so many times,
Mocked at by you and your generals, sons of Atreus,
Whose toady you now are!

But how did they get you to join their team? Ah?
How did they get you to Troy, Odysseus?
Trickery! Trickery that forced the yoke of servitude
Securely onto your bullish neck, Odysseus!
But I sailed freely, sailed of my own free will,
With seven ships in tow, only to be spurned,
Scorned, cast out on this desolate shore by you,
Each of you blaming the other!
And why, now, why now are you dragging me off?
What's the advantage to you?
To you I'm nothing.
For you I died long ago!

Evil, despicable wretch abhorred by the gods,
Am I no longer the cripple you once rejected,
Whose poisonous, noxious stench infected your camps?
How, with me on board, will you pour libations
And offer burnt sacrifices to the gods?
That was your pretext once for casting me out!
If there is any justice in the gods,
You'll have the miserable death that you deserve,
And I *know* you will, for what you have done to me,
I *know*, because some god has sent you here,
Some *just* god, how else would you have come here
To search out the miserable wretch I am
Without some goad of heaven driving you on!

O gods of my fathers' land, if you have pity,

Pity for me, take vengeance, vengeance on them all,
However late it comes! My life is torment.
But if I saw them dead, destroyed, annihilated,
I could believe that I had escaped by sickness.
LEADER: Bitter words from a bitter soul, Odysseus.
This man refuses to bend. He's stubborn.
ODYSSEUS: I could meet him argument for argument,
But time's against it.
All I'll say is this:
(To Philoktêtês.)
Whatever occasion demands, I am that man.
If justice and nobility are at stake,
No man will be more scrupulous than I.
Whatever I do, I set out to win.
Except this once.
Except with you.
Except in this case.
This victory I give to you.
(To the Sailors constraining Philoktêtês.)
Set him free. No one touch this man.
Let him stay where he is.
(To Philoktêtês.)
We don't need you. We have your arms.
We also have Teükros who'll know how to use them.
And I'm no mean shot myself;
I can wield it, aim it as cleverly as you.
So we don't need you.

Goodbye, Philoktêtês!
Enjoy your strolls on Lemnos!
It's all yours!
(To the others.)
We'll be going now!
(To Philoktêtês, indicating the bow.).
Who knows? This prize may bring me honor
That should have been yours.
PHILOKTÊTÊS: Oh, no! No! You'll take my—
Take my bow—and parade it before all the Greeks?
You and my bow before all the Greek army?

ODYSSEUS: I've had enough. I'm going.

PHILOKTÊTÊS: Nothing to say to me, son of Achilleus?

> Just sail away in silence?

ODYSSEUS: Turn away, Neoptolemos. I know your nature.

> One look and at him and goodbye to success.
> *(Philoktêtês turns to the Chorus of Sailors.)*

PHILOKTÊTÊS: Pity me, friends, pity me.

> Don't desert me.

LEADER: This boy is our captain, sir.

> What he says, we say.

NEOPTOLEMOS: Do as he asks, men. Odysseus will say

> I'm too soft-hearted. But if he has no objection,
> Stay till the ship is ready and we've made sacrifice
> For a fair wind. Perhaps by then our friend
> Will have changed his mind and think better of us.
> For now, Odysseus and I will go on ahead.
> When we signal, come quickly.
> *(Music fades in as Odysseus and Neoptolemos go off, right, with the Sailors. At the same time, the Chorus takes up a new position in the orchestra for the lyric dialogue.)*

PHILOKTÊTÊS: Constant companion in

> life, in death my friend, my
> home, my rocky home, my
> tomb! Hot in summer's
> sun, cold in winter's
> frost, my fate, my fate
> now is never to leave you,
> you who must witness my
> dying.
> O rocky hollow that
> sounded my pain and
> sorrow, what will my
> days be like? My dying
> days with you? What
> food-gathering hope have I?
> O birds that cowered above me
> once in the sky, cut through
> the shrilling winds with your
> wings, my arm is helpless

CHORUS:

now, helpless to
bring you down.

Unhappy man, the
choice was
yours. No higher
power brought
about your misfortune.
You alone
bear the blame.
Wisdom,
wisdom was
offered, but
you, you
chose
suffering.

PHILOKTÊTÊS: Ah! Then this is my fate!
Unhappy, alone, in pain,
no one to give me comfort, misery,
misery! Abandoned,
rejected, to waste and wither
away, to die! My strength
gone, my arrows to hit
their mark no more! My hands, my
empty hands, strong hands
once, bring home no
food for the starving
suppliant!
Aiiiiii!
Aiiiiii!
Defeated by lies and deceit,
trapped in the net of that
mind, that cunning mind!
If only he who snared me were
caught in the long
pain of my agony!

CHORUS: The fate that
snared you, my
friend, was
sent by the

gods. No
    trick of my hand
played any part.
   Don't lay your
    curses on me.
All I ask is
  friendship,
    friendship you
must not refuse.

PHILOKTÊTÊS: Oimoi moi!
    When I think of him
sitting there, on the shore of the
   gray sea, laughing at me,
    laughing, Odysseus, my bow in his
hands, brandished high
  above him, my means to
    life never touched by man! O
dear bow torn cruelly from my
  loving hands, if you can
    feel, pity me, pity
Heraklês' friend, never to
  wield you again! You
    now have a new master, a wily
deceitful man, whose every
  shameful deed you will
    see, and the countless ills his
treachery has aimed at me.

CHORUS: A man who
    defends the truth is
right, but once he has
  spoken, he must not
    sting with a
rancorous
  tongue. The
    man you
revile was
  chosen by
    many; he obeyed
orders made for the

public good.

PHILOKTÊTÊS: Birds of the air, wild
beasts whose bright eyes
      burn on the mountain, no
          need to flee from your
lairs. My hands are
      empty. Look, no
          arrows, no bow, no
power. I'm nothing. Roam
      freely, the island is
          yours, nothing to
flee from anymore. It's
      your turn now to
          gorge on my rotting
flesh; my blood for
      yours. Soon I will be
          dead. Where will
livelihood come from? How
      long can I live on the wind, no
          strength to gather nurture that
only earth can provide?

CHORUS: I beg you, if you
          regard your
friend, our
      master Neoptolemos,
          draw near him, he
comes in all
      kindness and loyalty!
          Consider, Philoktêtês!
You must consider!
      The power to
          change is
yours, to
      change your fate, to
          escape this
daimôn that
      eats away at you
          cruelly!
A cruelty you

    cannot ever—
     pain you can
   never endure!
PHILOKTÊTÊS: You are the kindest of
     all; the best who ever
   came here! Then why,
    again and again, do you
     waken my agony? Why
   destroy me like
    this? Why do you
     do this?
   Why?
CHORUS: Do what?
     Why do we do
   what?
PHILOKTÊTÊS: Take me back to Troy!
     It's what you hoped for!
   Troy! The land I
    hate,
     hate!
CHORUS: I thought it best.
PHILOKTÊTÊS: Then leave me here!
CHORUS: Whatever you say!
   Willingly!
    All right, men:
     back to the ship!
(They start off, causing Philoktêtês enormous anxiety.)
PHILOKTÊTÊS: No, no, by Zeus who
    hears men's curses,
     don't!
CHORUS: Easy, Philoktêtês,
     easy—
PHILOKTÊTÊS: Don't go!
   Stay! I
    beg of you!
CHORUS: Why are you
   calling us?
PHILOKTÊTÊS: Aiiiiiiiiiiiiiiiiiiiiiii!
    Aiiiiiiiiiiiiiiiiiiiiiiiii!

O daimôn, daimôn!
   I'm lost! Damn you,
      foot! Damn you! What do I
do with you? How can I
   live? O friends! Dear
      friends! Come
back, come
   back!

CHORUS: First you
tell us to
   go and
      now,
now
   it's something
      different?

PHILOKTÊTÊS: The pain I suffer,
   suffer—a raging
      storm—tears me!
Forgive me, friends,
   forgive what I said!

CHORUS: Poor man,
we hear you!
   Come! Come
      with us, then!
Come!

PHILOKTÊTÊS: Never! I'll never
   go! Never! Let the
God of Lightning
   strike me with his
      bolt and consume me in
flame, but I will never
   go! Never! Let the
      walls of Troy collapse and
crush the miserable
   enemy that cast me
      out, a cripple! Oh, but,
friends, grant me one
   prayer!

CHORUS: What is this prayer?

PHILOKTÊTÊS: Bring me a sword, an
                    ax, anything, anything,
                        hurry, anything,
                please, an
                arrow!
CHORUS: For what new insanity?
PHILOKTÊTÊS: To hack the flesh from my
                    limbs! Limb from
                        limb from—head,
                hands, feet! All I
                    want is to die!
CHORUS: But why?
PHILOKTÊTÊS: My father—
                    to find my
                        father—
CHORUS: Where?
PHILOKTÊTÊS: In Death's Dark
                        Kingdom—out of the
                light of the sun—o
                    city, city, my
                        country! Home of my
                fathers! To see you
                    again! What a fool I
                        was to leave your holy
                river, never to
                    see you again, sailing for
                        Troy to help the
                cursed, the faithless
                    Greeks! My enemies,
                        enemies!
                Nothing!
                    Now I am
                        nothing!
                Nothing!
        (He drags himself up the path and into his cave. The music fades out.)
LEADER: We should have left for the ship long ago.
        But here come Neoptolemos and Odysseus.
        (Neoptolemos enters, right, carrying the bow. Odysseus hurries after him.)
ODYSSEUS: Why the rush? Where are you going?

NEOPTOLEMOS: To undo the terrible wrong I did.

ODYSSEUS: And what would that have been, I wonder?

NEOPTOLEMOS: In obeying you and the Greek army.

ODYSSEUS: You did what that didn't suit you?

NEOPTOLEMOS: I cheated a man with lies and deceit.

ODYSSEUS: What new mad scheme are you up to now?

NEOPTOLEMOS: No mad scheme. To pay a debt—

ODYSSEUS: I'm almost afraid to hear what you're thinking!

NEOPTOLEMOS: —to Philoktêtês—I took his bow.

ODYSSEUS: What are you saying? You'd give it back?

NEOPTOLEMOS: Yes! I won it with shame and deceit!

ODYSSEUS: By god, boy, are you trying to mock me?

NEOPTOLEMOS: Yes, if it's mockery to speak the truth!

ODYSSEUS: Do you have any idea what you're saying?

NEOPTOLEMOS: How many times do I have to say it?

ODYSSEUS: I'd rather not have heard it the first time!

NEOPTOLEMOS: In that case, I've said all there is!

ODYSSEUS: I assure you there is a power to stop you!

NEOPTOLEMOS: A power to stop me? And what might that be?

ODYSSEUS: The Greek army, with me among them!

NEOPTOLEMOS: You were born clever, but you talk like a fool!

ODYSSEUS: All you say and do is foolish!

NEOPTOLEMOS: Foolish, perhaps, but at least it's just!

ODYSSEUS: To give back the prize my cunning helped win?

NEOPTOLEMOS: Steal, not win! I'm ashamed of that!

I'll try to undo it!

ODYSSEUS: No fear of the army?

NEOPTOLEMOS: With right on my side, your threats don't frighten me!

ODYSSEUS: And what if I use force? What then?

NEOPTOLEMOS: No force of yours could make me yield!

ODYSSEUS: Then it will be you we fight, not the Trojans!

NEOPTOLEMOS: So be it!

(Odysseus places his right hand on the hilt of his sword.)

ODYSSEUS: Do you see this?

(Still holding the bow, Neoptolemos does the same.)

NEOPTOLEMOS: As well you can see this! I'm ready!

ODYSSEUS: Why waste time? No. I'll go back.

Once I've reported this, they'll know what to do.

NEOPTOLEMOS: Very wise, I'd say. You've come to your senses.

Keep this up and you'll stay out of trouble!

(Odysseus goes out right. Neoptolemos turns toward the cave and calls softly.)

NEOPTOLEMOS: Philoktêtês, son of Poias, come out!

(Philoktêtês' voice resounds in the cave's hollow.)

PHILOKTÊTÊS: Who's calling now? Who's there?

What do you want of me?

(Philoktêtês appears at the cave's mouth.)

More misery! Are you here to add

More pain to the others you've brought?

NEOPTOLEMOS: Don't be afraid! Only listen!

PHILOKTÊTÊS: That's what frightens me!

I listened before, and the misery it brought,

Your "fair" words!

NEOPTOLEMOS: Is change impossible?

No room for repentance?

PHILOKTÊTÊS: You sounded the same, the same words,

When you stole my bow,

The same deceit in your heart.

NEOPTOLEMOS: But not now!

I'm asking, Philoktêtês:

Will you stay here and endure your pain,

Or sail with us?

PHILOKTÊTÊS: Enough! No more! You're wasting words.

NEOPTOLEMOS: Your mind is made up?

PHILOKTÊTÊS: More than you know.

NEOPTOLEMOS: I'd hoped to persuade you,

But if there's no chance—

PHILOKTÊTÊS: None!

Nothing you could say would change me now.

First you steal my life with your cunning words,

Strip me of my bow, and now you come

To lecture me! Hateful son!

That noble Achilleus should sire such a son!

I curse you all, curse you!

Sons of Atreus! Odysseus! And *you!*

NEOPTOLEMOS: No more curses, Philoktêtês.

Here's your bow. Take it. I give it to you.

PHILOKTÊTÊS: What are you saying? Another trick? Ah?

NEOPTOLEMOS: No, no trick. By the majesty of holy Zeus.

PHILOKTÊTÊS: Sweetest of words, if only they were true!

NEOPTOLEMOS: They're true, Philoktêtês. This will prove it.

(Philoktêtês comes slowly down the path to ground level where a silent, almost sacred, transfer of the bow is about to take place.)

NEOPTOLEMOS: Reach me your hand.

Be master again of your weapon.

(Odysseus, approaching, accompanied by several Sailors, is heard before he enters left.)

ODYSSEUS: No! I forbid it!

(Entering, right, before the bow is exchanged.)

I forbid it in the name of all the gods,

In the name of the sons of Atreus,

In the name of the army!

PHILOKTÊTÊS: Is that Odysseus' voice?

ODYSSEUS: Yes, and here beside you!

I'm taking you back by force, Philoktêtês!

Back to Troy no matter what this son of Achilleus

May have to say!

(Philoktêtês grasps the bow from Neoptolemos' extended hand and aims it with the agility of a great archer.)

PHILOKTÊTÊS: Not if this arrow finds its mark!

(Neoptolemos seizes Philoktêtês' arm.)

NEOPTOLEMOS: Philoktêtês, no!

PHILOKTÊTÊS: Let go of me, dear boy, let go!

NEOPTOLEMOS: I can't!

(Odysseus, followed by the Sailors, rushes off left during the struggle.)

PHILOKTÊTÊS: Why did you keep me from killing him!

I had him in my sight, my hated enemy!

NEOPTOLEMOS: Killing him dishonors us both.

PHILOKTÊTÊS: One thing's sure at least:

Those lying, so-called ambassadors of the Greeks,

Are brave with words, but cowards when it comes to fighting!

NEOPTOLEMOS: I agree. But the bow is yours now.

No reason for any further grudge against me?

PHILOKTÊTÊS: None.

You've shown your true nature, Neoptolemos:

The spirit of your father Achilleus,

Our greatest hero in life and death.

NEOPTOLEMOS: Thank you, Philoktêtês.

Praise like that from you makes me proud
Both for my father and me.
But I have another favor to ask. Please listen,
And be fair in your judgment.

We're only men, only mortals, we have no choice
But to live life with the fate the gods have given us.
But when we cling to sufferings we've brought on ourselves,
As you are doing now,
We can't expect pity from anyone.

You've become a savage; you refuse to listen to reason;
To talk, even. When someone tries to persuade you
In all goodwill, you turn and attack with a vengeance,
As if he were out to harm you; as if he were an enemy.
Even so, I'll say what I have to say,
With Zeus as my witness,
And ask that you take it carefully to heart.

This plague you suffer from came from a god.
You wandered into the roofless sanctuary of Chrysis
And disturbed the serpent that secretly guards her shrine.
You're poisoned now, and as long as day follows night
There will be no cure till you come to Troy
Of your own free will.
You'll find doctors there,
The famous sons of Asklêpios,
Who will heal your wound, and then, with your sacred bow,
You and I together will level Troy's towers.

I'll tell you how I know. We have a prisoner
From Troy, the noble prophet, Helenos,
Who pledges his life as forfeit if what he says
Fails to happen: that before the summer is out,
We are to take Troy.

There, I've said it all.
Knowing this, won't you give way?
The reward couldn't be greater.
To be recognized the greatest of the Greeks!
A cure for your wound!

But most of all, glory for yourself
By ending the agonized tale of Troy with victory!
PHILOKTÊTÊS: O hateful, detestable life!
Why am I forced to live, why can't I die!
Why not sink into death and darkness and Hades!
What can I do? How can I turn deaf ears
On the counsel of this kind friend? Do I give in?
If so, how can I leave this wretched life
To walk again in the sight of men?
Who will speak to me?
How can these eyes that have seen what they have seen
Bear to see me meet those brothers again,
Those brother-kings, sons of Atreus, who destroyed me,
Or evil-hearted Odysseus?
No!
It's not the pain of the past that stings me most,
But the suffering the future holds; for men's minds,
Once they have bred evil, breed only evil.
(To Neoptolemos.)
As for you, Neoptolemos, I wonder at you.
What reason could you have for going to Troy?
What reason could you have to take me with you?
They outraged you! They stole your father's arms
And gave them in honor to Odysseus! And now you'll go
And fight with them? And force me to do the same?
No, son! No! Be true to the oath you swore
To take me home. Then go to Skyros and forget them.
Leave those evil men to the evil end
They deserve. Do this, son, and you will reap
A double blessing, from me and from my father!
For no one will say you shared the evil of your masters.
NEOPTOLEMOS: I hear you, Philoktêtês.
Just trust in the gods and me and sail back with me.
PHILOKTÊTÊS: To Troy—with this crippled foot?
To my hated enemy, Agamemnon?
NEOPTOLEMOS: To doctors who'll heal your foot,
Cure your disease, and end your pain.
PHILOKTÊTÊS: What is this miserable advice?
NEOPTOLEMOS: The best advice for us both.
PHILOKTÊTÊS: Aren't you ashamed?

NEOPTOLEMOS: Ashamed to help my friends?

PHILOKTÊTÊS: Help? The generals or me?

NEOPTOLEMOS: You! I'm your friend, Philoktêtês!

PHILOKTÊTÊS: You've a strange way to prove it!

NEOPTOLEMOS: A little less pride would help!

PHILOKTÊTÊS: You'll be my death!

NEOPTOLEMOS: You don't understand!

PHILOKTÊTÊS: The Atreidai threw me out!

NEOPTOLEMOS: And now they'll rescue you!

PHILOKTÊTÊS: I'll never go back to Troy!

NEOPTOLEMOS: What more can I do? I give up.

> Go live your life as it is—
> past hope, past cure—

PHILOKTÊTÊS: Whatever there is to endure, I'll endure.

> But your promise, Neoptolemos!
> Take me home—home to Skyros!
> And never mention Troy again!
> I've suffered enough.

(For some moments Neoptolemos is inwardly torn; then speaks with calm resolution.)

NEOPTOLEMOS: All right. Let's go.

PHILOKTÊTÊS: Good for you, boy!

NEOPTOLEMOS: Walk firmly now.

PHILOKTÊTÊS: The best I can.

NEOPTOLEMOS: The Greeks will make me pay for this!

PHILOKTÊTÊS: Forget them, son!

NEOPTOLEMOS: They'll ravage my country!

PHILOKTÊTÊS: I'll be there.

NEOPTOLEMOS: To help? But how?

PHILOKTÊTÊS: The arrows of Heraklês.

NEOPTOLEMOS: I don't understand.

PHILOKTÊTÊS: They'll hold off invaders.

NEOPTOLEMOS: Take your farewell, Philoktêtês.

> Kiss the ground of Lemnos.

(Philoktêtês slowly sinks to his knees with the help of Neoptolemos and ex-tends his arms upward in silent prayer. In the distance is heard the low, con-tinuous rumble of thunder that creates a sense of mystery and expectation. Music fades in as Philoktêtês prostrates himself on the ground, kissing it. The thunder grows louder and is punctuated by claps of lightning. Neoptolemos bends over the silent, prostrate body of Philoktêtês as he whispers to him.)

NEOPTOLEMOS: Come. We must get to the ship.

(He helps Philoktêtês to rise. Unseen at first, the voice of Heraklês is heard slowly approaching from a distance from above and behind the cave's mouth. He comes gradually into view.)

HERAKLÊS: Philoktêtês, son of Poias.

> Stop. Listen to me.
>
> It is Heraklês you hear and see,
> Heraklês son of Zeus.
>
> I have come to you from my seat
> on high Olympos
> to tell you of Zeus' will:
> You must not make this journey.
> Listen to me now: hear my words.

(The vision of Heraklês is now fully revealed in a radiant epiphany above the mouth of the cave. He is an immortal, he is young, he is beautiful, and wears a wreath of laurel on his head to signify apotheosis. The thunder and claps of lightning fade. Neoptolemos and Philoktêtês in awe have assumed positions of worship.)

HERAKLÊS: I will tell you first of my own fortunes:
The twelve exacting labors I endured
Won for me this glorious immortality.
Your fate will be the same: labors to perform;
And out of great suffering: fame and glory.

You will go with this man to Troy and there be cured
Of your terrible illness. You will then be chosen by the Greeks
Their greatest champion. You will seek out Paris of Troy
Who began this evil encounter and you will kill him
With those my weapons. You will sack the city and receive
From your fellow warriors the treasured prize of valor.
You will carry home to your father Poias and your country
The spoils of battle; and a portion of those spoils
You will take to the heights of Oïtê and dedicate them
As a thank-offering for my bow.

I have words for you, too, son of Achilleus.
Neither of you alone can conquer Troy.
But like two lions who share a common ground,
Defend each other.

I will send Asklêpios himself
To heal your wound; and then, as destiny decrees,
Troy will be taken a second time by my bow.
But one thing you must not forget: When Troy is sacked,
Observe true reverence for the gods; for nothing else
Holds greater weight in the eyes of Zeus our Father.
Piety lives on in the hearts of men.
Men may die, but piety never dies.

PHILOKTÊTÊS: How long, how long I have yearned to hear your voice!
How long, how long I have longed to see your face!
You are my master! I obey!

NEOPTOLEMOS: And I!

HERAKLÊS: Hurry! The time is right!
The wind sits fair in your sail!

(The vision of Heraklês vanishes.)

PHILOKTÊTÊS: Lemnos, my island, my own
cave that shared with me
many a midnight watch!
And you nymphs of streams and meadows,
deep-throated roar of ocean and rock
that licked my head hidden from your blast!
And the Hill of Hermês that echoed my cries!
Goodbye!
And goodbye to you, Lykian spring!
I leave you now, leave you,
a hope I never harbored,
never embarked on!
Lemnos, goodbye; goodbye, sea-washed island!
Send me sailing in safety
where destiny, my friends' advice,
and the spirit of my master lead me!
It was he decided;
and now it is done!

CHORUS: Let us all pray
the nymphs of the sea
for a safe voyage,
a safe return!

(All leave to the right, Neoptolemos and Philoktêtês last. The island is empty. The gentle lapping of waves. Silence.)

OEDIPUS AT KOLONOS
(ΟΙΔΙΠΟΥΣ ΕΠΙ ΚΟΔΩΝΩΙ)

CAST OF CHARACTERS

OEDIPUS *once king of Thebes*
ANTIGONÊ *his daughter*
A CITIZEN OF KOLONOS
CHORUS OF CITIZENS OF KOLONOS
LEADER OF THE CHORUS
ISMENÊ *daughter of Oedipus and Antigonê's sister*
THÊSEUS *king of Athens*
KREON *king of Thebes and brother-in-law of Oedipus*
POLYNEIKÊS *son of Oedipus and brother of Antigonê and Ismenê*
A MESSENGER
GUARDS AND ATTENDANTS OF THÊSEUS
BODYGUARDS OF KREON

The lines of the Chorus, unless otherwise indicated, are to be delivered by individual voices and varied groups of voices.

OEDIPUS AT KOLONOS

Kolonos. The Sacred Grove of the Eumenides, a mile northwest of the Athenian Akropolis. It is a lush, green area, luxuriant with olive, laurel, and vine, with a rocky ledge jutting from the left. The skênê building with its large double doors is visible through whatever foliage is present. It represents the Brazen-Floored Threshold of Earth. A circular orchestra is flanked at the upper reaches of either side by an entrance, the left leading to the country, the right to the city. Centrally located in the orchestra is an altar with an unhewn throne-like rock situated near it. A large outcropping of rock dominates the area that demarcates the Sacred Precinct from the downstage and stage right areas. The heroic statue of a horseman is situated to the right. Oedipus enters, left, led by his daughter Antigonê, whose skin is browned by constant exposure to the sun, and whose feet are bare. Oedipus is old and his physical condition is in a sorry state. His life for many years has been that of a beggar, and he carries the traditional beggar's bag. His face is scarred with the hollows of his withered eye sockets. He is dirty, bent, and barefoot and presents the image of a wild outcast. And yet he possesses two attributes that age, time, and calamity have not deprived him of: nobility of mind and the imperious quickness to anger that typified him in his earlier days as King of Thebes.

OEDIPUS: Child of the blind old man, daughter, Antigonê,
   What land have we come to now, what town?
   Who will give scanty courtesy today
   To wandering old Oedipus? I ask but little,
   And receive still less; and yet I'm satisfied.
   Suffering and time, vast time, have taught me acceptance
   Of life's adversities, as has nobility of birth.
   But now, child, tell me, is there a place
   Where we might find a seat—
   On public ground or sacred?
   (Extending his hands to her.)
   Give me your arm; lead me there.
   And when I'm seated, we'll inquire where we have come to;
   As strangers we must learn from the local people
   And do as they do.

(Antigonê looks off to the right in the direction of Athens.)

ANTIGONÊ: Father, poor, tired, wandering old Oedipus—

 The towers that crown the city are a long way off.

 As for this place, it is surely sacred ground—

 You can sense it: heavy with olive, laurel and vine:

 A haven for the song and flutter of nightingales.

 (She leads him to a natural stone seat resembling a throne within the confines of the grove.)

 There now, rest a while on this rough stone.

 You've come a long road for a man of your years.

OEDIPUS: Help me to sit; care for the blind old man.

ANTIGONÊ: Time has taught me some things, too, father.

 (She backs him onto the stone seat, then arranges his clothes, perhaps placing his walking stick at his feet.)

OEDIPUS: Can you tell me what place this is?

ANTIGONÊ: The city off there is Athens.

 Here, I don't know.

OEDIPUS: We learned as much from travelers!

ANTIGONÊ: Shall I go ask its name?

OEDIPUS: Yes, child; and if anyone lives here.

ANTIGONÊ: Oh, that they do! But no need to leave.

 There's a man not far off: I can see him.

OEDIPUS: Is he coming in our direction?

 (A Citizen of Kolonos enters right and approaches them while also remaining outside the Sacred Precinct.)

ANTIGONÊ: He's here already.

 Say what you think right;

 He's by our side.

OEDIPUS: Stranger—my daughter, whose eyes serve us both,

 Tells me of our good fortune in meeting you here.

 I think that you have come to learn who we are,

 And perhaps can shed some light on—

CITIZEN: No, no questions! Not yet!

 First you must leave that seat at once!

 The ground you stand on is sacred;

 It mustn't be touched!

 Leave it now, please.

OEDIPUS: What ground is this?

 What god does it honor?

CITIZEN: It mustn't be violated; no one may live here:
     The Terrible Goddesses hold it in power:
     Daughters of the Earth, Daughters of Darkness.
OEDIPUS: Tell me, sir, by what dread name are they known,
     So that I may do them honor.
CITIZEN: We here call them the Gentle All-Seeing Ones;
     Though elsewhere they are honored by other names.
OEDIPUS: May they·receive me gently, then,
     For I will never leave this refuge.
CITIZEN: What are you saying?
OEDIPUS: My destiny is here.
CITIZEN: Well, if that's true, I don't dare turn you out;
     Not without word first from the city;
     Not before I report to them what you're doing.
OEDIPUS: In god's name, stranger, don't refuse
     A poor wanderer the knowledge that he seeks.
CITIZEN: Ask me what you want; I'll answer.
OEDIPUS: Tell me, what is this place we have come to?
CITIZEN: I'm glad to tell you whatever I know.
     Everything you see, the country round you,
     Is holy ground, held in protective power
     By mighty Poseidon; but the fire-wielding Titan
     Prometheus is honored here as well.
     The ground you rest on there is known by all
     As the Brazen-Floored Threshold of Earth, bulwark
     Of Athens. And the neighboring fields and the people
     Are known by the name of our founding father,
     The horseman Kolonos, whose statue you see there.
     This land of ours may not be honored in legend,
     But it has a place in the hearts of those that love it.
OEDIPUS: The people really live on their lands?
CITIZEN: Indeed they do; and named for their hero.
OEDIPUS: Who rules the people? A king or themselves?
CITIZEN: The King of Athens. He lives in the city.
OEDIPUS: Who is this king who holds the power?
CITIZEN: Thêseus, the son of King Aigeus before him.
OEDIPUS: Could someone be sent to him with a message?
CITIZEN: To deliver one or to call him here?
OEDIPUS: A small favor brings him great gain.

CITIZEN: What is to be gained from a man without eyes?

OEDIPUS: My every word will radiate light!

CITIZEN: Listen, stranger, I'm trying to help you here.

> I can see that you are of noble birth,
> Despite your luck.
> Stay where you are, right there,
> Don't move, and I'll go tell the people who live here.
> It is theirs to decide whether you leave or stay.
> *(He goes off right.)*
> *(Silence.)*

OEDIPUS: Child, Antigonê, has the stranger gone yet?

ANTIGONÊ: He has; you may speak freely now; we're alone.

> *(Oedipus rises from his seat and approaches the altar. Antigonê assists him. Once he is at the altar, facing outward, he shakes her hands from him imperiously and, bracing himself on the stone of the altar, slowly and painfully lowers himself to his knees. Antigonê retreats and, finally, kneels at a distance.)*
> *(Silence.)*

OEDIPUS: Dread Goddesses, you whose eyes are terrible,

> It is here on this seat in your Sacred Grove
> That I first find rest in this land.
> Be gracious to Apollo and to me:
> For when he cried aloud those prophesies of evil
> That would afflict my life, he also spoke
> Of this resting place to crown long years of suffering:
> A land at journey 's end where I should find
> A seat belonging to the Awful Goddesses.
> And there, too, he said, I would find a home
> To round out the days of my miserable being;
> Conferring on them who received me a great benefit;
> A curse on those who rejected me.
> As a sign,
> He assured me that there would be many portents:
> Earthquake, thunder, Zeus' holy lightning.
> But I know this: that without some true intimation
> From you, Dread Ladies, I would not have found
> The cool of your Holy Wood; nor met you,
> The first in all my wanderings:
> You who love no wine,

And I who drink none.
How else could I have found this sacred seat
Of unhewn rock?

Goddesses! Grant me, then—
Unless my life's afflictions seem too light,
I who suffer life's greatest calamities—
Grant me consummation, as the god foretold,
And the passing of life.

Welcome, Sweet Daughters,
Daughters of Original Darkness!
Welcome, Athens,
City of mighty Pallas, city of cities!
Pity the pitiful shadow of Oedipus,
for Oedipus is not the man he was.
(Silence.)

ANTIGONÊ: Shh! Some old men are coming
To see where you've taken refuge.

OEDIPUS: Then I will be still; just lead me clear of the path
And hide me in the wood, I will hear them from there.
Knowledge will tell us then what action to take.
(Music begins immediately as Antigonê leads Oedipus into the Sacred Grove and a Chorus of Old Citizens of Kolonos enters the orchestra from the right with their Leader. They remain outside the precinct as they search the area with a terrible frenzy. Here, as elsewhere throughout the play, they speak sometimes together, sometimes separately in varying combinations.)

CHORUS: Look for him!
            Look,
                look for the
            man! Who can he
            be? Where?
                Where is he
            hidden? Where?
                Reckless man!
                    Shameless!
            Look! Look for
            him! Every
                direction! A

wanderer, I hear!
   Stranger, I hear!
      Strange to this
place! Why
   else has he
      gone, why
else, into the
     Holy Grove? The
     Pathless
Grove? Sacred to the
    Maidens! Furies!
      Goddesses invincible!
Whose names we
   fear to name,
     tremble to name!
We pass with
   eyes cast
     down, voices
hushed, no word
   spoken, breathing
      pious thought only, in
veneration, in
   reverence!

LEADER: Now one is come,
or so we hear,
   one has come who
     knows no reverence,
devotionless, impious man!
   Where is he to be
     found?
Where?

CHORUS: I look!
     I cannot tell!
Cannot find him!
   Where is he?
    Where?
Where? Where is the
   man?
    Where?

(Oedipus, led by Antigonê, appears on the rocky ledge.)

OEDIPUS: I am that man, that
   stranger. I see by
     sound, as the saying goes!

CHORUS: Oh!
   Oh! Terrible,
    terrible! Dreadful
 sight! Dreadful to
  hear!

OEDIPUS: I beg you, don't
 see me as a
  lawless
   man.

CHORUS: Zeus protect us!
  Who is he, this
   ancient man?

OEDIPUS: Not one whose fate is
   enviable, o guardians of this
    land! Why else would I
 move with other's
  eyes? You can
   see, here! Why
 else would I lean my
  height on one so
   small? The weaker
 on the stronger?

CHORUS: Oh!
   Oh! Blind!
 Blind! Were you
  blind from birth? He is
   blind! Wretched,
 wretched and
  long, wretched and
   long is your
 life!

LEADER: But if I can prevent it,
   you shall not add
 this curse to your
  misery! You have

| | gone too |
| | far! |

CHORUS: Too far! Too
          far! Too
far!

LEADER: Take care!
CHORUS: Take care!
care!

LEADER: You mustn't intrude
    on the soft green
glade, the voiceless
    glade where the gentle
      hollow gathers softly flowing
streams; where swirling pure
    waters mix with the honey of
      bees!

CHORUS: It is a sacred
    place! You mustn't
      set foot there, man of
grief! Come out!
    Come out!
      Don't delay!

LEADER: How far the distance is
    between us! Can you
      hear? Come down, miserable
wanderer, if you have any
    word for us here!
      Leave that place
forbidden to men! Come
    down where all are
      allowed to speak!
Till then, be silent!

(The music changes character to a less frenzied mode.)

OEDIPUS: What way does wisdom
    point, my child?

ANTIGONÊ: To obey them, father,
    as custom demands;
      to give in and listen
to them, I think.

OEDIPUS: Give me your hand.
ANTIGONÊ: It's here.
               Do you feel it?
OEDIPUS: Strangers, I must endure no
                    wrong when I have
               left my refuge. I
                    trusted you.
LEADER: Never, old man, we
               will never force you to
                    leave this refuge
                    against your will.

(Oedipus begins to move forward tentatively, supported but not led by Antigonê. He then pauses.)

OEDIPUS: Farther still?
LEADER: Yes; farther!

(He takes another cautious step, then pauses again.)

OEDIPUS: Farther?
CHORUS: Yes; farther!
LEADER: Lead him, young woman.
                    You see and
               may trust us.
ANTIGONÊ: Come, let your
                    blind steps follow.
               Follow where
                    I'm leading.
LEADER: Stranger in a strange land,
               be warned, poor wanderer!
CHORUS: Hate what we
                    hate! Love what we
               love!
OEDIPUS: Lead me, then, child,
                    to the place where we may
               speak and listen;
                    to lawful ground. We
                    must not fight Necessity.

(He reaches the rocky outcropping at the edge of the Sacred Grove.)

CHORUS: There!
               There!
LEADER: No farther than the
               rocky platform.

OEDIPUS: Here, then?
LEADER: Yes, as I have said.
OEDIPUS: May I sit?
LEADER: Yes; a little to the
                        side. Crouch down. Sit
            now—the edge of the
            rock.
ANTIGONÊ: Father, let me help you.
            It's why I'm here.
                  Careful now.
                        Step by step.

(He stumbles and is caught by Antigonê.)

OEDIPUS: What—!
                  Oh!
ANTIGONÊ: Keep with me.
            Lean on my arm.

(She gently helps him down onto the seat of rock and moves away to the side.)

OEDIPUS: Cruel misery of a darkened soul!
CHORUS: Poor man, tell us,
            now you're at ease,
                  who are you? Your
                        parents? Why are you
            wandering in such terrible
                  pain? Where are you
                        from? What country?
OEDIPUS: Country?
            I have none.
                  But don't ask me—
LEADER: Ask you?
            What? Why
                  not, old man?
OEDIPUS: No, no! Don't
                  ask! Don't ask who I
                        am! Don't
            question!
                  Please!
LEADER: But why?
OEDIPUS: My birth was unspeakable—
LEADER: Tell us.

(Oedipus gropes about for Antigonê's hand.)

OEDIPUS: Antigonê—

         child—

           what shall I

             say?

(Antigonê takes hold of his hand, trying to calm him.)

LEADER: What is your

           family? Who was your

             father?

OEDIPUS: Child—

           child—what is to

             become of me—?

ANTIGONÊ: Answer them: you're

           driven to the edge.

OEDIPUS: I will speak, then—

        yes—no way

          to hide it—

LEADER: You have taken too long!

        Hurry!

OEDIPUS: You have heard of the

          son of Laïos?

CHORUS: Ioo!

        Ioo!

          Ioo!

OEDIPUS: Born of the family

        of Labdakos?

LEADER: Dear god!

OEDIPUS: Of wretched

        Oedipus?

LEADER: You're that man?

OEDIPUS: Don't let what I

        say frighten you!

(With a protracted shout of horror and loathing, the Chorus pulls back and turns away, faces hidden behind folds of clothing, scattering about the area as if to escape pollution.)

CHORUS: Ioo!

        Ooo!

        Ooo!

OEDIPUS: My destiny has

      been a misery!

CHORUS: Ooo!
                    Ooo!

OEDIPUS: My child, what
                    happens to us now?

LEADER: Go! Leave our land!
              Leave us!

OEDIPUS: And what becomes of your
                    promise?

LEADER: Fate doesn't punish
                  a man who returns
                    evil for evil! Deceit
              invites deceit and brings
                    pain, not reward!

CHORUS: Leave this place!
              At once! Go!
                    Go! Leave this land!
                    Hurry!

LEADER: Before pollution
                  falls on my
                    city!

ANTIGONÊ: Reverent men, whose
                  minds are just; you who
                    refuse to hear my agèd
              father's story because the
                  deeds done by him,
                    although unwilling, are
              too well known to you,
                  have pity, at least, on
                    me! On my unhappiness!
              I appeal to you for my
                  father. Not with eyes
                    that have no sight, but as a
              child of your own
                  blood might look, pleading
                    for care for the ancient
              suppliant!
                  In our despair we
                    turn to you as to a
              god! We ask you to

grant the unhoped-for
favor! I pray you by
what you love
most dearly: child,
wife, treasure,
gods! Search the world,
you will never find a
god-driven
man who
escapes his
fate!

(The Chorus disburses variously around the orchestra as the Leader approaches Oedipus and the music fades out.)

LEADER: Child of Oedipus, we pity your misfortune
The same as we do his. But we fear the gods.
What else can we say?

OEDIPUS: Then what is the use of great renown?
What is the use of a glorious name? What?
If it flows away to nothing?

Athens, praised the world over
For piety and readiness to rescue the wretched,
The exiles of every land, to give them shelter!
Yet what is my share of this? What refuge do I find!
First you uproot me from my rocky seat;
Then drive me out, and all for fear of my name!
What terror does this wretched body hold,
Or what have I done?
What I have done is suffer, more than act!
Oh, I could tell you, if it were fitting,
Tell you of my mother and father,
Of what they did, for that is why you fear me,
That much I know!

And yet, whatever my actions,
How, how in my nature was I evil?
I was attacked.
Was it wrong to repay an evil deed?
And even had I known,
I would not be guilty; but knowing nothing,

Nothing, I went on, went on my way.
Yet they knew! They who planned my destruction—
they knew!

And so I implore you, strangers,
Implore you by the gods, just as you
Displaced me from my shelter, protect me now;
And don't in one breath honor the gods,
And in the next deny them. Their eyes are fixed
On the godly man the same as on the ungodly;
And no godless man ever escapes them.

The gods be with you, then; and do not slander
The fame of glorious Athens by giving in
To unholy acts, but support me now as you promised,
And guard me to the end.

My face may be dreadful,
But I come here as one full of grace,
Bearing for your city and its people
Great benefit, as you will learn when he comes,
Your ruler, whoever he is. Meanwhile take care
To do me no evil.
LEADER: You plead your case well, old man. Your words
    Fill me with awe: they are not taken lightly.
    But I'll be relieved to let our leader decide.
OEDIPUS: Where is he, then, this ruler of yours?
LEADER: In Athens, the city his father ruled.
    The messenger who brought us has gone to fetch him.
OEDIPUS: Why should he trouble himself for a blind old beggar
    To come himself?
LEADER: Once he has heard your name, he will come.
OEDIPUS: Yes, but who will bring him that message?
LEADER: Athens is a long way off, and travelers
    On the road talk, rumor spreads. Your name
    Is known the world over, old man.
    The minute Thêseus hears who you are,
    He will abandon whatever it is he is doing
    And hurry here to see you.
OEDIPUS: Then let him come

And bring blessing both to his city and to me.

The noble man is his own best friend.

ANTIGONÊ: Dear god, father!

What should I say!

I can't believe it!

OEDIPUS: What is it, child?

What, Antigonê?

ANTIGONÊ: A woman!

A woman coming toward us, father,

On a fine Aitnian colt!

A Thessalian hat pulled down to shade her face!

What can I say? Is it or isn't it?

Am I dreaming? I just don't—Yes!

Oh, poor girl! Oh, it *is,* it *is!*

I see her eyes now, bright with greeting!

She's coming! Oh, she waving!

It's Ismenê! It is!

OEDIPUS: Oh, dear child, what are you saying?

*(Ismenê, well-dressed in contrast with Antigonê, enters, left, on horseback,
followed by a mounted Attendant. She dismounts and runs to Oedipus and
Antigonê.)*

ANTIGONÊ: It's your daughter, father, my sister Ismenê!

When you hear her voice, you'll know her!

ISMENÊ: Oh, my dear, dear father—dear sister!

Oh, there are no two words more precious to me!

How hard it was to find you, and now

How hard it is to see you through my tears!

OEDIPUS: Oh, child, have you come?

ISMENÊ: Ah, how old you are, father!

OEDIPUS: Yes, but you're here?

ISMENÊ: But not without difficulty!

OEDIPUS: Touch me, dear child!

ISMENÊ: Oh, let me hold you both!

OEDIPUS: My children! My sisters!

ISMENÊ: How wretched life is!

OEDIPUS: Hers and mine?

ISMENÊ: And mine, ours together!

OEDIPUS: Why have you come?

ISMENÊ: Concern for you, father.

OEDIPUS: Longing to see me?

ISMENÊ: Yes, and with news for you.

    I came with the only servant I could trust.

OEDIPUS: And the young men, your brothers, my sons,

    Where are they; where are they when needed?

ISMENÊ: They are—where they are—

    It's a grim time for them.

OEDIPUS: What! Are they Egyptians now, born and bred?

    In Egypt, they say, the men stay at home

    Weaving, keeping the house, while the women go out

    To earn the daily bread! Just so, these two,

    Your brothers, sit at home, idly, like girls,

    While you do their work for them, taking on

    Your unhappy father's sorrows!

    (Holding Antigonê's arm.)

    But my dear daughter, here, my dear Antigonê,

    Once she had left her childhood behind her

    And grown to a woman, with a woman's strength,

    Joined my wanderings, leading the way through forests,

    Hungry, barefoot, in pounding rain and heat,

    Scorning the comforts of home, only to tend

    Her father's needs.

    (Moving toward Ismenê.)

    And you, my dear child, my dear Ismenê,

    Came out more than once from Thebes, in secret,

    With all the latest news of the oracles

    Concerning me. You were my faithful spy

    When I was driven from home.

    But tell me, Ismenê,

    What brings you now, so far from home? I know

    You haven't come this far for no good reason.

    Some word of warning, perhaps? Some danger? Hm?

ISMENÊ: Father, I will pass over the difficulties

    I've had in finding you, for the pain of telling

    Would equal the suffering.

    What I have come with now

    Is news of the trouble that plagues your sons.

    They agreed at first that the throne should pass

To Kreon; and they reasoned well: to avoid
The city further pollution from the curse
That stains our family line for whole generations.
But now some evil rivalry, some furious
God and their wicked minds' lust for power
Has seized their hearts, and all that they can think of
Is the throne and reins of government.

Eteoklês, his younger, hot-headed brother,
Has stripped Polyneikês of his crown,
And banished him from Thebes.
But rumors has it
That Polyneikês has settled in the valleys of Argos;
That he is making new alliances through marriage,
And gathering friends and allies, warrior friends,
Telling them that Argos will occupy Thebes
In honor, or else die and be raised to the stars
In glory for so heroic and noble a deed.

These are no meaningless words, but terrible, painful
Truth! How long before the gods take pity
And deliver you, I don't know.
OEDIPUS: The gods take pity on me?
    Why would they do that?
ISMENÊ: The latest oracles say so.
OEDIPUS: What oracles? What do they say?
ISMENÊ: That the men of Thebes will soon search you out;
    That before and after your death they will want your help—
    That you are their protection.
OEDIPUS: Protection? From a man like me?
ISMENÊ: They say that the strength of Thebes is in you.
OEDIPUS: Strength? Ha! When I'm worn to shreds!
ISMENÊ: The gods who destroyed you are raising you now.
OEDIPUS: Raising a carcass destroyed in his youth?
ISMENÊ: Yes, and that's why Kreon is coming,
    For that very reason; and sooner rather than later.
OEDIPUS: Ah! Tell me! To do what, exactly?
ISMENÊ: To settle you near the border, father—
    Where they can control you and keep you from Theban soil.

OEDIPUS: What benefit am I, then, beyond the gates?

ISMENÊ: Your untended grave would curse the city.

OEDIPUS: It takes no oracle to teach us that!

ISMENÊ: It's why they want you near, to master you.

OEDIPUS: And when I die? Will they bury me in Thebes?

ISMENÊ: A man who spilled his father's blood?

OEDIPUS: No! They will never have power over me!

ISMENÊ: In which case Thebes is doomed to destruction.

OEDIPUS: When what has happened? Tell me, child.

ISMENÊ: When they come to your tomb and feel your rage.

OEDIPUS: Who told this to you, child, who?

ISMENÊ: Envoys returning from Delphi.

OEDIPUS: And Apollo truly said this about me?

ISMENÊ: According to them, these were his words.

OEDIPUS: Has either of my sons heard this?

ISMENÊ: Both of them, yes; they're well aware.

OEDIPUS: The scoundrels! To know, and still to choose power
 Rather than have their father back!

ISMENÊ: It's a terrible thing: it pains me to hear it;
 But, yes, it's true.

OEDIPUS: Gods, grant me that their ambitious rivalry
 Never ends! And give me the power, you gods,
 To decide the battle that even now they raise
 Their spears to begin! For then neither he who holds
 The scepter and throne would remain, nor would the exile
 Return to his city!

 These two, these sons,
 Saw their father uprooted from his native soil,
 Shamefully, and lifted no finger, opposed nothing,
 Offered no shield to my suffering, saw me driven
 From home and heard the heralds cry out my banishment!
 They did nothing!

 You say it is what I wished?
 That the city did right to grant me this gift?
 Not so! For on that day when my mind raged,
 I begged for death, death even by stoning,
 But no one helped me to that dearest desire.

No!

Only then, as time passed,
And the fever of my rage cooled, and I felt
My wrath had been too great for the wrongs I did—
So long ago—the punishment too harsh:
Then, only then, in its own good time,
Did the city satisfy my passion, and drive me out!
And they, they, those two who could have helped
Their father, their own father, did nothing, refused!
For want of a little word they might have spoken—
Those two! those sons!—I was cast out
From the land to wander, a beggar, to the end of my days.
(Reaching for Antigonê and Ismenê.)
Only these, these two, girls that they are,
As far as nature permits, provide me
With life's needs: food and safe conduct;
While their brothers turn deaf ears to their father's fate,
Choosing throne and kingdom over their father!
No, they will never win me, never win
Old Oedipus as their ally, never their champion
To win their war!

Good will never come of their rule in Thebes,
This much I know: for the prophecies brought by this girl,
And the deeply buried memory of those oracles
From Apollo's throne, have found fulfillment here.

So let them send Kreon, and whomever else
Is high and mighty in Thebes, to search me out.
And you, friends, stand by me now; and joined
With these Dread and Awful Powers protect this suppliant;
For then your city will win a grand defender,
And cause my enemies great and lasting pain.
LEADER: Oedipus, you have deserved our pity,
    You and your daughters. And since you offer yourself
    As our city's defender, let me give you good advice.
OEDIPUS: Stand by me, dear friend; I will do all you ask.
LEADER: First things first:

You must appease these deities
  Whose ground you violated.
OEDIPUS: Tell me by what rites.
  Instruct me.
LEADER: There is a fresh spring that flows forever:
  Clean your hands first, then bring libations.
OEDIPUS: And when I have it, the pure water, what then?
LEADER: You will find bowls by master-craftsmen;
  Wreathe both their rims and the handles.
OEDIPUS: With olive sprigs, or woolen stuffs?
LEADER: With a new-shorn tuft from a young lamb.
OEDIPUS: And how am I to perform the rite?
LEADER: Face the dawn and pour the libation.
OEDIPUS: Pour from the same bowls you spoke of?
LEADER: In three streams; but empty the last.
OEDIPUS: With what do I fill them? Tell me that.
LEADER: With water and honey; but add no wine.
OEDIPUS: And when the leaf-dark earth has drunk it?
LEADER: Lay down three times nine shoots
  Of olive branch and say this prayer.
OEDIPUS: The prayer; yes; the most important.
LEADER: "Gentle Ones, who are gentle of heart,
  Gently receive this suppliant in safety."
  You, or someone else taking your place,
  Should pray thus in a hushed voice;
  And then return without looking back.
  Do this and we will stand firmly by you;
  If not, I fear for you, friend.
OEDIPUS: Daughters, did you hear?
ANTIGONÊ: We heard them, father.
  What must we do?
OEDIPUS: One of you must go there in my place;
  One soul can pay a debt for many
  If it is performed with purity of heart,
  And I am too weak and blind.

  Quickly now!
  But don't leave me behind here alone;
  I have little strength and need a hand to guide me.
ISMENÊ: I'll perform the rite for you, father.

(To the Leader.)

But where do I go?

LEADER: Beyond this grove you will find a guardian to help.

ISMENÊ: Dear Antigonê, take care of father.

No pain is too great if done for a parent.

(Music begins as Ismenê goes off into the grove and the Chorus gathers around Oedipus.)

LEADER: It is dreadful, my friend,
                    dreadful, to waken
                          evils of the sleeping
              past! And yet I
                    long to know—

OEDIPUS: What now?

LEADER: Of the terrible anguish that
              knows no end; the
                    sorrow that is never
        lived through!

OEDIPUS: Be kind to the guest and
                    never touch the shameful
        wound he suffers from!

LEADER: The rumor spreads and
                    never dies! My friend, I
              long to hear it truly
                    told by you!

OEDIPUS: Omoiiiii!

LEADER: Bear with me,
              I beg you!

OEDIPUS: Féu! Féu!

LEADER: You have had your
                    wish, now grant me
                          mine.

OEDIPUS: I endured, friends, endured
              evils not willed by
                    me—god as my
        witness!—evil, unspeakable
              deeds I never
                    chose!

LEADER: What deeds?
              Tell me.

OEDIPUS: Unknown to me, unknown to

them, Thebes bound me to
    evil, to an evil
        marriage that brought me
ruin!

LEADER: I have heard but how can I
        believe—that bed—where
son and mother met
    in infamy!

OEDIPUS: Omoiiiiii!
Your words are
    death to me, friends! But
        these, these girls, are
mine—my
    blood—

LEADER: What are you—?

OEDIPUS: Children!
    Curse-bearers!

LEADER: O god!

OEDIPUS: Born of the same
    womb that bore
        me!

LEADER: Children sprung from your
    loins, but also—

OEDIPUS: Sisters—
yes—to their
    own father!

CHORUS: Ioo!

OEDIPUS: Ioo!
    Unspeakable evils
        pound at my soul,
again,
    again!

LEADER: You have suffered—

OEDIPUS: Things unforgettable!

LEADER: What you did—!

OEDIPUS: I did nothing!

CHORUS: Nothing?

OEDIPUS: A gift from Thebes!
        A prize to break the heart!

If only I had never
    served my city that
        day, never deserved
reward!

CHORUS: Unhappy man!

LEADER: And you also killed—

OEDIPUS: What more do you
    want? What more do you
      need?

LEADER: —your father!

OEDIPUS: Papaiiiiiiii!
    A second wound!
Wound upon wound!

CHORUS: Killed—

OEDIPUS: I killed,
but not without—

CHORUS: What?

OEDIPUS: Justice on my side!

LEADER: What are you—

OEDIPUS: I'll tell you.
    The man—the
man I murdered
    would have murdered
      me! Before the
law I am
    clear of this
      blood!
I came to this—
    came to it blind—
      ignorant—
unknowing!

(Thêseus, on horseback, has entered, right, during the above with his mounted Royal Guard as the music fades out.)

LEADER: But here is Thêseus,
  Our king, son of Aigeus;
  Come as you requested.

(Thêseus approaches Oedipus and stands for a moment in silence looking at him.)

THÊSEUS: Son of Laïos—yes, I have heard your story,

Heard it many times over in the past;
And if I had not been informed on the way here,
I would know you nonetheless by your sightless eyes,
As well as by your dress and tortured face.
And truly I'm sorry for you.

But tell me how I can help, why you called me,
What favor I and the city can do for you—
For you and your unfortunate companion.
Tell me, for it would have to be something dreadful
For me to deny comfort to you. Like you,
I was raised in exile, in foreign lands
And exposed to perils unknown to any man.
I, who once was an exile, as you are now,
Would never turn my back on such a man
As you and deny him help and comfort.
I am a man, no more, no less; and tomorrow
Brings me no better fate than yours is now.

OEDIPUS: Thêseus, you leave me little to say:
Your words and nobility express it all.
Who I am, who my father was,
What was my country, you know well enough.
The only thing that remains is my desire,
And there an end.

THÊSEUS: What is your wish?

OEDIPUS: I come here bearing a gift:
My beaten self; a sorry sight.
And yet its advantage is greater
Than any beauty.

THÊSEUS: What is this advantage?

OEDIPUS: You will know soon enough.

THÊSEUS: How long?

OEDIPUS: The day on which I die and you bury this body.

THÊSEUS: But what of the life between?

OEDIPUS: With that I have everything.

THÊSEUS: It is a small favor you ask.

OEDIPUS: Be careful. It is no small conflict.

THÊSEUS: The trouble with your sons?

OEDIPUS: They will force you to send me back.

THÊSEUS: If that is what you want, then exile is wrong.

OEDIPUS: But when I wished it, they refused!

THÊSEUS: Pride is a foolish thing when a man is in trouble!

OEDIPUS: First hear me out, *then* lecture me!

THÊSEUS: Then tell me; I shouldn't judge till I know.

OEDIPUS: I have suffered many wounds, Thêseus.

THÊSEUS: Your family's curse?

OEDIPUS: All of Greece knows that!

THÊSEUS: What, then? What wound?

OEDIPUS: To be driven out by my own sons!

 Never to return!

 Guilty of having killed my father!

THÊSEUS: Then how can they bring you back?

OEDIPUS: Forced to!

 The god's order!

THÊSEUS: And they fear what?

OEDIPUS: That Thebes is fated to fall to Athens!

THÊSEUS: But how could war exist between us?

OEDIPUS: Dear son of Aigeus!

 Only the gods know neither age nor death!

 Time, all-mastering Time, obliterates all.

 Earth wastes away, man's body wastes away;

 Faith dies, bad faith is born; the bonds

 That tie together friend and friend, city

 And city, are ever in flux, never steady;

 For some men sooner, for others later,

 Pleasure sickens, then turns again to love.

 Today between you and Thebes the sky is cloudless.

 But Time in its endless course gives birth

 To days and nights in untold numbers; and then,

 One day, for some slight pretext, all too trivial,

 A sword will shatter the peace that exists between you.

 On that day, if Zeus endures, and his son

 Apollo still speaks true and clear of voice,

 My body, cold in earth, in silent slumber,

 Will drink hot blood!

 But I must not speak of mysteries.

 Not yet. Ask me no more. But keep your pledge,

Give Oedipus shelter, here, on your land,
And you will never complain that he was ungrateful,
Unless the gods have tripped him up again.
LEADER: My lord, since before you arrived here,
This man has claimed he will carry out his promises.
THÊSEUS: Who could turn away this man's kind friendship?
First, by natural right, he is an ally,
Entitled to our hearth and hospitality.
He also comes to our gods here as a suppliant,
Bringing with him no small benefit to Athens
And to me. As I respect his gifts,
I won't reject him, but grant him all the rights
Of citizenship.

If our friend chooses to stay,
I leave him here in your care. Or if he wishes,
He may come along with me.
(Turning to Oedipus.)
Oedipus, I leave the choice to you.
OEDIPUS: May Zeus be generous to men like these!
THÊSEUS: What is your wish? Will you come to my palace?
OEDIPUS: If it were right, but here is the place—
THÊSEUS: To do what? I won't oppose you.
OEDIPUS: Triumph over those who cast me out.
THÊSEUS: Your presence is a great blessing.
OEDIPUS: Yes, if you keep the promise you made.
THÊSEUS: You needn't worry; I won't fail you.
OEDIPUS: As you are an honorable man,
I won't make you swear.
THÊSEUS: My word is my oath.
You have no more to gain.
OEDIPUS: How will you act?
THÊSEUS: What do you fear?
OEDIPUS: They'll come!
THÊSEUS: These men will see to that.
OEDIPUS: Beware that when you leave—
THÊSEUS: Don't lecture me!
OEDIPUS: Fear overwhelms me!
THÊSEUS: I have never known fear.

OEDIPUS: You don't know the threats.

THÊSEUS: But I know this much:

No one will ever take you against my will.
Men threaten with angry words, but let the mind
Master itself and all the threats vanish.

As for these Thebans, boasting they will carry you off,
I think that they will find the sea too wide
And heavy going. You needn't be afraid.
Not only do you have my firm assurance,
But it was Apollo who sent you to this ground.
You can rest assured that, even absent,
My name will be your shield.

(Music begins under the above and Thêseus goes off, right, with his mounted Royal Guard, and the Chorus, whose fears are quelled, at first gathers around Oedipus, then regroups for its ode.)

CHORUS: You have come, old friend, stranger,
                to a land of all lands the loveliest,
                beloved of horsemen for well-bred steeds,
                        white Kolonos;
                where never song of nightingale
                        ceases in green bowers;
                        nor sun's ray falls,
                        nor wind invades
                the wine-dark ivy heavy with berry;
                whose wooded hollow of laurel and olive
                        is sacred to the god,
                        reveler Dionysos,
                        with his bakkhic band
                and the whirling nymphs who nursed him.

                Refreshed by morning dew, the fair-
                clustered narcissus blooms in the crown
                of Great Goddesses Mother and Daughter;
                and sun-drenched crocuses burst into flame,
                weaving along the mirroring streams
                of Kephisos' never-sleeping rills,
                whose currents every day spread wide
                across the valley's fertile breast,

bringing rich abundant birth;
whose land the Muses never forsake,
nor Aphroditê's gold-reined chariot.

Oh, and what a marvel we have here,
unknown in Asia and Pelops' Dorian isle!
A glory self-creating, self-renewing!
Never vanquished terror of enemy spears!
The gray-leafed olive, nurturer of children,
undestroyed by youth or crabbed old age,
protected by Zeus of the Olives and gray-eyed Athêna!
But another gift now,
gift to mother Athens,
another gift, splendid
gift of god most great
that raises high our city,
city glorious for steeds,
mighty steeds and colts,
and might of majestic sea!
That gift I now must sing.
Praised be god Poseidon!
Son of Kronos, we praise you,
who granted to us first
use of bit and bridle
to curb the stallion's rage;
god who first fit oar
to hands that whip us onward
across the gray sea's surge
in the wake of numberless Nêrêdes!

(The Chorus disperses around the stage as the music fades out as Antigonê, looking in the direction of the left entrance, sees an offstage approach and rushes back to Oedipus.)

ANTIGONÊ: O Athens, praised above all, now is the time
To act and prove your words!

OEDIPUS: What is it, child?

(Kreon, a man of greater age even than Oedipus, enters, left, with four attendant Bodyguards and makes his approach to Oedipus.)

ANTIGONÊ: A man, father!
Coming toward us!

Yes, it's Kreon!
And an escort with him!
OEDIPUS: Kind old men,
I ask you now, defend me.
Give me proof of my safety!
LEADER: Don't be afraid, old friend.
I may be old, but the nation's strength
Hasn't yet fallen prey to age.
KREON: Gentlemen, citizens of Athens! I detect
A sudden fear in your eyes at my arrival.
But don't be troubled, don't be hostile. I come
In peace, not with ill will. And certainly
Not at my age. Besides, I'm well aware
This city has a power unmatched in Greece.

No, I have been sent, despite my age,
To persuade this man to return home with me.
I speak for Thebes, not for myself alone,
And because, as a relative, I have suffered
More than anyone else the pains of his fate.

Poor, unhappy Oedipus, come home!
Your people rightly call you back, and I
Most of all, for I would be the cruelest
Of men if I failed to grieve at your misery,
Old man, a ravaged wanderer, a stranger,
Begging, with one lone companion!

Could I have known, could I even have guessed,
That this poor girl would come to this: miserable,
Caring for you in poverty; unmarried,
Despite her age; yet open target for any
Rude assault.

Face the truth, old man,
The disgrace, not only for you, but for me,
For all of us, your family! Can a shame,
A public shame be hidden? No! And therefore,
Oedipus, listen to me! Listen for the sake

Of our fathers' gods! Cover your shame. Come home
To your fathers' house. Take leave of this kind city.
She deserves it! But Thebes who bore and nursed you
Has greater claim.
OEDIPUS: You would dare anything, Kreon!
There is no argument you would not twist
To your own cunning advantage! Why even try?
How can you think to snare me, a second time,
In a trap that leads to unspeakable misery?

There was a time long ago, a time
When I was sick to the death, sick with the pains
Of my private sorrows, and dearly longed to leave
My land and wander in exile; but you refused me!
Then!
      then!
            then when my soul had spent
Its share of passion in rage and grief;
                        then
When the boon of quiet and peace of my father's house
Was a treasure to me;
                then you saw fit to drive me
Out into exile! Caring nothing for our kinship!
Nothing for our family! The same family
Feeling that now you invoke to coax me with soothing
Words back to Thebes! Now when you see me
Welcomed and accepted by this kind city
And its people as one of theirs!
Soft words disguise hard thoughts!
What kindness forces friendship on the unwilling!

But consider it this way, Kreon: Suppose for a moment
That you were eager to gain some deep-held wish,
But had it refused; then later, when your heart was full,
That wish was granted: what sort of kindness is that?
What empty satisfaction?

And yet, your offer is no less empty a gesture;
No less evil.

I say it now to these men: I say you are evil.
You have come to take me away; but not to my home;
Not to my city; but to plant me outside its walls
As protection against a future threat from Athens.

But that you will never have!
This is what I give you:
My curse unto all generations of your city!
And as for my sons' legacies: They will inherit
Only enough of my country to bury them in.

Who now reads the fate of Thebes more clearly?
You or I? You? Or I who have
The best informants: Apollo and Zeus his father?

But you come here, your tongue slick with phrases,
Sharpened for double-edged politic thrusts, and yet,
Your words will get you nothing. Harm, not good!

Ah, but you don't believe me. I can tell.
Go, then; but I stay here.

Is it possible
A life that offers contentment can be evil?
KREON: Who do you think is hurt more by your tirade?
    Your words do greater harm to you than to me.
OEDIPUS: I'll be content if your words persuade these men
    As little as they do me.
KREON: Unhappy man! Time has taught you nothing.
    You shame your age!
OEDIPUS: And you have a wicked way with words, Kreon.
    I never knew an honest man who argued
    Both sides equally well.
KREON: A torrent of words doesn't always hit home!
OEDIPUS: And you speak little and to the point?
KREON: Not to a mind as dull as yours!
OEDIPUS: Leave us! All of us! These men, too!
    I shout it for them, too!
    Here is where I will live!

Stop this blockade!

KREON: I call on them, not you, to serve as witness

To how you answer to friends!

If I ever get my hands on you—

OEDIPUS: Take me? How? With these allies here?

KREON: There are other ways to make you suffer!

(Kreon signals vigorously to two Guards who rush off into the grove.)

OEDIPUS: What have you done to dare such a threat?

KREON: I have already taken one of your daughters;

This one I will have shortly!

OEDIPUS: Oimoiiiiiiiii!

KREON: You will soon have more to groan about!

OEDIPUS: You've captured my daughter?

KREON: And this one I will take soon!

OEDIPUS: Ah, friends!

What will you do? Abandon me?

Refuse to drive out this impious man?

LEADER: *(To Kreon.)* I want you out of this land, stranger!

Now! What you are doing,

And what you have done, is unjust!

KREON: *(To his Guards.)* You! Take her! By force if need be!

(Two Guards approach Antigonê.)

ANTIGONÊ: Where shall I run!

What gods or men can help me?

(Kreon goes rapidly to Antigonê and grasps her by the arm. Antigonê resists, but cannot struggle free.)

LEADER: Stop! What are you doing there?

KREON: I won't lay hands on the old man,

But this one is mine!

OEDIPUS: Oh, lords of this land!

LEADER: What you are doing is unjust!

KREON: What I'm doing is just!

LEADER: Just?

KREON: I'm taking back what is mine!

(Music begins under the above as Kreon signals the two Guards to take hold of Antigonê, whose arms they pinion behind her as she continues to struggle.)

OEDIPUS: O Athens!

LEADER: What are you doing?

Leave her!

Or you will have ample
proof of our strength!

(The Chorus approaches Kreon threateningly.)

KREON: Stand back!

LEADER: Not as long as you persist!

KREON: Harm me and your
action means war!

OEDIPUS: As I foretold—

LEADER: Let go of the girl!

KREON: Don't command where
you have no power!

LEADER: I said to release her!

KREON: And I say move out!

(The Guards roughly pull Antigonê toward the left exit.)

CHORUS: Men of Kolonos, come!
Come! My city suffers
violence! My Athens is in
peril! Come!
Help me!
I beg you!

(The music fades out.)

ANTIGONÊ: Help me! Friends!
They're dragging me off!

OEDIPUS: Child! Where are you!

ANTIGONÊ: Taking me by force!

OEDIPUS: Give me your hand, child!

ANTIGONÊ: I can't, father! I'm helpless!

KREON: *(To his Guards.)* Get her out of here!
Now! Do you hear?

(The two remaining Guards remove Antigonê through the left exit.)

OEDIPUS: Dear god, dear god!

KREON: One thing is sure at least, these two props
Will never guide your hobbling steps again!
But if you're so bent on conquering your people,
Conquering your city that sent me here,
Their king, then enjoy your little triumph!
You will learn soon enough that nothing you do
Or have ever done was just, raging your anger
Against your friends!

Anger and rage were always your downfall!

(Kreon turns to follow Antigonê and the Guards but the Chorus intercepts his exit without actually physically assaulting him.)

LEADER: Stop where you are!

KREON: Don't touch me!

LEADER: You're not leaving till those two are free!

KREON: Then Thebes will take a greater hostage!

I will take more than his daughters!

(Kreon has turned toward Oedipus who has again taken up refuge in the grove.)

LEADER: What are you—?

KREON: I'll take him, too!

The old man!

LEADER: Brave words to threaten with!

KREON: I will, I say!

Unless this country's king can stop me!

OEDIPUS: Hateful voice! You wouldn't dare

Lay a hand on me!

KREON: You, shut up!

OEDIPUS: No!—But if the Powers here permit,

I will lay down one more curse upon you!

You, you vile, despicable man who stole,

Cruelly stole, my darling that served as my eyes,

The eyes I lost so long ago! O god!

I wish, by that great eye of day, the Sun,

All-seeing Hêlios, and on all your race:

A life like mine and my terrible age!

KREON: Do you see this, men of Athens?

OEDIPUS: They see us both! Yes, and they see

That all I have for defense is words!

KREON: Enough of this! I may be alone,

Weak and slow with age,

But I will have him at any cost!

(Music begins as Kreon turns and slowly approaches Oedipus.)

OEDIPUS: Aiiiiiiiiiiiiiiiiiiiiiiiiiiii!

(The Chorus grows disturbed at seeing Kreon approach Oedipus. The Leader attempts to intercept him.)

LEADER: An arrogant spirit

                    led you here, stranger,

	if you think you'll succeed!
KREON:	I *do!*
LEADER:	Then Athens is finished!
	Athens is no more!
KREON:	With justice as a weapon
	the weak man triumphs!
OEDIPUS:	You hear his words?
LEADER:	Zeus knows he will fail!
KREON:	Zeus knows, not you!

(The Chorus is shocked as Kreon crosses the boundary of the Sacred Grove in pursuit of Oedipus.)

CHORUS: Outrage!

(As Kreon grabs the terrified and groping Oedipus, Thêseus enters, right, in haste with his Armed Guard unseen by the adversaries.)

KREON: An outrage you will bear!

CHORUS: Help!
               Help! Citizens!
                 Citizens! Men of
                   Kolonos! Lords of the
               land! Come! Come
                 fast! Come! Before they
                   cross our borders!

(The music fades out.)

THÊSEUS: What has happened here? Why all this shouting?
    Why have you interrupted my sacrifice
    To Poseidon, god of the sea, our city's protector?
    I don't like making such haste with no good reason.
    (Oedipus breaks from Kreon and rushes toward Thêseus.)

OEDIPUS: Ah! Ah! Dear friend! I know your voice!
    This man has caused me great suffering!

THÊSEUS: Who is he?

OEDIPUS: Kreon—the one you see—
    Has stolen my daughters! My only children!

THÊSEUS: What are you—?

OEDIPUS: Now you know all I have suffered!
    (Thêseus turns to his Guards.)

THÊSEUS: Quickly, one of you, hurry, go to the altar
    And end the rites! Tell them to move at once
    By foot and horse to the place where the highways meet!

Hurry! If the two women pass that point,
I am made a fool by this man's violence
As though I were an easy conquest.
Quickly, now!
(A Soldier rushes off right in the direction of the altar. Thêseus avoids turning toward Kreon and addresses the assembly.)
As for this—man:
If I treated him as he deserves,
He would already be smarting of his wounds.
However—he will be judged by the same laws
As those he brought here with him, and no other.
(To Kreon.)
And you: you will never leave this land
Until I see those two girls here before me.
You have disgraced not only me, but your people
As well as your country!
The city that you have come to honors justice,
And rules by the authority of law.
But you have come here and cast aside
The very principles that govern us.
You take what pleases you—
Take with violence—
As if the city were barren of men, or a city
Made up of slaves, and I no more than nothing!

It wasn't Thebes made you. Thebes doesn't breed
Lawless sons. Nor would Thebes be proud
If she learned that you plunder me, plunder my gods,
By dragging helpless suppliants from sanctuary!
If ever I set foot on your land,
I would never, no matter how just my cause,
Do so without the express consent of its ruler,
Whoever he might be.

Nor would I ever steal or plunder.
I would know how a stranger
Behaves in a foreign city and among its citizens.
You bring shame on a city that doesn't deserve it—
Your city, your native city. But all the years

That time has burdened you with have siphoned your wits.

What I said before, I will say again.
Those two girls, the daughters of Oedipus,
Will be brought here before me without delay,
Or you will take up residence in Athens
Against your will, an alien to the end.
This is no idle threat: I know my mind.

LEADER: Do you see now where this has brought you, stranger?
Thebes is honest, but you have acted wickedly.

KREON: No, son of Aigeus, I never thought your city
Lacking in manliness; nor do I think
My action rash, as you suggest. I acted
Thinking that surely none of your people were so
Enamored of kin of mine as to provide them
Shelter against my will.

I also knew
That no one here would choose to welcome a man
Polluted by the killing of his father,
A man—a man whose children are the brood,
The vile brood of his own mother!

And I knew that the wise council on the Hill of Ares
Would never condone sanctuary in Athens
For such a fugitive.

Certain of that, I seized my prey.
And yet, if he had not acted as he has,
Calling down curses on me and my family,
I would never have touched him. But being so wronged,
I thought the injury deserved reprisal.
Anger knows no age; only death
Cools its fervor: the dead feel no pain.
And yet, you will do as you see fit.
I'm weak, defenseless, however just my cause;
But old as I am, I will answer blow with blow.

OEDIPUS: Arrogant! Shameless!
Whose age do you think that you insult more,

Mine or yours? You spew at me words like bloodshed,
Incest, misery, all of which I have suffered
Against my will, the fury of the gods
Against my race from ages past!

And yet,
Look in me as deeply as human can,
You will find no secret guilt that made me
Bring this ruin on myself and on my own!

But tell me this, Kreon, this one thing:
Let us suppose a prophecy from an oracle
Came to my father that he should be killed by his son:
How with any justice could you blame me?
I who wasn't yet born, not yet conceived,
Innocent of my mother's womb? How?
Born to misery as I was! How? When I met
My father in strife, and struck him down, killed him,
Knowing nothing of who he was, nothing
Of what I did! How in justice can you blame me
For a deed done in ignorance?

Yes, and as for my mother, you miserable wretch,
Have you no shred of shame, you, her brother,
Forcing me to speak of that shameless marriage,
Which I will speak of now, no silence now,
Since you have shattered the bounds of decency!

She was my mother, yes, she was my mother—
Dear god, what a fate!—though neither of us knew!
And to her shame, she bore children to him
She once had given birth to!

But I know this:
Your slander of us, slander of her and me,
Is done with full knowledge; but had I known,
I never would have chosen to make that marriage
Any more than I choose to speak of it now.
No. I won't be judged guilty, not of this marriage,

Not of my father's murder, which you so ruthlessly
Throw in my face!

But answer me one thing.
If here, this very moment, you were approached
By a man intent on taking your life, would you,
Righteous man that you are, pause to inquire
If that man is your father, or would you strike,
Strike back in defense of your own life?

I think the latter. After all, you love life.
I doubt that you would search for justification.
But these were the sorrows the gods put upon me.
And if my father's spirit returned to life,
I think he would say the same.

But you, you who lack all goodness, you,
You who think it proper to speak whatever
Comes to your mind, speakable and unspeakable,
You blame me for these things in these men's presence!
You flatter famous Thêseus and well-ruled Athens
Because it suits your purpose. But you forget
One thing in all your praises: If any land
Knows how to revere and honor the gods,
It is glorious Athens surpasses them all.
And yet it is to Athens you come to seize me,
An old man, a suppliant, you who have stolen
And carried off my two—my dears!—my daughters!

And therefore I invoke the Great Goddesses,
Mother and Daughter, of this sacred grove,
To hear my prayers and supplications and join
With me as allies and take up my cause
And show to him the stuff this city's men
Are made of!
LEADER: This man is honest, my lord.
    He has suffered disaster, but deserves our aid.
THÊSEUS: Enough of this! While we stand discussing,
    The criminals are in flight!

KREON: What are your orders? I'm helpless now!

THÊSEUS: You will lead the way and I'll escort you.
And if the girls are hidden anywhere near,
Point them out to me. But if your men
Have fled with them, we will save ourselves the trouble.
My men are already in hot pursuit,
And none of yours will escape to thank their gods.
Forward!
Move out!
The captor is now the captive;
And fate has snared the hunter in his own traps!
What was taken in deceit will be taken back,
For there's no one now to help you as before;
That much I can assure you. You would never
Have reached the pitch of violence in your crime
Without assistance. No, there was someone else
That you relied on to carry out these deeds.
I must see to it. Athens will never depend
On one man's mercy. Do you understand me?
Or are my words as meaningless as yours
When you hatched your plot?

KREON: Say whatever you like on your own soil;
But once home, we will know what needs doing.

THÊSEUS: Threaten all you like, just move out!
As for you, Oedipus, you stay here;
Rest untroubled. I will return your children,
Or die in the attempt.

OEDIPUS: Bless you, Thêseus, you have a noble heart.
Bless you for the care you show me.

(Music begins immediately as Thêseus, Kreon, and the Royal Guard turn to go off left. At the same moment, the Chorus assumes a new position and bursts out exultantly in song and dance in anticipation of the victory.)

CHORUS: I wish I were there
                 when the enemy
                     turns,
              turns with brass-braying
                 clangor at the
                     Pythian
                 shore!

Or at the torch-lit
          coast of Eleusis
where Mother and Daughter
     goddesses,
          goddesses,
Dêmêtêr,
     Persephonê,
          and the ministering
Eumolpids, tend the
     sacred rites, the
          rites for mortals whose
tongues are
     locked by the
          golden key of
silence!
     Silence!
          There, oh, there!
Soon, soon, soon
     war-waking Thêseus,
          Thêseus,
somewhere,
     somewhere on the
          Sacred Way will
raise a rousing
     shout!
          Battle-rousing
shout!
     Engage the
          Foe with ringing
brass!
     And from the
          battle's midst,
from the battle's
     fray,
          deliver,
deliver
     the two virgin sisters
          still within our borders!
Or soon the enemy's

flight will cross,
        cross the pastures of
Oiatis' slope,
    westward the snowy
        rock, pounding,
pounding,
    pounding with horses,
        pounding with swift horses,
horses swift as wind,
    pounding,
        pounding,
or in chariots,
    nimbly,
        nimbly,
nimbly racing!
    But Arês,
        god of war, moves in,
Arês moves in, and
    down will fall,
        fall,
fall all
    before him in the
        skirmish!
Terrible,
    terrible the
        warriors of Kolonos,
and Thêseus' men,
    terrible in battle, whose
        bridles sparkle
pinshafts of light, their
    reins
        free, flying
free in the
    heat of pursuit, in
        honor of the
Queen of Horsemen:
    Athêna!
        And of the God of
Earth-Girdling Sea

Rhea's son:
Poseidon!

(Pause. Silence. No movement. Listening. Then in a more hushed mode, rising to fullness in the end.)

Has the battle begun?
Is it yet to be?
To be?
Be?
Hope rises to
see the sisters!
Terrible their torment,
terrible, terrible, at
kinsmen's hands!
But Zeus will birth,
will accomplish today,
victory!
Victory!
Victory in
combat!
I see it!
I see it!
See it!
O like a dove,
like a dove,
let me soar on the wind,
soar,
soar,
soar, to see with my
own eyes the mêlée,
with my own eyes!
Zeus!
Zeus!
Zeus, great
master!
Zeus!
All-seeing Zeus!
Grant our king,
Thêseus,
Thêseus, our land's

guardian,
triumph in battle, the
battle's prize!
Let him win,
win,
win the day!
And I
pray to Athêna,
mighty Pallas, your
daughter; and to
Apollo,
Apollo Hunter I pray;
and his sister Artemis
racing dappled deer
in heady flight!
Come o come!
Come twofold
strength to the
land's
rescue,
and to our
own!

(Before even the Chorus' ode has ended, Thêseus, followed by the Royal Guard, enters left leading Antigonê and Ismenê by the hand. At the sight, the Chorus Leader turns joyously to Oedipus, and the music fades out.)

LEADER: Wandering friend, call me a true prophet!

For I can see your daughters coming toward us—

And with an escort!

OEDIPUS: Where? Where? What are you saying?

ANTIGONÊ: *(Running to him.)* Father! Oh, father!

If only some god could give you back your sight,

To see this prince of men who has brought us back!

OEDIPUS: My child! Are you really here!

Both of you here!

ANTIGONÊ: Thêseus and his men saved us!

OEDIPUS: Child! Come to your father's arms!

Let me touch you!

I never thought I would hold you again!

ANTIGONÊ: Your wish is ours, too, father.

OEDIPUS: Where are you? Where?

ANTIGONÊ: We're coming together!

    Almost there!

OEDIPUS: My dear sweet girls!

ANTIGONÊ: All his children are dear to a father!

OEDIPUS: My only support!

ANTIGONÊ: Sharers in your sorrow!

OEDIPUS: My dear ones with me, I could die happy!

    Oh, my dears! Press me hard!

    One on each side!

    Let me rest from this dreadful journey!

    Tell your father in a few words!

    Youth should be brief.

ANTIGONÊ: It was Thêseus, father!

    Thêseus saved us! Listen to him.

    I can't be briefer than that.

    (Antigonê turns Oedipus to face Thêseus.)

OEDIPUS: Dear friend, don't wonder at the doting words

    I say to my children, but I never thought

    I would see them ever again. Yet here they are—

    The two of them! And yes, I know whose doing

    Gives me this joy! It was you who saved them.

    May the gods grant all that I wish for you,

    You and your city, for nowhere on earth have I found

    Such piety and open devotion to justice,

    Such honesty of speech.

    I know these things,

    And all I have to repay you with are words.

    Everything that I have has come through you.

    (Groping, he extends his hand to touch Thêseus.)

    My dear lord, give me your hand to touch!

    And, if I may, I would like to kiss your cheek.

    (Quickly pulling back his hand.)

    But what am I saying? How can a man so miserable,

    So corrupt, so stained with every evil,

    Hope to be touched by you? No, I won't have it!

    No, not if you asked. Only those

Who have borne my pain can ever share it with me.
Stay where you are; take my thanks from there,
And treat me kindly as you have done till now.
THÊSEUS: No, my friend, there is nothing to be wondered at
In the drawn-out delight you take in your daughters;
Nor that you should speak with them before me.
How could I blame you? There's no offense. Deeds,
Not words, distinguish my life, as you can see.
Here are your daughters as I promised them to you,
Living and unharmed despite the threats.
As to the battle and the winning of it,
Why boast of that? You'll hear of it from them.
But on my way here a small matter arose,
Small but strange; I would like you to advise me.
A man should ignore nothing as beneath him.
OEDIPUS: Tell me, then, Thêseus.
    What should I know?
THÊSEUS: It seems there's a man at Poseidon's altar,
    The altar that I was sacrificing at
    Before I came here.
    He asks for sanctuary.
OEDIPUS: Where is he from? What is he praying for?
THÊSEUS: I only know he asks to see you briefly
    On a matter of little importance.
OEDIPUS: What? To be a suppliant is no small matter.
THÊSEUS: All he asks is a word, and then to return
    Safely by the road he came.
OEDIPUS: But who can he be?
THÊSEUS: Do you have any relatives in Argos?
    Someone to ask a favor?
OEDIPUS: My friend! Say no more!
THÊSEUS: Tell me.
OEDIPUS: Don't ask!
THÊSEUS: Ask what? Tell me.
OEDIPUS: Your words just now!
    Argos, you said!
    I know who this suppliant is!
THÊSEUS: Who is he, then?
    Who? Tell me!

OEDIPUS: My son, King Thêseus!
My son—the hated son,
Whose words are more painful to me
Than any man's!
THÊSEUS: Hear him out at least.
You needn't act against your will.
Why should it pain you?
OEDIPUS: Even his voice is hateful.
Don't force me to yield, my lord, please!
THÊSEUS: But as a suppliant he has a right to be heard.
You owe it to the god, in reverence.
ANTIGONÊ: Father, listen to me.
I know I may be young, but let me persuade you.
Allow the king to satisfy his conscience
And give the god his due.

Let him come, let our brother come,
Ismenê's and mine, for our sake.

No, and don't be afraid;
Nothing he says can force you to change your mind,
Especially against your interests. What harm is there
In listening? Whatever ills he intends,
His own words will betray them. You're his father,
And nothing that he's done, however vilely
He's treated you, and the things that you have suffered,
You can't repay him in kind.

Let him come, Father! Other men
Have evil children they rage against, but when
Given friendly advice their mood softens,
Their anger is charmed away.

Think of the past, think of the pain you suffered
From your own parents. For then you can never deny
That evil always leads to more evil.
Think of your sightless eyes that will never see day.

Yield to us, father. It isn't right to allow

A just cause to go begging. It isn't right
   For one man to receive favor and then
   Deny it to another.
OEDIPUS: Your words touch me, child. And yet the pleasure
   That you have won from me will be my pain.
   —If it is your wish, so be it.
   (To Thêseus.)
   Ah, but if that man comes, my friend,
   He must never win control over me!
THÊSEUS: I have no need to hear this twice, old man.
   Your life is safe as long as mine is.
   *(Music begins immediately as Thêseus and his Royal Guard turn to go off
   right as the Chorus reassembles.)*
CHORUS: —Man who longs for length of days,
                unhappy with life's modest span,
                        is a fool.
            Long days lay up more sorrow
                        than joy,
            and pleasures fade when life's outlived
                        its term.
            Death, Deliverer, comes to all
            alike without a wedding-song
            nor any lyre nor singers dancing.
                        Death is all.

            —Not to be born is best. And then,
            second, to hurry whence he came.
            Youthful folly, once gone by,
            what pain, what grief is far behind?
            Envy, faction, strife, war,
            slaughter! And then, in the end, age,
            joyless, infirm, lonely, friendless,
            harbor of all life's evils.

            —So it is for him, for me,
            a northern shore lashed by gales
            of winter storms that know no end,
            buffeted from every quarter,
            suffering man, crashing swirling,

head to foot, no end, no end,
blasts that strike from setting sun,
blasts that strike from day's great eye,
blasts that strike from midday's peak,
blasts that strike from night's black hole!

(Polyneikês has entered, right, during the last section of the ode. His eyes are wet with tears, as he approaches Oedipus. The music fades out as the Chorus disperses.)

ANTIGONÊ: He's coming, father!
The stranger's coming!
He's alone—his eyes red with tears!

OEDIPUS: Who is it?

ANTIGONÊ: The very one we spoke of—Polyneikês!

POLYNEIKÊS: Ah, sisters, what should I weep for first?
My own miseries or those of my father here,
An ancient man in an alien land, an exile,
With you, both of you, clothed in rags so wretched
That the filth has become one with his agèd skin,
Rotting his sides, his withered ribs!

And here,
Over his sightless eyes, his hair, ragged,
Straggling in the breeze! And his beggar's bag,
As miserable as the old man himself—
Scraps for his thin and withered belly.
I'm so ashamed. I have learned all this too late.
(To Oedipus.)
I confess to you now, father, the wrong I've done you,
The terrible wrong, in not supporting you,
Not caring for you. You needn't hear it from others;
Hear it from me.

Consider, father: Mercy
Shares the throne of Zeus in everything he does.
Mercy may stand at your side, too, father.
I can heal the wrongs that I have done to you;
The worst is passed.
(Silence.)
Why so silent, father?

Speak to me, don't turn away.
(Silence.)
No answer?
None at all?
You would send me away with nothing?
Without a word? In hatred?
Without explaining the rage you feel against me?
(To Antigonê and Ismenê.)
Sisters! Daughters of this old man! Help me
At least to thaw our father's merciless silence.
Don't let him cast me off, humiliated,
A suppliant, unanswered.

ANTIGONÊ: No, you must tell him yourself, my dear.
Tell him why you have come, what you want.
A flow of words gives pleasure or rouses anger,
Touches the heart with pity, giving voice
Even to stony silence.

POLYNEIKÊS: Yes, I'll speak for myself, as you advise.
But first I call on Poseidon, my protector,
The god from whose altar the king of this land
Raised me and sent me here to speak and listen,
And then return unharmed the way I came.
I trust you will honor the same pledges, strangers,
And you, my sisters, and father.

I want to tell you now why I've come, father.
Being your firstborn son, I justly claimed
My right to your throne. But Eteoklês, my younger brother,
Exiled me from Thebes—not by force
Of argument or any test of strength,
But by winning over the city with persuasion.
All of which I blame on the curse that haunts us,
As prophets have borne out.

When I left Thebes, I went to Dorian Argos,
Where I took King Adrastus as my father-in-law,
Binding myself by oath with that alliance
To the land's finest families and best warriors.
With them I planned a seven-pronged attack

Of spearsmen against Thebes. Either I die
Together with these men in a just cause,
Or I drive out those who expelled me from my city!

All right, then, why have I come?

I'm here, father,
To beg you with all my prayers and all the prayers
Of my seven allies—comrades whose seven spears
Lead seven forces that at this very moment
Encircle the plain of Thebes in an iron grip!
Men like Amphiareos, matchless spearsman
And augur. And, second: Tydeus of Aitolia,
Son of Oineüs. Eteoklos comes third;
Born in Argos. And brave Hippomedon,
Sent to us by his father, Talaos, fourth.
Then Kapaneus, fifth, who boasts he'll level
Thebes with fire. Sixth, from Arkadia,
Parthenopaios, eager for the battle,
Named as the late offspring of his mother,
Faithful son of Atalantê. And I,
Last, your son, or if not your son,
Then spawn of some evil fate, and called your son,
Lead these fearless warriors of Argos
Into battle on the plains of Thebes.

We implore you now, father, by your children,
By your life, to renounce the terrible rage
You harbor against me as I go out to punish
The brother who robbed me and drove me from my country!
If oracles can be trusted, those you side with
And bless will in the end win the victory.

By all the holy springing fountains of Thebes,
By all of our gods, I beg you to listen to me
And soften your heart! We're beggars, both of us,
You and I, exiles! Both of us stooped
To courting favors from other cities! Both
Dogged by the same fate! While he, at home,

Lords it in his luxury—insupportable!—
And mocks us in his laughter!

But side with me,
And with little effort and in no time,
I'll scatter the strength of his forces to the winds,
And settle you once more in your own home,
And settle myself, once I have cast him out
By force of arms!

Join your will with mine.
It will be my boast. If not—
it's certain death.
LEADER: For the sake of Thêseus, old man,
    Say what seems right and send him off.
OEDIPUS: Ah, my friends, guardians of this place,
    Had it not been Thêseus who sent him here,
    He would never have heard the sound of my voice,
    But now he will, and he will leave having heard
    Such words that will never cheer his life.
    You, you depraved, most vile and despicable of men—
    When it was you who held the throne and scepter
    In Thebes, as now your brother holds them there,
    You cast me out, an exile, your own father!
    You denied me my own city, and gave me these rags,
    These beggar's rags, to wear, these rags that now
    Bring hot tears to your eyes, only now
    When you yourself have reached the same dregs
    Of misery as I!
    Save your tears!
    This burden is mine to bear as long as I live!
    And I will always remember you as my murderer,
    You who cast me out into misery,
    Who made me beg my daily bread from strangers!

    As for these my girls, my dear daughters,
    If they had not been born to comfort me,
    I would be dead, for all that you cared!
    But they have saved me, they support me, nurse me;

They are not women, but *men* in their loyalty to me!
And as for you, my *sons,* no *sons* of mine,
But *spawn* of some other seed!

There are eyes watching you carefully now,
But not yet as carefully as they will watch
If your troops are really on the march to Thebes.
You will never destroy that city.
No!
But you will be destroyed along with your brother
In a bloody bath, brother polluting brother.
These are the curses I laid on you long ago,
And now I call them again to stand beside me
And fight on my behalf! To teach you respect
For parents, and not to dishonor a father who's blind
And because he bore such pitiless sons as you!
My daughters never treated me this way!
So now, now, may all my curses outstrip
And overwhelm your prayers and supplications,
Your precious throne, if primal Justice and Zeus
Still share the throne of Eternal Laws!

Go now!
Go with my curse!
I spit on you!
I cut you off! I disown you!
You have no father!
You evilest of evil men!

Here are the curses I call down on you now!
Never to conquer your native land! Never
To return to hill-ringed Argos! To be killed
By your own brother, and to kill him in turn
Who cast you out! These are my prayers for you!

I call on the dismal depths of Tartaros
To take you home; and on the kind Goddesses
That dwell in this land; and on Arês Destroyer,
God of Strife, who planted in you both,

Brother and brother, such terrible, evil hatred!
Knowing this, go, now; spread the word
To all the men of Thebes, and to your allies
Girdling the Theban plain, that Oedipus
Divides among his sons such benefactions!
LEADER: Your journeys give me no pleasure, Polyneikês.
Go back quickly—as fast as you can.
POLYNEIKÊS: Ah, what a waste!
All this disaster, for nothing!
Our long march from Argos ends here!
Oh, my comrades!
And I can say nothing, to no one,
No friend, nor turn them back,
But go myself to meet this doom in silence.

Ah, but, sisters,
Daughters of the blind old man—you who have heard
Our father's cruel curses: in the name of the gods
I beg you, if ever his curses come true,
And you should find a way home to Thebes,
Don't dishonor me, but bury my body
With honor and the proper rites. For then
The praise you have from him, from this old man,
Whose pains you share, will be doubled by your kindness to me.
ANTIGONÊ: Polyneikês, listen, please!
POLYNEIKÊS: Dearest, tell me!
What is it, Antigonê.
ANTIGONÊ: Quickly, turn back your army!
Back to Argos!
Don't destroy yourself and Thebes!
POLYNEIKÊS: No! How could I lead them again,
Even backward, once I'm known as a coward?
ANTIGONÊ: Oh, but, my dear,
Why should you be angered again?
What will you gain by destroying Thebes?
POLYNEIKÊS: Shame provokes me, shame and dishonor.
Shame to be mocked by a younger brother.
ANTIGONÊ: But you're making your father's curse come true!
He said that you would kill each other,

Shed each other's blood!

POLYNEIKÊS: Then that must be his wish,
    But I can't give way.

ANTIGONÊ: But who would follow you now,
    Once they've heard our father's curses?

POLYNEIKÊS: They will hear nothing.
    Not from me.
    A good commander reports the good,
    Not the bad.

ANTIGONÊ: Oh, dear, dear brother!
    Then your mind is resolved!

POLYNEIKÊS: Yes.
    (Antigonê rushes to embrace him.)
    And you mustn't hold me back.
    (They embrace in silence.)
    It's a dark road I go down, but it's mine;
    Doomed by my father's curse and his Furies.
    (He extends his other arm to Ismenê who comes to him.)
    But as for you, dear sisters, may god bless you
    If you do as I ask once I'm dead,
    For there is nothing more you can do for me living.
    (He kisses them and gently releases their hold on him.)
    Let me go now.
    Goodbye, my dears.
    You'll never see me alive again.

ANTIGONÊ: Oh, my dear!

POLYNEIKÊS: You mustn't mourn.

ANTIGONÊ: How can I not,
    Seeing you rush headlong toward death?

POLYNEIKÊS: I'll die if I have to.

ANTIGONÊ: No, my dear, live!
    Just do as I ask!

POLYNEIKÊS: You can't persuade me.
    Don't even try.

ANTIGONÊ: But life without you is impossible!

POLYNEIKÊS: All that is in the hands of some dark destiny:
    Living, dying, who can tell? But I pray
    The gods that evil never cross your path.
    The world knows you don't deserve to suffer.

(Immediately, Polyneikês turns to go out left in the direction of Thebes. There is no movement anywhere. Silence. Then a barely discernible constant rumble of thunder in the distance that lends a mood of expectation, mystery, and growing advent of divinity to the scene. After a short time, music fades in and the Chorus comes slowly together in a tight unit, as though threatened, the Leader at its center.)

LEADER: New evils break from the blind man's curse,

        unless it is Fate's hand moving.

        For how can I say god's decrees are in vain?

        Watchful, ever watchful of those decrees is Time.

            Today he levels the prosperous;

            tomorrow again raises the lowly.

(A distant crash of thunder.)

CHORUS: Heaven's voice!

              Zeus protect us!

(The rumbling thunder draws nearer and grows, as does the sense of immanence.)

OEDIPUS: Children! Daughters! Is anyone near!

    Send him to bring me Thêseus, that best of men!

ANTIGONÊ: Why, father?

(A violent series of thunder claps very near.)

OEDIPUS: God's winged thunder, now, now, any moment,

    Will lead me down the way to Death!

    Send for him! Quickly!

(The growing storm now flashes with searing bolts of lightning that shake the earth and light the sky as the atmosphere grows increasingly darker. The Chorus in a state of terror darts about the stage.)

CHORUS: Listen! Listen!

        God-thrown

           bolts,

      unspeakable!

        tumble down the

           vault of

    heaven!

        Again!

          Again!

     Terror shakes me!

       Shakes me!

         Again! Again!

My spirit shrinks!
   Lightning
      tearing the
sky with
   fire!
      What will it
birth? Never in
   vain! What grave
     issue?

(Another terrible volley of thunder and lightning.)
   Majestic powers!
    Ah, Zeus!
     Zeus!

(The storm's display ceases momentarily, leaving in its place a silence heavy with portent. The Chorus cowers in fear. From here to his exit, Oedipus' anxiety, slowly at first, is progressively but quite visibly transformed into a resignation that betokens calm, security, and spiritual authority—but it is never less than total simplicity.)

OEDIPUS: Children, children,
Your father's end has come,
His destined end,
No turning away now.

ANTIGONÊ: But how can you know this, father?
How?

OEDIPUS: It's all so clear now.
But someone, quickly,
Bring the king—
At once—hurry!

(During the above speech, the rumble of thunder sounds again, and then a series of lightning flashes and thunder blasts more violent than any thus far.)

CHORUS: Éa!
      Éa!
        Blast upon
    blast!
      Roundabout me!
      Piercing voice!

LEADER: Great spirit, have mercy! Be kind, I pray you,
if you bring lowering gloom on our land!
Forgive if I have looked with pity

on this accursed, polluted man!
I pray you, save me from his misery!

CHORUS: Great Zeus, hear us!

(The blasts cease but the rumble of thunder continues under the speeches.)

OEDIPUS: Is he coming?
Will he find me still alive,
My mind still clear?

ANTIGONÊ: Why do you want him, father?

OEDIPUS: He was kind to me,
And the time has come
To give him the great gift I promised.

CHORUS: Ioo!
                    Ioo! Son,
                        listen! Come
            quickly!
                Quickly!
                    Leave the
            sea god's
                altar, the holy
                    rites of
            sacrifice! Come!
                Come! The stranger
                    says you are worthy,
            you! the city!
                the city's people!
                    to receive great benefit
            for all the kindness!
                Quickly!
                    Come!

(A loud blast of thunder that ceases immediately upon the entrance of Thêseus with his Attendants from the right.)

THÊSEUS: What is this outcry?
All of you and my guest, too?
Is it Zeus' thunderbolt frightens you?
Or is it the threat of rain and hail above us?
When a god sends such a tempest,
Nothing is impossible.

(The music fades out.)

OEDIPUS: Oh, how I have longed for you, my king!
   Some god prepares your fortunate coming!
THÊSEUS: What is it, son of Laïos?
   What has happened?
OEDIPUS: My life will soon be over—
   I want to honor the pledge
   I gave to you and Athens.
THÊSEUS: What sign have you had?
OEDIPUS: The gods tell me!
   Their own heralds!
   Signs they appointed long ago.
THÊSEUS: Tell me what they are, old man.
OEDIPUS: Thunder born of god!
   Incessant crash of lightning bolts
   From Zeus's unvanquished hand!
THÊSEUS: I believe you. None of your prophecies
   Has ever been false. Tell me what to do.
OEDIPUS: Yes, I will tell you now, son of Aigeus,
   What the ages hold in store for Athens
   That will never know decay.

   Soon I will lead you,
   Unaided, unguided by any hand, to that place
   Where I am to die. But you must never reveal it
   To any man, not even the region that hides it.
   Do so and it will be an eternal defense,
   Better than many shields, better than spears
   Of neighboring allies. These are mysteries no tongue
   Must ever profane. And when you come, alone,
   With no one else, to that place, you will see for yourself,
   And understand. For I will never utter them
   To any of your people, nor to my children,
   Love them as I do. You must keep them safe,
   And then when you come to the end of your life,
   Reveal them to your eldest son, and he
   In turn to his successor, and so forever.
   Do this, and your city will never be ravaged
   By the men of Thebes, sown of the Dragon's teeth.

Many a city, no matter how well governed,
May slide from virtuous supremacy
Down into vicious arrogance. The gods,
Though they strike hard, are slow to see and strike
When men abandon reverence to the gods
And turn to frenzied rage.
Don't let this happen to you, son of Aigeus.
I wanted to warn you;
Though I know you have no need for such instruction.

Let us go now where destiny leads us.
The god within drives me on.
We must not delay!
(*His apotheosis complete, Oedipus rises, unaided, from his rocky seat, though Antigonê and Ismenê rush to help him; but seeing the physical power of his renewed strength, they retreat a few steps. Oedipus, led by a profound inner force, with slow but secure steps, at first makes his way half-way toward the left exit, beckoning the others on, though no one moves but himself. He turns several times, slowly, suddenly not sure of his direction, then gradually seeks out the center of the orchestra. Again he turns, head raised as if listening to an unheard voice. The darkness of the storm passes rapidly and sunlight breaks through.*)

OEDIPUS: Children!
                    Come!
                        Follow me!
A strange marvel has come to pass.
I am now your guide who once was led by you.
(*Both daughters reach out to help him, a movement he senses unseen.*)
No! Do not touch me!
I alone will discover the sacred grave
Which Fate has destined for my burial ground.
(*He beckons to them again.*)
This way! Come! O come!
Hermes leads me, Guide of the Dead,
And Persephonê Queen of the Underworld!
(*He begins a slow progress towards the Sacred Grove.*)
O light I do not see!
Sunlight that once was mine!
I feel you one last time!

Warm this ragged body
As I go to close my life
In the dark house of Death.
(Turning to Thêseus.)
And you, truest of friends,
Be blest, you and your land
And all of your people,
And in your days of greatness to come,
Remember me in my death,
The seed of all your fortune
In time to come,
Ever renewing,
Forever new!

(Music fades in and continues to the end of the play as Oedipus turns up-stage once more toward the Sacred Grove and slowly goes straight into its center in the direction of the skênê: the Brazen-Floored Threshold of Earth, whose doors open slowly to admit him. He is followed at a distance by Antigonê and Ismenê, Thêseus behind them, and behind him an Attendant. When all have entered, the Chorus reassembles.)

LEADER: Goddess! Unseen Persephonê! If it is lawful,
let me honor you with my prayers!
And you, Ruler of Eternal Night!

CHORUS: Hear me!
Aïdoneüs!
Aïdoneüs!

LEADER: Grant our friend an easy passage—

CHORUS: free of pain,
unlamented,
to the dark land below,
fields of the dead,
all-enshrouding,
to the Stygian house!

LEADER: Uncounted sorrows came to him without cause.
I pray that some just god will exalt him in glory.

CHORUS: Daughters of Earth! Daughters of Darkness!
And you, dread
beast, unconquered,
ever-watchful
at the gates of many guests,

                    snarling at the cavern's jaws,
                    guardian of Hades' hall
                    as legend says—

LEADER: —and you, Death, son of Tartaros and Gaia,
                    restrain the beast and make the passage clear
                    as our friend approaches the endless Fields of the Dead!

CHORUS: On you I call,
                              god of eternal sleep,
                              lead him gently—
                              give him rest—

*(No movement. Then a Messenger enters through the doorway of the skêné
and comes forward into the orchestra.)*

MESSENGER: Oh, my fellow citizens, to tell you simply
    Would be to say that Oedipus is dead.
    But more has happened than can be simply said,
    Or said in few words.

LEADER: He's dead, then, poor man?

MESSENGER: I assure you. He's passed from life.

LEADER: How? By god's grace painless?

MESSENGER: This is the very thing that's such a wonder.
    You know, you saw it, how he left here,
    Led by no friend, himself leading the way.
    Well—when he had come to the steep descent,
    The Brazen-Floored Threshold of Earth that leads
    To the earth's roots, he paused at one of the many
    Branching paths, near the rocky basin that marks
    The covenant of Thêseus and Perithoüs.
    And there, midway between the hallowed basin
    And the Rock of Thorikos, with its hollow pear tree
    And marble tomb, he sat down and undid
    His filthy garments.

    He then called to his daughters
    To fetch him fresh water from the stream nearby,
    To wash himself and pour libations to the gods.
    We watched them climb the Hill of Dêmêtêr, goddess
    Of green things and growth, and soon return
    With the water to wash and dress him as custom requires.
    When everything was done according to his pleasure,

And none of his commands were left undone,
Zeus of the Depths made the earth moan
With subterranean thunder.

Frightened, the girls trembled and fell to their knees
Beside their father and wept inconsolably,
Beating their breasts and wailing. And when he heard
The piteous sound, he folded his arms around them,
And said: "Children: this day is your father's last.
All that I once was is no more,
And the burden that you bore of caring for me
Is lifted now. It has not been easy, my children;
That much I know. And yet, one word frees you
Of all your pain and grief: that word is Love.
Never will you know greater love
Than you have had from me.
Go now, and live the rest of life without me."

And so, clinging together, the three of them wept.
And when they ended, and no more was heard,
There was a silence, and from that silence, suddenly,
A voice cried out that stood our hair on end
In panic fear! The god called him—called him
Again and again, echoing all about us,
Urging him on with shouting: "Oedipus! Oedipus!
It's time! You stay too long!"

Knowing it was the god's voice, he asked
Thêseus to come and said: "Dear friend,
Give me your right hand as a solemn pledge
To my children; and you, children, give yours to him.
Swear to me that you will never betray them,
Never of your own will, but promise in kindness
Always to do what is best for them."
And to his friend Thêseus he swore—
As befits a king, and not giving way to grief—
That he would do as asked.

This done,
Oedipus reached his sightless hands to feel

For his daughters and said: "Children, prove yourselves
Noble and brave, and leave here, never asking
To see what law forbids, nor hear what must not
Be heard. Go quickly now. Only King Thêseus,
Whose right it is, may witness the mystery
That now begins."

This much we heard him say,
And came away, sobbing, with the girls.
But then a moment later we turned around—
And the old man was nowhere to be seen,
Only Thêseus, his hands before his face,
Shading his eyes as against some dreaded sight
So terrible as not to be endured.
And then, quickly, with no word spoken,
We see him bow in reverence, with a prayer
To earth and the gods above.

In what manner Oedipus passed from life,
No mortal man but one can tell: only Thêseus.
It was no fiery bolt from god, no whirlwind
Sweeping in from the sea that took him off;
But either some guide came from the gods,
Or the earth below opened its unlit doors
In love to receive him.

Whatever way, his passage
Was free of all lament, sickness, and pain:
If ever any mortal's end was wondrous,
His surely was.
If what I say sounds foolish,
Believe what you like.
I can say no more.
LEADER: Where are the children,
    And the others with them?
MESSENGER: Not far off.
    You can hear their lament.
    They will be here soon.

(Antigonê and Ismenê enter through the skênê doorway and into the orchestra, wrapped in each other's arms.)

ANTIGONÊ: Now, now we may weep
         o weep! Now is the time,
           forever the time,
      to weep our fate, forever
        to weep the blood curse
         of our father that
     pounds in our veins!
        For him we endured while
          he still lived, bore up our
     burden; but now at the last,
        what we have seen, what
          we have suffered, baffles
     beyond all knowing!

CHORUS: Tell us!

ANTIGONÊ: It can only be guessed!

CHORUS: Gone?

ANTIGONÊ: Gone; as you
         would have wished.
      Neither war nor sea
        took him off; but the
          unseen fields bore him
     away in a mysterious end.
        And now night dark as
          death falls on our
     eyes. How will we
        weather our wanderings in
          exile, on land and sea, begging
     our bread?

ISMENÊ: Dear sister, how can I
        tell! O Death, murderous
      Death, open, open your
        gates, let me share, poor
          creature, in my agèd father's
     death. How can I
        live this life of desolation
         without him!

LEADER: Faithful sisters, best of
                      all daughters, what god
                            dispenses must be borne. Lay no
                grief, no heavy grief on your heart:
                      The path you have come is
                            beyond all blame.
ANTIGONÊ: Oh, how I longed for
                      past sorrows, for
                            sorrows past to come
                again! Even in sorrow
                      there was joy, when I
                            held him in my arms!
                O my father, father
                      whom I loved, father
                            shrouded in eternal dark,
                not even there, in Death's
                      dark kingdom, will you
                            lack our love, mine
                and hers!
CHORUS: Is he happy?
ANTIGONÊ: Happy!
CHORUS: Tell us!
ANTIGONÊ: He died as he had
                      wished, on foreign soil,
                his grave shaded in eternal
                      sleep, leaving behind him
                            mourning and bitter tears.
                Our eyes are dark with
                      heavy grief, grief beyond
                            speech! You wished to
                die on foreign soil; but why
                      so lonely, no gifts from
                            my hands?
ISMENÊ: Poor, wretched sister,
                      what fate, what
                            new fate awaits us
                now, desolate, robbed of
                      a father?
LEADER: Children of the blind old man,

```
                    his end was happy as
                        ever man's was. No more
                            grief now. No man's life
                    is ever free
                        of evil fortune.
ANTIGONÊ:           Dear, we'll go back!
ISMENÊ:      Why?
ANTIGONÊ:     This longing that seizes me!
ISMENÊ:           For what?
ANTIGONÊ:  His dark home!
                    To see it!
ISMENÊ:           Whose?
ANTIGONÊ:  Our father's!
                    God help me!
ISMENÊ:           No! It isn't
             lawful!
                    Listen!
ANTIGONÊ:        Why do you rebuke me?
ISMENÊ:      Because—
ANTIGONÊ:     What?
ISMENÊ:           —there's no grave!
             No one saw!
ANTIGONÊ:     Take me there now!
                    Kill me!
ISMENÊ:      Aiiiiiii!
                    What misery life has become!
                        Where will I go?
                    Where? Helpless! Alone!
                        Miserable!
LEADER:           You mustn't be frightened.
ANTIGONÊ:  But where to go?
                    Where to escape?
LEADER:           Stay here where you're safe.
ANTIGONÊ:  From what?
LEADER:      An evil turn in your fortunes.
ANTIGONÊ:        I understand.
LEADER     Then what are you thinking?
ANTIGONÊ:      How to get home!
                    I can't tell!
```

LEADER: You mustn't even try!

ANTIGONÊ: Trouble hounds us—

LEADER: It did so before.

ANTIGONÊ: Then we were helpless—
                    this is far worse!

LEADER: I know—a sea of
                    troubles overwhelms you.

ANTIGONÊ: Yes, yes!

LEADER: I agree.

ANTIGONÊ: Féu! Féu!
                    Where to turn?
                    Zeus!
                    Where else, where will
                    fate drive me?

*(Thêseus enters through the skênê doorway. The doors close slowly behind
him as he enters the orchestra.)*

THÊSEUS: No more weeping, children;
                    not for those to whom
                        Death has been kind
                            in the darkness below.
                    The gods would be angry.

ANTIGONÊ: Son of Aigeus,
                    we fall to our knees!

THÊSEUS: What do you want, my dears?
                    I hear you.

ANTIGONÊ: To see our father's grave
                    with our own eyes.

THÊSEUS: It's not permitted.

ANTIGONÊ: But you are the King of Athens!
                    Why?

THÊSEUS: Your father made me
                        promise never again
                    to approach that place,
                        nor tell anyone, ever,
                            the site of his sacred tomb.
                    If I did this,
                        if I kept my pledge,
                            he said that I would
                    preserve my land

from its enemies forever.
I swore it then,
heard by Zeus and his son,
the guardian of oaths.

ANTIGONÊ:　　　If this was father's wish,
then we must honor it.
But, please, my lord,
send us home to Thebes;
we must do all we can
to stop the bloody slaughter
that threatens our brothers' lives.

THÊSEUS:　　You have my word.
I will do everything
in my power to help you
and give pleasure to him who
only now was swept
from our midst.
I will never fail you.

LEADER:　　　No lamenting.
No more tears.

CHORUS:　　　　All these things
are accomplished.

(Antigonê and Ismenê go off left, all others go off right.)

APPENDIX

By Anna Krajewska-Wieczorek

ON MODERN PRODUCTIONS OF SOPHOKLES'TRAGEDIES

Had England's Elizabeth I not cancelled an appearance at a special reception in her honor at King's College, Cambridge, in the summer of 1564, one might well claim that the production (albeit in Latin) of *Aias* prepared for the royal visitor by students and masters initiated the modern production history of Sophokles' plays. As it happened, the grand effort of Nicholas Robinson and his colleagues proved futile, and all those costumes, armor, and stage equipment brought from London were returned unused. But performance of Greek tragedy at Cambridge was not delayed forever, for Euripides' *The Phoenician Women* and Sophokles' *Antigonê* were performed there in 1566 and 1580 respectively. These, however, were the only Greek tragedies produced in Europe before the opening of the Teatro Olimpico in Vicenza with a performance of *Oedipus Tyrannos*.

This historically famous production of March 3, 1585 boasted, in addition to speaking actors, a chorus of fifteen, singers, and extras in excess of one hundred to represent attendants, ladies-in-waiting, pages, and servants. And no expense was spared on special effects, including spraying the air with perfume to simulate the burning of incense by the Theban suppliants. The play was performed in Italian, translated by Orsato Giustiniani, and directed by Angelo Ingegneri, with costumes by the painter Giambattista Maganza, and music composed for the chorus by Andrea Gabrieli. The role of Oedipus was performed by Niccolo Rossi, Teiresias by the famous Luigi Groto, and Iokastê and Kreon by Veratos. The architect Vincenzo Scamozzi, who completed the theater after the death of its original designer, Andrea Palladio, placed a profusion of oil-lamps around the theater to achieve the illusion of Thebes bathed in Mediterranean sunlight.

Nearly three centuries passed before new attempts were made at staging Greek tragedy in Europe. And even though comedies by Menander, Plautus, and Terence were performed frequently in Humanist centers during the Renaissance, the severe rules imposed upon tragedy by the French Neo-classicists made the plays of Aeschylus, Sophokles, and Euripides unacceptable.

Sophokles returned to the European stage at the time of the rediscovery and revival of the plays of Shakespeare. Ludwig Tieck, a German critic and writer of the romantic period, mounted a famous production of *Antigonê* in Potsdam in 1841 that opened the way to Sophokles' heroine in the theaters of Berlin, Paris, and London in the years following. Tieck's production concept, innovative for the time, rejected naïve pictorial realism and advocated the convention of an open stage. He was the first to replace painted flats with three-dimensional scenery designed in response to the particular character of a play. Tieck's *Antigonê* set borrowed the look of the ancient Greek *skênê* building as it was then understood, and in front of it allowed for an unobstructed stage floor, which extended beyond the proscenium into the audience.

The success of Tieck's staging inspired an American businessman by the name of Dinneford to produce it in April 1845 in New York. Directed by George Vandenhoff, *Antigonê* was first performed at London's Covent Garden and in Edinburgh and won considerable applause for the protagonists, though the chorus of sixty men was criticized for being visibly underrehearsed. The New York critics were somewhat less pleased. Apparently unaccustomed to the choice of repertoire, they viewed Dinneford's venture a failure, criticizing Vandenhoff for his directing, as well as for his portrayal of Kreon, and Miss Clarendon for her inability in expressing Antigonê's tragic style of "noble devotion." They also found Palmo's Opera House an inappropriate venue for a play written to be performed in the open and little appreciated the chorus performing to the "sublime music" of Mendelssohn.

Other productions of Sophokles followed closely in time both in Europe and the United States. *Oedipus Tyrannos* once again opened Vicenza's Teatro Olimpico, this time after an intermission of more than two centuries, on September 15, 1847. Gustavo Modena played Oedipus, the opera composer Giovanni Pacini wrote the music, and new choral lyrics were translated by Jacopo Cabianca, a local poet. Four years later, in 1851, a theater in Munich offered *Antigonê* in a carefully researched production by Franz Dingelstedt. The set, conceived by Simon Quaglio in the Doric style, sought "historic accuracy" and consisted of a centrally placed altar, two sets of steps placed symmetrically on both sides, and the façade of a temple in the background. It was evidently inspired by Tieck's famous 1843 staging of *A Midsummer Night's Dream* in Berlin. *Antigonê* in Munich was performed in a new translation by philologist Friedrich Thiersch and with Mendelssohn's music for the chorus.

In the late 1860s, Adolf Wilbrandt for the first time adapted as a trilogy the so-called Oedipus plays, *Oedipus Tyrannos, Oedipus at Kolonos,* and *Antigonê,* for the world-famous Meiningen company. The adaptation, which was initially produced on three evenings, later made a successful tour and in 1886 played to great praise at Vienna's Burgtheater. It is reported that Wilbrandt's directorial emphasis was on the psychology of the characters rather than on the virtuosity of Sophokles' plot. The choice was a wise one in winning over a large popular audience.

The Meiningen company made a strong impression on Stanislavsky when in the 1880s it performed *Antigonê* in Moscow during its European tour. It also encouraged Stanislavsky to include *Antigonê* in the 1898–1899 opening season of the Moscow Art Theater.

The French stage career of *Oedipus Tyrannos* began in 1858 in Paris with a production at the Théâtre Français. Of particular historical significance are the two mountings of the play in the 1880s and 1890s with the great actor Jean Mounet-Sully in the lead, who in 1893 also performed Kreon to the Antigonê of Julie Barthet. The fame of these productions led to an immensely popular European and American tour, which played to great acclaim in New York in 1894. In addition they also encouraged other European artists to introduce Sophokles' plays to their stages. Between 1869 and the 1920s, *Oedipus* and *Antigonê* were also frequently performed in celebrated productions in the ancient Roman theater at Orange in Southern France.

Two remarkable men of the theater were haunted for years by the memory of having seen Mounet-Sully's Oedipus. The first was the Polish playwright, painter, and theater director Stanislaw Wyspianski; the second, Gordon Craig. Wyspianski admitted in his letters to seeing Mounet-Sully as Oedipus four times in Paris and that it had fascinated him. In 1903 in Krakow he staged *Antigonê* with the famous Polish-born American actress Helena Modjeska as the protagonist. This, as well as his own play *Protesilas and Laodamia,* marked a decisive turn in the history of the Polish theater: *Antigonê* for the feast of colors in the Greek costumes designed by Wyspianski as well as for his revolutionary lighting design; *Protesilas and Laodamia* for the sparse set and Modjeska's simplicity of acting.

As for Gordon Craig, he never realized his directorial and design projects that had been executed for a production of *Êlektra* in 1905 with Eleonora Duse. The Italian star found Craig's set and costumes too complicated for touring conditions and cancelled the production.

The late nineteenth century in both Europe and the United States saw a proliferation of college and university productions of Greek drama. One such was a Harvard production of *Oedipus Tyrannos*, performed in ancient Greek, that made its way to New York's Booth Theatre in the winter of 1882. The professional and highly successful American producer Daniel Frohman bought into a drama that was not only barely comprehensible to popular audiences of the time, but which proved threatening to the American puritan sensibility. Still, one must consider that more than a few obstacles were set up along the way, not the least being that the role of Oedipus was recited in Greek by a Harvard graduate, George Riddle, while the rest of the cast of professionals spoke in English. The New York critics, who cautiously applauded the leading actors (Georgia Cayvan as Iokastê was praised for "fairly outdoing herself in depicting horror"), had neither the courage nor the vocabulary to deal with the incestuous motif of the Oedipus tragedy. One critic was inspired to condemn Sophokles' play as "overflowing with the most horrible and immoral incidents."

Somewhat more successfully, thanks to the enthusiasm and persistence of students and scholars who promoted ancient Greek culture in Poland, the plays of Sophokles slowly made their way to the professional theaters of Warsaw and Krakow. The Artistic Association of Classical Greek Drama, instituted in 1905 in Krakow's Jagiellonian University, organized student productions, inspired translators, and popularized ancient drama through public lectures. Henryk Sienkiewicz, after seeing *Oedipus Tyrannos* staged by students in Warsaw in 1899, encouraged theaters to produce *Antigonê*. But the next professional production of a Sophokles play (after Wyspianski's 1903 *Antigonê*) did not materialize until March 1910 in Lvov—a production of *Oedipus Tyrannos* directed by L. Heller, using a new translation by Kazimierz Morawski.

In nineteenth-century England classical Greek tragedy was promoted through college performances primarily at Oxford and Cambridge. Performances in Greek, or Greek and English, took advantage of professional advances in scenery and design, and the chorus recited and sang in ancient Greek to the music of Mendelssohn or Gluck. Imperfect as these student performances may have been, they undoubtedly had an impact on both professional theater and scholarship. College productions encouraged and tested new translations of Greek plays, exhibited formal aspects of the Greek chorus' performance in space as well as music, and instigated research in costume and scenery. On the other hand, the academics who tested Greek tragedy in modern performance at the turn of the nineteenth century were very susceptible to the style and interpretation of leading actors and the visions of theater directors. As much as Mounet-Sully had once affected his audiences in the late nineteenth century, the Austrian theater director Max Reinhardt inflamed theater-goers and inspired practitioners by his monumental spectacles based on the plays of Aeschylus, Sophokles, and Aristophanes.

Max Reinhardt was a visionary who captured the essential features of ancient Greek drama: its spatial form, its chorus, and its communal emphasis achieved through artistically orchestrated emotion. Although he began his work on the Greek classics in the intimacy of the Kleines Theater in Berlin, where he staged Sophokles' *Êlektra* in Hugo von Hofmannsthal's translation-adaptation in 1903, Reinhardt's unquestioned success came with his staging of *Oedipus Tyrannos* in 1910; first in Munich's Musikfesthalle in September, and two months later at the arena stage of the Zirkus Schumann in Berlin. This staging, mammoth in scale and irresistible in exerting its power over audiences throughout Europe, was like a Wagnerian opera brought to a circus arena, with famous actors and the most innovative effects of lighting, stagecraft, and individualized movement for the crowd.

Reinhardt's chorus consisted of twenty-six men, though he intensified the stage picture with the presence of a crowd of over five hundred extras. The crowd's movement within the enormous space as well as its position between the protagonists and the chorus created very striking effects of dynamic force that divided the performing space and enabled a constant confrontation between actor and chorus. The crowd of extras created a powerful opening scene before the appearance of Oedipus. Out of darkness, murky blue lights slowly revealed the Theban masses in a city being destroyed by plague, storming the gigantic palace doors with cries for help. At the play's end, the blind Oedipus, his face streaked with blood and gore, makes his exit from Thebes through the audience—a choice not usual at the time.

The dynamic and highly emotional tone of Reinhardt's production was achieved in two ways. First, by means of its musically orchestrated mixture of voices and sounds—drums, organ, trumpets—and then by the use of highly evocative lighting. Lighting as a means of defining interpretation had been introduced earlier by Stanislaw Wyspianski in Krakow; but its impact was so provocative and unusual that critics reacted to it with disoriented vehemence. In Reinhardt's production of *Oedipus Tyrannos,* lighting added a new dimension to the play's structure; it immobilized it and accentuated its rhythm. In addition to the conventional means of lighting, including the light of torches, Reinhardt used the spotlight in ways that were new and highly effective: to emphasize the actor in the theatrical space, to isolate the actor in his own space, and to "brush" the crowd of extras in order to show an isolated momentary action.

Except for Firmin Gemier's 1919 circus-based production of *Oedipus Tyrannos* in Paris, the scale of twentieth-century productions of Sophokles' plays has been smaller than that of Reinhardt. The conventional set for productions between the 1920s and the 1960s was the façade of a palace or temple frequently fronted by a row of Doric columns. And the proliferation of translations in all languages offered a greater range of interpretations for theatrical presentation than ever before. The size of the chorus, too, has varied, depending on the size of the stage and the proscenium. Sophokles' chorus numbered fifteen; yet for the production of Yeats' translations of *Oedipus Tyrannos* and *Oedipus at Kolonos* at Dublin's Abbey Theatre in 1926 and 1927, respectively, the chorus shrank to six.

The first decades of the twentieth century celebrated the revival of Greek tragedy staged in the open-air ancient theaters in Italy and Greece. In 1914, under the leadership of Count Mario T. Gargallo, the Greek theater in Syracuse became the site of the first festival of Classical drama, the Syracuse Festival, which continued until the outbreak of World War II in 1939. Several of Sophokles' plays were produced there: *Oedipus Tyrannos* in 1922, utilizing the methods of "rhythmic space" as laid out by Appia and Dalcroze; *Antigonê* in 1924, with its spectacularly successful choral dancing; *The Women of Trachis* in 1933, with an abstract set design; *Oedipus at Kolonos* in 1936; and *Aias* in a pompous military mode in the spring of 1939, under the influence of the Italian dictator Benito Mussolini, who took charge of the festival in the mid 1920s. The Fascist note in interpretation was also struck heavily in the 1937 production of *Oedipus Tyrannos,* when it was staged in an Italian colony in Africa in the ancient Roman theater at Sabratha.

Rediscovered ancient Greek theaters were used for productions in the 1930s at Delphi and in the 1950s at Epidauros and the Odeon of Herodes Atticus in Athens. The festivals in Delphi owe their inception to the enthusiasm of the Greek poet, Angelos Sikelianos, and his American wife, Eva Palmer. For the opening in 1927, the solemn production of *Prometheus Bound* was directed by Eva Palmer to music composed by K. Psachos, with the chorus' choreography based on gestural iconography found on ancient vases. Although the Sikelianos' initiative was short lived due to financial considerations (it reopened only once, in 1930), Delphi became the center of research and performance hosted by the European Cultural Centre of Delphi founded in 1964. From 1981 to the present, this organization has invited scholars of theater and ancient drama to participate in symposia enriched by theatrical festivals with productions of classical drama from around the world. Plays of Sophokles presented there range from *Antigonê* by an Eskimo group in 1985, to *Oedipus Tyrannos* from Peking, also in 1985, an *Êlektra* from Japan in Tadashi Suzuki's adaptation based loosely on both Sophokles and Euripides in 1995, and productions originating in Athens, Patra, and Thessaloniki.

Among Greek productions staged in Athens and Epidauros, the most memorable are those by Dmitris Rondiris, a student of Reinhardt, from Piraiko Theatro, who directed Katina Paxinou in 1952, and, in 1960, Aspasia Papathanassiou, with a superbly musicalized and choreographed chorus in *Êlektra*. Most recently there is the work of Theodoros Terzopoulos, who in *The Women of Trachis* (a part of his 1998–1999 adaptation *Herakles*) accomplished interesting results in his fusion of Greek and Japanese Kabuki motifs.

Productions of Sophokles' works, not to mention those of his colleagues Aeschylus and Euripides, have in the last four decades indicated a decisive turn from the archeologically based reconstruction of the form and style of ancient Greek theater toward a modern production style stripped of its ancient look and performed either on a bare stage or in a space dynamized by flights of steps and cubic forms. There is also a radical change in the delivery of Sophoklean rhetoric when one considers the difference between the 1935 Old Vic production with Laurence Olivier and the production of Sophokles from the late 1970s to the present in any world metropolis, from Japan to France, Poland, Brazil, or the United States.

As for the number of contemporary productions, it is so great that an accurate accounting of it is virtually impossible. A few of those productions resonated mightily on the international scene, central among them being Ariane Mnouchkine's 1992 *Les Atrides* with her Théâtre du Soleil company. And Britain's Royal National Theatre has mounted numerous major productions of Sophokles and his contemporaries. Two of Sophokles' plays, *Oedipus Tyrannos* and *Antigonê*, have always been his most popular, and this is particularly true of the present. In an age known for its indifference toward truth and independence, the search of Oedipus precisely for the truth at any cost is an endeavor of heroic dimension; and Antigonê's drama of necessary sacrifice has been a recurring inspiration in a world of political tension, of unabated tyranny and violated human rights. It is these two plays that have repeatedly stood as symbols of freedom of thought and invincible spirituality.

ON SOPHOKLES' CHORUS

When we read words of the Greek rhetorician Gorgias about poetry's capacity to deceive and at the same time bring pleasure, and then about the power of a poet to create illusion, we inevitably think of mimetic poetry. If we look at his statement carefully, we may find there a description of Greek tragedy along with its chorus.

"All poetry," says Gorgias, "I consider and define as discourse in metre. There comes over the audience of poetry a fearful horror and tearful pity and doleful yearning. By means of the discourse their spirit feels a personal emotion on account of the good and bad fortune of others." The "discourse" that works such wonders on an audience engaged in watching tragedy can be perceived either as the process in the spectators' minds (or, to be precise, first in their emotional faculties), or as a complex "discourse" between the protagonists and the chorus who partake equally in carving the emotions of the audience by means of the plot.

Critical works on Greek tragedy published in the last few decades have begun to emphasize the emotional impact of tragedy on its audience. After more than a century of distanced and sober assessments by Classical scholars who studied the original texts of Greek drama solely as literature while failing to see them as texts meant to be performed in a theater by actors in front of an audience, Classical scholarship is finally looking at these texts as works of living theater that encompass the entire theatrical experience, including the audience. This former disregard has prompted a misperception of the place and presence of the chorus in contemporary productions of Greek drama, along with a consideration of the considerable effect the chorus is able to exert on an audience.

T. S. Eliot writes the following in regard to the chorus in his play *Murder in the Cathedral*:

> I . . . became aware of my reasons for depending, in that play, so heavily upon the assistance of the chorus. There were two reasons for this, which in the circumstances justified it. The first was that the essential action of the play—both the historical facts and the matter I invented—was somewhat limited. A man comes home, foreseeing that he will be killed, and he is killed. I did not want to increase the number of characters, I did not want to write a chronicle of twelfth-century politics. . . . I wanted to concentrate on death and martyrdom. The introduction of a chorus of excited and sometimes hysterical women, reflecting in their emotion the significance of

the action, helped wonderfully. The second reason was this: that a poet writing for the first time for the stage, is much more at home in choral verse than in dramatic dialogue. [. . .] The use of a chorus strengthened the power, and concealed the defects of my theatrical technique. For this reason I decided that next time I would try to integrate the chorus more closely into a play.

Eliot's statement regarding the chorus "reflecting in their emotion the significance of the action" leads us directly to a discussion of the Sophoklean chorus. If we bear in mind that Sophokles wrote of the suffering and death of characters from Greek mythology and that therefore the action of his plays was removed from the time and life experience of his spectators, we may understand the essential role that his chorus played in affecting the emotions of his audience by means of the emotions performed in choral odes in the Athenian orchestra. And we know another important thing: that Sophokles, in the seven extant plays that survive, was not a neophyte playwright, but one with more than a few years of theatrical experience behind him.

A historian of the Greek theater would enumerate the functions of the Greek chorus as follows: (1) as the commentator on an action, (2) as the ideal spectator, (3) as the introducer of characters entering the acting area, (4) as the provider of time and space for the spectator to come to terms with his or her reaction to the plot being played out, (5) as the group that engages in dialogue with the protagonists, (6) as the co-singer of the *kommos* with the hero or heroine, and (7) as the group that dances and concludes the play with a moral *sententia,* while dancing away to the rhythms of the *exodos.* Rarely, however, does any Sophoklean chorus play out all these functions in performance.

One of the most crucial questions regarding the chorus in Sophokles' plays is the physical presence that this group of fifteen performers (including the leader) had in the spatial geography of performance. The role of the chorus in extended sections of the play where it has no lines is seriously misperceived by much contemporary criticism and performance practice. We must ask ourselves in all seriousness: What does the chorus "do" during these frequently extended passages? How would this group of fifteen that almost never leaves the stage once it has entered react to the momentous events that it is witness to? How would it react to the frequently lengthy messengers' narratives about death and suffering and the virtual monologues spoken by the protagonists? Anyone intimately involved with the theater ancient or modern has to conclude that this chorus "does" something. And David Wiles in his recent *Tragedy in Athens* goes so far as to suggest that the chorus, in addition to singing and dancing its odes, might conceivably also have acted out the story of those odes. An even more radical idea of his, and one that bespeaks a vibrant understanding of theatrical performance and utilization of a chorus' theatrical capacity, is that the chorus several times in a given Sophoklean play abandons its plot "persona" and becomes an "objective" acter-out of messenger narratives and protagonist monologues.

The importance of the chorus in the social and aesthetic consideration of Greek tragedy began with Lessing, who in 1759 was the first to enunciate the superiority of Greek drama over French neoclassical tragedy. This discussion continued in the letters of Goethe and Schiller and in Schlegel's lectures and found it's culmination in Nietzsche's *The Birth of Tragedy*. While German poet-playwrights analyzed the essence of tragic heroism and the artistic merit of the Greek chorus, Nietzsche perceived the chorus as the communal voice of Dionysos' celebration and as the intermediary in the ecstatic emotional eruption of societal expiation. The practical exegesis of the chorus as an emotional catalyst was conducted much earlier by Schiller in his heroic tragedy *The Bride of Messina* in 1803, which resulted in the following theoretical conclusion:

> The mind of the spectator ought to maintain its freedom through the most impassioned scenes; it should not be the mere prey of impressions, but calmly and severely detach itself from the emotions which it suffers. The . . . objection made to the chorus, that it disturbs the illusion, and blunts the edge of the feelings, is what constitutes its highest recommendation. . . . If the strokes which tragedy inflicts . . . followed without respite, the passion would overpower the action. We should mix ourselves up with the subject-matter, and no longer stand above it. It is by holding us under the different parts, and stepping between the passions with its composing views, that the chorus restores to us our freedom, which would else be lost in the tempest. The characters of the drama need this intermission in order to collect themselves; for they are not real beings who obey the impulse of the moment, and merely represent individuals—but ideal persons and representatives of their species, who enunciate the deep things in humanity.

I find Schiller's reflections very revealing today and appropriate to the understanding of the preëminent function of the Sophoklean chorus. It is in the "stepping between the passions with its composing views" and holding our emotions in control so that they do not "overpower the action" that Schiller touches upon the very core of the chorus' theatrical complexity, along with the irony that underpins Sophokles' plot and strategically orchestrated emotions, both triggered and calmed by the chorus.

GLOSSARY

Abai: site in Phokis of a temple-shrine dedicated to Apollo.

Achaia: ancient province in the northern Peloponnesos; general name for mainland Greece.

Achaioi: a name for the Greeks.

Acheloös: the largest river in Aitolia in central and northwestern Greece; a river god who in wooing Dêianeira took the form of a monstrous bull. In Greek myth river gods are male and frequently seducers and rapists.

Acheron: a river situated in northern Greece, which, because it ran underground in several places, was believed to be the river that led to the underworld, the sunless realm of the dead presided over by Hades, lord of the dead.

Achilleus: one of the central heroes of Greek myth; son of King Peleus and the nereid Thetis; father of Neoptolemos; commander of the Myrmidons on the side of the Greeks.

Agamemnon: a son of Atreus; king of Mykenê; husband of Klytaimnêstra; father of Orestês, Êlektra, Chrysothemis, and Iphianassa; brother of Menelaos; brother-in-law of Helen; supreme leader of the Greek forces in the war against Troy; murdered by his wife and her lover Aigisthos upon his return from Troy.

Aias: one of the strongest and bravest of the Greek warriors at Troy; killed himself when not awarded the armor of the dead Achilleus; son of Telamon; known as Telamonian or Greater Aias; commander of the Greek forces from Salamis.

Aiai: a cry of grief and pain; believed by Sophokles to be the source of the name Aias.

Aigaion Sea: the sea between Greece and Turkey; an arm of the Mediterranean.

Aigeus: king of Athens; father of Thêseus.

Aigisthos: son of Thyestes; brother of Atreus; cousin of Agamemnon; seducer of Agamemnon's wife Klytaimnêstra; co-murderer of Agamemnon; killed by Orestês in revenge for Agamemnon's death.

Aitolia: ancient region on the Gulf of Korinth.

Akropolis: fortified upper part of a city, as at Athens.

Alkmênê: queen of Thebes; wife of Amphitrion; mother of Heraklês by Zeus.

All-Seeing Ones: formerly the Furies; after the trial of Orestês for matricide, called the gracious or gentle ones; protectors of Athens.

Amphiareos: (1) his wife Eriphylê accepted a bribe of a golden necklace to convince her husband to join the expedition against Troy; (2) one of the seven against Thebes in the attack led by Polyneikês.

Amphion: Theban ruler who is said to have built the walls of Thebes by leading the stones to their proper place with the music of his lyre; husband of Niobê; took his life after the death of all their children.

Amphitritê: a nereid; goddess of the sea and wife of Poseidon; most likely the present-day Atlantic ocean.

Antigonê: daughter of Oedipus and Iokastê; sister to Ismenê, Polyneikês and Eteoklês; niece to Kreon.

Antilochos: son of Nestor, king of Pylos.

Aphroditê: goddess of love, beauty, and fertility; wife of Hephaistos and lover of Arês; said to have been born out of the seafoam; also known as Kypris after the island that was the seat of her cult.

Apollo: born on Delos; one of the twelve Olympian gods; symbol of light, youth, beauty; synonymous with music, poetry, medicine, and prophecy; his temple of oracular prophecy at Delphi in central Greece was the most famous in the ancient world; twin brother of Artemis; archer renowned for his unfailing aim.

Apollo Lykêios: see Apollo above; Sophokles believed the term *Lykêios* to be derived from the word for light; known to protect shepherds from wolves and pestilence.

Areopagos: rocky hill northwest of the Athenian Akropolis; site of the Athenian high court of justice that met there.

Arês: god of war unpopular among the Greeks; son of Zeus and Hera; lover of Aphroditê and probably father of Eros.

Argive: Homeric name for any Greek; a native of Argos; of or pertaining to ancient Argos.

Argos: ancient city in southeastern Greece in the northeastern Peloponnesos; in general terms, mainland Greece.

Arkadia: ancient pastoral district of the central Peloponnesos.

Arktouros: giant red star of the first magnitude, the brightest of the constellation of Boötes.

Artemis: daughter of Zeus and Hera; twin sister of Apollo born on the island of Delos; virgin huntress associated with wild places and animals; primitive birth goddess; known as an archer.

Atalantê: beautiful, swift-footed maiden who offered to marry any man who defeated her in a race.

Atê: the goddess personifying criminal folly or reckless ambition in man, bringing on him punishment by Nemesis.

Athêna: daughter of Zeus, who sprang fully armed from his head; goddess of wisdom, skills, and warfare; chief defender of the Greeks at Troy; particular defender of Odysseus; in competition with Poseidon, who produced the horse, she won the favor of Athens by producing the olive tree, considered the more valuable, for which she was made patron of Athens, her namesake.

Athêna Polias: epithet of Athêna as patron of Athens.

Athens: independent city-state in southeastern Greece; center of Greek culture in the fifth century B.C.E., when it was the capital of ancient Attika.

Atreidai: meaning sons of Atreus, the name applied to the brothers Menelaos and Agamemnon, leaders in the Greek war against Troy.

Atreus: king of Mykenê; father of Agamemnon and Menelaos; to avenge the treachery of his brother Thyestes, he killed Thyestes' sons and served their flesh to him at a banquet.

Attik: of or characteristic of Attika or Athens.

Attika: a peninsula of southeastern Greece; in ancient times, a region dominated by Athens, its chief city.

Aulis: ancient town in east central Greece, in Boiotia; traditionally the harbor from which the Greeks set sail against Troy.

Bakkhai: Female followers of Dionysos whose ecstatic frenzy was brought on by the god; free of human fears and conventions, they roamed the mountains in celebration of the god, tore up trees by the roots and devoured raw flesh; known also as Maenads.

Bakkhant: follower of Dionysos; *see* Bakkhai.

Bakkhos: one of the several names of the god Dionysos.

Boiotia: province of east central Greece northwest of Attika; dominated by Thebes.

Bosporos: the strait between the Sea of Marmara and the Black Sea.

Boötes: a northern constellation including the bright star Arktouros.

Boreas: the north or northeast wind; at times appears as a horse; also appears as a bearded old man, as depicted on the Tower of the Winds in Athens.

Brazen-Footed Threshold of Earth: any place that allows a passage from earth to the Realm of the Dead or Hades.

Cape Kênaion: headland or promontory by the sea on the island of Euboia.

Centaur: wild creature, half-man, half-horse; inhabitant generally of mountainous regions, in particular Mount Pelion in eastern Thessaly, northeastern Greece; identified with primitive desires; antisocial; known for drunkenness and chasing women; probably pre-Homeric.

Chalkodon: a contemporary of the father of Philoktêtês.

Chance: in Greek *tychê;* luck either good or bad; fortune; fate.

Cheiron: wisest and most humane of the centaurs; famous for his knowledge of medicine; taught Asklepios, Achilleus, and Heraklês.

Chorus: in Greek drama, a group of actors with a specific identity that sings, dances, and at times narrates.

Chrysê: island in the northern Aigaion Sea; a daimôn worshipped there.

Chrysothemis: one of the daughters of Agamemnon and Klytaimnêstra; sister of Êlektra and Orestês.

Chthonian Hermês: epithet regarding Hermês as leader of the souls of the dead into Hades.

Daimôn: divine being; an attendant or ministering spirit; frequently associated with bad luck that shadows one from birth; fate; what is unexpected and outside of one's control.

Danaë: daughter of Acrisios, king of Argos; locked in a bronze tower by her father upon learning that a male child of hers would kill him; Zeus visits her in the tower as a rain of gold, which gives birth to Perseus, who accidentally kills Acrisios while throwing a discus.

Danaians: another name for the mainland Greeks.

Daughters of Darkness: see All-Seeing Ones.

Daulia: city in Phokis, near Apollo's shrine in Delphi, originally Pylos.

Dêianeira: daughter of Oineüs; wife of Heraklês; mother of Hyllos.

Delian: a native or inhabitant of Delos; of or relating to Delos.

Delos: Greek island in the southwest Aigaion Sea; traditional birthplace of Apollo and Artemis.

Delphi: Greek city on the southern slopes of Mount Parnassos; site of the most famous oracle of Apollo.

Dêmêter: goddess of agricultural fertility; protector of marriage and women; sister of Zeus; mother of Persephonê.

Diomêdes: son of Tydeus; king of Argos; instrumental with Odysseus in returning Philoktêtês to the Greek forces at Troy.

Dionysos: god of divine inspiration and the release of mass emotion; associated with wine, fruitfulness, and vegetation; son of Zeus and Semelê; leader of the Bakkhai; bestower of ecstasy; worshipped in a cult centered around orgiastic rites and veiled in great mystery; also known as Iakkhos and Bakkhos.

Dirkê: a river near Thebes.

Dodona: Greek town in Epiros in northwestern Greece; site of an ancient sanctuary and oracle of Zeus.

Dorian: a member of or relating to one of the three branches of the Greeks, particularly those in the Peloponnesos.

Dread Daughters: *see* All-Seeing Ones.

Dryas: father of Lykourgos.

Echidna: mother of Cerberos; see Three-Headed Hound below.

Echo: a nymph deprived by Hera of speech, thus able only to repeat the words of others; pined away when spurned by Narkissos till only her voice remained.

Eisodos: entrance and exit on either side of the Greek theater structure.

Êlektra: daughter of Agamemnon and Klytaimnêstra; sister of Orestês and Chrysothemis.

Eleusis: town in Attika fourteen miles west of Athens; site in classical times of a mystical religious festival, the Eleusinian Mysteries, in which initiates celebrated Dêmêter, Persephonê, and Dionysos.

Elis: ancient city-state of southwest Greece in the northwest Peloponnesos; site of a temple-shrine dedicated to Zeus where ancient games were held.

Enyalios: epithet of Arês; personification of war.

Erechtheus: in classical times considered the first or an early king of Athens; raised by Athêna; associated with earth; worshipped with Athêna on the Athenian Akropolis.

Eriboia: mother of Telamonian or Greater Aias.

Erinyës: snake-haired goddesses of vengeance, usually three in number, named Alekto, Tisiphone, and Megera, who pursue unpunished criminals; Furies.

Erinys: singular of Erinyës; *see also* Erinyës.

Erymanthian Boar: one of the twelve labors of Heraklês; a gigantic beast from Mount Erymanthos, which he carried back alive to Mykenê on his shoulders.

Eteoklês: son of Oedipus and Iokastê; brother of Antigonê, Ismenê; killed his brother Polyneikês in a battle at Thebes over right to the Theban throne; killed by Polyneikês in the same battle.

Eteoklos: one of the seven against Thebes in the attack led by Polyneikês.

Euboia: island in the west Aigaion Sea; second largest island in the Greek archipelago.

Eumenides: *see* All-Seeing Ones.

Eumolpids: a priestly clan at Eleusis which held a major hereditary office.

Evenos: river in Greece across that the centaur Nessos ferried men in his arms.

Eüoi: a cry of joy and exaltation most frequently used by the Chorus.

Eurydikê: wife of Kreon and mother of Haimon.

Eurysakes: male child of Aias and Tekmêssa.

Eurystheus: grandson of Perseus, who, through the favor of Hera, inherited the kingship of Mykenê, which Zeus had intended for Heraklês; taskmaster of Heraklês.

Eurytos: king of Oichalia on the island of Euboia; father of Iolê.

Fates: the three goddesses who control the destinies of humans.

Fire-god: *see* Hephaistos.

Furies: *see* Erinyës.

Gaia: goddess of the earth.

Goddess of Vengeance: Nemesis; a power of retribution and vengeance.

God of Death: Hades; *see also* Hades.

Golden Apples: one of the twelve labors of Heraklês; the golden apples of the Hesperides guarded by a dragon.

Golden Rain: *see* Danaë.

Great Bear: Ursa Major; an extensive conspicuous constellation in the northern hemisphere.

Hades: underworld abode of the souls of the dead; lord of the kingdom bearing his name; also known as Pluto; son of Kronos and Rhea; brother of Zeus, Dêmêter, and Poseidon; husband of Persephonê.

Haimon: son of Kreon and Eurydikê; fiancé of Antigonê.

Hekatê: a primitive goddess of the underworld later associated with Artemis; connected with sorcery and black magic.

Hektor: eldest son of King Priam of Troy; supreme commander of Troy's forces in the Trojan War; killed by Achilleus.

Helenos: son of King Priam of Troy; prophet; captured by the Greeks; foretold the fall of Troy through Philoktêtês.

Helikon: mountain in Boiotia, Greece, the source of poetic inspiration and the home of the Muses.

Hêlios: sun god; a Titan; drives his chariot east to west across the sky; later identified with Apollo.

Hellas: classical Greek name for Greece.

Hellenes: classical Greek name for the people of Hellas.

Hephaistos: god of fire; son of Zeus and Hera; husband of Aphroditê.

Hera: goddess; daughter of Kronos and Rhea; sister and wife of Zeus; associated with women and marriage.

Heraklês: son of Zeus and Alkmênê; of outstanding strength, size, and courage; known for the performance of twelve immense labors imposed upon him.

Hermês: god; son of Zeus and Maia; messenger and herald of the gods; associated with commerce, cunning, theft, travelers, and rascals.

Hippomedon: one of the seven against Thebes in the attack led by Polyneikês.

Hyllos: son of Heraklês and Dêianeira.

Iakkhos: deity invoked during the Eleusinian Mysteries; most likely a name for Dionysos.

Ida: mountain and range southeast of ancient Troy; a favored seat of Zeus.

Ikaria: Greek island in the Aigaion Sea.

Ikarian: of or relating to Ikaria.

Io: a maiden loved by Zeus and turned into a white heifer by her to deceive Hera.

Iokastê: wife of King Laïos of Thebes; mother and wife of Oedipus; mother of Antigonê, Ismenê, Polyneikês, and Eteoklês.

Iolê: daughter of King Eurytos of Oichalia; one of the captive maidens brought home by Heraklês as a concubine.

Iphianassa: daughter of Agamemnon and Klytaimnêstra; sister of Chrysothemis, Iphigenia, Êlektra, and Orestês.

Iphitos: son of King Eurytos of Oichalia; brother of Iolê.

Ismenê: daughter of Oedipus and Iokastê; brother of Antigonê, Ismenê, Polyneikês and Eteoklês.

Ismênos: (1) river near Thebes; (2) worshipped as a son of Apollo by a Theban cult in a temple southeast of Thebes.

Istros: the lower Danube River.

Itys: son of Aëdon, accidentally killed by her while she tried to kill a son of Niobê.

Ixion: a Thessalian king punished by Zeus for his love of Hera by being bound to a perpetually revolving wheel.

Justice: in Greek Dikê; goddess.

Kadmeian Thebes: Thebes founded by Kadmos; *see also* Kadmos.

Kadmos: son of King Agenor who killed a dragon, planted its teeth, from which sprang a host of warriors who fought each other until only five re-mained, who joined Kadmos in founding Thebes.

Kalchas: seer and priest of Apollo who accompanied the Greek forces to Troy.

Kapaneus: one of the seven against Thebes in the attack led by Polyneikês.

Kastalia: a spring on Mount Parnassos sacred to Apollo and the Muses and believed the source of poetic inspiration.

Kênion: *See* Cape Kênion.

Kephallênian: an inhabitant of Kephallenia, an island off western Greece; an inhabitant of Ithaka or one of several neighboring islands.

Kephisos: river in Attika whose water never fails.

Kithairon: a vast range of mountains stretching between Korinth and Thebes.

Klytaimnêstra: wife of Agamemnon; mother of Êlektra, Chrysothemis, Iphigenia, Iphianassa, and Orestês.

Knossos: city in north central Krêtê.

Kolchidian Phasis: the Rioni River in the Caucasus.

Kolonos: village north of ancient Athens.

Korinth: port in southern Greece in the northeastern Peloponnesos.

Korykian: named for the famous caves above Delphi.

Kreon: successor to Oedipus as leader of Thebes; brother to Iokastê; uncle to Antigonê, Ismenê, Polyneikês, and Eteoklês.

Krêtê: largest of the Greek islands in the eastern Mediterranean.

Krêtan: of or relating to Krêtê.

Krisa: city in Phokis.

Kronos: Titan; son of Uranos and Gaia; father of Zeus who dethroned him.

Kyllênê: mountain in Greece associated with Pan.

Kypris: goddess of love, beauty, and fertility; wife of Hephaistos and lover of Arês; said to have been born out of the seafoam; also known as Aphroditê.

Labdakids: members of the house of Labdakos; *see also* Labdakos.

Labdakos: father of Laïos; grandfather of Oedipus.

Laïos: king of Thebes; father of Oedipus; husband of Iokastê.

Lakonian Hound: from the country in southern Greece in the southeast Peloponnesos of which Sparta was the capital.

Laërtês: father of Odysseus.

Laomedon: founder and ruler of Troy; cheated Apollo and Poseidon of their wages for constructing Troy's walls; father of Priam.

Lête: the mother by Zeus of Apollo and Artemis.

Lemnos: island in the northeastern Aigaion Sea; famous for its medicinal earth; place of Philoktêtês' exile.

Lernian Hydra: one of the twelve labors of Heraklês; a monster with nine heads, each of which, when struck off, was replaced by two new ones.

Libation: a pouring out of wine or some other liquid in honor of a deity; liquid so poured out.

Libya: north African country on the Mediterranean.

Lichas: the herald of Heraklês in *The Women of Trachis*.

Lord of Death: *see* Hades.

Lord of Cries: Dionysos.

Loxias: Apollo; a cult epithet that possibly refers to him as one who speaks in riddles, indirectly, through his oracle.

Lydia: region on the coast of west Asia Minor.

Lykêian King: *see* Apollo Lykêios.

Lykomêdês: king of Skyros; father of Neoptolemos' mother.

Lykourgos: King of the Edonians; the first to reject the cult of Dionysos, for which he was blinded, driven mad, and imprisoned.

Maenad: means raving, frenzied; a Bakkhant; *see also* Bakkhai.

Magnesia: the southwestern peninsula of Thessaly.

Maia: eldest of the seven Pleiades; mother by Zeus of Hermês.

Megareus: son of Kreon and Eurydikê; killed during the attack of the Seven against Thebes.

Melian: inhabitant of or relating to Melis in southern Thessaly.

Menelaos: son of Atreus; king of Sparta; husband of Helen; brother of Agamemnon.

Menoikeus: father of Kreon and Iokastê.

Meropê: queen of Korinth; wife of Polybos; foster mother of Oedipus.

Muses: nine sister goddesses, daughters of Zeus and Mnemosynê, each a protector of an art or science; sources of artistic inspiration.

Mykenê: city in the northeast Peloponnesos on the plain of Argos, north of the city of Argos; Agamemnon's capital.

Mysioi: the northwest corner of Asia Minor.

Narkissos: a beautiful boy who fell in love with his own water-reflected image; ignored the advances of Echo, who died for love of him; he in turn pined away and was changed into the flower.

Necessity: in Greek, *anankê;* fatal necessity, which even the gods could not undo.

Nemean Lion: an enormous lion strangled by Heraklês as the first of his twelve labors.

Neoptolemos: son of Achilleus.

Nessos: the centaur killed by Heraklês for attacking Dêianeira.

Nestor: oldest and wisest of the Greeks in the Trojan War.

Nike: goddess of victory.

Niobê: queen of Phrygia whose six sons and six daughters (in some versions seven) were killed by the gods Apollo and Artemis because she boasted they were more beautiful than the two gods.

Nymph: female spirits of nature endowed with long life.

Nysa: mountain on the island of Euboia stretching along the Attic and Boiotian coast.

Odysseus: son of Laërtês; father of Telemachos; leader of the Ithicans at Troy.

Oedipus: son of Laïos; son and husband of Iokastê; father and brother of Antigonê, Ismenê, Polyneikês, and Eteoklês.

Oichalia: city on the island of Euboia ruled by King Eurytos and destroyed by Heraklês.

Oineüs: father of Dêianeira.

Oïtê: mountain above Thermopylai with a precinct sacred to Zeus.

Olympos: mountain in northeastern Thessaly; seat of the Olympian gods.

Omphalê: queen of Lydia whom Heraklês was made to serve as a slave for killing Iphitos.

Orestês: son of Agamemnon and Klytaimnêstra; brother of Êlektra, Chrysothemis, and Iphianassa.

Ortygia: island in the Ionian Sea off Syracuse.

Ortygian Artemis: *see* Ortygia.

Paktolos: river in Lydia that delivered up gold dust.

Pallas: name for Athêna of unknown derivation.

Pan: Arkadian god; son of Hermês; a man with goat's legs, horns, and ears; god of fields, woods, shepherds, and flocks.

Parnassos: mountain in central Greece in northwest Boiotia; sacred to Dionysos, Apollo, and the Muses; on its slopes are Delphi and the Kastalian Spring.

Parthenopaios: one of the Seven against Thebes in the attack led by Polyneikês.

Patroklos: a warrior friend of Achilleus killed in the Trojan War by Hektor.

Pelasgian: of or relating to the peoples who inhabited Greece and the islands and coasts of the Aigaion Sea before the arrival of the Bronze Age Greeks.

Peleiades: the priestesses of Zeus at Dodona; also called doves.

Peloponnesos: peninsula forming the southern part of the Greek mainland.

Pelops: king of Argos; father of Atreus; grandfather of Agamemnon and Menelaos; gave his name to the Peloponnesos.

Peparêthos: island southwest of Lemnos.

Perithoüs: hero who descended into the underworld with Thêseus to rescue Persephonê.

Phanoteüs: ally of Klytaimnêstra and Aigisthos.

Philoktêtês: hero in the Trojan War in which he killed Paris with the bow and arrows given him by Heraklês; exiled from the Greek encampment at Troy and marooned on the island of Lemnos because of a noxious and festering snake-bite wound on his leg.

Phineias: king of Salmydessos in Thrake; put his first wife away and married a second time; the second wife blinded his two sons by his first marriage.

Phoibos: epithet of Apollo meaning "shining, bright."

Phokis: area in central Greece neighboring Boiotia.

Phrygia: country of west central Asia Minor.

Phrygian: an inhabitant of or relating to Phrygia.

Pleuron: city in Aitolia on the Gulf of Korinth.

Poias: father of Philoktêtês.

Polybos: king of Korinth; husband of Meropê; foster father of Oedipus.

Polydoros: son of King Priam of Troy; killed by Achilleus.

Polyneikês: son of Oedipus and Iokastê; brother of Antigonê, Ismenê, and Eteoklês; invaded Thebes at its seven gates to wrest the throne from his brother Eteoklês.

Poseidon: god of the sea; son of Kronos and Rhea; brother of Zeus.

Priam: king of Troy; son of Laomedon; father of Hektor and Paris.

Prometheus: Titan who stole fire from Olympos to give to mankind.

Pylades: friend of Orestês; son of Strophios of Phokis who received Orestês for safe-keeping from Klytaimnêstra during Agamemnon's absence at Troy.

Pythia: priestess of Apollo at Delphi who transmitted the oracles.

Pythian Games: the second most important Panhellenic festival celebrated in the third year of each Olympiad near Delphi.

Pytho: the ancient name of Delphi sacred to Apollo.

Salamis: Greek island in the Saronic Gulf off the coast of Athens; home of the Greater Aias.

Sardis: city of west Asia Minor; capital of Lydia.

Selloi: prophetic priests in the service of Zeus at Dodona.

Semelê: Theban princess; mother of Dionysos by Zeus.

Seven Gates: Thebes was fabled for its seven gates.

Sigeion: a promontory near Troy.

Sipylos: mountain in Lydia in Asia Minor.

Sisyphos: it was rumored that Odysseus was not the son of Laërtês, but of Sisyphos, king of Korinth, who had seduced his mother.

Skamander: principal river of the plains of Troy.

Skyros: Greek island in the Aigaion Sea.

Sounion: the southern promontory of Attika.

Sparta: city in the southern Peloponnesos known for its discipline and military prowess; the home of Menelaos and Helen.

Spercheios: river in Melis over which Philoktêtês' father Poias rules.

Sphinx: winged monster with a woman's head and a lion's body; situated outside Thebes, she destroyed young men who could not answer her riddle; when answered by Oedipus she killed herself.

Strophios: inhabitant of Phokis to whom Êlektra sent the infant Orestês for safety's sake during Agamemnon's absence at Troy.

Stygian House: underworld kingdom of Hades across the river Styx; see Hades.

Suppliant: one who expresses entreaty or supplication.

Tantalos: king of Phrygia; father of Niobê.

Tartaros: the utter depths of Hades where the Titans were imprisoned; a part of Hades reserved for evildoers; that part of Hades where Zeus imprisoned his defeated enemies.

Teiresias: blind Theban prophet.

Tekmêssa: Trojan captive assigned to Aias.

Telamon: a king of Salamis; father of the Greater Aias and Teükros.

Teleütas: father of Tekmêssa.

Terrible Goddesses: the Eumenides; see All-Seeing Ones.

Teükros: brother of the Greater Aias; son of Telamon.

Thebes: chief city of Boiotia in east central Greece northwest of Attika.

Themis: goddess of established law and custom.

Thersitês: ugliest and most evil-tongued fighter on the side of the Greeks at Troy; killed by Achilleus for mocking him.

Thêseus: son of Aigeus; hero of Attika known for his many great deeds; king of Athens who welcomed the aged Oedipus to Kolonos.

Thessalian: an inhabitant of or relating to Thessaly.

Thessaly: region of east central Greece on the Aigaion Sea; extensive fertile plain ringed with mountains.

Thestoros: father of Kalchas.

Thorikos: a town in Attika.

Three-Headed Hound: Cerberos guarded the entrance to Hades; one of the twelve labors of Heraklês.

Thyiads: maenads; see Bakkhai.

Thorikos: a town in Attika.

Thrakian Salmydessos: city in Thrake.

Thrake: Thrace; north of the Aigaion Sea and the Hellespont.

Trojan: inhabitant of Troy.

Troy: city in northwest Asia Minor.

Trachis: city in Thessaly, near the Spercheios River.

Tydeus: one of the Seven against Thebes in the attack led by Polyneikês.

Zeus: king of the Olympian gods; son of Kronos and Rhea; brother and husband of Hera; brother of Poseidon; father of many of the gods and mortals as well; has many epithets arising from his host of functions.

SELECTED BIBLIOGRAPHY

Bieber, Margarete. *The History of the Greek and Roman Theater*. 2nd ed. Revised. Princeton: Princeton University Press, 1961.

Bowra, Maurice. *Sophoclean Tragedy*. Oxford: Clarendon Press, 1944.

Else, Gerald F. *The Origin and Early Form of Greek Tragedy*. Martin Classical Lectures, Vol. 20. Cambridge: Harvard University Press, 1965.

Fergusson, Francis. *The Idea of Theater: A Study of Ten Plays, The Art of Drama in Changing Perspective*. Princeton: Princeton University Press; London: Oxford University Press, 1949.

Hornblower, Simon and Anthony Spawforth, eds. *The Oxford Classical Dictionary*. 3rd ed. Oxford: Oxford University Press, 1996.

Kirkwood, G. M. *A Study of Sophoclean Drama*. Ithaca: Cornell University Press, 1958.

Kitto, H. D. F. *Form and Meaning in Drama: A Study of Six Greek Plays and of Hamlet*. 2nd ed. London: Methuen, 1964; New York: Barnes and Noble, 1968.

———. *Greek Tragedy: A Literary Study*. 2nd ed. New York: Doubleday, 1964; 3rd ed. London: Methuen, 1966.

———. *Sophocles, Dramatist and Philosopher*. London: Oxford University Press, 1958.

Knox, B. M. W. *The Heroic Temper: Studies in Sophoclean Tragedy*. Sather Gate Lectures, Vol. 35. Berkeley and Los Angeles: University of California Press, 1964.

———. *Oedipus at Thebes: Sophocles' Tragic Hero and His Time*. New Haven: Yale University Press, 1957.

———. *Word and Action: Essays on the Ancient Theater*. Baltimore and London: The Johns Hopkins University Press, 1979.

Kott, Jan. *The Eating of the Gods: An Interpretation of Greek Tragedy*. New York: Random House, 1973.

Lattimore, Richmond. *The Poetry of Greek Tragedy*. Baltimore: The Johns Hopkins University Press, 1958.

Lax, Batya Casper. *Elektra: A Gender Sensitive Study of the Plays Based on the Myth*. North Carolina and London: McFarland and Company, Inc., 1995.

Lloyd-Jones, Hugh. *The Justice of Zeus*. Sather Gate Lectures, Vol. 41. Berkeley and Los Angeles: University of California Press, 1971.

Neils, Jenifer. *Goddess and Polis: The Panathenaic Festival in Ancient Athens*. Princeton: Princeton University Press, 1992.

Segal, Charles. *Tragedy and Civilization: An Interpretation of Sophocles*. Martin Classical Lectures, Vol. 26. Cambridge: Harvard University Press, 1981.

———. *Sophocles' Tragic World: Divinity, Nature, Society*. Cambridge: Harvard University Press, 1995.

Steiner, George. *The Death of Tragedy*. New York: Alfred A. Knopf; London: Faber and Faber, 1961.

Taplin, Oliver. *Greek Tragedy in Action*. Berkeley and Los Angeles: University of California Press; London: Methuen, 1978.

Vernant, Jean-Pierre and Pierre Vidal-Naquet, eds. *Myth and Tragedy in Ancient Greece*. New York: Zone Books, 1990.

Walcot, Peter. *Greek Drama in Its Theatrical and Social Context*. Cardiff: University of Wales Press, 1976.

Waldock, A. J. A. *Sophocles the Dramatist*. Cambridge: Harvard University Press, 1951.

Walton, J. Michael. *The Greek Sense of Theatre: Tragedy Reviewed*. London and New York: Methuen, 1984.

———. *Greek Theatre Practice*. Westport and London: Greenwood Press, 1980.

Webster, W. B. *An Introduction to Sophocles*. Oxford: Clarendon Press, 1936; 2nd ed., London: Methuen, 1969.

Whitman, Cedric H. *Sophocles: A Study of Heroic Humanism*. Cambridge: Harvard University Press, 1951.

Wiles, David. *Tragedy in Athens*. Cambridge and New York: Cambridge University Press, 1997.

Winkler, John, and Froma I. Zeitlin, eds. *Nothing to Do with Dionysus*. Princeton: Princeton University Press, 1990.

Winnington-Ingram, R. P. *Sophocles: An Interpretation*. Cambridge and New York: Cambridge University Press, 1980.

CARL R. MUELLER has since 1967 been a professor of theater at UCLA where he has taught in the areas of theater history, criticism, and playwriting. He has won the Samuel Goldwyn Award for Dramatic Writing, and in 1960–61 was a Fulbright Scholar in Berlin. A translator for over forty years, he has translated and published works by Buchner, Brecht, Wedekind, Hauptmann, and Zuckmayer, among others. For Smith and Kraus he has published *Arthur Schnitzler: Four Major Plays*, *Frank Wedekind: Four Major Plays*, and *August Strindberg: Five Major Plays*. Forthcoming are *Kleist: Three Major Plays* and *Pirandello: Three Major Plays*. His translations have been produced in every part of the English-speaking world.

ANNA KRAJEWSKA-WIECZOREK is a theater historian, critic, dramaturg, and translator. A graduate in Classical Philology, she received her doctorate in Poland and has taught at Jagiellon University in Krakow and The School of Performing Arts in Warsaw. She has published numerous essays on Greek and modern drama and theater as well as theater reviews in both Europe and the United States. She currently teaches European theater history, dramaturgy, and aesthetics at UCLA.